The
REASON
DRIVEN
Life

The REASON DRIVEN Life

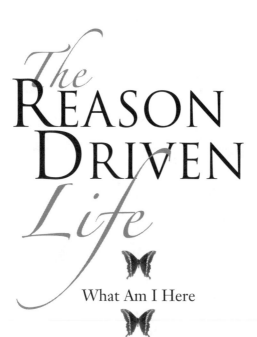

What Am I Here

on Earth For?

Robert M. Price

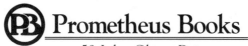 Prometheus Books

59 John Glenn Drive
Amherst, New York 14228-2197

Published 2006 by Prometheus Books

Inquiries should be addressed to
Prometheus Books
59 John Glenn Drive
Amherst, New York 14228–2197
VOICE: 716–691–0133, ext. 207
FAX: 716–564–2711
WWW.PROMETHEUSBOOKS.COM

10 09 08 07 06   5 4 3 2 1

Library of Congress Cataloging-in-Publication Data

Price, Robert M., 1954–
    The reason-driven life : what am I here on earth for? / by Robert Price.
        p. cm.
    Includes bibliographical references.
    ISBN 13: 978–1–59102–476–7 (hardcover: alk paper)
    ISBN 10: 1–59102–476–5 (hardcover: alk paper)
    1. Christianity—Controversial literature. I. Title.

BL2775.3.P75 2006
211'.4—dc22
                                                                                2006016169

Printed in the United States on acid-free paper

Contents

Foreword

Whenever I'm around Bob Price, I think "Thank God for him." And then I remember that I really mean, "Thankfully, we have a Bob Price" and God probably had nothing to do with it. Bob Price is such a rare individual. He really gets it: the value of religious stories, the value of the community, camaraderie, and sense of communal spirit that religious organizations provide. He has great respect for the Bible as a repository of ancient wisdom and a source of the narratives we tell ourselves about how we came to be and how we see our struggles with nature and with each other. Bob Price isn't just a scholar of Christianity; he often references Buddhist parables, too. He can bring up just the right story to provide a counterpoint or add emphasis to an idea. And not just Buddhism, psychology, too: he can call on Jungian theory when it's meaningful and appropriate.

Most important, he knows bull when he hears it.

This book is not just a polemic against Rick Warren's *The Purpose-Driven Life*. It's a beautiful, inspired, insightful work in its own right. I walked around for days after reading it filled with new ideas and a better way to look at my own life's predicaments. Then I read it again, and I got even more out of it.

For almost my entire life, I was much like some of the people Price describes in this book. I was a Christian by default, and I didn't take it seriously enough for it to cause me any real trouble. Bob says that the most well-adjusted Christians he knows are those who don't take it seriously. (Whether they are exactly conscious of this or not!) I think that was me. I think I was well adjusted. But that doesn't mean that I wasn't also stunted in my maturity by the side effects of benignly believing in the Christian stories and the childlike idea of a loving God who was pulling all the strings.

Then, there came a time when I was in crisis and I looked to my Christian faith to guide me. And it worked . . . at first. But then I looked closer and closer at what I professed to "believe" in and realized that if you followed the Bible's own logic and reasoning, if you expected it to stand up to even a modicum of scrutiny, you were going to be bitterly disappointed. I began to think that even Jesus, if he existed, would have to agree that the Bible itself was a house built on sand. Ultimately, I had to discard my faith. Bob Price says that, for him, this moment was simultaneously a relief and a great disappointment. Exactly. That's what I felt, too—maybe more disappointment than relief. But my discarding of my faith was based mostly on science and psychology and history. I didn't take the time to go over the Christian viewpoint again and decipher what made those religious ideas so compelling, so insidious, and so seductive. I didn't have the scholarly background or the patience to look into each seemingly harmless evangelical belief and find out where it came from and why it deserves to be thoroughly trashed! But Bob Price has that background! Which means that I especially enjoyed and learned so much from reading this book.

This past February, I attended and spoke at the annual Technology, Entertainment, and Design (TED) conference in Monterrey, California. Rick Warren was also one of the speakers. The organizers had included his book, *The Purpose-Driven Life*, in our packets of goodies. I read most of it the night before he was scheduled to speak. The first thing that struck me was Warren's liberal—and really disrespectful—paraphrasing of Bible quotes and reinterpretation of Bible stories. I had recently reread the New Testament gospels myself (for my monologue "Letting Go of God") and much of what I read in *The Purpose-Driven Life* seemed utterly unlike anything I had read in the Bible. In any case, I was eager to hear Pastor Warren speak.

Chris Anderson (who hosts the TED conferences) introduced Rick Warren saying that *The Purpose-Driven Life* "was the second-best selling nonfiction book ever, and that's if you count the Bible as a nonfiction book, which Rick Warren certainly does." Warren wore a Hawaiian shirt and sported a goatee; he's likable and approachable. He began as I expected, telling us that he didn't think we were accidents and that God planned for us to be alive and in fact even planned for us to hear his speech. But then Warren said something that surprised me. He said he thought his book was so popular because,

"Most people never think it through. They don't codify it or quantify it, and say this is what I believe and why I believe it."

I was astonished that Rick Warren was so aware of why his book was so effective. I think he is right: most people don't think it through. I used to be one of those people. I was handed a moral code by my culture and religion, and I was overtly and subversively not encouraged to think out my own morality. It was given to me from above, first from the sisters at the Catholic grade school I attended, then from the Jesuits who gave it the polish and feel of something intellectual, and then by my family who equated our rituals and culture with ethics and morality, and therefore questioning one part of this was tantamount to questioning all of it. Completely out of the question!

So for Rick Warren, "people who don't think it through" means "people who haven't accepted the fundamentalist Christian worldview based on the Bible." Those who never ask themselves "why I believe it" are people who just don't listen to their evangelical pastors telling them exactly what to believe and how to "serve" the church with their "gifts."

Bob Price has the intelligence and the persistence to tackle all these contradictions. He's spent the time looking at what Bible translations Warren uses, and Price addresses the deeper, darker side—the shadow side—of what Warren is really proposing. Price points out that encouraging people to deeply think about "why they believe what they believe" causes individualism to triumph over conformity, creativity over subservience, and empowerment over "joining the flock." Additionally, I was delighted to read along as Price nails Warren time and time again for his ridiculous, even comical use of Bible passages and quotations (as "translated" for a "modern" audience).

So, this book you're reading is a deeply thought out, theologically accurate, heartfelt dismantling of Rick Warren's (and all evangelicals') worldview. Even the ideas that seem, on the surface, to be unassailable (like Warren's call to a life of service to others) Price takes apart, reveals each for the sham it is, with elegance and charm and disturbing accuracy.

It almost makes me glad that Rick Warren wrote *The Purpose-Driven Life* so that Bob Price could write *The Reason-Driven Life*! I look forward to having this book on my shelf and as a reference tool in the coming years. So, sit back and enjoy. And be disturbed (because you will be very disturbed). Then be inspired. As Price says, human divinity is really human potential. Human potential is what each of us has innately. We have an enormous amount of control over how we view ourselves in relation to this world and to our fellow passengers on this planet.

For added pleasure, imagine Rick Warren reading this book and really getting it. Of course, it's highly unlikely to happen. But we can dream, can't we?

Julia Sweeney
Saturday Night Live star and author of
God Said, "Ha!" and *My Beautiful Loss of Faith Story*
June 6, 2006

Introduction

REMEMBRANCE OF FAITHS PAST

Rick Warren's super, bestselling book *The Purpose-Driven Life* is apparently meeting a great spiritual hunger among Americans these days. People, it would seem, want purpose. He does not extol the notion of living according to *some* chosen purpose. He has a very particular one in mind. For Pastor Warren, the purpose of all human lives is to be a fundamentalist Christian. That, he says, is why God created you. Really, now? Pardon me for wondering if the many fans of *The Purpose-Driven Life* are like the Israelites rebuked by the prophet: "Why do you spend money for what is not bread, and your wages for what does not satisfy?" (Isaiah 55:2, NASB).

From 1965, when I prayed to receive Jesus Christ as my personal savior, till 1977, while a student at Gordon-Conwell Theological Seminary, I did my best to live the Christian life. After that I abandoned evangelical, or "born-again," Christianity and explored liberal Protestant theology. For a great deal of that time I was pretty much an agnostic. It was years later, during my pastorate of a liberal Baptist church, that I realized I had rejected theism altogether. Since then I have lived what I would now call "the reason-driven life," one still under construction and filled with experiment. While a born-again Christian, I was a soul winner. I had daily "quiet time" devotions, attended church at least weekly, and studied the Bible with great zeal. I received Campus Crusade for Christ training more than once. I was chapter president for InterVarsity Christian Fellowship. By now I can look back on both of my "lives," both "incarnations" as believer and as nonbeliever. Perhaps by comparing them you and I can both learn something.

A MIGHTY FORTRESS IS OUR MENTALITY

In my experience, the born-again Christian life is one of narrow-mindedness, and narrow-mindedness raised to the status of a virtue, not a vice. One assumes a position of invulnerable stonewalling, a case of the "true believer" described so well by Eric Hoffer. Some idea comes up and Joe Christian is told, perhaps by his own well-trained conscience, not to go speculating down that path because it can only be Satan sowing seeds of doubt. If an unsaved friend stumps one with a question, one is coached to sidestep it: "Say, that's a good question! I'll ask Dr. Craig for the answer and get back to you. In the meantime, why not get saved anyway?" As if *any* objection could budge the born-again Christian or his Jehovah's Witness twin from his dogmatic party line. As a loyal Christian, one has no intention of giving the other guy a fair hearing. As he speaks, one is already looking for weak points on which to refute him, since one knows automatically one must be right. The Christian is automatically certain the unbeliever holds his view as a mere smokescreen to avoid repenting. While we are in that pocket universe, why can we never recognize our stance as the very essence of narrow-mindedness? Because those blinders are themselves part of the equipment of narrow-mindedness! No one has any problem recognizing narrowness as a vice in any other area of life. How can it suddenly become a virtue in this one area?

PETER PAN PIETY

Sigmund Freud spoke of religion as a neurosis and an illusion. To be religious, in his view, was a refusal to grow up and to accept certain harsh facts of life. That is probably too sweeping a generalization to apply to all forms of religion, but it does seem to me to describe quite well the born-again Christian experience as I have lived it and seen others live it. The born-again experience prolongs immaturity in at least three ways. *Morally*, one remains forever on the lowest rungs of character development as Eric Kohlberg and others map it out: a prisoner to dogmatic commandments that, out of fear, one dare not disobey. On the one hand, one never refines one's own moral sense because the supposed truth is provided already, and infallibly. On the other hand, with the threat of hellfire, one can never arise to a nobler motivation for morality. One is necessarily always mindful of saving one's butt from toasting! How could you not be?

Second, one's *intellectual* growth is halted, at least when it comes to religious matters, because God is imagined as a peevish theology professor who will damn you to hell for filling in the wrong answers in your final exam book. "Sorry, Mr. Jehovah's Witness! Tough luck, Miss Mormon! Bad break, Mahatma Gandhi! You get a big red 'F' for *fry!*" If that's the way things are, it is safest not to question, safer to sit down and shut up. This explains why so many born-again Christians can attain sophistication in many professions and disciplines and yet retain a sealed-off nursery school of religious beliefs.

Third, born-again Christianity stunts one's *personal* growth. As Eli Chesen (*Religion May Be Hazardous to Your Health*) said, it gives you a slate of answers before it has even occurred to you to ask the questions.[1] Embracing a party line of morals, beliefs, and opinions, you do not learn to think for yourself. You are told the only ideal to pursue is to be a "good Christian," not a mature person, and the two aren't the same thing (though neither is a bad thing). What else is it, in the long run, but a strategy for protracting immaturity when the Christian is told to take his problems and "leave them with the Lord," "leave them at the altar"? Not even God can grow up for you. You have to do it, and no devotional scheme can provide a shortcut. What a relief *and* a disappointment it was for me the day this simple insight finally penetrated my thick skull.

JESUS CHRIST SUPERSTITION

I fear Freud was right about born-again Christianity: it is at least highly conducive of "obsessional neurosis."[2] At least it is true the more seriously you take it. Many of us have been trained in what the old preachers called "up-to-the-minute confession." As soon as an unkind thought or lustful imagining flits into your mind, you must stop what you are doing or thinking and confess it to God lest you suffer an ever-increasing alienation from him and wind up "out of fellowship." That will drive you to distraction in short order. Oh yes, I knew many fellow Christians who lived bright and breezy lives untroubled by such introspective scruples, but then they were blessed with not having taken any of it seriously. That disparity itself should have told me something.

And the more strict one's pious conscience grows, the less it takes to offend it. Watchman Nee (*The Normal Christian Life*) offers a blueprint for misery when he suggests that anything at all that means much to you automatically becomes an idol you must smash to prove to yourself (and to God) that nothing rivals God in your life.[3] Once Nee or some like-speaking preacher poses the question, the poor pietist is caught in a vicious catch-22. His mind at once goes to some innocent amusement or relationship or possession. "If God wanted me to forsake it for his sake, would I?" In that moment, what was formerly innocent *becomes* an idol simply by virtue of the introspective question raised. And then it must be smashed, forsaken. And such a jealous god, really such an omnivorous conscience, begins hungrily to look around for the next potential "idol." Soon one is left with naught but religion, little suspecting that it has become the greatest idol of all.

Christ becomes an idol, German American theologian Paul Tillich says, when the Christian is preoccupied with nothing but religion. That is too narrow a basis for personal integration, and eventually the pious Christian will be left wondering why life has passed him by. Of course being a Christian soldier provides an exciting sense of purpose—for the adolescent who sees life still in simple, storybook terms. The born-again Christian has the same tendency as the Trekkie. He needs to move out of his parents' basement (or his church's) and get a life! His or her *own* life, not the life of Jesus to be lived through the Christian.

CRYSTAL BALL BUSTER

As Christians, we called ourselves blessed because, unlike the poor unsaved wretches around us, we knew the very will of God. I used to, but now I am relieved and happy to call myself as agnostic about God's will as Job was. Born-again Christians tell you that you must remain "in the center of God's will," straying neither to the right nor to the left, or the consequences will be grave: the wrong career, the wrong life partner, a life on the sidelines of Christian service. For some this means one must heed any subjective "leading" one feels, a risky matter. For others it means following a complex list of steps to divine the will of God, reminiscent of the priestly Urim and Thummim. One reads events in one's daily life, whether a headache, a flat tire, a compliment or insult, as a sign sent from God, and it is up to you to figure out what God is trying to tell you by it. I call this divination, superstition. What does it mean for one's daily life to be such a shadow-play filled with coded oracles and charades from a God who speaks only in the least reliable language of inner subjectivity? Are we merely rats in a Skinner box? Is one's life merely a training program, with God as the scientist putting one through one's paces? The fact that this God ostensibly loves us does not solve the problem. If he loves us, let him give us some breathing room. Let's put out a restraining order on him!

And does it ever even work? How many times had we been confident we had arrived at God's will on some decision, only to have it blow up in our face later? When that happens, there is always the default mode: "How foolish of a mere mortal to think he could read the mind of God!" But we were just covering our tracks, because next time we'd be following those same steps the same way, not daring *not* to, lest we stray from the perfect will of God.

LACKLUSTER SALVATION

Born-again Christian writers and preachers know it will sooner or later come to this; they make evangelistic promises they know will not be fulfilled, so when it falls through, they have the hitherto-unsuspected next step ready. "Defeated Christian," we will be solicitously told, "you have been striving to live the Christian life in the pitiful strength of the flesh! In order to live the *victorious* Christian life, you must cease striving and learn to rest in God's power. Let go and let God!" How are you to do this new thing? How do you cease striving and rest, carried along in a steady stream of sanctified consciousness? Well, er, one, um, *strives* to rest! You are back at square one. And soon this routine is seen for what it is: another gimmick to paper over the inevitable failure of overexaggerated promises, promises that born-again Christians will live a life of power, joy, and freedom.

I remember the moment it first occurred to me: How can I witness to people about a life of glowing joy and assurance when mine is filled with guilt for not working up the guts to witness to every guy I sit by on a bus? When I am always afraid of making a misstep, or of feeling or thinking the wrong thing? Likewise, how many years could I stand suppressing the patent truth that my "personal relationship with Christ" was just subjective projection, praying to a mental image of Jesus drawn equally from scripture and from stained-glass windows, pretending he was listening. Wasn't this Jesus construct merely an imaginary playmate that spoke with the voice of my own overtender conscience? I finally realized I was doing no one any favors by trying to get them to embrace the same exasperating set of mind games that had kept me so immature for so long.

GOD IS MY HIJACKER

Now what of reason and the life predicated upon it? You will not have missed the pun on Rick Warren's title. We often use the words "purpose" and "reason" pretty much as synonyms. What is the purpose of that law? What is the reason for that rule? Tell me the reason for your action, and I will tell you the purpose of mine. But there is a subtle difference. A purpose can denote a guiding aim, as it does in Warren's *The Purpose-Driven Life*, but a reason-driven life denotes a life lived by means of rational thinking and choosing. As Plato and Aristotle said, the chief excellence of humanity is its rational faculty, and so if we are to fulfill ourselves as human beings, we must live by that rational faculty. We don't absolutely *have* to. We could, for example, live a life of unbridled physical passion, but that wouldn't make any sense. It wouldn't be rational. And we would learn that too late by seeing first-hand the destructive results. One may choose among any number of purposes or goals for one's life, but any way you cut it, a truly human life must be a reason-driven life. In the present book I am trying to lay bare the shortcomings of Rick Warren's model of the fundamentalism-driven life. But I do not want to criticize without offering practical alternatives. I call upon my readers to rethink their commitment to the Warren-driven life and to contemplate the reason-driven life as I will set it forth.

I believe Freud was correct: maturity depends on realizing there is no Creator, no divine lawgiver, no author of destiny and meaning, and no giver of eternal life. One must come to view this humble, naked earth as one's true home. "Imagine there's no heaven, above us only sky." A morally neutral universe upon which we may place our stamp, as individuals and as a race.

Let me, however, mention a major problem I have with atheism. For many it is a sterile life of negativity and denial. It is the stance of the *apostate*, as Max Scheler described it in his shrewd book *Ressentiment*. The apostate is one who has turned away from a faith he once held without genuinely or deeply turning *to* anything else. Otherwise we should call him "a convert to" rather than "an apostate from." The apostate's life is a committed struggle of mere negativity, a campaign of continuous guerrilla war against the system of faith he once espoused and now so regrets having embraced.[4] The apostate is still Hoffer's "true believer"; he has merely switched teams in the same game. By contrast, the convert gets out of the game and leaves the stadium. He seeks another game that will satisfy him better.

I know many mere apostates, people who are for this or that reason very mad at religion and want to destroy it. Ironically, they retain many of the disadvantages of being a religious zealot. They are still burdened by an urge to save the world. They still divide the human race into the good guys and the bad guys, only they have just switched whom they put in which group. They still mark themselves out from their fellow men and women by means of bumper stickers, buttons, and T-shirts. I hope they are having fun. But the meaning of their lives seems to me parasitic upon that which they reject. If all religion were to vanish tomorrow, what would they do? If you are free from religion, I ask my atheist friends, what are you free *for*?

SOMETHING TO BELIEVE IN

"Atheist," though I do not disclaim it, is not my description of first choice because it merely indicates what I no longer believe, not what *else* I have since come to believe. It says what I don't stand for anymore. But I would rather be known for what I do stand for. I urge on the apostate what I urge on the born-again Christian: get a life!

I am trying to. Personally, I consider myself a humanist. I view myself as a would-be philosopher, with leanings toward Friedrich Nietzsche and Jacques Derrida. I'm not in a hurry to find a label that will fit just right. I do not hate religion. I even go to church for the rich pageantry and the moral challenge (more of this later). I am pleased, in the rural South, to live among fundamentalists and to appreciate them as people. I try to view their beliefs nonjudgmentally, as an anthropologist would. I have rejected those beliefs, but that does not compel me to view those who hold them to be my enemies. I am happy to share interests with them and, if need be, to avoid certain sensitive topics.

So I do not relish the life of the apostate, one I have overcome with difficulty. But I do relish certain aspects of the nontheist existence.

IS NOTHING SACRED?

For me, the notion of a Creator who somehow constructed this great and wonderful world is not only a false, pat answer to the question of how or why it got here; belief in creation tends to stifle the very sense of wonder that raises the question. "Huh," we say, as when we watch some TV special on the making of our favorite special-effects movie, "*that's* how they did it. Oh well." We can file that one away, give ourselves permission henceforth to take it for granted, and fall back into our mundane coma. Again, think of the Skinner box. If we must view the wide world as a great, big stage setting put up by God, instead of an autonomous reality in its own right, we are evacuating the world and life of meaning. It is all *maya*, then: illusion. And I don't think it is.

For me, the notion of a divine lawgiver is both pernicious and superfluous. Those who call on scripture to provide a full range of infallible answers turn out to be in no better position than the rest of us who make no such claims, for the simple reason that life always casts up new issues and shades of moral nuance never covered in the ancient books. How does the Bible give the biblicist any advantage at all when it comes to the maddening question of surrogate motherhood? Artificial insemination? White lies? Even abortion is never explicitly mentioned there. Christian ethicists have to debate these issues pretty much the same way their secular counterparts do. The claim to have a revelation *is* dangerous, though, since it can so easily function as an excuse for Reverend Bigmouth to claim that you don't need to evaluate *his* opinions *as* opinions, just accept them by faith.

Why are moral systems basically the same in all societies? It's just that morals and laws arise on a pragmatic basis as sets of rules that will enable people to live together most easily. We can breathe easier, no matter where we live, no matter what language we speak, no matter what totem we worship, if we can reduce theft, murder, rape, libel, and so on to a minimum. As Thomas Aquinas readily admitted, we hardly need a revelation to tell us that it is better not to do these destructive things.

I believe we live in a morally neutral universe, that the moral laws and grids of meaning through which we see it are artificial impositions by our various ancestors, for reasons I just mentioned. The universe is not rooting for things to come out any particular way. It is all the same to the Universal Void whether good or evil, as we define them, triumphs. It is the great privilege and challenge of the human race to work out the best rules we can, the best standards of good and evil we

can muster, and to strive to impose them on the universe. We are set-
tlers in a cosmic wilderness. The world was not put here for us, and
not all of it will ever prove amenable to us or to our scales of meaning.
But we must carve out a moral space where our culture and civilization can live. We are part of Chaos, and we begin, little by little, to
impose our own order and meaning upon it. There is no already-
determined meaning somewhere else, in the mind of some God
viewed as a kind of heavenly Bureau of Weights and Standards.
Where else could meaning be but in the eye of the beholder? And that
is in you. That is in me.

PRECIOUS LITTLE

Feuerbach was right, I think: the only God is humanity, and we must
not shirk the cross of our own terrible greatness by blaming gods and
devils for our own works. You and I are the Creator: we face the blank
canvas of our lives and decide what meaning, what artwork, we will
trace thereon. Nothing less befits human dignity.

And yet, we are mortal gods. We must die in the end, and the end
will come soon. Some object that human life is rendered meaningless
if it must end in death. An abrupt dead end makes all before it a sense-
less sentence fragment. But does it? I have never been able to see how
an otherwise meaningless life would suddenly become meaningful if
you added an infinite amount of it. If it has any meaning at all, it ought
to be discernible, now. And it *is*: to enjoy the world around us, to live
out the familiar patterns of family life and personal growth, to do the
wonderful things human beings have always done. Nothing fancy.

It won't last forever, but that lends a bittersweetness to it, an ines-
timable quality that life would never have if it lasted forever. The
words of Psalm 90 strike deep for the nontheist: human life is too
soon over, and we must budget our days. We must strive to do something that will outlast us, that will leave a mark of our passing, of some
improvement of the world. That isn't much. But unless one harbors
delusions of grandeur, thinks that life owes us an eternity, it is, I think,
more than enough.

Won't you explore with me the vast differences between the purpose-driven life of Rick Warren and the reason-driven life I advocate? I do not much care what you end up believing, partly because you should not jump to conclusions. Part of living the reason-driven life is that you no longer feel the false urgency to make up your mind *right now* what you believe. You realize you are not under any deadline. Nor are you likely *ever* to arrive at some definitive truth. Your thinking about the meaning of life will be an ongoing project, its own reward. And the conclusions you do reach will be tentative and always open to revision in light of new insights you may encounter. I would be delighted if *The Reason-Driven Life* helped you in that process, but your findings are none of my business. Will you be a theist? An atheist? An agnostic? A Christian? Obviously, that's up to you. I just want to be clear: I'm not trying to get you to agree with me. That wouldn't be rational. I merely aim to provide food for thought that you might not otherwise have considered.

Though it hardly matters whether you read a chapter a day or not, I have followed *The Purpose-Driven Life*'s ground plan of forty brief chapters or meditations to respond more specifically to the points made there. Sometimes I address a number of points Warren makes in the corresponding chapter; other times I focus on a single issue, especially if, as sometimes happens, he is reiterating some theme from one of his previous chapters. So *The Reason-Driven Life* is designed as a direct rebuttal and alternative to *The Purpose-Driven Life*. But I think my book makes sense by itself. When you have to know what it is in Warren's book that I am discussing, I begin by summarizing or quoting the relevant statements from *The Purpose-Driven Life*. Also, since Warren is merely recycling standard, one might even say *stale*, fundamentalist teaching, you may read my rebuttal as an answer to fundamentalism in general. If you are familiar with that, you haven't missed much if you are not familiar with *The Purpose-Driven Life*. So you needn't worry about having to make sense of half of a phone conversation.

Robert M. Price
July 9, 2005

NOTES

1. Eli S. Chesen, *Religion May Be Hazardous to Your Health: A Psychiatric Guide to the Uses and Abuses of God, Prayer, and the Church or Synagogue* (New York: Collier Macmillan, 1973), p. 28.

2. Sigmund Freud, *The Future of an Illusion*, trans. W. D. Robson-Scott, rev. ed. by James Strachey (Garden City, NY: Doubleday Anchor, 1964), pp. 70–71.

3. Watchman Nee, *The Normal Christian Life* (Wheaton, IL: Tyndale House, 1977), pp. 105, 145–48.

4. Max Scheler, *Ressentiment*, Marquette Studies in Philosophy IV, trans. Lewis B. Coser and William W. Holdheim (Milwaukee: Marquette University Press, 1994), pp. 47–48.

It *Is* about You

Man is the measure of all things: of the things that are, that they
are, and of the things that are not, that they are not.
—Protagoras

If one has to choose between different authorities, not they *but* oneself *is ultimate authority for oneself, and this means: there is no*
authority for him.
—Paul Tillich, "'By What Authority?'"

JUMPING OUT OF YOUR SKIN

In any journey, including especially one's life journey, it matters as
much where you begin as where you end up, or hope to end up. In *The*
Purpose-Driven Life, Rick Warren is rightly adamant on this point. Yet
he is wrong, in my humble opinion, as to what the proper starting
point *is*. He assumes, and he wants you to assume, the least likely
standpoint for a mortal human being, namely, a God's-eye view.
Weary of human speculations about the meaning and purpose of life,
Reverend Warren urges us to jump out of our mortal skins and join
the Almighty Creator, from whose side we may look down from Mt.
Sinai or Olympus or Asgard and see what we could not see from a
position too close to the ground: the reason we have been placed here
and the goals we ought to pursue. He tells a shaggy dog story eventu-
ating in the well-known quip, "You can't get there from here." You
see, Reverend Warren had once gotten lost on a mountain climb and
finally found someone from whom to ask directions. The man told
him just how lost he was: his destination was on the other side of the
range, and he would have to *begin on the other side* if he hoped to arrive
at his destination. Presumably, like J. R. R. Tolkien's Gandalf finding

his way through the Mountains of Moria, Warren did find his way to the other side. But he doesn't seem to catch the implications of the humorous cliché he quotes: what if you *can't get there from here*? What if you can't reach the Olympian vantage point of a god?

Warren seems to think it a simple matter for mere mortals to know the will of an invisible divinity. He is like a despairing parent on Christmas Eve, facing down a pile of parts for a complex toy for his child. He can make no sense of the mess, and so he redoubles his quest for a sheet of assembly instructions. There *must* be one in there somewhere! And, by golly, there is. Let's just hope whoever wrote it had a good command of the English language. And for Warren, who despairs at making any sense of *life* and its purpose using his own wisdom, there must be an instruction manual for that, too, one provided by the manufacturer: the Bible. Now maybe we can stop wasting time and get with God's program for us.

But not so fast. Warren seems hell-bent on discovering a definitive and infallible set of instructions, and this ought to give us pause for at least three reasons. First, Warren makes a colossal, and colossally dubious, assumption that there *needs* to be a single, uniform purpose or goal for all individual human lives. The variety of gifts and abilities and interests that characterizes the gloriously diverse human race may be a clue that different individuals have different life-purposes. Personally, I doubt very much whether one can say Albert Einstein, William Shakespeare, and Elvis Presley all had the exact same purpose in life. Granted, all of them lived to express their creativity and acted to enrich human experience. But even then, we're talking about wide generalities, not about specific trajectories for individual persons. And then again, there is nothing to say it is incumbent on each person to be creative or to enrich human life. There is presumably a place for passive enjoyers and consumers. Nothing wrong with that, is there?

Warren speaks dismissively of self-help books. I suspect one reason is that there are so many of them, all taking different approaches, and he will be satisfied with nothing less than a single, universal Purpose. He wants to play a tune to which all may march in lockstep. I do not much care for the implicitly totalitarian echoes I hear in *The Purpose-Driven Life* and the old-time fundamentalism it recycles. Why not let a hundred flowers bloom?

"I Took Jesus as My Savior—You Take Him, Too!"

My guess is that *The Purpose-Driven Life* appeals to readers who are afraid of taking responsibility for the direction of their lives and would therefore prefer to take someone else's orders. They have no confidence in their own ability to look at their lives and to decide what to do with them. They look to self-help tapes or seminars for direction, but these "surefire" programs may not work for them. They look at another book or course, and that is disappointing, too. They can see some people are shaped up by Anthony Robbins or by Thomas Harris's *I'm Okay, You're Okay*, some by something else. But they are tired of looking, and they want results *now*. And here comes a dogmatic preacher or writer who offers a magic alternative that will work for everybody, and they know it will because it represents no mere human guesswork but the very revelation of God.

Have you ever told a pushy evangelist that his faith is fine for him, but that you prefer another way? Why do you have to go *his* way? The answer, the real, psychological answer, is, "It has to be the way for everybody without exception. If it's only for some people, I won't know if I am one of the ones it will work for!" Sometimes, like Paul who claimed to have been the chief of sinners, an evangelist will say, "If it worked for me, it can work for anybody." But what this really means is, "Since it will work for everybody, then I can be sure, deductively, that it will work for me." The revival chorus celebrates "All sufficient grace for even me." I must have certainty! So for me to be sure the gospel will redeem me, I have to believe that you need it, too. Hence I cannot be satisfied thinking you might not need it. If I admit that something else might do the trick for you, I have to suspect that something else might work better for me, too. And since the much-vaunted claims that "Christ changed my life" are usually more statements of faith than accurate descriptions of experience, this suspicion would be fatal. I might then have to recognize that Christ is not living up to the advertising rhetoric and get back on the road looking for another panacea. And I'm sick of that.

NO ESCAPE FROM CHOOSING

Let me explain the two other factors I mentioned that cast severe doubt on Warren's approach. My second ground for hesitation is that one can by no means take for granted that any particular book, much less the Protestant Bible, *is* a set of truths revealed by God. Few will deny (certainly I will not) that the Bible is a repository of ageless wisdom. But that is a very different thing from making the Bible as a whole and in every part a communication of propositions from God. While it's not within the scope of this book to enter into biblical debate, I will simply stress that there is, and always has been, a very wide debate on the divine inspiration of the Bible. There are many more or less probable arguments on behalf of biblical inspiration and infallibility set forth by scholars like B. B. Warfield, René Pache, John Warwick Montgomery, Josh McDowell, and others. But there are also many other Christian understandings of the Bible that do not see it as a divinely inspired answer book. Some think the Bible's function is to teach the good life but not to deal with matters of scientific or historical fact. Others say the Bible need only treat basic matters of salvation but otherwise need not be doctrinally uniform. Still others esteem the Bible as the product of wise Jewish and Christian writers, but not the product of special inspiration at all. Other, non-Christian views reject the authority of the Bible, period.

My point is this: every one of the fascinating theories that still circulate among serious Bible students is fully as much a product of human speculation as are the life-purpose theories that Rick Warren dismisses piteously as fallible and speculative and thus unworthy of his readers' time. There is no way to simply jump over to the other side of the mountain, as if you had the equivalent of a *Star Trek* transporter. We cannot transcend human theories about things, even the issue of whether there is a word from God. You see, Warren is telling you, in effect, "Let's escape the bewildering puzzle of which psychological approach to take, by taking refuge with the Bible!" But he's only pushing the problem back a step, because now you have all the bewildering options for understanding the Bible to sift through and choose from. You *still* have to listen to all the candidates and then take your best shot. You're only human. You have no right just to close your ears to possibilities you don't like and then pretend you know which one is right automatically, as if *you* were God. Paul Tillich nailed you: "unable to stand the loneliness of deciding for ourselves, we suppress the fact that there is a split authority. We subject ourselves to a definite authority and close our eyes against all other claims."[1] And Walter Kauffman mapped out where you are:

> Those who pit commitment against reason and advise us to blind and destroy our reason before making the most crucial choice of our life are apologists for one specific set of doctrines which, to use Paul's word, are "foolishness" to those who have not taken leave of reason. They say their doctrine is infallible and true, but ignore the fact that there is no dearth whatsoever of pretenders to infallibility and truth. They may think they chose their doctrine because it is offered to us as infallible and true; but this is plainly no sufficient reason: scores of other doctrines, scriptures and apostles, sects and parties, cranks and sages make the same claim. Those who claim to know which of the lot is justified in making such a bold claim, those who tell us that this faith or that is *really* infallible and true, are presupposing, in effect, whether they realize this or not, that they themselves happen to be infallible. Those who have no such exalted notion of themselves have no way of deciding between dozens of pretenders if reason is proscribed. Those who are asking us to spurn reason are in effect counseling us to trust to luck. But luck in such cases is unusual.[2]

My third qualm is similar to the second. Let's assume for the moment that we do have a divinely inspired book in our hands. Reverend Warren, like all fundamentalists, plainly imagines that it is clear to all just what the Bible text means. Here please remember my analogy with the complex device Dad or Mom is desperate to assemble before Christmas morning: suppose the instructions are *not clear*. Maybe the factory worker who wrote them up in Hong Kong did not have the best grasp of English—you know you've been in that situation. Even with the instructions in hand, you may be far from out of the woods! And it is the same with the Bible. Why do you think there are thousands of Christian denominations? Sooner or later it all boils down to the ambiguity of scripture. Bible readers cannot agree on what the Bible says on many, many important points. An inspired and infallible passage whose meaning you cannot be sure of is not much more useful than an *un*inspired, *fallible* passage. In fact, I cannot see what the allegedly precious worth of such inspiration is supposed to be. I assume you know that it isn't just a question of widely differing sects in view here, say, Plymouth Brethren versus Greek Orthodox, groups that might be expected to divide on bigger, cultural grounds. No, even born-again Christians have taken to debating among themselves over whether a true believer must accept Jesus Christ simply as "Savior" or as "*Lord and* Savior" in order to be saved. The text of the Bible is just not clear enough on the point. And if it is not clear enough on *that* one, I'm not sure one can risk citing it, like a cop citing the traffic code, to determine anyone's direction in life.

To underscore my point, let me remind you that Rick Warren is happy to quote from no less than *fifteen* different translations or paraphrases of the Bible. You know what that means, don't you? They are so different that he has a lot of shopping to do before finding one that will make the Bible appear to say what he wants it to teach. One of his favorites is an extremely loose paraphrase called *The Message* that makes Kenneth Taylor's *Living Bible* look like the King James version by comparison.

And now we begin to discern what is really going on when a mortal like ourselves appeals authoritatively to a book, written by mortals, translated variously by mortals, and interpreted by a mortal, namely, the one quoting it to us. *That mortal, in this case the well-meaning Rick Warren, is himself assuming the mantle of a divine oracle.* It is his voice that is magnified through the medium of special effects, like the Great and Powerful Oz. It is Pastor Warren who, hardly realizing it, is Jacob wearing the Esau mask of "biblical authority" to persuade his old, blind father. What an irony! Fundamentalists, who denounce humanism and scorn the pathetic subjectivity of mere human opinions, have no other stock to trade in, and so they make the Bible into a ventriloquist dummy to speak with their own voice.

And thus we must ask, just *whose* purpose does Rick Warren want to be driving your life? God's purpose, as best as Warren can distill it from the Bible as he reads it. It is no less a miserable human specula-tion than yours or mine or anyone else's. So why not go with *yours?* Nothing else will be authentic.

TELL ME WHO I AM

The great danger of Warren's approach, and that of the fundamen-talist Christianity he represents, is an alien imposition of a self-con-cept and life agenda *from without*, no different in principle than the discredited Communist attempt to mint a new species of "Soviet Man." What is "human nature"? What is *your* nature? Who can ulti-mately decide but *you?* Even if there is a creator God who engineered your life, how else can he expect you to discern what you are here for—except by a long, hard, and continuing look at your own life? You, like many readers of *The Purpose-Driven Life*, may be tired of looking and looking, but that is no excuse for choosing the next thing you find and deciding you believe in it. What if the only way to find your purpose is to study yourself, as you live your life? I daresay that you will never be satisfied with a "canned," ready-made "purpose" handed you by another, no matter how many glowing endorsements it comes packaged with.

It's just like Billy Graham and his fellow evangelists always say: "God has no grandchildren." You can't ride the coattails of another's faith. Or, as John the Baptist told the self-complacent crowds, "Do not presume to say to yourselves, 'We have Abraham as our father'; for I tell you, God is able from these stones to raise up children to Abraham!" (Matthew 3:9, RSV). No, you must choose your own faith, it cannot be secondhand faith, or it will not be *your* faith. All right, sure: the wisdom of that is plain. Why isn't it equally obvious that you have to discover your *purpose* for yourself? You cannot possibly rely on someone else to do it for you, *not even God*, and that is because of the kind of thing a purpose is. As long as you let someone else sell you a bill of goods about how some book can tell you your purpose, you will be the puppet of that person, even if, like Rick Warren, he means only to help you. As Socrates said (Jesus, too, according to the Gospel of

Thomas), "Know yourself." There is no substitute, because otherwise you will be taking someone else's word for who you are. According to Harvey Cox's fascinating essay, "On Not Leaving It to the Snake," that was the original sin: Adam and Eve wimping out and letting someone else tell them who they were and what they ought to be about.

If you have been associated with fundamentalist, evangelical, born-again Christianity for long, you will have noticed what a turnover rate there is. Not only is there a constant stream of new converts coming in, there is also a steady stream going out. You are led to believe these poor souls have just "backslid." Just got tired of the straight and narrow life of Christian discipline. It might be so. But I suggest you try to follow up with some of them. You may find that many of us jumped ship because in the end we could no longer act out some script someone else pushed in front of us. We decided to discover for ourselves our purpose, or *purposes*. We decided it might be a better idea after all to start looking where we are, not where we aren't.

Day One

Point to Ponder: It *is* about me.

Quote to Remember: "If you will not know yourselves, you are in poverty; indeed, you are poverty." (The Gospel according to Thomas, saying 3)

Question to Consider: Why can't I get it through my head that a religious self-help program, even one that quotes some Bible verses, is just as subjective and debatable as a secular one?

NOTES

1. Paul Tillich, "'By What Authority?'" in *The New Being* (New York: Scribners, 1955), p. 86.

2. Walter Kaufmann, *The Faith of a Heretic* (Garden City, NY: Doubleday Anchor, 1963), p. 86.

You Are a Work of Art

*The atheist believes there is no God. The superstitious man believes
there is but wishes there weren't.*
—Plutarch

Fundamentalism feeds its adherents a set of mixed signals and so
places them in a desperate double bind. One soon realizes the disparate elements of belief can never be synthesized, worked into a
coherent system of thought. If there were an eternal and infinite
divine reality, of course it would be no surprise that there might well
be much more to it than poor mortals could understand. But then
don't try to map it all out. The wonderful Buddhist parable of the
blind men and the elephant makes that point well. In it, six congenitally blind old men make their way to a zoo where they hope to understand the reality of a strange creature they have heard of all their lives.
What on earth is this "elephant," and how can it possibly live up to all
the things told of it? So the old men circle the elephant. One grasps
the tail and concludes the elephant is like a rope. The second takes
hold of the trunk and announces that the elephant is like a snake. The
third, feeling of the mighty leg, decides the elephant is like a tree
trunk. Number four is convinced, as he fingers the beast's ear, that the
elephant is like a fan. The fifth blind man leans against the creature's
side and insists that the elephant is like a wall. The sixth, gingerly
feeling the sharp tusk, dogmatizes that the elephant is like unto a
spear. All are right in part, but all are wrong in their hasty generaliza-
tions, insisting there is no more to the truth than what they have personally experienced.

31

Now one might wish fundamentalists would keep this parable in mind when it comes to the question of other religions, for they might not be so quick to damn everyone else to hell. But they *are* quite quick to invoke holy paradox, blessed antinomy, when their own theology forces them into a corner. And it often does. For instance, in his second meditation, Rick Warren tells us that God not only *has* love but that he *is* love (as 1 John 4:16 tells us). All Christians will agree with this cheery sentiment, until, that is, the topic of eternal damnation comes up. At this point, they spout pious talk about how God would be unjust and remiss if he did not torture even minor sinners for eternity. How could a loving God, you ask, be worse than Hitler in *eternally tormenting any*body? Some will dismiss the question as a good old antinomy; others will try to get God off the hook by maintaining that sinners knew good and well what was coming and *asked* for it. That is so ludicrous as to require no rebuttal. But it is worth mentioning because it is a good example of how fundamentalists cannot seem to maintain their faith without a thousand self-deceptions. To protect the Truth, as they view it, they are coached to indulge in endless implausible excuses and dodges, the embrace of which thoroughly imbues them with an unnamed cynicism to the point where reason means nothing and propaganda means everything.

Reverend Warren assures us right off the bat that all that we are, in every detail, is the result of God's conscious artistic choice. Like a designer at Disney Studios planning a new animated epic, God labors over every minute detail of a character's appearance, voice, role, and amount of screen time. The upshot is the ancient belief, which Stoics also held, that one ought to strive to be content with the lot dealt one by Divine Reason and play the role assigned. It is an ethic of absolute duty: conformity to the will and command of the Creator. As with many aspects of fundamentalist Christianity, I want to suggest, the more seriously one takes this notion and its logical implications, the more absurd as a belief system and the more crippling as a philosophy of life the whole thing becomes.

Once one steps into the mire of predestination, the belief that all things happen in minute conformity to the design of God, one has inherited a world of trouble, created not by God (if there is one) but by fallible human theologians (the only kind there are). If you say God is the cause of every effect, then you perforce land in bed with St. Augustine and John Calvin, who clearly understood the implications: God determined beforehand that human beings should sin in order to justify sending Jesus Christ to save them. One cannot logically clear out a zone of free will so as to make sinful acts the free decisions of human sinners, with God merely "allowing" them. Theologians love to make an illusory distinction between the "decretive" and the "permissive" will of God, but Calvin saw through this dodge. It is like saying that the assassin pulled the trigger on the gun but only *allowed* the bullet to find its target. One cannot so easily rend the fabric of causality. Of course, Warren is not at the moment interested in that aspect of the matter. He only uses predestination to comfort his readers that, as the slogan goes, "God don't make no junk." He gave you every wart, and that for some good purpose. You ought to thank him for it.

But, again, this belief entails a dangerous sacrifice of the intellect. It opens a can of worms that the believer will not even bother chasing down and replacing in the can. And for neglecting to tidy things up, he or she fails to realize he or she is not really holding a belief at all, rather just a pleasant attitude reinforced with a high-sounding piece of gibberish. Let me explain.

Whether one worries about one's ugly kisser or the various tragedies of nature, including tsunamis and earthquakes, the issue is really the same: how does the loving control of God cause these things to occur? The bottom line is always that God had a purpose. Let's leave aside the nasty implication that for God the end justifies any means, no matter how horrifically painful or destructive. Let's ignore the terrible implication that the ostensibly loving God is really something of a Nazi concentration camp scientist, employing the most torturous methods either to "perfect" you or to teach you a lesson. Instead, let's cut to the chase: what sort of a "purpose" is this suffering, this ugliness, this tidal wave, supposed to be achieving? The answer is the old standby: "When we get to heaven, God will tell us." Don't you see what a dodge this is? Granted, it is a self-defense mechanism. It is an attempt to lick the wound, to soften the blow. But it is an admission that *there is no discernible purpose at all*. It is the same as saying "God *knows* why it happened!" In other words, *no one* knows. There is no answer. It is as if you had stayed up till the wee hours to see who won the Best Actor Oscar, and they handed the host an envelope, and he announced to the camera, "Well, *some*body won! There's a name in there, all right! Thanks for watching, folks! Good night!" Apparently, simply believing that there *is* a purpose, though none is ever given, is better than the angst of believing there is *no* purpose, that things happen unscripted.

But is it? Is Job not comforted only when he learns from the Whirlwind's mighty voice that no mortal can second-guess God? That Bildad and Eliphaz and Zophar are as wrong to say God is punishing Job as Job himself is to blame God for victimizing him? What a comfort to realize that misfortune *just happens*, and that God does *not* have a bullet with your name on it! What a comfort not to be hagridden by the superstition that God is plaguing you with a test, a trial, an ordeal! And that is precisely the superstition peddled by fundamentalist gurus like Bill Gothard, Merlin Carothers, and many others who tell us to practice the masochism of the battered wife who meekly responds to every imagined divine blow with "Thank you, sir! May I have another?"

Why are people content to comfort themselves (though it seems to me *cold* comfort) with these notions that an all-seeing God is subjecting you to the regimen of the experimental rat in the Skinner box? Another psychologist, Sigmund Freud, explained it pretty well, it seems to me, as a refusal to "put away childish things." We grow accustomed to the cloying reassurances of childhood that our parents are omniscient (*they* seem to think so, don't they?), fair, wise, and able to protect us. As we grow up we sooner or later come to the unpleasant realization that they are not what they were cracked up to be. We blame them for not being more than mortal parents could be. If we are unable to mature, unable to swallow hard and learn life's lessons on our own, we will insist on believing that we were only asking the *wrong parents* to be infallible. We will believe in a heavenly mommy and daddy (if we are Catholics) or at least a heavenly daddy (if we are Protestants) who *can* provide infallible answers without our having to trouble our heads and risk getting it wrong. We believe the heavenly daddy can protect us from all harm and that if he doesn't we must have deserved it, or that he must have been teaching us the hard way, and so on.[1] At least it's better than looking unflinching into the Void, isn't it?

Uh, *no*. No, it *isn't*. It's best of all not to be deceived, not to retreat into word games that promise answers that are never forthcoming, not to gull oneself with superstitions. But does such honesty result in a life of nihilistic despair? Is that what we're stuck with if we don't believe we are a coloring book page with God working the crayons? Again, no.

Okay, first, it is true that you didn't choose the way you look, your menu of talents, or the circumstances of your birth. These things were determined, almost completely, by genetics and the plain facts of when your parents conceived you. These things, even though there were no puppet strings of predestination, even though they were random occurrences in the broad picture, did determine how you would emerge and develop. It happened according to a definite recipe, but no one sat down and planned it out. Think of the movie *Back to the Future*. Marty's birth was the result of an improbable and haphazard meeting between his geek father-to-be and his racy teenager mom-to-be. No one planned it. But when he went back in time and unwittingly disturbed those very circumstances, he tipped over the house of randomly dealt cards, and he began to vanish from the family portrait. Things had to have occurred as they did, or there would have been a very different result, but nothing dictated that they happen that way. It's the same with you. It is only in *retrospect* that it had to happen just as it did, to get the result that you got, not in *prospect*.

And this lesson contains another, a wonderful one. It means that your birth, with all your particulars, is a wildly improbable event, and hence precious. You won the sweepstakes by being born at all. Think of all the wallflower sperm and egg cells. You made it, buddy. Whew! What a staggering wonder! What a thing to rejoice in! The lottery wasn't fixed! God didn't rig it! You won fair and square! What a miracle!

True, you might have been prettier or more talented had you created yourself. But you didn't, and you couldn't. I've got my own Bible quote for you: "Why kick against the ox-goads?" (Acts 26:14). God didn't design you in micro detail or in broad outline. And remember, if you want to say he did, you've got some explaining to do: all those birth defects; anacephalic babies; kids with no limbs; two-headed, conjoined twins. Pardon me if I'm not so politically correct as to say these are all hunky-dory. But that's what you're stuck with, my friend, if you want to believe everybody, including every horrific mutation, turned out just the way a loving God wanted them! I don't have to explain them except as reproductive misfires. I, unlike you, believe there are genuine *tragedies*. No theology or "sensitivity" doctrine compels me to pretend otherwise.

But I say you are nonetheless a work of art. And so am I. And it makes much better sense to say so if you do not bring in the mythology of a Geppetto who made you like Pinocchio. You are not a completely blank slate. Your parents' genes dealt you the hand you're holding, but it's up to you to play it. Or, to switch metaphors, you stand before the blank canvas of your life. Thanks to your parents and your position in time and space, you have a palette of particular colors in your hand. It is up to you to create the life you will live. It is up to you to create your own meaning. How could it be otherwise? Meaning and beauty are in the eye of the beholder. Where else could they be? They are anything but objective, aren't they? Whatever something means, it means *to someone*! If there is a God, he may have his own opinion as to what your life ought to be used for, what it means. But your life can have no meaning for you other than what it means *to you*, not him. You have to create it!

I like what Albert Camus said about art and why it must be gratuitous, why it must serve no purpose, neither to educate nor to propagandize: the artistic creation is a gesture of freedom, and toward freedom. It serves no purpose, obeys no command, does not labor to convey a message. It does not promote agendas. This is why, for example, we look askance at the old Socialist Realism of the USSR. That stuff was little more than sculpted political slogans. It was not art for art's sake. But that's what the artwork that is your life ought to be. A wonderful splash of creative joy and freedom. Not a tool for God.

How close to the mark Rick Warren comes! He correctly sees that it would make no sense for us to say God *had* to create the world or the human race. That would mean God felt need, was not sufficient to himself. He cannot have created us to love because he was love-starved. No, Christian theology says he created simply to share the wonder of his love with a wider audience. Hindu theology puts it slightly differently: God created the universe as an act of *play*. Either way, theologians understood Camus's point: if God were to create at all, it must be a gratuitous creative act. It must be for art's sake.

I will not take for granted that there is a God, but I prefer coherent God concepts to incoherent ones, theologies that make some sense to those that are merely blind assertions of superstition and mythology. And whether or not there is a God, there is a creator of your life: you! You stand before the canvas with brush in hand!

Day Two

Point to Ponder: I won the sweepstakes just by being born!

Quote to Remember: "The universe was not pregnant with life, nor the biosphere with man. Our number came up in a Monte Carlo game." (Jacques Monod)

Question to Consider: There are things about me that I don't like. Do they really make much difference? Which are worth trying to change? Can I see my way to resigning myself, with a laugh, to the rest?

NOTE

1. Sigmund Freud, *The Future of an Illusion*, trans. W. D. Robson-Scott, rev. ed. by James Strachey (Garden City, NY: Doubleday Anchor, 1964), p. 35.

One-Track Mind?

We are what we think.
All that we are arises with our thoughts.
With our thoughts we make the world.
Speak or act with a pure mind
And happiness will follow you
As your shadow, unshakable.

"Look how he abused me and beat me,
How he threw me down and robbed me."
Live with such thoughts and you live in hate.
"Look how he abused me and beat me,
How he threw me down and robbed me."
Abandon such thoughts, and live in love.
—Dhammapada: Sayings of the Buddha

An ass which turns a millstone did a hundred miles walking. When
it was loosed, it found that it was still at the same place. There are
men who make many journeys, but make no progress anywhere. . . .
In vain did the wretches labour.
—Gospel of Philip

BACKSEAT DRIVERS

In his third meditation, "What Drives Your Life?" Pastor Warren sets forth a poison menu of things that motivate too many people, with the result that their lives never get anywhere, and they never achieve any important goal, much less happiness. With most of these diagnoses no right-thinking person will disagree. I sure don't. Besides seconding the motion, my goal here is a modest one: to remind or inform the reader that the Bible is not the only source of wisdom when it comes to these questions. Permeating *The Purpose-Driven Life* is the assumption that the Bible alone holds the answers, even that it holds *the* Solution, singular with a capital, as if finally there is but one single Problem with a capital P.[1] That is going too far. Thankfully, nobody, no one thinker, no one religion, has a corner on the market of wisdom, and it is foolish to think otherwise. Beyond this, I want to indicate a few places where the fundamentalist piety Reverend Warren espouses actually seems to contradict or undermine the biblical wisdom he seeks to dispense.

Many poor souls are driven, or, one might say, paralyzed, by *guilt*. They feel, whether they think to use the term or not, that they have committed the unpardonable sin. As a result their sense of self-respect plummets, and they remain under a cloud of depression. If the offense (real or imagined) was especially traumatic, as Sigmund Freud said, the mind may "repress" any memory of the deed.[2] Or it may minimize its importance by editing our memory of it. But the subconscious mind is a stomach that cannot easily digest such poison, and it will try to throw it back up, often in the form of a vague sense of guilt or anxiety whose source we cannot seem to place. Deep down, we know exactly what's wrong, but we fear it would just hurt too much to recognize it. Psychoanalysis is a strategy for flushing out the villain, facing it down, and learning to move on. It is a path of wisdom and self-discovery. And it is well worth checking out if one is still haunted by guilt even after thinking better of what one has done (which, by the way, is what "repentance" means, the underlying Greek word being *metanoia*: "to change one's mind").

Once I had a student in a philosophy class who confided to me that he agonized over having badgered his pregnant girlfriend into getting an abortion. In retrospect he could not forgive himself. I reminded him of the Parable of the Prodigal Son (Luke 15:11–32), in which a man has disgraced himself and his family during years of squandering his fortune and sowing his wild oats. He finally slinks home, hardly daring to face his father for shame, asking only to be hired as a field hand so as not to starve. His father will have none of that and welcomes him back into the embrace of the family. The righteous older brother is none too eager to see this development, and the story closes with the father trying to reconcile the two brothers. I suggested to my student that if he considered Jesus any sort of authority in these matters, which I certainly do, he ought to see there was hope for him.

And the parable has a lot to tell us whether we are believers in the Christian God or not. What I mean is, the story, like all ancient stories of two estranged brothers, can be read as a psychological allegory for the two estranged sides of a single personality.[3] It is what happens when our heart becomes divided over, oh, let's say, guilt. Whence this division? Why are we afraid of *forgiving ourselves*? For a very good reason, I think. We are secretly aware of the danger that, if we wipe the slate clean, we will have gained relief at too small a cost. We will have minimized our guilt: "I guess it wasn't so bad after all, what I did to her." And we know that way lies moral paralysis. If we start down that path, we may find before long that it takes more and more to mortify us, less and less of a rationalization to get us off the hook of conscience. And, after a while, nothing bothers us. The news is full of people who have reached this tragic condition of total moral frostbite.

But there is a way to avoid that danger, to forgive ourselves without just blowing off what we did. It is a simple principle: we need *to forgive but not to forget*. We must remember what we were, and still are, capable of. We need to learn the sobering lessons of our history so as not to repeat them. Think of yourself as forgiven, not innocent.

If you have wronged someone else, of course you need to make restitution, to seek forgiveness. If you don't, you are letting yourself off way too easily once again.

But is there anyone *else* whose forgiveness you need to seek? Like maybe God's? I don't think so. I find sociologist Emil Durkheim to have been pretty wise when he began to suspect that the sense of an ever-snooping, finger-wagging God is a handy creation of society to keep its less reflective members in line.[4] The authorities can't keep the whole population under surveillance all the time (though our society may be moving in that direction!). So we indoctrinate our kids with the best morality we know until they internalize it. They develop a conscience to do the finger wagging when we're not around. And so far so good; if we don't do that, you know what we get: sociopaths and psychopaths, incapable of empathizing with their intended victims and heedless of society.

But then we go further: we get kids to believe Somebody is always watching them even if they escape *our* notice, and this God will see to their punishment even if, in the eyes of fellow mortals, they manage to commit the perfect crime. It's just like George Orwell's classic *1984*, in which the cowed subjects of a totalitarian regime have two-way TV screens in their rooms. Big Brother may be watching them any or all of the time. You never know when the set's on in your direction, so you better watch out, you better not cry. However useful, the God as Big Brother idea is probably what Durkheim said it was: an internalized peer pressure gimmick. Have you ever switched churches (or any other peer group) and noticed after a while that you don't feel self-conscious about certain things anymore, but you do feel self-conscious about a whole *new* set of things? It just shows how you, like everybody else, are easily affected and shaped by peer pressure. Not that that's a bad thing! But it does suggest we don't need belief in God to explain how morality (or forgiveness) works.

But some folks *might* need such a belief. It may be that their faith in the Nation of Islam is all that's keeping them from going back to dealing drugs. Maybe the fear of an avenging God is all that's keeping some guy from beating his wife. Well, in such cases, I welcome them to keep right on believing. I think they are making a logic jump, but I'm planning to keep that little opinion to myself. In fact, if this is *you*, why don't you just put away this annoying book right now!

Mixing up God with the issue of forgiveness only muddies the water. How very strange it sounds when preachers tell you how you cannot be forgiven unless you believe all the orthodox affirmations in the Nicene Creed. I know, that's not how they put it, but Reverend Warren closes his chapter by reminding the reader that one day he/she will face God's judgment bar, and a failure to acknowledge the truth of evangelical Christianity will send one down the shoot to a boiling hell. How can fundamentalists fail to see how wild a swerve they have made? What does believing in Jesus Christ as the divine savior, sacrificed on the cross, or any other religious belief, have to do with the psychological and emotional business of forgiving oneself or others? Believers in some other religion have no right to feel forgiven if they don't convert to fundamentalism? Again, I know Warren would never put it that way. He would and does retreat directly into the theological realm, as if he were an astronomer pointing out constellations to the uninformed. *It's not denominational affiliation that allows entrance into heaven. It is acceptance of the atoning death of the Son of God, since that deed was the only means of atoning for sin.* But that is just mystification. That is like a politician wrapping himself and his demagoguery in the flag, so you will not think to question whether good Americanism is automatic agreement with him. Gee, wouldn't you think such a forgiving deity could see his way to forgiving your theological mistakes?

Resentment is the favorite poison of other miserable folk. They cannot get over what others have done to them. They cannot forgive *others*. But they must. Matthew's Parable of the Unmerciful Servant (Matthew 18:23–35) isn't very helpful here, I'm afraid. In fact, it puts us in a maddening double bind by telling us that, unless we manage to forgive our sinning brother from our heart, God will hand us over to the torturers (most English translators are afraid of that word and soften it to "jailors" or some such euphemism). Do you see the paradox here? I hope you are reading your Bible carefully enough not to speed by this logical train wreck without noticing. This time, do some rubbernecking, okay? It is a case of what Paul Watzlawick calls the "Be Spontaneous" paradox.[5] Can spontaneous behavior be commanded? Can unrehearsed behavior be prescribed? Can off-the-cuff actions be scripted? No, obviously they cannot. And for precisely this reason one cannot (even God cannot) command and obtain sincere forgiveness under threat of torture and damnation. Can I forgive from my heart, motivated by threats? It is as if a man approached a woman and asked for a declaration of love while pointing a revolver at her face. What's she going to say? Sure, but is she going to mean it? She better hope the guy is stupid enough to believe her. But is God so stupid? Are you?

You see, the whole idea of forgiveness, whether divine or human, is essentially one of *grace*. No one owes you forgiveness. You don't owe it to them. The guilty party has burned the bridge. The offended party is under no obligation to take the trouble to rebuild it from his side, even if the offender has rebuilt his half. If you have to forgive whenever someone asks you, you are vulnerable to manipulation. No, like choosing the one you love, your decision must be an act of free choice, of grace. That is why it means so much once granted. We are used to hearing that God was under no obligation to forgive the human race. Right! And neither are you! Forgiveness is the kind of thing that cannot be required and commanded, or it is not forgiveness.

But on the other hand, it is stupid and self-destructive *not* to forgive, because, as Pastor Warren says, you will only be hurting *yourself.* You just have to forgive and put the past where it belongs: out to the curb. "But don't I have the right *not* to forgive? The right to nurse the grudge?" Sure you do. And you also have every right to refuse life-saving surgery, but I don't know why you'd want to.

But it is not so simple, is it? Some preachers tell you that if you do decide to forgive, you will immediately feel different. I have tried that, only to be frustrated and disappointed—and still bitter. Finally I learned that such emotional miracles are as rare as real physical healings at an Ernest Angley rally. It takes time to heal such wounds, just like physical ones. You do have to take your stand and decide by force of will that you will forgive the offender, love the unlovable. And eventually your emotions will realign themselves. It will speed the process if you can reestablish contact and make yourself go through the open-handed motions of friendship. Your feelings and attitudes will eventually accommodate themselves to what they see you doing. And finally you will *feel* you have forgiven. It will feel great!

Fear drives most of us at one time or another, some people most of the time. I wholeheartedly agree with Rick Warren's entreaty that the slaves of fear throw off their shackles. They/we need to get straight one simple fact: the future need not be a replay of the past. It will be so only as long as we guarantee it by our fear that it will be so. In fact, that is the only factor mighty enough to cause the past to replace the future. Otherwise, there is only *change*: you change, your circumstances and opportunities change. If you let them, your experiences will change *you*, and the more you open up to experience, the more it will change you. It is a simple fact. Just stop carrying the past like a chip on your shoulder. The free dawning of the future is natural; your blockage of it is what is unnatural. That's the thing you have to go to the trouble to *make* happen. The future will happen by itself. So let it!

SUNDAY DRIVERS

And maybe the most important example of letting the future bring healthful change is to be open-minded in your opinions. Don't go into the coming months or years with your mind and thoughts foreclosed. Religious beliefs are the most difficult ones to change. People are incredibly stubborn when it comes to religious doctrines, thinking it a virtue to be closed-minded. Do you bristle at this suggestion? Then I'm saying the shoe fits. Don't you think it best to be open to reason, that is, to possibly changing your mind, when it comes to brand loyalty, politics, whatever else? Isn't it a sign of good character and of wisdom when someone is broad-minded and willing to listen? Don't we admire that? Then how can it be virtuous to slam the door and switch the sign from OPEN to CLOSED when it comes to this, the most important of life's questions?

I do not mean to cast scorn on anyone, but I think most people's tenacious loyalty to the beliefs they were taught as children (or during the tender period of realignment after a stressful conversion) is the same as what happens to baby ducks.[6] It's called "imprinting." The duckling thinks the first thing its newborn eyes behold is Mommy, and little Daffy or Daisy or Donald will march lockstep behind "Mommy" even if Mommy turns out to be a cocker spaniel or a lawn mower. It is a hard bond to break, even though there is a good chance of being mistaken. And so it is with inherited or indoctrinated religious beliefs. I mean, what are the chances that only you, and not, oh, say, some Buddhist in Burma, were born with the one true religion?

I have encountered many, many students over the years who refused even to consider other faiths (which I only asked them to do for the sake of a "walk a mile in their shoes" essay) because they felt it would be disloyal to their parents. Talk like that tells me they have already relegated their beliefs to the vestigial position of an ethnic background, ancestral roots in some Old World country they have never seen and feel no particular desire to visit. How seriously can they take such a religion? But then they probably don't think much about it. What amazes me is the religiously committed students who try their best to live out their faith—and yet are equally unwilling to consider a rival doctrine. What are they afraid of? I'll tell you. And it's not just students and young people.

Fundamentalists or evangelicals (you do know the difference, right? An evangelical is a fundamentalist who'll let you go to the movies) are afraid of being damned to hell. That's why many of them embraced the faith in the first place. Tell me it's not so. Tell me I'm wrong. You know I'm right. "Repent or perish! Come to Christ tonight or spend a Christless eternity in hell! Your friends will wait for you! Come down to the altar, or you might die and go to hell on the way home tonight!" Such dear souls, terrorized into belief, heave a sigh of relief once they believe themselves safely within the fold. So imagine what they think when some sneaky professor tries to get them to consider a range of views: it must be a clever ploy of Satan to tempt them outside the charmed circle where the devil can get to them.

To use a different metaphor, they seem to think of God as an irate and peevish theology professor, and, just as Rick Warren and countless other clergy assure them, the Final Exam is on its way! You will look over a multiple-choice test and come to the question, "Which is the real savior?" Suppose you check off Amida Buddha. Yikes! You've already flunked. It's an unending Summer School in hell for you, my poor friend! Or if you left that one aside for the moment and pondered, "Which is the true God?" and you checked "Allah," same result. Or suppose you got as far as the True or False section, and up comes the Trinity: true or false? You mark it "F," and again you're headed for hell.

Rick Warren quotes 1 John 4:18 (or at least, I *think* he does; it's difficult to tell, with all the sloppy paraphrases he quotes; here's the Revised Standard Version): "There is no fear in love, but perfect love casts out fear. For fear has to do with punishment, and he who fears is not perfected in love." I'm not sure Warren should be quoting this text. He has by no means cast out fear. One might even say his religion is based on it.

Immanuel Kant was right: you have to get rid of the fear of damnation to think clearly about faith. I like the way he put it. One acts morally only when one "acts for the sake of duty," that is, because it is the right thing to do. By contrast, one's deed is morally worthless so long as one merely "acts in accordance with duty," that is, because you're afraid of getting punished if you don't. Sure, it's better for society if a would-be crook controls himself for fear of jail, but we don't give him a medal for it. Real morality is not the product of fearing a spanking. But what does fundamentalist hell-belief encourage? It retards any developing moral judgment by freezing moral maturity right at the most primitive, most childish, stage: the fear of retribution—and fundamentalism threatens one hell of a spanking.

How can you talk about God's love as long as you believe, essentially, that he will damn you to eternal torment for failing to get your theology straight? For being a pious Buddhist instead of a pious Christian? A Mormon instead of a Southern Baptist? Some will go even that far, while others will go considerably farther in separating the sheep from the goats. At this point, fundamentalists will often start backpedaling, rationalizing, which only shows they are ashamed of this belief. But that doesn't stop them from continuing to hold it.

Or think again of the gun-toting guy asking for a date. He might actually love you, but as long as he's also got the gun trained on you, it's a kind of love you don't really want. Fundamentalists offer us a "loving" God who is some kind of divine stalker. They think they have to. If they started revising their theology, they fear they'd wind up in hell for daring to touch the holy ark (2 Samuel 6:6–7).

THE PURPOSE-DRIVEN LIABILITY

So we can agree at least that guilt, resentment, fear (Warren rightly adds materialism and fear of others' opinions) ought not to be the big motivating factors in our lives. But what *should*? Of course, the whole premise of Rick Warren's famous book is that our lives, all of us without exception, ought to be devoted to serving God and forwarding his agenda as defined by evangelical Christianity. I will return to this point in a subsequent chapter, where I will try to show how even Warren's understanding of what the Christian mission is proceeds from nineteenth-century fundamentalism, not from careful biblical exegesis. Thus I characterize what he prescribes not as the "biblical" purpose of life, but rather as the evangelical purpose. I'm not ready to give him the Bible that easily.

Let me say, first, that I regard Warren's prescription as more of an emergency measure appropriate for people in dire straits than a plan for the healthy, normal life. As all theologians do, Warren tends to get melodramatic. Everything in life is seen in Technicolor, with a cosmic scope, and packaged in high-tension rhetoric. You are told you are playing a role in a cosmic drama. Everything casts a long shadow. Nothing is mundane. Religion comes from a magic storybook and assigns the believer a role, even if a brief cameo appearance, in a magic story.

I am putting it pretty bluntly, but I don't think I am distorting the nature and function of religious narrative. All of them, whether the *Iliad*, the *Mahabharata*, or the Bible, attempt to impart meaning to life by imposing an artificial structure on life. That structure is dramatic and narrative in form.[7] That is good, the great genius of narrative. But we don't have to take it literally. We ought to arm ourselves not with a creed, but with an agenda, a list of tasks. For instance, for the world to see that the good guys win and the bad guys lose, we have to *make* it happen that way. We must act out the heroic story of justice, its upset, and its restoration. The world does not seem to be a loving nest for the human race. It is cold and hard—except as we superimpose upon it our own vision, our own beautiful fiction, so to speak, of a world of love and warmth.

As caring human beings, we are duty-bound to humanize the world. Sometimes, as in a war against tyranny, that goal pushes everything else onto the back burner. But when things are normal, healthy, copacetic, when we are "at ease in Zion," the pressure is off. It is still our duty to conduct ourselves in a just way, honoring others and deferring to their freedom, loving others and enjoying their friendship in return, but I would call these the conditions of the good life, not exactly a purpose for life.

The difference is: what is the goal you start each day hoping to accomplish? That defines your purpose—or purposes. For most people, there are many goals, and they do not compete. Of course, you don't want them to conflict, which could cost you your integrity. And all alike may be thrust aside when emergency calls.

But it is not always during emergencies that goals must be put aside. For adolescents and teenagers it may seem that way, granted. Life may seem to be one big soap opera or fantasy role-playing game, but that, most of us think, should not be the norm. For those who think it is, we want to plead with such too-intense individuals to "get real," "to get a life."

I think Rick Warren, like most clergy and religious writers, is promoting this sort of hyped-up adolescent fixation. Why? Winston Davis, an anthropologist, explains how virtually all religions like to oversimplify life's problems as stemming directly from one particular root Problem.[8] They do this so they can then offer a particular, copyrighted one-size-fits-all Solution. In the case of fundamentalism, the one Problem is Sin, and the one Solution is coming to faith in Jesus Christ, by which they mean embracing the lingo and fellowship of fundamentalist Christianity. If you do that, every preacher repeats, then you will have the key to solving all your problems.

For whom is life so simple? For the distressed who have lost control of their lives, for the down-and-out, for those who subsist in chaos. They need radical surgery. They need extraordinary measures to get the worms back into the can. But this is not the normal state. Most mature individuals are not like this and thus do not need the radical surgery. Walter Kaufmann writes in response to Paul Tillich, but I think his words apply equally well to Rick Warren and the "old time religion" he represents: "Who really has a single ultimate concern? If that phrase has any definite meaning, it would seem to imply a willingness to sacrifice all other concerns to one's sole ultimate concern. Having only one ultimate concern might well be the recipe for

fanaticism. It is the mark of a humane person that he has several ultimate concerns that check and balance each other."[9]

Reverend Warren tells us that having "God's" purpose will sim-
plify our lives. That it will! But perhaps it *over*simplifies them. It may
even lobotomize them. Warren tells us that knowing the purpose of
our lives gives meaning to our lives. Really, that's almost a tautology,
like saying, "A bachelor is an unmarried man." Your meaning and
your purpose are the same, right? And then the question becomes:
how do you find it? Again, I am sure you must find it yourself, or no
matter what you come up with, it will not be your authentic purpose
at all. And some of us think it is the journey that matters more than
the destination anyway. How's this: "Looking for your purpose, creating your purpose, gives meaning to your life." Amen.

Day Three

Point to Ponder: Becoming is better than being.

Quote to Remember: "Why do you not judge for yourselves what is
right?" (Luke 12:57, RSV)

Question to Consider: What decisions have brought me to where I am
today, whether I like that place or bemoan it? Was I even aware of
making those decisions? Did I let others make them for me?

NOTES

1. Winston Davis, *Dojo: Magic and Exorcism in Modern Japan* (Stanford,
CA: Stanford University Press, 1982).

2. Sigmund Freud, *A General Introduction to Psychoanalysis*, trans. Joan
Riviere (New York: Pocket Books, 1953), pp. 304–307.

3. Bruno Bettelheim, "Tales of Two Brothers," in *The Uses of Enchantment: The Meaning and Importance of Fairy Tales* (New York: Vintage Books,
1977), pp. 90–96.

4. Emil Durkheim, *The Elementary Forms of the Religious Life*, trans.
Joseph War Swain (1915; repr., New York: MacMillan, 1965), pp. 297–99,
306–307.

5. Paul Watzlawick, *How Real Is Real? Confusion, Disinformation, Commu-*

nication: An Anecdotal Introduction to Communications Theory (New York: Vintage Books, 1976), pp. 19–21.

6. Thanks to Ed Babinsky for this analogy.

7. James W. Fowler, *Stages of Faith: The Psychology of Human Development and the Quest for Meaning* (San Francisco: Harper & Row, 1981).

8. Davis, *Dojo.*

9. Walter Kaufmann, *The Faith of a Heretic* (Garden City, NY: Doubleday Anchor, 1963), p. 83.

Sons of Dust

He knoweth our frame; he remembereth that we are dust.
—Psalms 103:14 (KJV)

*His disciples say to him, "When will the repose of the dead begin?
And when will the new world come?" He says to them, "What you
look for has already come, but you fail to recognize it."*
—Gospel according to Thomas, saying 51

TICKET TO HEAVEN

I think we are really getting bum advice in Rick Warren's fourth chapter, "Made to Last Forever." This is what I'd have to call *the purpose-driven lie*, except that he believes it. It is the notion that your life here on earth is mere calisthenics before the big game, the rehearsal before the play. Warren warns us that we have an unending afterlife awaiting and that, by comparison with it, our present life of eighty to a hundred years will one day seem like an implausible dream. And so that's the way it ought to seem to us now! I hardly know where to begin, but I might as well start with the Bible, the source of Reverend Warren's unshakable conviction on the matter.

My guess is that right here we have the mother lode, the major value people see in the Bible and why they insist it is a direct revelation of information from God. They know that, as mere mortals, they can never know what lies on the other side of the grave until they get there. And even then, there may be nothing to know, unless someone from the other side tells them so. If the Bible is a telegram from Beyond, then their desperate curiosity is satisfied. They view the Bible much as adherents of UFO cults like the Aetherius Society view their channeled "revelations" from "Space Brothers": namely, as a word from without, what in the science fiction epic *Dune* they call "the Voice from the Outer World." We could never plumb the depths of space to find life there, but if aliens came to earth, why, then we'd know! Then the mysteries of Beyond would be settled. And these people so desperately want it to be settled that they defend the "eye-witness accounts" of the supposed flying saucer crash at Roswell with the same stubborn insistence as evangelical apologists defending the inerrancy of scripture.

The same eager anxiety accounts for the great zeal of Christian apologists to defend the historical fact and character of the resurrection of Jesus, come hell or high water. It once again boils down to the desperate desire for certainty about life after death. You've heard the cliché: "Well, nobody's ever come back to tell us about it!" But if the resurrection of Jesus really happened, its proponents claim, somebody *did* come back from beyond the veil to tell us it's okay, it will turn out happily ever after. The same fears made Spiritualism, the nineteenth-century séance religion, wildly popular. People, understandably, experience great fear and anxiety when they think about not being here to watch TV anymore.

You see, this is why evangelicals, even sophisticated ones, hate the more liberal theology of people like Rudolf Bultmann, who, by the way, did believe in an afterlife; he believed in universal salvation.[1] But he rejected any literal belief in the resurrection of Jesus. For Bultmann, the resurrection is a symbol of the ever-present availability of the cross in Christian preaching, always offering the grace of God to the hearer. But that version of the gospel might as well be raw Satanism if you ask an evangelical or a fundamentalist. What's wrong with it? If the resurrection accounts of the gospels are sacred legends, as critical scholars think, or even just rumor and hallucination, as outright skeptics think, then we are left without any guarantee of surviving the grave ourselves. The return of Jesus from the dead, like the inerrant inspiration of scripture, serves as our guarantee of an afterlife. And you're going to have to pry that belief out of many people's cold, dead fingers. Whether they'll be watching you do it from their stadium seats in heaven, who knows?

If the Bible didn't guarantee a ticket to heaven, would most fundamentalists even care about it? Or if it left the question open? I doubt it very much, at least from the way they talk about it. Suppose the Bible taught mortality, no life after death. Many people would part company with it right there. Rick Warren says, in his fourth chapter, that if there were nothing beyond this life, we could be excused for throwing ethical concerns to the wind and using what time we have left for unabashed hedonism. (That, it seems to me, is an amusing spectacle to contemplate. Fundamentalists like James Dobson or Pat Robertson even enjoying the *idea* of whooping it up in some bar or den of iniquity?)

What if the Bible were just a collection of evolving and competing opinions of ancient thinkers on the subjects of death and the afterlife? No, that wouldn't satisfy fundamentalists either, because that sort of a Bible would no longer be a revelation in the sense they cherish. They don't want a Bible that merely offers food for thought. They are tired or afraid of thinking. They know good and well that no certainty could result from using one's poor human brain to philosophize on the matter. Don't philosophers disagree about everything? They sure do! And the fundamentalist, like Rick Warren, is in it for the certainty. He wants the teddy bear security of knowing his purpose in life and that it will take him to a comfy heaven.

Well, I'm afraid I have bad news about the Bible, a book I love very much and have spent the greater part of my life studying. You can keep insisting till you're blue in the face that it is inspired by God. And maybe it is, though I find the notion unhelpful: it doesn't tell you how to interpret anything. For the Bible does turn out to offer us a series of very different ideas about death and the afterlife. That tells me the book is in fact a collection of pious thoughts and theories, not a revealed textbook of doctrine. But if God did inspire or dictate it, he has a funny way of making himself clear. I don't see how an inspired but ambiguous book is any more helpful than an uninspired book. Even if you want to retreat to the old dodge that the Bible contains only "apparent" contradictions, you're not out of the hole, because then you've got to decide what is your basis for taking some verses literally and harmonizing the others as if they all agreed? Finally, you wind up interpreting the text through the lenses of your favorite church's tradition or creed. And that just shows you were kidding yourself when you thought you were going only by the Bible, getting your beliefs from it rather than imposing them onto it. But what *does* the Bible say about death and afterward? There is quite a menu of options.

UNCERTAIN SOUND

First, the Bible certainly teaches *mortalism*: no life after death. It teaches it right out of the starting gate, in the Garden of Eden story, which seeks to account for the dismaying fact of death, offering no comforting hints of postmortem hope. God hands out the punishments to Adam, Eve, and the Serpent, and they include species-wide capital punishment. "By the sweat of your face you will eat bread, till you return to the ground, because from it you were taken; for you are dust, and to dust you shall return" (Genesis 3:19, NASB). And there's nothing saying, "Stay tuned for the complete reversal of this verdict later in the book!"

And don't give me the nonsense about the "seed of the woman" crushing the head of "the seed of the serpent" in Genesis 3:15, that it hints at salvation on that future day when Jesus smashes Satan. The Bible never identifies the Edenic Serpent with Satan, and to make this verse refer to Jesus Christ, with no more explanation than this, is just the sort of wild allegorizing Martin Luther used to ridicule the Catholics for. And even if this verse *did* constitute some sort of prophecy of Jesus versus Satan (or as Roman Catholics read it, Mary versus Satan), it doesn't say anything about life after death. Boy, am I sick and tired of people claiming to take the Bible literally and then resorting to ventriloquism like this to get out of a tight spot.

Psalm 90, one of the most poignant passages in the Bible, shares the pessimism of the Eden story. It laments the irrevocable death sentence as the result of God's well-deserved ire. But it tries to make the best of it, asking God's help to awaken us from the complacent torpor in which we sleepwalk away our lives. We seem to be oblivious of the fact that we have but seventy or eighty years to live. If we were to gain wisdom from God, we would begin to use our scant time judiciously, inventorying our remaining years and spending them as constructively as we can. I want to come back to this wisdom in a moment.

Second, the Old Testament often speaks of a half-conscious *post-existence as a shade or a ghost amid the shadows of Sheol*, as one of the disembodied *Rephaim* floating on the currents of the *Tehom*, the vast, universal ocean existing under the flat earth (Job 26:5–6). Sometimes, as in the Gilgamesh epic, written in the same neighborhood as the Bible, Sheol is pictured as a great, dim city whose gates never open again after they receive the souls of the dead (as also in Job 7:9–10, 10:21–22). The woeful inhabitants of the place are not mindful of God (Psalms 6:5, 22:29, 30:9), nor he of them (Psalms 88:3–5). The righteous as well as the wicked wind up there, as Jacob resigns himself to do (Genesis 44:29). The kings of the earth cannot escape exile there (Isaiah 14:15–20).

Notice that, during this early period, it is assumed that the very righteous dead do not die and go to heaven to be with God. No, there are rare individuals who do manage to cheat death, but they have to ascend into the sky still alive. This is what happens to both Enoch (Genesis 5:24) and Elijah (2 Kings 2:11). Many thought Moses, too, ascended into heaven, which is probably why he is shown appearing from there along with Elijah in the gospel Transfiguration stories (Matthew 17:3, Mark 9:4, Luke 9:30) and in Revelation 11:5–6. There would be no reason for this if it were commonly assumed that the righteous dead always went to heaven when they died.

Third, we begin to see the doctrine of the *resurrection of the dead* emerge during the sixth century, around the time of the Babylonian Exile. It was an attempt to explain the perennial puzzle of undeserved suffering. It seems that, at first, nobody in ancient Israel and Judah chafed at the problem of the suffering of the innocent. People saw themselves less as individuals than we do, partly because, as in primitive societies even today, there was simply little to occupy oneself with, outside of scraping up the necessities of life. What could you collect? What music preferences could you have? What hobbies were available? If you had talents, how would you know? There was little to differentiate you from the person next to you, either in their eyes or yours. So the ancients existed in a state of what is called "corporate personality," as often in tribal societies today. If adversity struck you and your group, too bad, but no one agonized, saying, "Hey, *I* didn't do anything to deserve this!" Maybe the misfortune was hitting as a result of what the previous generations had done (Exodus 20:5–6), but so what? You were all members of the same body. Everyone suffered or rejoiced together, whether contemporaries or successive generations.

But this way of thinking began to change. Deuteronomy 24:16, Jeremiah 31:27–34, and Ezekiel chapter 18 all signal the abandonment of this philosophy: henceforth, they all proclaim, the individual will suffer only for his own sins, no one else's, and he or she will be rewarded for what he or she has done. Sounds good! Sounds fair! But it didn't work. This philosophical realignment only made things worse, because things didn't change. People who had seemingly done nothing bad kept right on suffering the effects of what others had done. Or they just found themselves the victims of random evil. How could a just God allow this? The problem now became more acute than ever, as we see in Job, where we witness the terrible agonies of a righteous man suffering inexplicably.

This dilemma, felt in other ancient societies, too, issued in three parallel beliefs: heavenly reward, resurrection, and reincarnation. Logically they were all equivalent, positing future innings during which the righteous would be compensated for their suffering and the wicked would get what they deserved. That way everything would work out smoothly, or so one would have to suppose. God was off the hook for permitting innocent suffering, and the righteous would receive their reward. The moral balance of the universe was restored. Or at least one's belief in it was, so long as one accepted any of the three beliefs. Actually, Hebrew belief would one day harmonize all three: eventually various thinkers believed that, immediately upon death, souls would rise or sink to intermediate heavens and hells, where they should stay till Judgment Day called them forth and reunited them with their bodies, in time for a final division of the righteous and the wicked into a permanent heaven or hell. In early medieval Judaism we also find the notion that people who died with important work unfinished might be reincarnated for a chance to finish it. But this was exceptional.

Resurrection, according to some biblical savants, might be the fate of the righteous only, and not even all of them at that. Daniel 12:2 anticipates the resurrection of some of the righteous. The Isaiah apocalypse (chapters 24–27) envisions the resurrection of righteous Israelites, excluding their heathen oppressors (Isaiah 26:14, 19–20). And 1 Corinthians 15 seems to equate resurrection with salvation, with the unrighteous dead simply left to rot. On the other hand, Acts 24:15 and Revelation 20:11–12 expect that both the righteous and the wicked will arise to face the judgment.

"But how are the dead raised? With what kind of body do they come?" (1 Corinthians 15:35, RSV). A good question. The gospels appear to suppose that wounds received in the present life will mark one for eternity, which is at least better than being thrown into hell in good shape (Mark 9:43–48)! Even the resurrected Jesus bears livid wounds (John 20:25–27). 1 Corinthians 15:44, on the other hand, thinks of the resurrected body as "spiritual," not composed of crude flesh, hence, presumably, no wounds.

In the meantime, Sheol has somewhere along the line morphed into hell, by way of both the Greek Hades and Tartarus, underground realms where the Giants and Titans were chained up. The New Testament actually just takes over the two hells with their Greek names Hades in Matthew 11:23, Luke 16:23, and so on, and Tartarus in 2 Peter 2:4. Also, we read in the Gospels (and the Koran) of a fiery hell called Gehenna, or the Valley of the Sons of Hinnom, originally simply a dump site to which not only garbage and unclean animal carcasses were consigned, but also where the notoriously wicked were stashed, since a decent burial in hallowed ground was forbidden them. We don't know exactly when Gehenna went from a geographical reference to a literal postmortem hell of flaming torment. Passages like Mark 9:43–48 could easily mean either one.

And it is interesting that Paul never once mentions anybody going to a hell, though he does expect that persecutors of Christians will perish in flames on the day Christ returns (2 Thessalonians 1:6–9).

Looking at all these possibilities, is it any wonder that even biblical literalists cannot agree on what the afterlife is like? I would submit to you that the Bible just does not supply a single, definitive answer to the question of what, if anything, comes after death. Maybe it would be best to embrace Paul's pious agnosticism in 1 Corinthians 13:12 and admit that this is one of those things we just cannot at present know.

IMAGINE THERE'S A HEAVEN; IT'S NOT SO EASY IF YOU TRY!

Warren admits that the measly human noggin can by no means grasp what a never-ending existence in heaven would be like. And for good reason. Nothing we are familiar with from the only life we know would seem to hold good there. It all comes back to what Paul says in 1 Corinthians 15:50, "Flesh and blood cannot inherit the kingdom of God" (RSV). That one sentence speaks volumes. It is not only that the frail and decaying human body is not sturdy enough to outlast the eons, and must be replaced by some hardier mechanism, a body made of sterner stuff, like Superman's. No, if you think about it even for a few seconds, it becomes apparent that there is *no aspect* of the life of mortal men and women that makes sense if you try to stretch it out into an unlimited eternity. Will you be joyfully reunited with your family? Uh, how far back? Will you gladly greet Uncle Zeke from the Civil War? Aunt Mamie from the Colonies? Uncle Alley-Oop from the Cro-Magnon cave civilization? That sounds like a lot of fun: being stuck at an eternal family reunion with plenty of folks you have never met and with whom you have nothing in common, not even language. (But, then, I guess we'd have telepathy. Sure, why not?) Start chopping it into manageable nuclear families, and you're stuck with a dilemma like Solomon's: you're going to have to cut a lot of people right down the middle, since plenty of people bridge successive nuclear families.

Are you going to spend eternity strumming a harp? Warren laughs that off as the cliché it is. But, I ask, if that is *not* what it will be, at least the *kind* of thing it will be, then what *will* the redeemed be doing to kill time? Exploring other planets at the speed of thought? I have heard that one suggested. But what's the point, once you have transcended physical, bodily confinement anyway? It was only a big deal to dream of going to Mars when you were stuck on Earth!

Will you accumulate a literally endless, infinite memory? Will your personality change? You won't need recreation, but there'll be no work to do either, since heaven is already perfect. You might try to escape these conceptual embarrassments by positing that heaven will be some sort of nontemporal "eternal now" moment. Then one would experience no duration at all, right? How is that even life? What is life without change?

How about the damned? I have heard sadistic Calvinists suggest (one even worked it into a wedding homily) that in hell the poor wretches will be outfitted with asbestos bodies with double the nerve endings! But you'd just lose your mind after a while. (Sounds like somebody already has!) Everything about us is defined by its limitations. In fact, that's what "*defin*ition" means! We have to trace out a thing's limits, its "*fin*ish lines," before we know what it is. The human being is a mortal, limited in life span, attention, power, and awareness. To posit an unthinkable heaven in which we will be at home is to drastically transform "us" beyond recognition. Will we not have to become unlimited ourselves in order to experience limitless afterlife, whether in heaven or hell? And then we are talking Buddhism, Hinduism, Jainism. We become the Godhead. I don't imagine Reverend Warren has thought it out that far. He has stopped at the point before his security blanket starts fraying.

But don't miss the irony here! Here is a man who tells us to predicate everything on a greater, more real reality that makes this one strictly preliminary and penultimate in importance. But of this greater life he admits there is virtually nothing to be said! Yes, it "passeth understanding." But that might be for either of two reasons: it is too deep for us, or it is just gibberish, a bundle of contradictions, less than meets the eye. I see no reason to give it the benefit of the doubt, since I have no idea what "it" is supposed to be!

LIFE IS BUT A DREAM—OR IS IT?

Given the uncertainty of the matter, whether philosophically or scripturally, I think it best to stick with the perspective of Psalm 90. Our working assumption ought to be that we have but a fleeting life here on earth, one full of irreplaceable opportunities. We ought to use our few years as wisely as we can. We ought to strive to make some mark on the world for the better. But we ought also to take the time to savor being in the world with all its beauty and mystery. We did not ask to be here. Our presence in it is a gift, even if there should prove to be no personal Giver. We ought to pause to marvel that there should be something rather than nothing at all. Think of the famous Buddhist tale of the monk who, fleeing from a ravening lion, plunges over a cliff and manages to grasp a hanging branch. As it begins to split, he sees below him a second hungry lion. Finally he spots, growing from his precious branch, already starting to divide in two, a luscious straw-berry. And he fills his awareness with the beauty of the strawberry. End of story. That's us: we're here for the briefest of spans, but what shall we occupy ourselves with? Fretting over impending blackness, like unto that from which we first emerged, or the beauty we see, however fleetingly, around us *right now*, the only moment that will ever exist?

You see, it is not only that Rick Warren's advice is built on the sand of wishful thinking, appropriating only what he likes in the Bible; what is really pernicious is the way in which he devalues and discounts the absolutely crucial character of *this life*, the one we're suited for, the one we find ourselves in, the only one we can be sure we have! To hear him tell it, this life amounts pretty much to a window of opportunity to accept the salvation scheme of his religion and then to kill the rest of your time by getting others to convert, too. What a miserably washed-out view of life! I'm sure you know people who devote themselves to nothing but "spiritual things" and witnessing to the unsaved, to the neglect of their talents (unless, of course, they can use them opportunis-tically for an evangelistic ministry or some such). They are hard to be around, in my experience. Basically cultists. You also certainly know plenty of other Christians who are not so fanatical. But that only means they know better than to go all the way with the religious rhetoric they espouse! If they took it seriously, they, too would be door-knocking fanatics. I have found, in my many years of membership and leadership in evangelical Christianity, that the people who take it all most seriously are the ones sooner or later disillusioned with the misery, burnout, and frustration of the thing. That is the purpose-driven lie.

A moment ago, I mentioned a Buddhist story. Fundamentalists

tend not to appreciate such alternate sources of ideas. But, ironically, the view of life Pastor Warren advocates comes astonishingly close to a Hindu and Buddhist worldview he would certainly repudiate if the bottle had their label on it. What I mean is that he has reduced this present life to a kind of *maya*, or illusion. It is not quite real. It is only the run-through, the rehearsal, the practice, not quite the real thing. That "realer" world awaits us after we awaken at death. Sounds like Shankara the Vedanta mystic to me.

But we don't even need to go that far afield to see what's tragically wrong with Warrenism's fundamentalism at this point. Have you ever found yourself living a life that seems to be nothing but *anticipation*, like the Carly Simon song on the old ketchup commercial? It's making me wait. It's keeping me waiting. Maybe you find yourself in school, training for a job. Maybe you're in a job that you view as a stepping-stone to a better one. You live in a "starter home," not the one you hope someday to move into. Or perhaps Spring has come, thawing the soul with its sweet-scented whispers, and you think to yourself: "If I only had a lover, I could really enjoy this. Until then, I'm just on the sidelines." If you think this way, you are secretly regarding your present life, your present time, as *all prelude, all practice, not the real thing*. I believe one of the key insights needed for us to find satisfaction is that *this is it*! This is the real thing! Not the rehearsal! This is the big game, not the training season. This is as real as it is ever going to get. You may in fact live long enough to get that promotion, that mansion, that relationship. But that will be reality tomorrow. *This* is reality today, and you need to learn to recognize its joys and its potential and its beauty and its glory. Because, *if you don't, no matter how good things get in the future, that will not seem to be "the real thing" either.* You will have settled into a mode of fixed expectation, and it will prevent you from recognizing what is right in front of you.

A MATTER OF PERSPECTIVE

Rick Warren assures us that, once we are confident we are going to live forever, we can gain a healthier, humbler perspective on this life. We can grow past the pesky little things that bug us from our worm's-eye viewpoint. When we take into account the vast tapestry of eternity, we can look back upon the petty problems and worries we once thought such a burden, the microscopic sorrows we once thought so burdensome, and we can laugh at them, and at our myopic foolishness. I quite agree. But one need not imagine oneself to possess eternal existence for this to work. One can lift up one's eyes to see the horizon of eternity and think, "How foolish I am to be preoccupied with such trifles!" In fact, that foolishness may be all the more apparent when you realize, in the grand scheme of things, just how little time you have to waste. Are you sure you want to sit there watching game shows or soap operas? Do you really have enough time for that, all told? As Psalm 90 advises, "O Lord, teach us to number our days, that we may apply our hearts unto wisdom!" (Psalms 90:12). What's that? You mean we don't have to count our days? We're going to live for an infinite number of days, up in heaven? Well, then, never mind. Hand me the *TV Guide*.

Day Four

Point to Ponder: Maybe I really am a mortal.

Quote to Remember:
> As for the days of our lives, they contain seventy years,
> Or if due to strength, eighty years,
> Yet their pride is but labor and sorrow;
> For soon it is gone and we fly away.
> Who understands the power of your anger
> And your fury, according to the fear that is due you?
> So teach us to number our days,
> That we may present to you a heart of wisdom.
>
> Psalms 90:10–12 (NASB)

Question to Consider: Would I bother with Christianity if I knew there was no life after death?

NOTE

1. Walter Kaufmann, *The Faith of a Heretic* (Garden City, NY: Doubleday Anchor, 1963), pp. 96–97.

My View Is God's View

Jesus says, "Do not lie, and do not do what you hate, for everything is observed from heaven."
—Gospel according to Thomas, saying 6a

"You ought to" means "I want you to," so why not say so?
—Hugh Prather, *Notes to Myself*

Rick Warren suggests that, if you look closely enough at your life, you will be able to discern some particular metaphor that governs the way you live your life. What a sterling insight! James Fowler, in his classic *Stages of Faith*, makes a similar point, only the way he puts it, each of us is living out the pattern of an implicit narrative, or story.[1] The two observations are compatible and complimentary. I believe that we do adopt basic images, whether static metaphors or dynamic stories, by which to live our lives. We may have adopted these scripts consciously ("Say, that's the kind of life I'd like to lead!") or we may have picked them up unconsciously, letting them rub off on us from our reading or from observing other people. We may have been programmed by authorities who wrote our script for us when we were too young to write it ourselves. Joseph Campbell (*The Hero with a Thousand Faces*) made a good case that all stories and myths of the heroic quest are scripts that inspire us to live our own adventures and to overcome whatever challenges may stand in our way. The story we are living may be a good one or a bad one, a tragedy or a comedy, with a happy ending or a stage full of corpses. In any case, I believe the meaning of our lives is narrative in nature. It is a matter of living out archetypal symbols that are buried deep in our unconscious minds, as Carl Jung said. The epic of Jesus Christ, conveyed to us by the gospels, is perhaps the very best example of such a narrative that we may choose to impart meaning to our lives. And of course it is up to each individual to take responsibility for the ruling metaphor or narrative he or she will live out. If we let someone else choose it for us, we are copping out.

THE ULTIMATE AUTHORITY

But this is where I part company with Pastor Warren. For it is just at this point, as soon as he finishes explaining the centrality of life-metaphors, that he dumps most of them into the toilet and blithely informs us that we must live out the metaphor mandated in the Bible, at least as he reads it. In this way, he assures us, we will not be taking any risks. No, we will be viewing and evaluating our lives *from God's viewpoint*. Now, that is some tall claim!

I am just amazed at the hubris taken for granted here. Reverend Warren seems entirely oblivious of what he (like all other fundamentalist preachers) is doing. *He* takes a look at the Bible and makes some inferences. He takes his best shot. And henceforth his best guess qualifies as the infallible will and word of God. If you put it that way, he'd most likely deny it. But that's what I mean about obliviousness. Isn't he saying that his reading of the Bible ought to govern your whole darn life? Again, all fundamentalists do this. "Well, friend, there's *your* view, and then there's *God's* view,"[2] because God is smart enough to agree with me. I bet you've seen the fundamentalist bumper sticker that says, "God said it! I believe it! That settles it!" It must be a typo, because what the driver really means is, "I said it! God believes it! That settles it!"[3] The fundamentalist is the ventriloquist, and Almighty God is his dummy. They believe in an infallible book, and so they naturally assume that whatever they think it says must be equally infallible. Karl Barth described so well what Warren is doing when he pontificates from his Bible: it is just like a man who shouts into a cavern; he hears his own echo and thinks someone else is replying to him. Similarly, the fundamentalist hears his own voice magnified through the Bible and mistakes it for the word of God.

MESSED-UP METAPHORS

I suspect that the Bible being the word of God is itself little more than a metaphor, but let's get back to Warren's decrees from scripture. In his fifth chapter he concentrates on two biblical metaphors for life. One is life as a *test* or series of tests; the other is life as a *trust*, a stewardship to do your best with another's goods entrusted to you. These are, I readily agree, very powerful and helpful metaphors. But, as usual, I think Warren's fundamentalism undermines the wisdom he is trying to convey. Like many of the insights in *The Purpose-Driven Life*, they are stuffed into the meat grinder of fundamentalist dogma and come out as a less-than-appetizing meatloaf. The main problem, as I see it (sorry, I can't claim to occupy God's Olympian viewpoint), is that Warren sees the whole of this earthly life as a test or set of exams determining your postmortem fate. You will receive rewards or punishments of some undefined type. Naturally the main test is the theology test. You have to manage to believe in a particular salvation religion (among many available), namely, Christianity, and not just Christianity, but fundamentalist Christianity. Otherwise, it's down the shoot to Gehenna.

Just as we saw in the last chapter, Warren sees this whole life as merely preparatory for the indefinable, unimaginable life to come rather than an end in itself. It seems to me that the value of regarding life as a series of tests is the potential this metaphor holds to help us improve our lives while we are living them, here on terra firma. These tests are challenges to prompt us to become more and better than we are, so we may live better, more noble lives in this world, being better parents, citizens, friends, workers, and so on. Life is a vocational education and a vocation at the same time. We are engaged in on-the-job training. It is not an apprenticeship befitting us for heaven. How the heck could it be the latter when, as even Warren admits, this life and the next are so dissimilar that we cannot even begin to describe the next life? How is anything you learn here going to train you for that? Harp lessons?

Again, the metaphor of life as a stewardship is extraordinarily powerful, but it is a metaphor. As a fundamentalist, Pastor Warren can't help taking everything literally, so he assures his readers, on the basis of Luke 16:10–12 and 19:17,[4] that a life well lived will net them some kind of authority or possessions in the future life. Here we are dealing with fantasy. What, is the good fundamentalist who has had daily devotions and witnessed enthusiastically to be put in charge of a few planets in the world to come? We are verging on the extremes of Mormonism here. No, the Parable of the Talents likens your life to a loan simply in the sense that you must one day yield it up.

> For it is just like a man about to go on a journey, who called his own slaves and entrusted his possessions to them. To one he gave five talents, to another, two, and to another, one, each according to his own ability; and he went on his journey. Immediately the one who had received the five talents went and traded with them, and gained five more talents. In the same manner the one who had received the two talents gained two more. But he who received the one talent went away, and dug a hole in the ground and hid his master's money. Now after a long time the master of those slaves came and settled accounts with them. The one who had received the five talents came up and brought five more talents, saying, "Master, you entrusted five talents to me. See, I have gained five more talents." His master said to him, "Well done, good and faithful slave. You were faithful with a few things, I will put you in charge of many things; enter into the joy of your master." Also the one who had received the two talents came up and said, "Master, you entrusted two talents to me. See, I have gained two more talents." His master said to him, "Well done, good and faithful slave. You were faithful with a few things, I will put you in charge of many things; enter into the joy of your master." And the one also who had received the one talent came up and said, "Master, I knew you to be a hard man, reaping where you did not sow and gathering where you scattered no seed. And I was afraid, and went away and hid your talent in the ground. See, you have what is yours." But his master answered and said to him, "You wicked, lazy slave, you knew that I reap where I did not sow and gather where I scattered no seed. Then you ought to have put my money in the bank, and on my arrival I would have received my money back with interest. Therefore take away the talent from him, and give it to the one who has the ten talents. For to everyone who has, more shall be given, and he will have an abundance; but from the one who

does not have, even what he does have shall be taken away. Throw out the worthless slave into the outer darkness; in that place there will be weeping and gnashing of teeth." (Matthew 25:14–30, NASB)

As Job said, "Naked came I into the world, and naked shall I one day go hence" (cf. Job 1:21). What will your biography, your epitaph, your eulogy read? If you have lived well, if you have lived as a "good and faithful servant," why, the life thus lived will obviously have been its own reward. Do you have to be paid for it, too?[5] This is what comes of the silly notion of your life being nothing but a preparation period during which you are earning your merit badges.

THE STIFF UPPER LIP

I am always amused to hear people say that American society and Western culture are built upon Christian, biblical values. It is half true at most, and that is because New Testament ethics are derivative from pre-Christian, Classical paganism, especially from Stoicism.[6] Named for the Stoa, a well-known portico where adherents gathered (cf. John 10:23 and Acts 5:12), this philosophical school was founded by Zeno of Citium shortly after the time of Socrates and sought to carry on his legacy. Thus it was around for some centuries before Christianity and had already permeated Mediterranean Judaism by New Testament times. It was a popular creed spread by street-corner soapbox preachers. Stoics are mentioned as taking an interest in Paul in Acts 17:18. Stoicism turns out to be perhaps the most important source of New Testament ethics, at least as important as the Old Testament or the teaching of Jesus (which, by the way, closely echoes Cynic teaching,[7] the more radical prototype of Stoicism). Let me briefly survey Stoic thinking, and you will see the similarities.

Stoicism was more than anything a doctrine of Divine Providence. Having applied the tool of allegory to Greek scriptures including the *Iliad*, the Stoics demythologized Zeus, king of the Olympian gods, interpreting him as an impersonal divine force underlying all things. They were pantheists, believing that all things are made of God, are forms of God. This means that everything that happens occurs according to the divine Logos, or reason. God does not sit in a study somewhere in heaven, charting out how things will go. God is beyond the limitations of personality. Rather, the rational principle inherent in God orders all things and governs the proportion and rate of change. Everything happens just as it should, both in the universe at large and in the lives of mortals, who have a special spark of that divine Logos. Reason is awake in human beings, though it is present everywhere.

Human beings are the only rational creatures. Thus they alone of all beings face moral choices (animals act by mere instinct), and they alone have a sufficient portion of the Logos to see the right thing and to do it. (See John 1:9, where the Logos, the Word, "enlightens every one that comes into the world.") Insofar as they fail to do so, it is because they have not bothered to sharpen their reasoning skills, allowing their appetites to control them. But the enlightened person who sees the divine hand at work in all things rejoices in whatever befalls him. (Paul says the same in Romans 8:28.) The proper Stoic does not protest and complain (does not "kick against the goads," as in Acts 26:14) when he does not like a particular turn of events, because he knows he cannot know better than God. Specifically, the Stoic has come to understand that there is only one true good to be desired (cf. Luke 10:41–42), and that is virtue. All things, pleasant or unpleasant, but especially the latter, must be welcomed as new opportunities to exercise virtue or to grow in virtue (precisely as in James 1:2–4). If material possessions or interpersonal relationships loom too large in your affections, then the sudden, even catastrophic loss of these things is like a hammer and chisel knocking away the rough edges, and you will emerge a more perfect diamond of virtue (1 Peter 1:6–7). Thus the Stoic trusts God no matter what happens. It is not that he believes God will shield him from suffering, but that if suffering comes, it will be salutary and should be welcomed.

As we live our daily lives, we need not renounce family, friends, possessions, and home (as the more radical Cynics urged). Granted, the only "thing" of real importance is virtue, and to everything else one must cultivate indifference and inner detachment. This means that the Stoic, while he does not have an ascetic phobia of wealth and loved ones, does practice "sitting loose" to them (just as Paul prescribes in 1 Corinthians 7:29–31). He allows himself to enjoy them, but if he is one day stripped of all of them, as Job was, fine and dandy. "Shall we indeed accept good from God and not accept adversity?" (Job 2:10, NASB).

Stoics believed that no one could believe himself truly virtuous, short of moral perfection. One sin, one vice, was enough to deny one the status of "righteous," just as in James 2:10. Eventually they softened this stance and spoke not so much of the righteous versus the unrighteous but rather of the unrighteous versus "those on the way." The latter was much like the status Søren Kierkegaard claimed for himself: not yet a Christian but seeking to become one.

Stoics did not believe in an afterlife; that element comes into the New Testament from Judaism, Platonism, and other sources. But Stoics did believe in a periodic destruction and re-creation of the universe. It would be consumed in a cosmic fire, only to reemerge again, commencing an exact repetition of the previous cosmic cycle. As Woody Allen quipped: "Great! That means I'll have to sit through the *Ice Capades* again!"[8] In 2 Peter 3:10, the reader is reminded of the Stoic cosmic conflagration in the certainty of the "second coming."

METAPHORS ARE NOT LITERAL

Well, I think we need to do to the Bible what the Stoics did with the *Iliad*: we need to interpret the mythology of scripture figuratively, because if we take it literally, we wind up not only in contradictions but with superstition as well. For instance, is life a test? Yes and no. Sure, life presents us with a series of hurdles that show us what we're made of and afford us opportunities to grow. We would be fools to cry over spilled milk, to refuse to learn whatever lessons we can from our mistakes. We ought to prize our integrity (our "soul") above all else, as that which can never be stripped from us against our will. We should be willing to, as Martin Luther said, "let goods and kindred go; this mortal life also." These are solid insights. And I think they are the distillation of both Stoic and New Testament ethics. But in order to learn and believe these lessons, one hardly need believe that the events in your life are actually planned as bolts from the blue, sent special delivery from a deity who is testing and training you like a lab rat! And that is what we are saying when we fretfully ask, "What can God be trying to teach me through this tragedy?"

It is one thing to decide to learn what you can from a tragedy; it is quite another to say someone has arranged the tragedy because they thought you needed an object lesson. Such a god must be a mad scientist, making his human test subjects jump through the hoops. And that is the perverse teaching of fundamentalist gurus like Bill Gothard, Merlin Carothers, and Rick Warren, who tell you to thank God for his educative thrashings. Jesus says, "It is inevitable that stumbling blocks come; but woe to that man through whom the stumbling block comes!" (Matthew 18:7, NASB). Why should that apply less to God than to human beings? If you take the "testing" metaphor literally, as Warren does, you quickly wind up blaspheming, making God into B. F. Skinner, training his rats, or, worse yet, into Josef Mengele, tormenting his inmates.

Day Five

Point to Ponder: My life is about what I say it is.

Quote to Remember:

My prayer is: I will be what I will be
And I will do what I will do.

All I want to do, need to do, is stay in
rhythm with myself. All I want is to do
What I do and not try to do what I
don't do. Just do what I do. Just keep
pace with myself. Just be what I will be.

I will be what I will be—but I am *now*
what I am, and here is where I will
spend my energy. I need all my energy to
be what I am today. Today I will work

in rhythm with myself and not with what
I "should be." And to work in rhythm
with myself I must keep tuned into myself.

God revealed his name to Moses, and it
was: I AM WHAT I AM.

Hugh Prather, *Notes to Myself*

Question to Consider: What story am I living as my life's script? Do I like it? Did I choose it? Is it too late to change it?

NOTES

1. James W. Fowler, *Stages of Faith: The Psychology of Human Development and the Quest for Meaning* (San Francisco: Harper & Row, 1981).

2. Thanks to my old friend Richard Abate for this way of putting it.

3. My seminary pal Tony Glidden first put it this way as far as I know.

4. "He who is faithful in a very little is faithful also in much; and he who is dishonest in a very little is dishonest also in much. If then you have not been faithful in the unrighteous mammon, who will entrust to you the true riches? And if you have not been faithful in that which is another's, who will give you that which is your own?" (Luke 16:10–12, RSV).

"And he said to him, "Well done, good servant! Because you have been faithful in a very little, you shall have authority over ten cities.'" (Luke 19:17).

5. In his *Meditations* (9:42), Stoic Roman emperor Marcus Aurelius says the same: "Is it not enough to have obeyed the laws of your own nature, without expecting to be paid for it?"

6. Abraham J. Malherbe, *Paul and the Popular Philosophers* (Minneapolis: Fortress Press, 1989).

7. F. Gerald Downing, *Cynics and Christian Origins* (Edinburgh: T & T Clark, 1992).

8. *Hannah and Her Sisters*, written and directed by Woody Allen. Orion Pictures, 1986.

No Changes Are
Permanent, but Change Is

What I must do is die now. I must accept the justice of death and the injustice of life. I have lived a good life—longer than many, better than most. Tony died when he was twenty. I have had thirty-two years. I couldn't ask for another day. What did I do to deserve birth? It was a gift. I am me—that is a miracle. I had no right to a single hour. And yet I have had thirty-two years. Few can choose when they will die. I choose to accept death now. As of this moment I give up my "right" to live.
—Hugh Prather, *Notes to Myself*

Mariam says to Jesus, "Who are your disciples like?" He says, "They are like young children who have made a place for themselves in someone else's field. When the owners of the field come, they will say, 'Get out of our field!' They strip off their clothes in order to vacate it to them and to return their field to them."
—Gospel according to Thomas, saying 21

INAUTHENTIC EXISTENCE

Chapter 6 of Rick Warren's *The Purpose-Driven Life* strikes me as pretty good Buddhism, though, as always, there's a fly in the ointment. He sums up earthly life as a "temporary assignment," something short and over soon, with which to busy ourselves before we check into the unseen afterworld that will last for eternity. If this is all life is, then, Warren reasons, it would be pretty silly to become too attached to it. When it is over, the worldly fool will be left holding the bag, just like a plantation owner after the Civil War with a suitcase full of Confederate money.

My first thought on reading this meditation was that, once again, one hardly needs belief in an afterlife to accept this wisdom. I remember ten years ago, just after my beloved father, Noel B. Price, died, how I sat sorting through various old papers of his. I found pages of notes, of pros and cons, deliberating whether he should change jobs. How important it must all have seemed at the time. But what a diversion it appeared years later, after his death. I couldn't second-guess his thinking, but it made me resolve to keep the perspective of death in mind whenever I began to take certain choices way too seriously.

Another time, at one of the Heretics Anonymous discussion groups my wife, Carol, and I host in our home, I recall how Berkeley Leeds, a hale and hardy young man in his eighties, commented that he now looked back on a life full of civic and social involvements and wondered just how much of it was really worth the time. I decided to remember that remark, too.

Again, I recall how, when I was a Baptist pastor, our congregation's moderator told me she was thinking of skipping some interminable board meeting so she could be with her sick daughter. I pointed out the obvious: one day, on her deathbed, she would regret the time she might have spent, but hadn't spent, with her family far more than having missed some committee meeting. The brevity of life is enough to provide the sort of perspective Reverend Warren rightly urges upon us. We are fools to act as if we've got all the time in the world. But that implies not one thing about the possible existence of an eternal afterworld right around the corner of death.

Philosopher Martin Heidegger went so far as to claim that no one can live authentically until he faces and accepts his own imminent death. One must face one's own mortality and start making some decisions, ranking some priorities, taking the remainder of life into one's own hands and not leaving it to the masses or to "the authorities" to decide for you, and certainly not to Bible-quoting traffic cops who threaten you with hell for not adopting their reading of scripture as your life's guide. Warren seems oblivious of the serious danger of allowing a belief in eternal life to undermine the gravity with which we undertake life in this fleeting world. After all, if it's only preliminary, what the heck? If a job's not worth doing, it's certainly not worth doing well.

STUMBLING ALONG THE DHARMA PATH

What is Buddhistic about Rick Warren's advice in this chapter? Just about everything. I think this is worth pointing out since, reading *The Purpose-Driven Life*, one might pretty easily get the idea that only the Bible holds wisdom about life, that if you find any wisdom in Reverend Warren's prescriptions (and of course you will) you ought to buy the whole fundamentalist Christian package. I'm mighty glad he is as wise as he is, but I regret his unwise narrowness.

And speaking of the wise, Gautama the Buddha (the "Enlightened One") ranks near the top of the list of wise men. He sought the cure for universal human suffering. He found the answer in the principle of *impermanence* (*anicca*). All things are *becoming*, not being. There is nothing immune to change, even if it takes longer than we can discern for the change to become visible, like the slow erosion of mountains. We seek satisfaction, and so we latch onto worldly things we imagine will satisfy us once and for all. But nothing can do that, since everything is fleeting and changing. What looked so bright this morning will have tarnished by the evening, even if only through the contempt that familiarity breeds. Because of this, life swings like a pendulum back and forth between extremes of frustration (until we get what we seek) and disappointment (once we get it). Nothing in this fleeting world satisfies forever! How *could* it? How could an impermanent world filled with impermanent things possibly satisfy us permanently? We live as dogs barking up the wrong tree.

Buddhism says the satisfaction we seek can only be found in Nirvana, a meditative state of bliss. It may be obtained already during this life if one focuses consciousness via meditative arts and divests oneself of the illusion of the ego, desiring nothing, having no vested interests, playing no favorites, accepting whatever comes. Nirvana is not an afterlife exactly; it cannot be squeezed into a worldly, temporal sequence like that. But Nirvana is *analogous* to an afterlife because at least it does put an end to reincarnation in *Samsara*, this vale of tears, this theatre of wearying and futile reincarnation. Nirvana short-circuits the merry-go-round of lives so you can get off. What awaits you then? We can't say, since there is no longer any private ego that might enjoy a vacation in heaven. It's not like *that*. But we can't say what it *is* like. In fact, Warren admits much the same about his own, Christian, afterworld, but he hamstrings himself by insisting that we "go to" it as if it were a place, as atomistic individuals, conscious selves.

The earliest Buddhists thought that, to avoid the distracting temptations of Samsara, they had better retreat behind monastic walls to seek Nirvana in isolated silence. They were pretty world-negating. They felt as hostile to the outside world as Rick Warren does. Warren pictures the Christian as God's ambassador to a hostile country. The Christian will be a disloyal traitor insofar as he or she deems the world a nice place to live. This sounds like the drastic "us-versus-them," chip-on-the-shoulder mentality we should expect to find among the Amish, or that guy I used to see in the Port Authority Bus Terminal singing hymns, clutching a Bible, and sporting a sandwich sign.

Eventually Buddhism arrived at a less neurotic view of the world. It was the second-century CE philosopher Nagarjuna who came up with a negotiated truce between Nirvana and Samsara. It is one of the most profound and revolutionary religious insights known to me. Nagarjuna saw that one need not loathe, fear, or even be disappointed by the fleeting samsaric world as long as one understands and appreciates it for what it is: a shiny and beautiful soap bubble, here one instant, gone the next. There is real, albeit transitory, beauty in it, and its impermanence does not change that. Samsara is only a bewitching distraction so long as one imagines it is or ought to be permanent, as long as one clings to it. One cannot cling to the fleeting, and so if one tries, one will always, inevitably, be disappointed. But if you've learned not to cling, you realize the mistake was yours, not the world's! Do not blame it for not being what it was never supposed to be.

In fact, Nagarjuna reasoned, one can go further to the insight that one need not flee Samsara, the world of impermanence, in order to experience the unchanging Nirvana. One can actually learn to see through the thin, illusory veneer of Samsara to the Nirvana beneath all things. It would be like one of those digital perspective posters so popular some years back: you have to look through the surface design, which seems to depict nothing in particular, and then you can see a striking three-dimensional scene beneath it.

It was this realization about the fleeting world of impermanent but real beauty that gave birth to Buddhist art. Sometimes that art uses special means to drive home that lesson, as when Tibetan Buddhists make fantastically elaborate "sand paintings" of complex mandalas, and then leave them intact only for a few minutes before scattering the colored sand again. Beauty is fleeting and must be caught on the fly! It will not stay, so we mustn't try to force it to stay. We must have the wisdom that Johann Wolfgang von Goethe's Faust learned the hard way: in the shifting cavalcade of the world's beauty, we must go with the flow and not try to arrest it. We must never dare say to it, "Pause a while; you are so beautiful!" Because the merry-go-round will not pause. We will only be thrown off it and on to our behinds. Rick Warren's fans need to learn what he does not tell them: that life, like beauty, is all the more precious because it is so fragile, so rare, so fleeting.

Buddhism is much like Stoicism, discussed in the preceding chapter: in both, one learns to glimpse and to appreciate the divine in the midst of what at first would seem to be its opposite; one glimpses the divine as the Ground of Being of the world. Maybe it's just me, but I prefer looking at it as a two-layer cake, rather than Reverend Warren's "present versus future" worldview where we're like Jews in a Nazi concentration camp, waiting impatiently for the Allied liberators to come free us.

Don't get me wrong: I doubt that very many readers of *The Purpose-Driven Life* really feel this way, like strangers in a strange land. I bet they are largely well adjusted, at ease in Zion, singing, "This is My Father's World." Once again, I would suggest that a fundamentalist is going to be more healthy-minded the less seriously he or she takes the rhetoric of fundamentalism. If you're well balanced, as many or most are, you are (consciously or not) taking the whole thing with a grain of salt. Good for you. But it might be even better to switch to a philosophy you can actually live out consistently.

By the way, do you see what I'm *not* arguing for here? I am sharing some helpful wisdom from Buddhism, but I'm not suggesting that if you see the truth of it, you ought to go the whole way and convert to Buddhism. Why should you have to? Good insights thrive within many systems of thought and belief, but that doesn't mean they can't be transplanted. Or, better, think of individual Bible, Stoic, Buddhist, and so forth insights as delicious fruits on various trees in an orchard. You don't have to swallow the whole darned tree to eat the fruit! Nor is anything stopping you from picking fruit from several of the trees.

HAPPINESS AIN'T SO BAD

Rick Warren tells us many times that it is a big mistake to adopt the pursuit of happiness as the purpose to drive one's life. I think the mistake is his. But I need to back up and take a running start at it.

Albert Schweitzer, known to most people as a medical missionary and humanitarian, was, among many other things, one of the greatest New Testament scholars in history. In fact, he studied medicine and built a hospital in French Equatorial Africa to heed Jesus's command to lay down his life for the gospel. In his books *The Mystery of the Kingdom of God* and *The Quest of the Historical Jesus*, Schweitzer tried to make sense of those sayings of Jesus that most of us prefer to skim over and forget: turn the other cheek, give away your possessions, invite the street people to Thanksgiving instead of your friends and family. You know the ones I mean. Schweitzer wondered what would have led Jesus to issue such demands. He finally concluded that they were all predicated on Jesus's preaching that the End Times were at hand, the Tribulation, the Final Judgment, the resurrection of the dead. His contemporaries would live to see it—and had better get ready for it! They lived in a crisis period immediately preceding the end. Thus they had the need and the opportunity to be *perfectly* righteous, heedless of worldly consequences. In other words, ordinarily you'd think twice about giving away your savings to the poor since you're going to have to pay for your children's education. You'd be reluctant to adopt nonresistance lest evil triumph, and so on. But now, with the end of the world at hand, none of that weighs on the scale anymore. The only thing your money is good for now is to feed those in immediate danger of starving. So you'd best fork it over. This was also why Jesus had nothing to say about government or economics: those things were business as usual, and he saw all such matters as reshuffling the deck chairs on a sinking ship. Schweitzer called it an "interim ethic," a set of extreme measures uniquely appropriate to a time of crisis, with mundane priorities fading into insignificance.

Whether Schweitzer was right in assessing the intentions of Jesus, I will not argue here. I bring up the theory only to show a surprising parallel with Rick Warren's approach, for it seems to me he, too, is operating on the basis of an interim ethic. He doesn't necessarily think the world is ending that soon. But he does think that, with your life sure to end at least relatively soon, there's no time for much else than fundamentalism: you know, Bible reading, witnessing, praying, and so on. Seeking happiness would be a colossal waste of time. "Only one life; 'twill soon be past; only what's done for Christ will last!" You know the drill.

But I disagree. I believe Warren is prescribing emergency measures when in fact we do not live most of the time in a state of emergency. Warren and his colleagues are crying wolf, and I don't believe them anymore. As you grow up and start to mature, you realize there are many important things that are just the natural gratifications, preoccupations, and interests of adult life. You calm down. And you no longer imagine yourself to be Frodo on the way to Mordor. You've put aside thoughts like, "If I, personally, don't witness to those people over there *right now*, they may wind up in hell, and it'll be my fault!"

If we want an ethical guide to a normal, healthy life, we might want to look for a moment outside the martyr-sect world of the New Testament. We might want to look at what the Greek philosophers were saying. They wrote about the good life in a world of normalcy. And some of them said happiness *is* the proper goal of human life. Aristotle pointed out that everything everybody does is a means of making them happy, sooner or later, closer or farther down the line: eating dessert or going on a diet, investing money or spending it, depending on the circumstances. What do we do in a day that is *not* aimed at increasing our happiness? This is even true of Rick Warren, who sure wants to wind up amid the eternal bliss of heaven, the ultimate happiness as he conceives it.

Aristotle shrewdly warned that it never works if we pursue happiness *in itself*. No, it is always something in particular, some activity, some condition, that makes us happy, that provides satisfaction, almost as a by-product. It will differ with every individual, depending on his or her makeup. But if we are to be the best person we can be, we will rightly pursue what will bring us satisfaction. And, among other things, that includes helping other people, sharing friendship, shouldering one's fair share of life's burden. (Don't you feel like a jerk if you don't?) Epicurus had very similar ideas. Why should I have friends? Because it brings me pleasure. But that's not inordinately selfish, because my friendship makes my friends happy, too. Epicurus said I ought to pursue my own pleasure (judiciously and with foresight, of course), and you ought to pursue yours. That way, each seeking his own good, we will arrive at symphonic harmony, each one playing his own instrument, reading her own music, and not tending to someone else's.

Most of life is not particularly heroic. We don't face the challenge of shouldering the martyr's cross every day. And until that day comes, I'm saying we need guidance like Aristotle's and Epicurus's. When and if the crisis comes, and it's no longer business as usual, okay, let's mobilize!

Rick Warren explains how biblical injunctions to martyrdom make a lot of sense once you realize you aren't giving up much, that the martyr's cross or stake or bullet is really the magic doorway into heavenly bliss. But isn't that a gross trivialization of martyrdom? It sure doesn't sound like the ultimate sacrifice anymore. I mean, if you are able to count on everlasting life, even after martyrdom, what are you really giving up?

I think of martyrdom as a proposition of giving up either your life or your integrity. Dying for your country would be a good case. Or for your family. Once a pal of mine I hadn't heard from in some years called me up. By this time we had both married and had young children. Out of the blue, he said, "This may sound weird, but suppose you had to sacrifice your life for your children. You'd do it without hesitation, wouldn't you?" I replied that, yes, I had thought the same thing many times. It is a measure of how much you love your own flesh and blood. Even with no prospect of heavenly reward, what parent would not gladly give his or her life for his or her children?

This kind of duty is what Immanuel Kant called a "categorical imperative," an absolute obligation, no matter what. Here we hit the foundation. Our back is against the wall. There is no room for maneuvering. You face one of these situations; you realize the jig is up. The Grim Reaper has kept his appointment with you. It's your time. But it sounds to me that Warren, like Christians generally, is making martyrdom into what Kant called a "hypothetical imperative." This is not a matter of moral calculus at all, but a mere strategic option. If you want to get to Pizza Hut, what's the route you "ought" to take? It is merely prudential, tactical. "Hmmm, I could save my life in the short run, but if I bit the bullet and let myself get martyred for Christ, I'd get eternal life in pretty cushy circumstances. Not bad!"

How ironic that the thrust of Rick Warren's chapter is ostensibly the brevity of life as a "temp job" in this world, when in fact he is really implying the exact opposite: you are an immortal godling who will live forever (provided you espouse the right theology). The result is that even the important things in life, such as life-and-death decisions, are relativized, even trivialized. No one who believes what Warren tells us to believe can take the tragedy of death seriously. Instead, the believer in heaven will retreat to the infantilism of the child whose daddy tells her comforting lies like, "Mommy's . . . uh, gone on a long trip." To heaven. That is inauthentic existence. Get real, and don't shield yourself from the inevitable harshness of things. That is the way of all the earth.

Day Six

Point to Ponder: This world is fleeting, and so am I. Maybe I should learn to surf instead of drowning.

Quote to Remember: "I cannot 'make my mark' for all time—those concepts are mutually exclusive. 'Lasting effect' is a self-contradictory term. Meaning does not exist in the future and neither do I. Nothing will have meaning 'ultimately.' Nothing will even mean tomorrow what it did today. Meaning changes with the context. *My* meaningfulness is here. It is enough that I am of value to someone today. It is enough that I make a difference now." (Hugh Prather, *Notes to Myself*)

Question to Consider: Paul said that "if in Christ we have hope only for this present life, we are of all men the most miserable" (1 Corinthians 15:19). But Blaise Pascal said the Christian life would still be well worth living even if it turned out there was nothing after death. Who was right?

The Mystery of Everything

As for the Christian theology, can you imagine anything more appallingly idiotic than the Christian idea of heaven? What kind of deity is it that would be capable of creating angels and men to sing his praises day and night to all eternity? It is, of course, the figure of the Oriental despot, with his inane and barbaric vanity. Such a conception is an insult to God.
—Dialogues of Alfred North Whitehead

Celebrant: Forgive us, Lord, for this, our dreadful toadying.
Congregation: And bare-faced flattery.
—Monty Python's The Meaning of Life

SHOCKING AWARENESS

As philosopher Martin Heidegger put it, "The first question of philosophy is, Why is there something rather than nothing?" That is what many call the primary experience of "ontological shock." If you have never experienced even a touch of the shock I am talking about, I daresay it is because you have never paused from your round of busy activities to notice that, yes, you are alive in this world when in fact you might not be, and that there is a world, a reality, for you to be alive *in*, when, for all you know, there might as well not be!

There are two different but related reactions to the Mystery of Being. One is simply to stand in awe of it; the other is to surmise there was a Creator, and to transfer one's awe to him (or her or it). The second impulse, that of worship, glorifying the Creator, is Rick Warren's option. I think that is a crude, mythological version of the first option. And it is another case where the literalism of mythology, not seen as a metaphor, actually subverts the initial impulse that gave rise to it.

81

I consider all doctrines of the divine creation of the world spiritually dangerous, essentially antireligious. Please note that I am not simply saying that religious fundamentalists have no right to ignore and suppress science in the name of biblical myths. I do believe that, but I am making a rather different point: those who insist on a creation doctrine are sinning not only against science but even against religion. For the believer in divine creation, the open question of the Mystery of Being is like an open wound. It stings and gapes, and the believer cannot rest till it be healed up, closed up, smeared with the soothing balm of an answer, even if his doctrine be a sophisticated one like Aquinas's or that of the latest Liberal Protestant theologian.

But I say every supposed answer to the Mystery of Being is not a healing balm but rather a sedative, even a blinding dose of spiritual poison. For the minute you fill in that blank, you are exorcizing the chief source of religious awe. What once one gaped at in astonishment and unbearable awe, one now relegates to the file drawer of solved cases. Eric Hoffer, as always, has the fundamentalist "true believer" pegged: "To be in possession of an absolute truth is to have a net of familiarity spread over the whole of eternity. There are no surprises and no unknowns. All questions have already been answered, all decisions made, all eventualities foreseen. The true believer is without wonder and hesitation."[1]

The Bible and the Koran both picture us gazing at the great dome of the heavens, sprinkled with stardust, wide with untold worlds and nebulae, and just as quickly the scriptures choke off the precious sense of wonder with a fairy tale. "Oh, you're wondering how to account for such a grand thing? You're puzzled? Dumbfounded? Well, friend, don't worry! It's really pretty simple! You see, the world was made by an invisible watchmaker named God. See? Now don't trouble your head about it again. From now on, you can take it for granted."

Well, of course, to think you've explained anything by saying "God created it" is absurd. It's like Erich von Däniken "explaining" the mystery of the pyramids by saying space aliens built them. You can't "explain" one enigma by an even bigger enigma. It's like the old Hindu myths in which the world rests on the back of an elephant, which rests on the back of a tortoise, which rests on the back of something else. But that's not the real problem. When you think you can account for the origin of the world by chalking it up to a Creator, don't you see that you're draining away the wonder of the thing? You're just giving yourself an excuse to take the whole thing for granted and to sink into a worldly stupor in which you can actually get bored. Imagine! Bored? In this world? Is it all so pat, so old hat to you? Ennui overtakes you? If it does, it's because you have already benumbed yourself.

William Wordsworth's "Ode" puts it very powerfully.

I

> There was a time when meadow, grove, and stream,
> The earth, and every common sight,
>> To me did seem
>> Apparelled in celestial light,
> The glory and the freshness of a dream.
> It is not now as it hath been of yore; —
>> Turn wheresoe'er I may,
>> By night or day,
> The things which I have seen I now can see no more.

II

>> The rainbow comes and goes,
>> And lovely is the rose,
>> The moon doth with delight
> Look round her when the heavens are bare;
>> Waters on a starry night
>> Are beautiful and fair;
>> The sunshine is a glorious birth;
>> But yet I know, where'er I go,
> That there hath past away a glory from the earth.

Once we sported in the glory and wonder of the Mystery of Being as a dolphin in the sea foam. But then "a glory faded from the world." The prison walls of adult perception, rote perception, dull perception, began to close in, and now it is hardly perception at all. What happened? Or rather, how did it happen? I think the Russian Formalist critic Victor Shklovsky was right on target:

> As perception becomes habitual, it becomes automatic. . . . In this process, ideally realized in algebra, things are replaced by symbols. . . . Habitualization devours work, clothes, furniture, one's wife, and the fear of war. "If the whole complex lives of many people go on unconsciously, then such lives are as if they had never been." And art exists that one may recover the sensation of life; it exists to make one feel things, to make the stone *stony*. The purpose of art is to impart the sensation of things as they are *perceived* and not as they are *known*. The technique is to make objects "unfamiliar." . . . Art removes objects from the automatism of perception.[2]

I am sure this is right, both the diagnosis and the prescription. What has happened to us? We no longer *perceive*, because we have learned to *know*, to recognize. We are mostly like a surveillance camera, like a computer that apprehends data, thus "knows" it, but does not *know that* it knows, does not *perceive*. It does not experience that it knows something. And neither do we. Oh, once we did. When we first fell in love, and we delighted in the charms of our beloved that were new every morning. At least for a few mornings, and then that little smile, that gesture that once so charmed us, it becomes routine—and thus invisible. It is filed away in the memory bank.

The Zen masters say we fail to perceive the world anymore because it has become habitual. We let words and concepts substitute for things. It is like the changeover from barter to currency, exactly like it. We used to exchange actual things, squealing goats, pungent herbs, fabrics smooth or rough, things we could see and feel and hear—and could not help but see, feel, hear. But now all we do is exchange coins and bills that *stand for* value. And then it is checks, then plastic credit cards, soon computer clacks.

And this might not be bad, but it is the same for our whole lives! As Shklovsky said, habituation devours everything! And our whole life is scanning a text. We are inured to everything, numbed to everything. Shklovsky prescribed art, literature, as the cure, art that strips away the blindfold of familiarity and forces us to perceive again the things we know.

Perhaps this is why Jesus is depicted in the gospels not as some dull pulpit preacher, feeding his audience with more concepts, more sleeping pills, but as an artist, a reciter of poetic couplets and a spinner of riddles. When asked why on earth he didn't just use straight talk, he said, "Because seeing they do not see, and hearing they do not hear" (Matthew 13:13, RSV). In other words, like Shklovsky said, the truth is so familiar to them, they're so habituated to it, that they can no longer see it at all. Familiarity breeds invisibility. And so Jesus must use the language of artistry to make the stone be perceived again as stony, the soul as soulish.

Rudolf Bultmann spoke of the need to "demythologize" the gospel for the benefit of modern man. But I think Victor Shklovsky was closer to the truth. We need to "defamiliarize" the gospel. Since concepts and words merely substitute for the Real, the Zen masters knew they had to find some other way to strip off the veil. So they taught with slaps in the face, sermons of silence, teasing riddles designed to force you to theology's dead end. If we want to learn to see again, even if for a moment, the glory that has faded from the world, we must seek the paradox, the volatility, the unstable explosiveness, the inherent absurdity of our religious myths and symbols. If we do this, they may be able to help us. Otherwise they will only get in the way. They are only ladders to be climbed up and then jumped off. This is why I am in the habit of treating sacred things with levity, lest they become idols.

Those psychologists who study sleep patterns tell us that people get the most irritated when deprived of sleep. When they are trying to grab a few needed winks and the experimenter prods them awake, they get surly fast! And it has been my experience that the same is true in the spiritual realm. When the alarm clock of some new religious shock goes off, people don't want their "dogmatic slumber" (as Kant called it) disturbed. They grab the clock and with a cry of "Heresy!" or "Blasphemy!" they pitch it out the window. You probably remember throwing a few clocks out yourself. I know I have.

Awe at the Mystery of things is the key to a religious attitude. It is the source of freshness of perception. Do not kill it and nail it into a coffin called "God." Do not even mummify it in a mummy case called "the Mystery of Being"! Because it is not an "it." That's taking the first step to labeling it and filing it away.

THE SUPEREGO

If the mythical notion of "God the Creator" saps the vitality of our faculty for wonder, I believe it does more and worse. It produces an unworthy and superstitious God concept, as Alfred North Whitehead said. Let's suppose there is a God of some sort. Classical theology has posited that God possesses the attribute of "aseity." This means God is self-sufficient and unaffected. God cannot be harmed by anything demons or humans or space aliens or ogres or anything else may think to do to him. Think of the disproportionate power we would be giving human beings if we really thought God could be plunged into depression by one of us rejecting him. Yeah, that has to be a blow to the Infinite, Absolute, Universal Being! He must be really shook up at that. Or imagine, as the Bible constantly does, that some crummy mortal does or says something that royally ticks off the Almighty Lord of All Things. "Why, you little flea! I'll see you tormented in hell for this!" he might say. It's just absurd, unless you want to worship a god who is no greater than Zeus or Odin or, come to think of it, some Juju totem. No, it's this sort of thing in the Bible that has forced theologians including St. Anselm and John Calvin to speak of "accommodation" and "analogy" in our speech about God, since no God worth our worship could peevishly demand it. Surely Meister Eckhardt was right: God is humble! He may be imagined as rejoicing in his perfection, but maybe that's even going too far, since it would seem to imply an element of pleased surprise. Does the sun exult in its expenditure of hydrogen? Psalms 19:4–5 so depicts it, but no one denies that is an analogy.

The implications of God's aseity are explosive. Among other things, God's self-contained invulnerability, as Hosea Ballou saw, simply rules out the whole basis for the theology of the atoning death of Christ on the cross. How? The traditional understanding of the atonement is that we have offended God by our sins, injured his majesty, as if a serf flipped the bird to the king. But that, again, is grossly mythological. The myth of the Divine King symbolizes the exceeding greatness of the Mystery of Being. It is literalism that muddies the water, mistaking the metaphor for literal description. And so theology winds up with a God who thunders in his petty irritation against helpless, hapless mortals, reducing them to masochistic servitude if they hope to escape the ultimate doom of eternal torture.

Yes, the worship required by this God quickly ceases to be the unbridled and spontaneous awe we feel looking at the night sky and instead becomes an obsequious cringing before a tyrant. His grace means his arbitrary whim of mercy. Nero did, after all, occasionally decree "thumbs up" in the arena, but it was always a surprise. And we lick God's boots in worship, thanking "him" for not damning us. We butter him up, stroking his ego. Not that he has one, right? That's my point: how ugly the myth becomes. Human dignity is smashed just like the Taliban fanatics smashed those ancient Buddha statues in Afghanistan. Poor Job makes a good showing of asserting his dignity before a persecuting God, but even he is cowed once his tormentor shows up in force.

Paul Tillich once remarked how worshiping a divine tyrant can never be heartfelt. It will always more or less mask the resentment the worshiper feels deep down. And if he doesn't? If he is happy to negate himself? The worshiper has become victim to the Stockholm syndrome: the tendency of captives to follow the path of least emotional resistance and identify with their captors and tormentors. Think of the wizened old scarecrow in *Monty Python's Life of Brian* who is manacled to a mossy dungeon wall and quips, "Crucifixion? Best thing the Romans ever did for us!" Or think of Patty Hearst, locked in a closet by the Symbionese Liberation Army until she came to see it their way and joined in the bank heists. How about poor Winston Smith, antihero of George Orwell's masterpiece *1984*: the Thought Policeman O'Brien tells him that strict obedience to Big Brother is not enough; Smith must convert. He must embrace the party line with enthusiasm. That is the cowed worship of the mythical Jehovah, and it is idol worship. It reduces both deity and worshiper to subhuman proportions. "Forgive us, Lord, for this, our dreadful toadying" indeed.

HAVING A LITTLE TALK WITH JESUS

You knew Pastor Warren would get around to it sooner or later: his seventh meditation closes with an evangelistic invitation to any "unsaved" reader who may have slipped into the audience. To become a bona fide child of God, it seems it is not enough to be a mere human being. No, one must "receive Christ into one's heart." Man, you can believe the Nicene Creed till you're blue in the face. You can take communion till it's coming out your nose. But that means nothing to born-again Christians. No, for them, you must adopt a particular, historically conditioned, devotional idiom, or you are not saved. Your religious life must employ the imagery and lingo of "a personal relationship with Jesus," henceforth your "personal savior." No matter what your heartfelt Christian belief, for these people, if you don't invite Jesus into your heart as your Lord and Savior, you are going to hell. Essentially this notion is no different from that of fringe Pentecostals who claim that anyone who fails to speak in tongues is no real Christian and is headed for the Inferno.

The fairy tale speaks of the emperor with no clothes, and here we are dealing with the naked King of Kings. How is it that, for all their much-vaunted Bible reading, fundamentalists never seem to recognize that their "personal relationship with the personal savior" rhetoric *never occurs in the Bible at all.* Jesus never speaks this way in the gospels; nor does Paul in the epistles. The oft-repeated demand for "belief in Christ" certainly carries no implication of an inner dialogue with Jesus. In fact, this kind of sentimental "personal savior" piety is no older than the eighteenth-century Lutheran Pietist movement in Germany, from whence it passed into Methodism. And yet, to born-again Christians, this particular mind game is the be-all and end-all of Christianity. Only after one is safely in the 700 Club of evangelical Christianity will God welcome one's worship.

I think fundamentalists fail to notice the absurd enormity of their claims just because there are so many of them who make them. Everyone in their preferred circles shares the same notion, so it never occurs to them how outlandish it ought to seem. I recall how back in 1975, as an InterVarsity Christian Fellowship leader at Montclair

State College, I was reading apologetics literature, and it was having the opposite effect than intended, as my doubts only grew bigger and bigger. But then I studied that summer at Wheaton College, a bastion of evangelical education. While there, I felt the old doubts, once so nagging and plaguing, melt away, and I experienced a spiritual high like none previously. For some odd reason, the sensation did not last once I returned to my old surroundings in September. Perhaps the reason was as Peter L. Berger described in his *Heretical Imperative*:

> In principle, the quest for religious certainty is bound to be frustrated "in this world," except for momentary experiences that can only be maintained precariously in recollection. . . . Put in phenomenological terms, there are indeed experiences of contact with the supernatural that carry with them absolute certainty, but this certainty is located only within the enclave of religious experience itself. As soon as the individual returns from this enclave into the world of ordinary everyday reality, this certainty is retained only as a memory and as such is intrinsically fragile.[3]

Once you dare peek outside the charmed circle of "Christian fellowship" with its unquestioned assumptions and its passwords, you begin to realize how odd and arbitrary many things seem. Like the Rapture. If you believe in the Rapture, do you have any business smirking at the belief of flying saucer cultists that they are about to be beamed up to the mother ship? They're practically your coreligionists! You also begin to realize that the cluster of beliefs in evangelical Christianity only seems to cohere because you accepted them as a package when you converted. You bought the whole bill of goods. An elementary knowledge of church history and the development of theology will show the various doctrines have about as much integral connection as the contents of a curiosity shop.

One more thing knowledge will show, I think, is that the sociologist Emil Durkheim was right: the God evangelical Christians worship so fervently is evangelicalism itself, externalized and made into a totem.

Day Seven

Point to Ponder: What difference could it possibly make to an all-sufficient Being whether I worship him or not?

Quote to Remember:
Oh Lord, please don't burn us,
> Don't grill or toast your flock,
> Don't put us on the barbecue,
> Or simmer us in stock,
> Don't braise or bake or boil us,
> Or stir-fry us in a wok
> Oh please don't lightly poach us,
> Or baste us with hot fat,
> Don't fricassee or roast us,
> Or boil us in a vat,
> And please don't stick thy servants Lord,
> In a Rotissomat . . .
>
> *Monty Python's The Meaning of Life*

Question to Consider: How long has it been since I have meditated on the vast extent of the universe or the complexity of the subatomic world?

NOTES

1. Eric Hoffer, *The True Believer: Thoughts on the Nature of Mass Movements* (New York: Harper & Row, 1951), p. 80.

2. Victor Shklovsky, "Art as Technique," in *Russian Formalist Criticism: Four Essays*, ed. and trans. Lee T. Lemon and Marion J. Reis (Lincoln: University of Nebraska Press, 1965), p. 12. Italics in original.

3. Peter L. Berger, *The Heretical Imperative: Contemporary Possibilities of Religious Affirmation* (Garden City, NY: Doubleday Anchor, 1980), p. 138.

God: Planned for Our Pleasure

*But if cattle or lions had hands, so as to paint with their hands and
produce works of art as men do, they would paint their gods and give
them bodies in form like their own—
horses like horses, cattle like cattle.*
—Xenophanes

*If you examine the object to which he is attending, you will find that
it is a composite object containing many . . . ingredients. There will
be images derived from pictures of the Enemy as he appeared during
the Incarnation. . . . I have known cases where what the patient
called his "God" was actually located . . . inside his own head. . . .
[He] will be praying to it—to the thing that he has made, not to the
Person who has made him.*
—C. S. Lewis, *The Screwtape Letters*

The sentimental syrup only thickens when we reach Rick Warren's
eighth meditation. What a target he makes of his religion! Is this a
caricature of religion, or the real thing? Or is the real thing a caricature? This chapter of *The Purpose-Driven Life* leaves you wondering.
There are four major themes that invite brief comment during this,
our own eighth meditation.

PITIFUL SELF-ESTEEM

In his great psychological work *The Courage to Be*, Paul Tillich diagnosed the prevalent woes of post–World War II men and women as a
sad trinity of anxiety, guilt, and meaninglessness. His existential
analyses of these maladies framed the question he believed the Christian gospel must answer for his generation. Well, in our day, the
gospel must apparently tackle the half-imaginary problems of narcis-

sism, and of these the greatest appears to be self-pity, the lack of self-esteem. Pastor Warren seeks to apply the balm of his own gospel to this wound. And his formula is pretty much the caption one once saw on cartoons depicting a bruised-elbowed tyke hiding behind his forearms, his smudged face and tousled locks still visible: "I must be worth somethin' 'cause God don't make no junk."

Now that is a piece of what we call "cold comfort." Pretty cold indeed. It is the perfect example of a piece of deductive reasoning: *Major premise: God maketh no junk. Minor premise: God made me. Conclusion: I am not junk.* No one resorts to such desperate tactics to dispel his self-loathing unless he has altogether failed to find any other positive reason for liking himself. If he had, why, he would be happily framing an inductive proof of his acceptability. He would be pointing at evidence of his worth. Some winning trait, some virtue or talent. But no, the poor schlemiel can find no sign of even minimal worth, so he resorts to pulling it out of a hat: "I *must* be worthwhile, right? Because why would God have wasted a hundred (or two hundred) pounds of matter on me?" It's sort of like inferring the existence of black holes somewhere in space, not because anyone has discovered one, but because somebody's abstract theory entails their existence, at least on paper. Well, whatever gets you through the night.

Thus does Reverend Warren assure his readers of God's beaming, proud-papa love for them. "The moment you were born into the world, God was there as an unseen witness, smiling at your birth,"[1] presumably passing out cigars to the angels. This is a warmed-over Me-Decade version of the Calvinist notion of "unconditional election." To safeguard the principle of salvation by grace apart from works, Calvin taught that God's choice of individuals to be saved owed nothing to any actual or foreseen merit of theirs. God's choice of you for salvation had not a blessed thing to do with any worth or worthiness of your own, because you haven't *got* any, get it? Now just be glad you're not frying in hell.

This doctrine is reinforced with the use of the word *agape*. This word was originally merely one of a number of Greek synonyms for "love," used interchangeably with *phileo*, there being no real distinction between them. But agape got hyped up in Christian preaching to denote a special love in which the lover loves the beloved without regard for any inherent worth or attraction of the beloved. Wacky old Bishop James Pike was about the only one with the guts to point out that this supposed virtue—that is, this special love—is really a case of blatant condescension. Looked at critically, it means that God's supposed love for us is such as to imply not a high value for us as his beloved, but a very low one. Remember the cliché, "Price has a face only a mother could love?"

I cannot help suspecting that Warren's loving God is a projection of the desperate wallflower who can find no other grounds for self-esteem. I see the bumper sticker saying, JESUS IS MY BEST FRIEND, and my immediate reaction is: "You poor bastard!" Like Eric Hoffer's "true believer," the born-again Christian gladly sloughs off the burden of a self he hates, happily volunteering for duty as "one more brick in the wall" of the church.

MADE IN OUR IMAGE

Reverend Warren's God knows no theological sophistication (no more than any of the readers who champion his dreadful book), though Christian clergy might try to tell you otherwise. Warren's God is cut directly from the broad cloth of myth. According to Warren, "We often forget that God has emotions, too. He feels things very deeply. The Bible tells us that God grieves, gets jealous and angry, and feels compassion, pity, sorrow, and sympathy as well as happiness, gladness, and satisfaction. God loves, delights, gets pleasure, rejoices, enjoys, and even laughs!"[2] Well, of course he doesn't. Not unless we're talking about Zeus or Damballah or maybe Baal. For over a thousand years Christian theologians have seen the problem, the sheer impossibility, of ascribing such emotions to God. God is supposed to be eternal and unchanging. God is not supposed to be subject to cause-and-effect, nor to be confined to the time stream. Ask St. Augustine, St. Anselm, St. Thomas Aquinas, or John Calvin. Thus God cannot change his own emotional or volitional states. He cannot be made to react. Being perfect, he cannot pass from a state of potentiality to actuality. Thus he cannot be potentially angry until someone sins, then actually angry once they do. God "cannot" do any of these things for the same reason he "cannot" sin. They are beneath "him" as an eternal, self-existent entity.

This is why Anselm, Aquinas, and the rest maintained that we can use all such affective terms of God only as metaphors or analogies. We cannot, strictly speaking, say even that God loves us. "Love God whether *he* is loving or not, and certainly not *because* he is loving, for he is nonloving, being above love and affection" (*Meister Eckhart*, Fragment 42).[3] We can only know that the "benefits" (as Philip Melanchthon called them) of God toward us, the provision of salvation, providence, and so on, imply some positive disposition that is more analogous to the love of one person for another than anything else we know. Of course, that analogy may not be very close, since, for example, when we attribute "justice" to God, it does not seem to exclude the possibility of his causing genocidal warfare or allowing devastating plagues. What's sauce for the human goose need by no means be sauce for the divine gander. And then you have to wonder why you're even using the same word for what we're like and whatever God is like.

I confess that I have lost patience with such contradictions. I do not think a coherent God-concept survives them, and a god of raw mythology such as Warren promotes is simply unbelievable. Warren is stuck in Sunday School–level, pretheological fundamentalism. It is religious infantilism of the kind that led Freud to conclude that religion is nothing more than neurotic wishful thinking and the refusal to grow up. I believe there is a good bit more to religion than that, but I'm afraid Freud was right about Warrenism. It is a piñata, made of brightly colored paper, filled with sweet candy, and too easily knocked apart.

FEEDING GOD'S EGO

Reverend Warren warns us in this chapter that "worship is not for your benefit." Perish the thought! "We worship for God's benefit. When we worship, the goal is to bring pleasure to God, not ourselves"[4] You know, I think I'd rather go with Paul's opinion in Acts

17:25 that God "does not live in shrines made by mortals, nor is he served by human hands, as though he needed anything." Of course, Paul means to deny that God needs to consume food, as the ancients supposed when they sacrificed animal meat to their gods/God, and the sweet savor went up to the nostrils of the Almighty (Genesis 8:21). Aristophanes, a contemporary of Socrates, lampooned this notion in his comedy *The Birds*, in which the birds hatch the scheme of setting up tollbooths in the clouds to catch and trap the sacrificial smoke, starving the gods till they agree to the birds' demands. Warren knows God doesn't chow down on Doritos or caviar. What he fails to see, however, is that there is no difference in principle between the old animal sacrifice theology and his own. Surely the same principle applies to emotional gratification. He is still manifestly talking about the care and feeding of God. His God, like an insecure boyfriend, seems to need emotional stroking.

One might try to defend worship by consistently pursuing the rationalizing logic of Aristophanes and Paul. If worship does not serve the needs of God, since he doesn't have any, who *is* it for? Well, who is left? Us! It is quite reasonable, it seems to me, to understand worship as Friedrich Schleiermacher did, as an occasion for us scatterbrained human beings to take time out from all the things that so easily distract us from God-awareness during the week, to come together and sing and think together about the divine. So, yes, of course, worship must be for our benefit, not God's. What could he possibly get out of it? "The Sabbath was made for man, not man for the Sabbath," after all.

Have you ever heard someone praying in church as if he or she were giving God a theology lesson? "O God, blessed and eternal Father, we know that you have sent your Son Jesus Christ to save mankind. We believe you sent the Holy Spirit to sanctify us, and you have given us the Bible so that we may show ourselves approved workmen, etc., etc." After a while, you open your eyes and mutter, "Does he think God doesn't know this stuff? Why's he chewing God's ear with it?" But, of course, he's really addressing the congregation, reminding them of these beliefs, to make them appreciate God more. He's trying to help them contemplate God instead of the upcoming football game, their romantic or financial problems, and so forth. Of course worship is for the benefit of the congregation. Who else could it be for?

HE WALKS WITH ME AND HE TALKS WITH ME, AND WE'RE PLANNING TO ELOPE RIGHT AFTER CHURCH

For Reverend Warren, like all evangelical Protestants, it finally all comes down to that saccharine "personal relationship with Christ." He writes, "This is what real worship is all about—falling in love with Jesus," daily "carrying on a continual conversation with him."[5] Okay, Warren has here plumbed the depths of religious infantilism. Jesus Christ has become an imaginary playmate with whom one may hold imaginary conversations, as when a little girl, plastic plates spread on the plastic table, asks her dolly what she would like for dinner.

Don't get me wrong. It's not as if Warren were an innovator here. Indeed, the greatest puzzle of *The Purpose-Driven Life* is how its warmed-over fundamentalism became such a national craze, as if born-again Christians had not already been surfeiting on a steady diet of the same pabulum for generations.

There is much less to the whole business than meets the eye. Fundamentalists have just never thought the thing through, any more than it occurs to a child to wonder how Santa Claus can visit all those homes during a single evening. Is the Risen Jesus still an individual human consciousness, with whom one may have a "relationship"? Then how can he possibly be imagined as carrying on millions of conversations with competing pietists jamming the lines every second of the day? A brilliant *Saturday Night Live* skit depicted Jesus (Phil Hartman) appearing one morning in the kitchen of a born-again housewife (Sally Field) and asking her if she could maybe hold off on praying about daily trivia like this: "Jesus, be with Timmy as he takes his exams today." There's just too much claim on his attention. But this obvious problem never bothers born-again Christians, which just shows what a mind game it is.

In the end, the whispering voice of one's personal savior is nothing more than the internalized norms and neuroses of one's particular church. Jesus tells a woman in a Holiness Church not to wear a simple hair ornament lest she be damned for the sin of vanity, but he assures Tammy Faye Bakker she can wear enough mascara to be mistaken for a raccoon. Jesus becomes the ventriloquist dummy for one's own conscience, which has very likely been flogged to raw hypersensitivity from the pulpit.

As I noted in the previous chapter, the greatest irony of the whole thing is that the "personal savior" piety to which Warren reduces the whole of Christian worship, indeed the whole of Christianity itself, is never so much as intimated in the New Testament. Where do you propose to find it? Granted, you can find all manner of passages requiring the sinner to repent and sin no more, to believe that God raised Jesus from the dead, that you must come to the Father through Jesus, and so on. But where does Jesus or anybody else say a single word about having a personal relationship with a personal savior? Does John 15:1–11, the True Vine discourse, discuss it? "Abide in me, and I will abide in you"? No one is denying Christianity involves some sort of spiritual union with Christ, but the crucial element of personal, back-and-forth communication is conspicuous by its absence here. Surely the passage deals with the Eucharist, the Lord's Supper, Holy Communion, given the Dionysian imagery of the fruitful vine and its grapes.

Does John 10:1–15, the Good Shepherd discourse, have anything to do with a personal relationship with Jesus? I can't see how, unless you read it in between the lines. Jesus says that his own sheep recognize his voice and respond to his call, while members of Satan's flock turn a deaf ear to him. This is simply an alternative metaphor, saying the same thing as the parable of the seeds and the soil in Mark 4:3–20. Both metaphors depict the glad reception of the gospel by certain hearers, precisely as in 1 Thessalonians 1:4–5 ("We know, brethren beloved by God, that he has chosen you; for our gospel came to you not only in word, but also in power and in the Holy Spirit and with full conviction." RSV). The same contrast is drawn, using other metaphors, in 1 Thessalonians 2:13, 1 Corinthians 1:18, and 2 Corinthians 2:14–16. But what about when he says, "I know my own, and my own know me"? It simply means the same as Mark 13:5–6, 21–23: Jesus's disciples will be able to distinguish him from rival, false prophets and pseudomessiahs (mentioned in John 10:8, too). There is simply nothing implicit or explicit in such texts suggesting that the believer has an ongoing personal acquaintance with Jesus.

Revelation 3:20 ("Behold, I stand at the door and knock; if anyone hears my voice and opens the door, I will come in to him and eat with him, and he with me." RSV) is perhaps the last resort, but I'm afraid it is irrelevant to the "personal savior" business, too. If you look at the context of the verse, you will see that it appears in the letters of John to the seven churches. Notice how each letter makes reference to the End-Time events depicted on a grander scale later in the book. In Revelation 2:7, the Risen Christ promises that anyone in the Ephesian church who heeds his warnings will be allowed to eat from the Tree of Life in the Paradise of God, the privilege of all the saved in 22:2. The faithful of Smyrna are promised kingly crowns, anticipating those of the Twenty-four Elders in 4:4 and 10, as well as immunity to the Second Death (2:11) of which we read more in 20:14. The unrepentant in Pergamum are threatened with the word/sword of the Lamb in 2:16, already anticipated in 1:16 and seen in 19:15 as a missile aimed at the Antichrist. The faithful of Pergamum will partake of the manna (2:17) hidden in the heavenly Ark that shelters the souls of their fellow martyrs (6:9–11 and 11:19). Thyatiran heretics will be thrown into the sickbed of their seductive mistress Jezebel, the false prophetess (2:22), who foreshadows the doomed Harlot of Babylon in chapter 14. The righteous in Thyatira, however, can look forward to sharing the iron-rod scepter of the Lamb (compare 2:27 with 12:5). They will also receive the Morning Star (2:28), a title of the victorious Christ himself in 22:16. Sinners in Sardis are warned of the thieflike stealth of the coming judgment in 3:3, echoing the apocalyptic warning of Matthew 24:43–44. Their opposite numbers, the faithful in Sardis, will receive white robes (3:4–5), as later in 6:11 and 7:9. They need not worry about their names being erased from the heavenly ledger of the saved (3:5) on the day of the final assize (20:12–15). In 3:12, righteous Philadelphians are promised a fate like that of the blessed Baucis and Philemon from Greek myth, who, upon death, became columns upholding the temple of Zeus. The Philadelphians, as residents of the New Jerusalem, will uphold God's living temple in the new earth (21:1–4), just as Cephas, James, and John were the pillars of the old Jerusalem (Galatians 2:9).

This brings us at last to the letter to Laodicea, where the "Jesus on the doorstep" scene appears. When the Risen One says that he stands at the door, calling on those within, hoping for their sake that they hear his voice, we are, on the one hand, back with the Good Shepherd who calls his flock to salvation's pasture (see also John 5:25 and 18:37). And, on the other, we find ourselves on the very verge of the Second Coming, as in Mark 13:29 ("When you see these things taking place, you know that he is near, at the very gates." RSV) and James 5:9 ("Behold, the judge is standing at the doors." RSV). In all these cases "standing at the door" language denotes the imminence of the Second Coming and the Final Judgment; it has nothing to do with devotionalism or an evangelistic appeal. The supper he promises them (Revelation 3:20) is no cozy, devotional klatch such as Robert Boyd Munger envisions in *My Heart, Christ's Home*,[6] but rather the Marriage Supper of the Lamb at the end of the age (Revelation 19:6–7). Apparently he is offering them a chance to participate in the final slaughter of the wicked (19:17–18: "Come, gather for the great supper of God, to eat the flesh of kings, the flesh of captains, the flesh of mighty men, the flesh of horses and their riders, the flesh of all men, both free and slave, both small and great." RSV), which will keep the vultures supplied with carrion for many days to come.

YOUR SAVIOR

Once I attended a fan convention and was prowling through the colorful bazaar called the Dealer's Room. I was on the lookout for interesting old science fiction paperbacks, monster movie videos, and whatnot. Some people at these events just cannot seem to resist the impulse to show up in costume. All of a sudden I spotted a guy dressed as Jesus. So I could not resist the impulse to accost him with a smart remark. I walked up to him and asked him, "Excuse me, but have you accepted yourself as your personal savior?" I don't even remember what he answered, because it suddenly hit me: that is the crucial question everyone must face: *Have* you accepted yourself as your personal savior? Because that's the only savior who can do the job! *You* are your personal savior, without whose aid you will never get anywhere. Unless this savior intervenes on your behalf, nothing anyone has done to help you will do any good. You are going to have to decide to heed the advice some wise man gave you. You are going to have to decide the time has come for you to make an about-face. It is you, not me, nor anybody else, not even Rick Warren nor Jesus Christ, who can discover the meaning of your life. Only you can answer the question why you are not doing what you know you must do. Only you, not your church or some other peer group, can save you. That is the cross you must bear: free decision and responsibility for the results.

Day Eight

Point to Ponder: How about a bumper sticker that says JESUS IS MY IMAGINARY FRIEND.

Quote to Remember: "It is of course not difficult for an imaginative person so to conjure up the Person of Christ before himself that the picture shall take a kind of sensuous distinctness. . . . Someone thinks he sees Jesus Himself, and consequently begins to commune with Him. But what such a person communes with in this fashion is not Christ Himself but a picture that the man's own imagination has put together." (Wilhelm Herrmann, *The Communion of the Christian with God*)

Question to Consider: Am I listening to the inner voice of the Holy Spirit? Or am I listening to my own? Do I need to pretend to be speaking for Jesus in order to take my inner voice seriously?

NOTES

1. Rick Warren, *The Purpose-Driven Life: What on Earth Am I Here For?* (Grand Rapids, MI: Zondervan, 2002), p. 63.

2. Ibid., p. 64.

3. Meister Eckhart, *Meister Eckhart*, trans. Raymond B. Blakney (New York: Harper & Row, 1961), p. 248.

4. Warren, *The Purpose-Driven Life*, p. 66.

5. Ibid., p. 67.

6. Robert Boyd Munger, *My Heart, Christ's Home* (Downers Grove, IL: InterVarsity Press, 1954), pp. 8–9.

What Makes Me Sick

Then the human race began to multiply and progress. The Archons
met to consider the matter and resolved: "Come, let us unleash a
deluge with our hands and wipe out all flesh, from man to beast."
But when the Archon of the forces was apprised of their plan, he said
to Noah, "Make yourself an ark from some wood that does not rot
and conceal yourself inside, you and your offspring and the beasts and
the birds of the sky, from small to large, and set it up on Mount
Seir." Then Norea approached him, intending to come aboard the
ark. But he refused to allow it, and she blew upon the ark, causing it
to be consumed by fire. Then he built the ark a second time.
—Hypostasis of the Archons

"You're lucky: you believe your own twaddle."
—Plog the smithy, in Ingmar Bergman's *The Seventh Seal*

Once, when I was a pastor, I sat listening to our small but cherubic
kids choir sing some ditty about Noah and the Flood. It returned
again and again to the theme of God placing the rainbow in the sky,
promising never to inundate the world again. The song was called
"Rainbow Valentine." Maybe you've heard it. When I did, it struck
me as the height of black comedy. "Rainbow Valentine"? It should
have been titled "Rainbow Epitaph." The cheery verses did not linger
on the prospect of the drowning of nearly the whole human race by a
deity who regretted his decision to create them in the first place. I
couldn't help thinking of "Rainbow Epitaph" when I read Rick
Warren's ninth chapter, "What Makes God Smile." In it he uses the
story of Noah's Flood to illustrate how we are to try and please God,
our doting Father. Noah's Boy Scout behavior made the big old Softy
in the sky smile. Everyone else on earth got a rather different reaction
from God. He drowned *them* like rats. Like the kiddy song, Warren
doesn't really mind. Once Reinhold Niebuhr commented that, while

101

one may no longer be able to take the Bible literally, one still ought to take it quite seriously. No matter what you may think of Niebuhr's advice, it seems to me that Rick Warren's approach is the worst possible: here is a guy who takes the Bible *literally but not seriously*. Otherwise he'd never be able to treat the text the way he does.

SO THIS IS THE TALE OF OUR CASTAWAYS, THEY'RE HERE FOR A LONG, LONG TIME

Reverend Warren believes the story of Noah is literally true, the historical account of eight survivors, together with a floating menagerie of animals, of a world-devastating flood. "God said, 'This guy brings me pleasure. He makes me smile. I'll start over with his family.' Because Noah brought pleasure to God, you and I are alive today."[1] "He trusted God completely, and that made God smile."[2] I can't help but feel I am back amid the kiddy choir.

Are we all adults here? Then let's get one thing straight: the Genesis story is a myth. It's not as if there were no great floods in the ancient Near East. There was a whopper in 12,500 BCE, for instance. But the story of Noah is not a record of it. *First*, it is a derivative version of demonstrably much older flood epics from the same area, including the Gilgamesh epic, the Atrahasis epic, the story of Xisuthros, and that of Deucalion and Pyrrha, all of whom survived the world-devastating flood by setting sail in a protective ark, most of them bringing the animals along for the ride. We find all the familiar details: The decision of the gods to flood the world for some offense committed by the human race, the stipulated dimensions of the ark, the provision for the animals, the onset of the rains, the number of days the flood lasted, the naming of the spot the ark came to rest, the sending forth of birds to find dry ground, the emergence of the refugees, their sacrifice, and the promise of the gods never to doom the world thusly ever again. It's all there, at least most of it in most versions.

Second, there are blatant contradictions within the biblical version. Here we read the Flood lasted forty days (Genesis 7:4, 12), then receding for three weeks, for sixty-one days all told. But then we read the whole thing took one hundred and fifty days (Genesis 7:24, 8:3). First we find Noah bringing aboard a pair of each nonkosher species and seven pairs of kosher species (which he could dine on and sacrifice in the meantime, Genesis 7:2–3). Then we read of him bringing only a single pair of all species (Genesis 6:19–20). What is going on? While these discrepancies would indeed be gross self-contradictions in a single work by a single author, human or divine, they are rather signs of the combination of two originally distinct stories. The biblical editor had two different versions of the story, both esteemed sacred by many people already, so he dared not cut anything out. Yet he was compiling a single narrative and could not afford to leave the absurd impression of one flood story ending in a promise never again to flood the world, and then commence another in which the world appears to be flooded again, immediately thereafter. So his only option was to splice the two together, which accounts for both the contradictions and the redundancy of the stories.[3]

Third, the story was originally not about Noah at all. In the other versions of the story, the hero who builds the ark and prevails over the rain is a sun god or other immortal character, and the flood story tries to account for his immortality. The biblical "Noah" seems to have been confused by scribes with "Enoch," whose name is nearly identical, only one letter off, in Hebrew. Noah was at first cast as the inventor of wine, the means by which he brought the human race "relief from out of the ground" for the toil to which God had consigned us after Eden (Genesis 5:29 and 9:20–21). After a hard day's work, they'd lift a few, saying, "It's Noah time!" Enoch was originally a sun god, one of many Hebrew deities who were reduced in rank to ancient human heroes as Judaism inched toward monotheism. His solar character is made clear from his "life span" of three hundred sixty-five days, his "walking with God," that is, along the rim of the firmament daily, and his rising into heaven. It would fit the myth pattern better if Enoch, not Noah, were the original Hebrew Flood hero.

Fourth,[4] the engineering of the ark is grossly anachronistic. In the envisioned period people had only reed rafts and hollowed-out logs for water travel. And if God did give Noah such advanced nautical technology, why didn't Noah pass it on? It would be many, many centuries before ancient sailing vessels caught up with Noah's fanciful ark.

Fifth, the Genesis writer naturally had no remote idea of the complexity and variety of the accommodations Noah would've had to have built into the ark for the various animal species to survive. Did he have leather slings to keep giraffes upright? Did he have different types of floor surfaces to accommodate different species without injury? Were the window bars spaced appropriately for all manner of different horned species? Were feeding troughs at various reachable distances up off the floor (where they wouldn't be fouled)? How did he deal with the terrific amount of toxic sewage? How did he keep the animals, some of them the natural prey of others, apart for the duration? And if he did, did he also bring extra animals for the carnivores to eat? Where did he keep the unthinkably vast stores of food that would be needed even for the shorter, forty-day duration? And what about the different environments required by polar and tropical animals?

Sixth, how did Noah come by penguins from Antarctica, Australian marsupials, and other far-flung life-forms that had never made an appearance in ancient Mesopotamia? Did they all travel to the Middle East aboard smaller arks first?

Seventh, a flood of the world-covering magnitude described in Genesis would have stirred up undersea currents so mightily that they would have driven all oxygen out of the water and suffocated all sea creatures. I'm afraid that's the end of the food chain and thus of all life on earth. Poor Noah would have come out of the ark only to starve to death after his last can of sardines was empty!

THE WEATHER STARTED GETTING ROUGH THE TINY SHIP WAS TOSSED

You can always suggest that God could have miraculously taken care of all this. He could have placed all the critters in a state of suspended animation so they wouldn't starve or eat each other or keep poor Noah up all night with their intolerable noises. Or maybe he could have solved the space problem by shrinking the animals down with the reducer ray Brainiac used to shrink the city of Kandor in *Superman* comics. I mean, he's almighty, right? What can't he do?

But, don't you see? Then you're writing a whole new story. God could have done anything, true, but the story never intimates him doing anything like these wonders, compared to which the Flood itself would seem the merest parlor trick. For that matter, if you want to come up with your own Flood story based on what God *could* have done, why not dispense with the ark altogether? Just have God erect force fields over certain well-stocked areas on each continent. Why not, if you don't feel bound by the constraints of this story you insist is the infallible word of God? Anything goes.

Or you can just close your eyes blissfully and leave it to God. Somehow it's all true anyway, despite the fact that it makes no sense. Well, then I have to ask you: what is it you believe? What do you have in mind? If, thanks to all the scientific difficulties, you admit the straightforward reading doesn't make sense, in what sense is it still true "anyway"? I think at this point the blind-faith believer has come merely to affirm his emotional loyalty to the story, as a part of scripture, a rather different thing from "believing" it all actually happened. Hey, I'm loyal to it, too! I love the story! It just isn't a piece of history.

But Reverend Warren believes the story literally. How closely has he studied the matter? The implied superficiality of this man's—this book's—grasp of the Bible is frightening. Given the power of quoting the Bible to its fans, this is like seeing a nursery school tyke holding a loaded gun.

So Warren takes the Flood myth literally. But he does not take it seriously. The benign chumminess he predicates of God, depicting him as a smiling Father like Fred MacMurray on *My Three Sons*, just does not reckon with the enormity of this cruel power that destroyed the whole human species! You can't maintain that the whole human race deserved extermination. Was every one of the ancients a sadist? A Nazi? A cannibal? Even the *kids*? As with the other genocidal jihads in the Old Testament, this one makes no distinction between adults and children. Suffer the little children to sleep with the fishes. Of course, these ancient race wars are most likely fictions, too. At any rate, the whole idea of an entirely evil race is itself a mark of fiction, like the Orcs in *The Lord of the Rings*.

Warren is treating the story as if it were an illustrative fiction. That is when you feel free to dismiss features of the story as irrelevant to your point. For instance, when we read the Parable of the Lost Sheep (Luke 15:4–7), some wag might say, "Hey, this guy's a pretty lousy shepherd! He goes off looking for one measly sheep and leaves the other ninety-nine to fall to predators?" But we say he is missing the point of the story. The parable portrays God's concern for the lost and straying. You aren't supposed to take every detail literally. If you did, you would ruin the story. That's because that's all it *is*: a story. And so's the Flood story! Deep down, Warren must know that, but it doesn't occur to him to say so, since for him reality is a matter of trying to situate yourself in a fictive, imaginary world of magic and miracles. The Warrenite Christian is like a *Star Wars* geek who dresses up in costume and dearly wishes he lived in the Star Wars universe. Sometimes such a fan will even spend as much time as he can in weekend costume conventions. For Warrenites, that's going to church.

HAPPY HAPPY, JOY JOY

"God smiles when I trust him."[5] Is it really possible that Karen Hughes, undersecretary for public diplomacy and public affairs, and Neil Cavuto, business editor for FOX News channel, enjoyed and endorsed this book? It says so on the dust jacket. Could I have gotten the children's edition by some mistake? Rick Warren makes Robert Schuller look like Nietzsche. Nietzsche, as you know, proclaimed that God is dead. But for Rick Warren, God is apparently senile. And yet Warren urges us to "trust" this cosmic genocidal maniac. Okay, that's unfair. He has forgotten all about the Mr. Hyde side of the Genesis deity. That's not the one he wants us to trust (though if we *don't*, we'll probably be meeting him and his wrath soon enough). Warren wants us to ask ourselves, "Since God knows what is best, in what areas of my life do I need to trust him most?"[6]

This is traditional pietist rhetoric. I am not surprised to read it. But I do wonder what it is supposed to mean. A great deal of fundamentalist lingo, I believe, has no descriptive reference. In fact, I suspect that for many, even the much-vaunted "personal relationship with Christ" does not refer to anything they can point to. Such lingo instead functions as in-group jargon, a superficial screen to make one's group seem different from outsiders. In the same way, I wonder what Warren has in mind, if anything, when he tells us to trust God with various areas of our lives. If I were a born-again Christian, what would Reverend Warren want me to do with all this "trusting"? I can think of two possibilities. Actually, I've been pondering the question for many years, almost as long as I've been urged to do this "trusting."

First, he may intend that one need not worry about the future. "Will I find love? Will I succeed in my chosen field (Uh-oh, excuse me—the field God has chosen *for* me)? Will I live a long and healthy life? Will my loved ones be kept safe?" We might worry about these things. Everybody does at one time or another. Eventually we grow up and realize that it is morbid and completely useless to dwell on such anxieties. When we worry, we are already living, in some measure, as if the worst had already happened. We are trying to acclimate ourselves to disaster so we can soften the blow when it one day strikes. But that's counterproductive. We are only summoning the shadow of what we fear. And as we mature we learn to resign ourselves to the future and the fact that we cannot control it. We'll have to hope we will have developed sufficient strength to roll with the punches when the time comes. And if not, we'll deal with it then. Might as well enjoy the sunshine now!

I regard living in the moment as a realistic accommodation to reality. But is that what Warren has in mind? Yes and no. As I read the evangelical rhetoric of prayer and trust in the care of God, I get the impression there is a kind of bait-and-switch tactic in play. In order to make the Christian life more attractive, preachers offer the promise that you will dwell in the protective hands of God where nothing can touch you. "A thousand may fall at your side, ten thousand at your right hand, but it will not touch you" (Psalms 91:7, NASB). But this is naïve, and it is never long before the disillusioned pietist approaches his pastor asking why things are not coming up roses as promised. Then we fall back to Stoicism: actually, the "best" thing *did* befall you, because rotten luck brings you into closer dependence upon God. Besides cultivating an attitude of masochism, this rationale is a malicious joke on the earnest believer, whose peace of mind is being sacrificed as a face-saving maneuver on behalf of the party line. But after the believer has learned the lesson of Stoic resignation and given up naïve hopes of a brighter outcome, his "trusting God" amounts merely to equanimity in the face of life's vicissitudes. There is a degree of wisdom in that, and yet, no matter who says it, Christian, Stoic, or Buddhist, I must confess I wonder if such resigned pessimism is not essentially a cowardly move, an emotional disengagement so as to avoid risks. Some risks are worth taking in life, and life will never be fulfilling without them.

Second, Pastor Warren might have in mind the person who knows what "God's will" (i.e., the born-again policy) is supposed to be in a particular matter, but he thinks he is going to be handicapped if he adopts that policy. Some more worldly course of action might seem preferable in the short run. The Christian ethic might seem counterintuitive, so you are tempted to obey common sense, or what looks like common sense at the moment. To trust God in a situation like this would then imply that the Christian way is the best policy despite appearances, and if you just hang tight, you will be glad you did. An example would be the (I think wise) ethic to avoid promiscuous sex. You'll be glad you did. That makes a lot of sense to me, though I don't think it is so much a matter of "trusting God" as of simply having foresight and trusting the greater experience of those who advise you. And if the advice is sound, presumably it will make sense to the person being advised. It ought to "click." You ought to be able to see what you didn't see before, why so-and-so would be foolish. Maybe you *can't* see the wisdom of it, but your dad or your pastor says, "Look, I've been at this longer than you have. I know what I'm talking about. Don't make this mistake!" I think you ought to give the person the benefit of the doubt, because it's not a request for blind faith and obedience. They *have* lived through more of life than you.

Similarly, suppose Reverend So-and-so says, "Trust the Bible on this one! This is what God says!" The Bible is very often wise, and there are many cases of things having turned out best when people followed its teachings on this or that point. But do you see what that means? In such cases, it turns out *not* to be a simple demand for blind-faith obedience. Again, there is a long record of *experience* we can point to. Nothing arbitrary there.

But! Suppose some clergyman tells you to trust God when he (allegedly) says a wife must submit even to a bullying brute of a husband because that is the divinely established pecking order. Maybe hubby will react like the British Empire against Gandhi's minions, who got pummeled because they didn't defend themselves. The Brits felt ashamed and went home to tea. But in cases of domestic abuse, in which case the woman is asked to "trust God," a battering husband is unlikely to stop abusing his wife out of shame. In essence, the woman is really being told to become a martyr for the sake of biblical inerrancy. To hell with that. Bible or no Bible, "trusting" God on this one is just playing sucker for the sake of an institution's policy.

There are other examples where your piously "trusting God" is more a matter of not rocking the boat, serving the institutional interests of your sect, not your interests, not God's—as if the Almighty, Eternal God could *have* any interests. I am thinking of the universal fundamentalist ban on Christian teenagers dating non-Christians. I don't mean louts or Lotharios. I want my daughters to avoid them, too. I mean good people who happen not to be born-again Christians. Why the ban? The Christian getting emotionally close to the nonbeliever would be risking eroding the illusion that only one's co-sectarians are loving and noble. One would soon get the impression that morality and character are not the property of any one faith, and that they are not necessarily dependent upon faith at all. No, the church wants her children to stay within the tribe, so as to keep the walls up high. I can readily see why a small religious community, like Judaism, would be concerned about this. Interfaith marriage threatens to destroy American Judaism. But there is a big difference between being concerned about interfaith marriages (like Jews) and forbidding them (like born-again Christians). And besides, certainly American fundamentalism is in no such danger of being destroyed. And if one "trusts God" on dating in this manner, one will again be manipulated against one's own interests for the sake of an institution.

In short, I just don't trust anyone who suggests I set aside my own better judgment in favor of some prepackaged set of rules, the wisdom of which I cannot already see. Remember, "I said it! God believes it! That settles it!" To invoke God's authority is to smuggle in your own. God may not be smiling when I refuse to trust Pastor Warren's pontifications made in his name. But I'm afraid I can't help that. I cannot set aside my moral autonomy for the sake of any dogma. That would implicate me in an inauthentic existence and cost me my integrity. And that is a sickening prospect.

Day Nine

Point to Ponder: I smile when I trust myself.

Quote to Remember: "But he [Jesus] said to him, 'Man, who appointed me a judge or arbitrator over you?'" (Luke 12:14, NASB)

Question to Consider: Why does Rick Warren quote only Bible paraphrases that already smuggle in the evangelical interpretation?

NOTES

1. Rick Warren, *The Purpose-Driven Life: What on Earth Am I Here For?* (Grand Rapids, MI: Zondervan, 2002), pp. 69–70.

2. Ibid., p. 71.

3. The verses derived from the Yahwist (J) account are as follows: Gen. 6:5–8; 7:1–5, 7–10, 12, 16b–17, 22–23; 8:2b–3a, 6–12, 13b, 20–22; 9:18–19. The Priestly version consists of Gen. 6:9–22; 7:6, 11, 13–16a, 18–21, 24; 8:1–2a, 3–5, 13a, 14–19; 9:1–17, 28–29.

4. Much of what follows I owe to Robert A. Moore, "The Impossible Voyage of Noah's Ark," *Creation/Evolution* 11 (Winter 1983).

5. Warren, *The Purpose-Driven Life*, p. 76.

6. Ibid.

The Achilles' Heel of Worship

*So our coming of age forces us to a true recognition of our situation vis
á vis God. God is teaching us that we must live as men who can get
along very well without him. The God who is with us is the God who
forsakes us (Mark 15:34). The God who makes us live in this world
without using him as a working hypothesis is the God before whom we
are ever standing. Before God and with him we live without God.*
—Dietrich Bonhoeffer, *Letters and Papers from Prison*

*For freedom Christ has set us free; stand fast therefore, and do not
submit again to a yoke of slavery.*
—Galatians 5:1 (RSV)

Pastor Warren tells us in his "The Heart of Worship" chapter that the
essence of worship is total surrender to God. He knows he has his
work cut out for him, since surrender is a dirty word, and, like the
French Army or the Democratic Party, he must now make it sound
good. Like the World War II propagandist Axis Sally, he tries to tell
us that surrender is no shameful thing, especially when one is surrendering to such a kind captor as God. God loves us, so we ought to be
ready to surrender to him. That is a bad analogy, as if one partner in
a marriage agreed to yield him- or herself to the other in abject subservience. That would be a sick situation, codependency and then
some. But Warren tries to negotiate the surrender of his reader to his
God by telling the former how much the latter loves him.

CROSS TALK

According to Warren, "If you want to know how much you matter to
God, look at Christ with his arms outstretched on the cross, saying, 'I
love you this much! I'd rather die than live without you.'"[1] Uh, where
in the gospels does Jesus say anything like this? Of course Warren

111

does not mean to be quoting scripture; he provides no citation. But he is, in effect, creating his own scripture. Just as the gospel writers did in their crucifixion accounts, Warren is putting words into the mouth of the crucified Christ in order to set forth his own understanding of the so-called salvation wrought there. But his view of the atonement is far from clear. And that only raises the larger question of whether *any* of the proposed explanations of the idea of "Christ dying for our sins" makes any sense. C. S. Lewis in *Mere Christianity* offers to us that basic faith (shall we call it a "lowest common denominator"?) which is content merely to believe that the cross of Jesus saves but demands no particular theological explanation of *how* it saves.[2] Such doctrines are secondary, he urges. Nothing to divide the church over. But, as often with Lewis, he is too facile. There is a deeper problem than Christian factionalism here. Why is there all that debating over cross doctrines? Simply because all of them are beset with severe problems. If any one of them made any sense, everyone would probably be happy to agree on it.

Is it any help to say that Jesus's death was an *expiation*, that is, that his shed blood cleansed us of sin in the same way that the blood of a helpless, squealing sacrificial animal supposedly washed away the sin of the ancient Israelite? The animal sacrifice idea is itself no more intelligible than the cross business. You wind up trying to explain one puzzle by means of another.

Is it any better to say Jesus's death is a *penal substitution*, letting John Wayne Gacy go free if Mother Teresa were willing to take his place in the gas chamber? Hardly! What sort of justice is this? If you piously believe this one, maybe you never notice the problem, any more than Gacy would question the propriety of the substitution as he packed his bags and left death row behind. Don't kick a gift horse in the mouth.

How about Athanasius's doctrine that God had to live a truly mortal life (including a death) in order to infuse mortals with his own immortality? Sounds good, but besides the questionable business of picturing immortality like some kind of a permeating grease, this one runs aground on the rock (as Thomas Altizer noted)[3] that no mortal dies for only a couple of days. This theory would work better if there were no resurrection in the story. Now that would be a real death.

Gregory of Nyssa formulated a theory whereby Jesus's death was a scam to outwit a kidnapper named Satan, who held the whole (sinful) human race hostage. God the Father knows how much Satan would love adding Jesus's immortal soul to his collection (think of Mr. Scratch with his collection of moths in *The Devil and Daniel Webster*), so he offers to barter Jesus's death for the return of the hostages. Satan falls for it, poor dope, not realizing that he can't keep a good man down. Jesus rises from the dead, escapes Satan's domain, and leaves the poor devil holding the bag. The crass mythological characterization hardly requires comment. We have only lengthened the line of defense here, not shortened it.

Peter Abelard tried to short-circuit all these theories (and more like them) by saying simply that Jesus's death saves us by demonstrating the love of God. But this, the "moral influence theory," is exceedingly lame. How does an avoidable death show love? The death could only show love if dying were the only way to save us. If I jump in front of a speeding car to get you out of its path, and I die, then my death will indeed show my love for you. But if you are not in any danger from a car and I say, "Watch this!" and jump in front of a car, I'm just crazy. Abelard was making Jesus into John Hinckley.

Rick Warren's peculiar quip ("I love you this much!") shares the weakness of Abelard's moral influence theory: how on earth does the gratuitous death of an innocent man demonstrate anyone's love in any way? Warren is just too used to hearing that it does. He has come to take the arbitrary juxtaposition for granted and assumes we will, too.

Old Washington Gladden hit the nail on the head: "The figures used by these theologians are so grotesque that it is difficult to quote them without incurring the charge of treating sacred themes with levity."[4] Again he says, "It is easy to see why these theories have either perished or become moribund. It is because they are morally defective. They ascribe to God traits of character and principles of conduct which are repugnant to our sense of right. It is because men are compelled to believe that the Judge of all the earth will do right, that they cannot believe these theories."[5] To these morally reprehensible atonement doctrines one must add any doctrine of the cross that leads to the conclusion that people will be damned to eternal torture for not believing in it.

SCHIZOID CREATOR

And that seems to be what Warren believes. Either this man is a devious huckster, soft-pedaling the negative aspects of his gospel, or he is "blind" in the way Jesus condemns the Pharisees for being blind. He does not mean, I think, that they are cynically pretending to a piety they laugh at in private, a peculiar charade. Rather, I take him to mean that their casuistry has run away with them, distorting their perspective so that they can no longer see how their extrapolations from the Torah get in the way of scripture instead of facilitating our obedience to it. The scribes didn't *mean* to dishonor parents (Mark 7:9–13). They just embroidered the commandment so much they could no longer catch sight of its original point. I think Warren has completely lost perspective in the same way. In the same chapter he says two very different things. First, "God is not a cruel slave driver or a bully who uses brute force to coerce us into submission. He doesn't try to break our will, but woos us to himself so that we might offer ourselves freely to him."[6] But then just five pages later we find him saying how, thanks to Bill Bright, founder of Campus Crusade for Christ, "more than 150 million people have come to Christ and will spend eternity in heaven."[7] Say, Rick old buddy, what do you suppose is going to happen to the considerably more than 150 million who have *not* "come to Christ"? Are we to imagine them just hanging around on the shore of the River Styx? No, we know good and well what Bill Bright and Rick Warren think will happen to them: they are going to spend a "Christless eternity" roasting on a spit in the pit of hell, tortured day and night forever and ever. Make up your mind, pastor! What is it going to be? A God who terrorizes people who don't happen to belong to his (your) favorite religion? Or a God who respects people's choices and accepts only love freely offered? If you want the latter, then you just have to give up the scare story of hell.

Warren claims that "Surrender . . . does not mean giving up rational thinking. God would not waste the mind he gave you! God does not want robots to serve him."[8] Then I guess he'll respect it if I come to an honest conclusion that differs with his (yours)? I guess the criterion of salvation will *not* be my acquiescence to a creed about the death of Jesus for my sins?

DEMEANING MEANING

But why would one equate spiritual exaltation with "surrender" in the first place? Why do power relations have to have anything to do with it? Ultimately I think it is a question of priestcraft, as the old Freethinkers used to call it. Religious institutions do not trust their members to think for themselves. Nor do most believers *want* to think for themselves. They'd as soon be free of the burden of responsibility and autonomy, and they will mortgage their freedom to the church in exchange for assurances of salvation, handed out like the dole by the Roman Caesars. Fyodor Dostoyevsky was right on target when he spelled that out in *The Grand Inquisitor*. Note the intimidating rhetoric used by the apparently genial Warren (quoting E. Stanley Jones): "If you don't surrender to Christ, you surrender to Chaos."[9] "Surrender is not the *best* way to live; it is the *only* way to live."[10] That is utter nonsense, as five minutes' conversation with any average non-fundamentalist will confirm. Everybody has problems, even born-again Christians (as their own mass of self-help books demonstrate eloquently), and everybody has joys, triumphs, and rich experiences.

Warren believes that only abject surrender to God, Christ, the Bible, and the earthly spokesman for this trinity is the only way to slough off the dead snakeskin of selfish vice and to cultivate virtue. Short of such surrender, he says, we are like so many Satans coveting the throne of God. Listen, just because one has his own delusions of grandeur, he needn't project them onto everyone else.

As far as I can tell, surrender hasn't got a thing to do with it. What matters is *maturity*. And one need not even call it "*spiritual* maturity." Nothing wrong with that phrase except that it's redundant. It is simply maturity to reach the point where you are no longer insecure and can rejoice at the success of others. When you don't have to make others look bad for you to look good. The mature person is not defensive and readily yields when his opinion is refuted, because he just wants the truth to emerge, and it doesn't matter from whom. The mature person, whatever her religious identity or lack of it, knows that her own interests include those of others and do not compete with them. The mature person automatically seeks to put others at ease, feels no need to dominate conversations, and patiently views detractors as merely childish until and unless he is forced to conclude they are evil. The mature person hopes to be given the benefit of the doubt and knows he must give it to others, if only to avoid jumping the gun and being mistaken.

The mature human being is humble yet rejoices in his strengths, no longer thinking to pat himself on the back for them. He does not fish for compliments or make sure everyone knows of his good deeds. To do otherwise would not be sinful, only gauche. He does not feel impelled to set others straight and correct their opinions, believing instead that others will learn gradually and at their own pace as he himself has done. When struck or insulted, the mature person is secure enough not to return wrath or harm (unless, out of self-defense, he must repel serious violence). He knows that, as Proverbs says, "A soft answer turneth away wrath" (15:1). When criticized, the mature one will first ask himself if the complaint is true, and, instead of resenting it, he will take it to heart. If you are mature, you will shrug off offense and look for every opportunity for reconciliation. None of these traits depends upon any religious belief. It is just a question of growing in wisdom as one grows older. One must be willing for it to happen, but it is not a miracle. Nor does sincere moral maturity ever think of deserving or receiving some reward for doing the right thing.

Let me say a word in favor of *im*maturity. As Carl Jung mapped it out, each of us, on his or her road to mature "individuation," must first seek to consolidate his or her ego. One begins to exercise autonomy of will. One dares to think for oneself, usually sloppily at first. One becomes bull-headed and rebellious against adults. One criticizes authority figures one used to respect. Once-cherished opinions are dropped simply because they were inherited and not chosen. It is all embarrassing and quite sophomoric. Most people do foolish things during this period. But this stage is necessary. One must establish some sort of stable ego to use, as it were, for a launching pad for the next stage of growth, individuation, the progress from ego to Self.

As one nears maturity, one's sympathies and interests broaden out. The center of the circle expands on its way to becoming equal to the circumference. Those who live for others are the most mature. They do not see themselves as having sacrificed self-interest for the sake of others' interests. No, it is rather that they can no longer tell any difference. These are the saints and the bodhisattvas. Few of us get that far. But then when we navigate by the North Star, we don't expect to actually *reach* the North Star. Jesus Christ—or Gautama Buddha or no one name or face—may function as that North Star of individuation and maturity. No one has the copyright. There is no need for there to be a copyright. No one has a corner on the market, just as no one owns the air or the sunlight.

If we are the children of God, is it likely that God would want to keep his children in a mode of infantile dependence upon him? Wouldn't we be a bit worried if our own growing children should say to us, "I need thee every hour"? "You must increase, but I must decrease?" Isn't it just the opposite, that we as parents are the most fulfilled when we see our children assuming maturity and autonomy? It is common for devotional writers to compare the human soul to a green plant, worship to photosynthesis and heliotropism. The plant turns naturally toward the source of its light and life so it may thrive. But perhaps that is not the appropriate metaphor for human beings. We are not passive vegetables. As mature sons or daughters must at length seek to live apart, on their own, grateful for the long years of tutelage and care in their parents' home, so, I believe, mature adults need to put aside infantile religious doting and dependence. Actual worship of *anything* should be anathema to mature adults.

Religion admits that it deals with invisible realities that we must take on faith. Thus it is hard to evaluate religious claims by anything but faith. But occasionally we are lucky enough to find an empirical factor that we can use to test the validity of religious claims. Here is one of them: if a particular approach to moral responsibility presupposes a state of arrested moral and emotional development, then we can reject that approach. The approach is plainly revealed as a product of minds that have not yet reached maturity. And that is incompatible with a divine origin. Reverend Warren's faith is one predicated upon moral immaturity. That alone should be enough to discredit it.

Day Ten

Point to Ponder: What do power relations have to do with spirituality?

Quote to Remember: "And such thought makes us free men; we no longer bow before the inevitable in Oriental subjection, but we absorb it, and make it a part of ourselves. To abandon the struggle for private happiness, to expel all eagerness of temporary desire, to burn with passion for eternal things—this is emancipation, and this is the free man's worship." (Bertrand Russell, "A Free Man's Worship")

Question to Consider: Is there any difference between maturity and sanctification? Can there be one without the other?

NOTES

1. Rick Warren, *The Purpose-Driven Life: What on Earth Am I Here For?* (Grand Rapids, MI: Zondervan, 2002), p. 79.

2. C. S. Lewis, *Mere Christianity* (New York: Macmillan, 1960), p. 57.

3. Thomas J. J. Altizer, *The Descent into hell: A Study of the Radical Reversal of the Christian Consciousness* (New York: J. B. Lippincott, 1970), pp. 106–107, 116–19. Walter Kauffman agrees: "the sacrifice of a few hours' crucifixion followed by everlasting bliss at the right hand of God in heaven, while millions are suffering eternal tortures in hell, is hardly the best possible symbol of love and self-sacrifice." Walter Kaufmann, *Critique of Religion and Philosophy* (Garden City, NY: Doubleday, 1961), p. 202.

4. Washington Gladden, *How Much Is Left of the Old Doctrines?* (Boston: Houghton Mifflin, 1899), p. 178.

5. Washington Gladden, *Present-Day Theology* (Columbus, OH: McClelland, 1918), p. 162.

6. Warren, *The Purpose-Driven Life*, p. 79.

7. Ibid., p. 84.

8. Ibid., p. 80.

9. Ibid., p. 82.

10. Ibid., p. 83.

Becoming Imaginary Friends with God

*Then they took the ox which was given them and they prepared it
and called on the name of Baal from morning until noon, saying "O
Baal, answer us." But there was no voice and no one answered. And
they leaped about the altar which they made. It came about at noon
that Elijah mocked them and said, "Call out with a loud voice, for
he is a god; either he is occupied or gone aside, or is on a journey, or
perhaps he is asleep and needs to be awakened." So they cried with a
loud voice and cut themselves according to their custom with swords
and lances until the blood gushed out on them. When midday was
past, they raved until the time of the evening sacrifice; but there was
no voice, no one answered, and no one paid attention.*
—1 Kings 18:26–29 (NASB)

*The Jesus Prayer has one aim, and one aim only. To endow the
person who says it with Christ-Consciousness. Not to set up some
little cozy, holier-than-thou trysting place with some sticky, adorable
divine personage who'll take you in his arms and relieve you of all
your duties and make all your nasty Weltschmertzen and Professor
Tuppers go away and never come back.*
—J. D. Salinger, *Franny and Zooey*

MONOTHEISM AND MONOMANIA

In chapter 11 of *The Purpose-Driven Life*, Rick Warren has an all-too-temporary moment of clarity when he observes: "It's difficult to imagine how an intimate friendship is possible between an omnipotent, invisible, perfect God and a finite, sinful human being."[1] Except that "difficult" is hardly the word. "Impossible" is more like it.

119

"He is a God who is passionate about his relationship with you." This is supposed to be Exodus 34:14, which in an actual translation from the Hebrew reads: "The LORD, whose name is Jealous, is a jealous God." I prefer quoting from the New American Standard Bible, which happens also to have been translated by a committee of evangelicals, but these translators left theological interpretation to others and actually rendered what is in the Hebrew and Greek texts. Warren likes to quote from, in this case, the New Living Translation, one of several fundamentalist paraphrases of the Bible that seek to increase the ancient text's usability for born-again devotionalism by transposing the original into the idiom of that brand of piety. Just look at the context, and you will readily see how Warren and his fellow ventriloquists have hijacked the meaning of the text. Originally it formed part of the dictates of Jehovah commanding his people to overrun and vandalize the old hilltop shrines ("high places") sacred to other deities such as Asherah. The text is about what we would today call religious intolerance (but as long as it's in the Bible, fundamentalists are okay with it). It has nothing whatever to do with the storm deity Jehovah being our pal. In fact, it was looking at such passages that led Harry Emerson Fosdick to comment, "One does not go into one's room and shut the door to commune in secret with such a deity."[2]

As Fosdick also pointed out, we do in fact have a number of Old Testament stories (the same ones Warren likes to quote) in which mortal men and women talk with God as one mortal talks to another. Thus Abraham, Enoch, and Moses can be called "friends of God." But, Fosdick says, these stories are like those in Homer in which Achilles, Odysseus, Agamemnon, and the others are on familiar terms with their deities who walk onstage in human form. These stories, whether in Homer or the Bible, are grossly inappropriate as models for the spiritual experiences of moderns. While one might reasonably believe an unseen God is monitoring one's prayers, the element of personal interaction between equals that is absolutely crucial to a friendship is impossible, even grotesque to suggest. There are some individuals today who are quite serious about having a literal relationship, literal interaction and conversation, with God. They are schizophrenics who hear voices and nurse delusions of grandeur about being so favored. I'm afraid your choices are either some spiritual exercise to which the term "relationship" does not really apply, even as a metaphor (e.g., contemplative prayer or centering prayer), *or* cultivating the inner echoes of unseen and imaginary friends.

Forgive me for saying so, but I believe that the techniques prescribed by Reverend Warren are awfully close to inviting insanity. He wants you to "practice the presence of God" all day, every day, on the job, at work or play, filling every spare mental moment with a brief mantra like "You are with me," "I receive your grace," "I'm depending on you," "I want to know you," "I belong to you," "Help me trust you," "For me to live is Christ," "You will never leave me," and "You are my God."[3] He points to seventeenth-century lay monastic Brother Lawrence who consciously made every swab of floor mopping a sacrifice to God (exactly as the Hindu Bhagavad Gita suggests). Another good example would have been the anonymous Russian itinerant who wrote *The Way of a Pilgrim*, who covered all of Russia, keeping himself warm by quietly chanting "Lord Jesus Christ, Son of God, have mercy on me, a sinner." The pilgrim was trying to meet Warren's dilemma ("How do you 'pray without ceasing'?"). But it is evident from his own account that the pilgrim became what Warren's readers would become if they took him seriously: a shuffling, muttering eccentric with his head in the clouds.

PRACTICING THE ABSENCE OF GOD

Why does one person believe in God, while another does not? Both may be equally aware of the equivocal arguments for and against the existence of God. Both live in the same world and see the same events. And to one the heavens declare the glory of God, the firmament showeth his handiwork, but for the other, the universe is a void. Why?

I suspect one either intuits the existence of God or one does not. One has a sense of God, the other does not. And yet this is not quite right. To leave it at that implies that the one who intuits God is like a person who has an ear for music, while the one who does not sense

God has a theological tin ear. The radio waves are being broadcast, but the atheist just doesn't happen to have his antenna up.

In my experience, the atheist does not merely fail to pick up on God. No, one may actually intuit the absence of God. One may sense that there is no God. Indeed, that is how it seems to me. My experience, though there is nothing particularly dramatic about it, is of a universe empty of God, a rarefied atmosphere of metaphysical emptiness.

Am I saying that I know God does not exist, because of my intuition? Of course not. I do not want to jump the gun and conclude that whatever seems clear and distinct to me at this moment must therefore be true. Ultimately, the universe we sense and taste is the one within our head. We can't get past it.

And why is it that we intuit God or intuit no God? I have no idea! Partly it may have to do with your success in developing a superego, with your relations with your father. Whether you are pessimistic or optimistic. There must be causes, though we cannot easily see them. And despite not seeing any God, the ancients posited predestination. It must be the electing decree of God that decided what nothing apparent seems to decide: who will believe and who will not believe. And this is another example of the usage of "God" to stand for what we do not know. Who knows why we believe? "God knows." In other words, *no one* knows. Who or what determines whether we will believe? "God"—in other words, nothing we know of.

That brings me back to Brother Lawrence and his book *Practicing the Presence of God*. I have come to think, by contrast, that what is needful is "practicing the absence of God." To bathe and bask in the emptiness, the lack, the void.

Baruch Spinoza and Mansur al-Hallaj, both pantheists, reasoned that if God exists at all, then God must be all that exists. If God is infinite, then that means nothing can form the boundary of his existence. If anything else, so much as a single microbe, were to exist, then God would be limited to that degree. Now it is plain that many things do exist, so pantheists deduced that all things *are* God. All things are forms of God, not truly what they seem to be. Monists go a step further and declare that all individual things that seem to exist in reality do not. All but God, Brahman, is illusion.

But can we believe that the universe is an illusion? A shadow play? I feel uneasy with this claim, especially since the cash value, the result of it, is to say that religion alone is important and that, insofar as we recognize the beauty, the grandeur, the glory of a thing, we must hasten to translate it into God. We hasten from the thing to God, and thus we cancel out the thing. By calling it a "creation," we signal that we are interested only in the creator.

I have said before that I believe any doctrine of creation is inimical to the sense of wonder, which I regard as the central spiritual experience. Why? Because we prematurely answer the question of where the world came from by referring it to a Creator, a pseudo-answer that leaches the amazement from an amazing thing.

In the same way, if the meaning of life is dictated by a concept of God, if morality is settled by reference to the supposed will of God, then life has no meaning in and of itself. It is derivative, secondhand. You haven't the chance to decide what it means for yourself.

We must, I say, *practice the absence of God.* As the mystics of the Kabbalah said, God must contract, withdraw into himself, for there to be room left over for the world to exist. God must retreat. He must decrease for you to increase. So you must exorcise God!

Freud said that we imagine God as watching over us, protecting us, having the answers to give us, setting the rules for us to follow—all because we are neurotically fixated on the illusion that our parents could provide these securities, these assurances. Life has shown us that our parents, mere human beings, are not up to the challenge. We ought to reduce our expectations, accept the limitations of our parents as mere humans. Even more important, we ought to accept the limits of our own existence as human beings with all the contingency and uncertainty that implies. But we can't bear to do that. So instead we elevate nostalgia to divinity and believe in heavenly parents who will guarantee eternal life and providential protection. We want guardian angels who will come to us in the cold night and rock us back to sleep with promises that everything is all right.

Freud administered the bitter medicine of reproof: we must renounce such illusions if we are ever to achieve maturity and wisdom. We must learn to live with merely mortal wisdom, merely human resources, though of course those are quite considerable and far greater than religion wanted us to realize. Religion sought to keep us as mewling infants, mortgaged to dependency. Religion was a drug, its assurances comfortable opium dreams. And there will be withdrawal pains if we wish to break that addiction. We must learn to live without God, without illusion.

You may reply that I have defined God too narrowly, and you may go on to redefine God as meaning, oh, let's say, human potential. When you are done, the word "God" will bear very little relation to any traditional use of it. I wonder why you feel you must continue to use the outworn, outmoded word at all? Why is it so important? Why can you not let it go? Isn't your very insistence on hanging onto it at all costs evidence that it is, after all, a security blanket? If you are enamored of speaking of "God within," why can't you just talk about "human nature within"? Human greatness within? Why isn't that enough?

Take your liberal redefinition of God and paraphrase it. Call it something as impersonal and abstract as it deserves, and declare a moratorium on the word "God." See, after a while, whether it makes any difference. If you have lost nothing besides a name, a word, then I guess it *was* just a name. As I suspect, you may be more of a closet atheist than you wanted to believe!

Whenever I hear people say that they do not just *believe in* God but *experience* God or Christ as a watchful presence in their lives, I am not impressed with the reality of their faith. Rather, I fear for their sanity. They are cultivating a delusion. Even if there *is* a God, what else is going on in their heads but the cultivation of a delusion? It must be a psychological projection. I know there are ways for sophisticated believers to assimilate this fact and make the best of it. Tillich said we must inevitably create a symbol for God since God is infinite and we cannot grasp that. So we make our images of God, our symbols for God, and we try our best to remind ourselves that God is always more than the image, the figment.

But I think that is trying to have your cake and eat it, too. If we can adequately account for a phenomenon, in this case, the "personal relationship with Jesus," as simple psychological projection, then why suppose there is anything else, anything more "mysterious," to it? It is arbitrary and superfluous to think there is. It would be like a child getting a sneak peek at his parents putting the presents under the Christmas tree and rationalizing that, well, Santa must be busy and has sent Mom and Dad the kid's Christmas list, telling them to take care of it. Why not just face it? The God that you seem to experience is essentially an imaginary playmate. And you would be better off without it. Just as when you were a kid and gave up your unseen playmate it was a step toward maturity. Say good-bye to the imaginary playmate called God. Practice the absence of God.

In practicing the absence of God you will be laying down a heavy burden. What I mean is this: inevitably the world and life disappoint your beliefs in divine Providence. The world refuses to conform to our expectations. And we will seemingly do anything to avoid accepting that we were wrong, that the universe is morally neutral and indifferent to human welfare. We fear the universe would be a frightening and uninhabitable place if we believed there was no God pervading and permeating it. But would it? I think the opposite is true.

When tragedy strikes, when loved ones die, is it comforting or edifying for you to imagine that God had some reason for killing them? Was the suffering of Job alleviated or was it compounded by his belief that God must have had a purpose in it? Why make tragedy worse by elevating it to the outrage of cosmic injustice? The Moody Blues song "A Question of Balance" asks indignantly, "Why do we never get an answer" to the problem of evil? Well, what kind of answer did you have in mind?

It is like Samsara and Nirvana. Reality only looks so bleak because you had exaggerated expectations for it. Samsara isn't so bad once you realize it was never supposed to be Nirvana. The world operates as if there is no God. Why continue to suffer from the static, the friction, of swimming against the ontological current? Get rid of the headache that comes from the never-ending cognitive dissonance of insisting there is a God in a Godless universe. How long can you keep it up? How long will you stay in denial? Recovery groups like to talk about the problem a dysfunctional family never faces as "the elephant in the living room." No one will admit it's there, but there's just no way it's not going to make a difference! Well, in this case, the problem is that the elephant, the God, is nowhere to be seen in the living room, yet the family insists it's there.

Day Eleven

Point to Ponder: Pascal said it was worth living for God even if there is no God. Perhaps it is worth living without God even if there is one. Maybe that's even his will.

Quote to Remember: "Can God deliver a religion addict? Yes he *can!*" (Marjoe Gortner)

Question to Consider: If my immediate reaction to this chapter is fear of going to hell, what is my faith really based on?

NOTES

1. Rick Warren, *The Purpose-Driven Life: What on Earth Am I Here For?* (Grand Rapids, MI: Zondervan, 2002), p. 87.

2. Harry Emerson Fosdick, *A Guide to Understanding the Bible: The Development of Ideas within the Old and New Testaments* (New York: Harper & Brothers, 1956), p. 210.

3. Warren, *The Purpose-Driven Life*, p. 89.

Providence and Superstition

*O nobly-born, the Great Glorious Buddha-Heruka, dark brown of
color, with three heads, six hands, and four feet firmly postured . . .
will come forth from within thine own brain and shine vividly upon
thee. Fear that not. Be not awed. Know it to be the embodiment of
thine own intellect. . . . Simultaneously with the recognition,
liberation will be obtained.*
—*Bardo Thödöl* (Tibetan Book of the Dead)

THE DEVOTIONAL BIBLE VERSUS THE DEVONIAN BIBLE

"God . . . is bored with predictable, pious clichés."[1] I know *I* am, and as
a result I'm having trouble getting through *The Purpose-Driven Life*.
One of those clichés is that "if you want a deeper, more intimate connection with God you must learn to honestly share your feelings with
him [and] trust him when he asks you to do something."[2] To back this
up, Pastor Warren quotes 1 Samuel 15:22, or what passes for it in the
New Century Version), "What pleases the LORD more: burnt offerings and sacrifices or obedience to his voice? It is better to obey than to
sacrifice." Reading it in Warren's context, one might think the passage
had something to do with the bubbly picnic of the Christian's ongoing
adventure with his divine pal, God. Quite a different light is shed upon
the verse when one reads it in context. The Ayatollah Khomeini–like
prophet Samuel had commanded King Saul to go forth and execute the
long-destined wrath of Jehovah upon the nation of Amalek. God had
held a lively grudge against them since their ancestors' refusal to allow
migrant Israelis to pass through their territory on their way to the
Promised Land. Now it was time for payback. Samuel tells Saul, "Now
go and strike Amalek and utterly destroy all that he has, and do not

spare him; but put to death both man and woman, child and infant, ox and sheep, camel and donkey" (1 Samuel 15:3, NASB). That is what God wanted his buddy Saul to do. Saul did see to the butchery of every human being but one: he spared Agag, king of Amalek, as well as some sheep to feed his hungry troops. Oops! *That* was the disobedience Samuel complained about, and it cost Saul the crown!

I point this out for two reasons. First, Reverend Warren is completely out of touch with the actual book he is constantly and opportunistically quoting. One would have not the faintest idea of what the Bible was about if all one read was Warren's comically out-of-context snippets from it. Similarly, he accounts for the origin of the great hymnal of Judah, the Psalter, in this trivial fashion: "To instruct us in candid honesty, God gave us the Book of Psalms . . . every possible emotion is catalogued in the Psalms."[3] Talk about the dog gobbling up the crumbs that fall from the table (Mark 7:28)! The Psalms are a treasure trove for understanding the mythology, the liturgy, and the royal God-king ideology of ancient Judah. The emotional utterances to which Warren refers are all dramatic lines, formulaic scripts, probably intended for the ritualistic use of the king during times of national crisis or triumph. I suppose one needn't say the texts have no further interest or use. My point is, however, that "the Bible" as Warren presents it bears little resemblance to the ancient book that so fascinates scholars. It might as well have been written in the 1970s or 1980s for born-again Christians. Come to think of it, given the raft of new, gooey devotional paraphrases he likes to cite, *it was!*

Second, Warren's choice of the Amalek genocide passage to illustrate how Christians need to heed and obey the commands of their smiling pal God shows just how dangerous the whole business would be if one took it seriously. What I mean is: precisely how is one to know when God is speaking to him, and not his own neuroses and fears—and hates? Can we really believe a true and existing God told the ancient shaman and his client warlord to exterminate every single Amalekite baby? Hold on! Wait a minute, my friend, before you begin to defend the gruesome act as an act of God, lest you utter some cold-blooded enormity you otherwise would never entertain. Apologists have too often come off sounding like Nazis at just this point.

Naïvely believing that the stories of Abraham, Samuel, and the others are provided as case studies for how we ought to cultivate friendship with the Almighty Pal, there have been numerous examples of sad souls stuffing squalling infants in the oven at what they supposed was God's whispered behest. Warren, of course, would never countenance such a thing. I know that. My point is that the rhetoric he and his colleagues always use—"Look at Abraham for an example of being God's friend!"—logically opens the door to those of a more adventuresome bent than he. All Warren has in mind, probably, is his suburban reader "obeying the voice of God" as he reads some challenging ethical advice in the epistles of Paul. Then that's what he ought to say, without all the Technicolor. Again, the more seriously one takes the rhetoric, the deeper the trouble one is asking for.

THE DIVINE STALKER

The divine drama of a Christian's walk with God, its gradual development, the progress of learning, testing, and sanctification—is all taking place in the pietist's head. It is a mind game. His friend God is no more real than Harvey the giant rabbit whom no one but Jimmy Stewart could see and hear. Let me be clear: I do not mean to say that there is no God somewhere out in the universe. How could I possibly know a thing like that? It's just that the possible existence of God in no way bears on the imaginary "relationship" the born-again Christian is having inside his head, with himself.

Like every cultural primitive, the evangelical seeks for signs and portents in the trivia of everyday life and asks, "What is God trying to tell me through this flat tire, this missed TV program, this stomach ache?" If you have read a page of Merlin Carothers's *Power in Praise* or attended Bill Gothard's Institute in Basic Youth Conflicts or absorbed the preaching in any average evangelical church, you know I am by no means exaggerating. Honestly, can you tell me why we ought not to call this kind of thing by its rightful name of "superstition"? Durkheim once suggested that the Protestant Reformation had "disenchanted the world" of medieval Christendom in which the heavens were full of ascending and descending angels, saints, mediators, and spirits. Any place might be a holy place, filled with numinous radiance and worth taking a pilgrimage to upon one's bleeding knees as one fingered one's rosary. Protestantism evacuated the heavens and the earth of the Holy by restricting divine mediation to Jesus Christ and the Bible, relegating miracles to ancient history. The rationalist reductionism thus unleashed continued to snowball into Unitarianism, Protestant Liberalism, and Modernism, and on into Secular humanism. But popular religion has never felt at home in such a barren universe and has always tended to restore the invisible traffic between heaven and every square foot of earth.

Accordingly, the born-again Christian pauses to listen for heavenly telegrams and to watch for divine charades acted out in everyday events, the divine provision of parking spaces (even as children in Bangladesh die of starvation),[4] the multiplication of precious coincidences that "confirm" some nudge to one's feelings felt that morning during one's devotional "quiet time" (even though the Ebola virus devastates whole towns across the world, an event not worthy of God's interest and intervention). Earthquakes swallow up hundreds of innocents because God was too busy pantomiming signals to his favorites in suburban America through shattered vases or toothaches. It is the job of God's would-be chums to discern what he is telling them. And if they are unusually thickheaded, he may have to take off the gloves to make his intentions clear: "he will do whatever it takes to bring you back into fellowship with himself."[5] This kind of talk sounds ominous, and Warren knows it. As always, he tries to coat the brick of divine terror with the velvet of psychobabble euphemism: "Your problems are not punishment; they are wake-up calls from a loving God. God is not mad at you; he's mad *about* you."[6] We feel like Job: how can I get a restraining order put on this "lover"? Nor is this impression merely the result of some poor choice of words on Warren's part. It is a consistent theme of obsessive love. We must show ourselves true friends of Jesus by *obeying* him.[7] If that is not the classic language of abusive, manipulative relationships, what is?

But one *can* slap a restraining order on the Divine Stalker. Just laugh him off, along with Reverend Warren's sugar-coated threats.

Practice the absence of God. Rejoice in the fact that you live in a morally neutral universe in which events fall into your life like random raindrops instead of divine bullets with your name on them. Of course you can learn from adversity; you'd be a fool not to. But you don't have to live a hag-ridden life of superstitious fear, wondering what God's going to hit you with next! You don't have to fall victim to the Stockholm syndrome, becoming grateful for your tormentor's degrading attentions. Warren tells us, "It is likely that you need to confess some hidden anger and resentment at God for certain areas of your life where you have felt cheated or disappointed. Until we mature enough to understand that God uses everything for good in our lives, we harbor resentment toward God over our appearance, background, unanswered prayers, past hurts, and other things we would change if we were God. . . . Bitterness is the greatest barrier to friendship with God: why would I want to be God's friend if he allowed *this*? The antidote of course, is to realize that God *always* acts in your best interest, even when it is painful and you do not understand it."[8]

No, the answer is to stop personifying life as an individual being, God, who has conscious control over the events of your life. The answer is to see that these things *just happened*, and that *no one* caused them. No one aimed them at you. There is no one to resent for it. Resentment is misplaced. When we posit a God to resent, we are like some primitive positing a god who caused the monsoon, or some savage who imagines angry ancestor spirits spoiled his crops. Neither is there anyone, by the same token, to trust to make things come out for the best.

This God is a demon infesting your imagination. Cast him out like spoiled meat from your refrigerator. Cast him off like a reeking garment. Because the stalking lover of your soul is only haunting your head. He is not in the world. There may be plenty of challenges out there, but the obsessive friend called God is not one of them. There are people like Warren's God. Jim Carrey played one of them to perfection in *The Cable Guy*. The Cable Guy is a classic nerd who cannot easily make friends and tries to win them by giving them gifts of free service and (possibly hot) electronics. His visits and phone calls are obsessive and annoying. He inevitably alienates his unrequited friends, and when they begin to withdraw, he shows his displeasure by malicious tricks, trying to show his still-loved "friends" how wise it would be to return to his good graces. This, of course, only makes things much, much worse. Warren is making God into the Cable Guy. I say, cancel the service.

Day Twelve

Point to Ponder: Whoever thinks he can give you commands is not your friend.

Quote to Remember: "Verily, it is a blessing and not a blasphemy when I teach: 'Over all things stand the heaven Accident, the heaven Innocence, the heaven Chance, the heaven Prankishness.'" (Friedrich Nietzsche, *Those Spoke Zarathustra*)

Question to Consider: Have you ever decided, however reluctantly, that it was time to break off an abusive relationship? Maybe that time has come with God.

NOTES

1. Rick Warren, *The Purpose-Driven Life: What on Earth Am I Here For?* (Grand Rapids, MI: Zondervan, 2002), p. 94.

2. Ibid., p. 92.

3. Ibid., p. 94.

4. Richard Abate drew this contrast for me once, and I have never forgotten it. Who could?

5. Warren, *The Purpose-Driven Life*, p. 98.

6. Ibid., p. 98.

7. Ibid., p. 95.

8. Ibid., p. 94.

Worship That Creates God

*He waved loosely at the darkly gleaming shelves of religious curios in
the handsomely carved traveling case rising beyond the end of the
table. He frowned a very different frown than his business one.
"There are more things in this world than we understand," he said
sententiously. "Did you know that, son?" The Great Man shook his
head, again very differently. He was swiftly sinking into his most
deeply metaphysical mood. "Makes me wonder, sometimes. You and I,
son, know that these"—He waved again at the case—"are toys. But
the feelings that men have toward them . . . they're real, eh?—and
they can be strange. Easy to understand part of those feelings—brats
shivering at bogies, fools gawking at a show and hoping for blood or
a bit of undressing—but there's another part that's strange. The
priests bray nonsense, the people groan and pray, and then something
comes into existence. I don't know what that something is—
I wish I did, I think—but it's strange." He shook his head.
"Makes any man wonder."*
—Fritz Leiber, "Lean Times in Lankhmar"

*I love even churches and tombs of gods, once the sky gazes through
their broken roofs with its pure eyes, and like grass and red poppies, I
love to sit on broken churches.*
—Friedrich Nietzsche, *Thus Spoke Zarathustra*

WHEN WORLDS COLLIDE

Over the years in my Heretics Anonymous groups, one of my favorite
discussion starters has been a juxtaposition of two passages on the
same subject by two writers of very different persuasions, two writers,
in fact, who were probably blissfully unaware of each other's existence.

133

They are Rudolf Bultmann and Oral Roberts. I want to set up a dilemma posed between Bultmann and Roberts and then show a way out marked by the sociologists Peter Berger and Thomas Luckmann. First, from Bultmann's essay "New Testament and Mythology":

> A blind acceptance of New Testament mythology would be simply arbitrariness; to make such acceptance a demand of faith would be to reduce faith to a work. . . . Any satisfaction of the demand would be a forced *sacrificium intellectus,* and any of us who would make it would be peculiarly split and untruthful. For we would affirm for our faith or religion a world picture that our life otherwise denied. . . . We cannot use electric lights and radios and, in the event of illness, avail ourselves of modern medical and clinical means and at the same time believe in the spirit and wonder world of the New Testament.[1]

Next from Oral Roberts's autobiography, *The Call*:

> When I was a young, struggling pastor in the mid-1940s, I kept wrestling with a deep sense of discontent. I felt frustrated and dissatisfied in my work. It seemed to me that my ministry and the outreach of my church were making no real difference in the lives of the people of our community. . . . Though I was only in my late twenties I felt I was dying on the vine. Each week began to be more and more of a struggle. How could I get up and preach about Jesus making the lame to walk, the dumb to talk, the deaf to hear, the blind to see, the leper to be cleansed, and the dead raised to life and then let it all be treated as something in the past, something irrelevant to our life and time? How could I talk about the Bible being in the NOW? I began to be consumed with a passion either to have a ministry like Jesus or to get out of the ministry. What good did it do to tell about events that weren't happening in this world, in the now?[2]

What was the nature of the crisis of faith faced by young Oral Roberts? He had come to experience in a personal way the inconsistency pointed out by Bultmann: he saw too clearly the stark disjunction between the world he talked about on Sunday mornings and the world he and his parishioners seemed to have no choice but to live in the rest of the week.

In the sixties a group called the Vogues did a song called "Five O'clock World." In it the singer says how bored and aggravated he is in his job every day, day in and day out. But he can stand it, he can get through it without losing his mind, because he looks forward to a different world awaiting him when the whistle blows: a five o'clock world. A self-contained world where he can do and say what he wants to, a minizone in which for a few precious hours he can find regeneration and respite. He cannot cause his two worlds to interpenetrate. He merely endures the one till he can escape into the other.

Oral Roberts felt he could no longer live for most of the week in the mundane world waiting for his "eleven o'clock Sunday morning world." He decided that by hook or by crook he had to somehow extend the boundaries of sacred time, church time, what Bultmann calls "the spirit and wonder world of the New Testament," to cover the rest of the week. So Roberts began a ministry of tent revivals and healings, to drag the New Testament myth-world kicking and screaming into the secular twentieth century.

Did it work? It is plain that it did not, that he chose the wrong option. Years later, as you know, this man was claiming to have seen a Jesus as big as Godzilla appearing to him, telling him to build a hospital that, after he built it, proved impossible to fill, a superfluous white elephant. And then he woke up in the middle of the night, feeling himself throttled by the devil. And then he heard God's ultimatum to have him rubbed out if he didn't raise a certain amount of cash by a designated date. He had confused God the Father with the Godfather.

Like Bishop Pike, Oral Roberts found himself wandering in a desert of delusion. I want to explore why that happened, and what he could have done instead. And the reason I want to do this is that I think it will suggest something quite important about the nature of faith itself as well as the life of faith. That is because *spiritual experience* presents us with the same problem Oral Roberts faced in another form.

JACK AND JILL WENT UP THE HILL

Have you ever had a "mountaintop experience" at a particularly poignant church service or at a spiritual retreat? You feel you have been present with Jesus atop the Mount of Transfiguration, and you are hesitant about leaving. And yet you must leave. You must return, if not to the depth of the valley, if not to the Valley of the Shadow of Death, then at least to the flat, dull, dusty roads of Palestine. There, you may walk with Jesus himself, but the heat of the midday sun and the choking dust and the plaguing flies and the length of the road till the next inn make you forget that you walk with Jesus. You just want to make it to the end of the day and to rest your weary feet. You have left the zone where, like Moses, you had to put off your shoes from your feet for you stood on holy ground. You have fallen, like Paul, from the acme of the Third Heaven where you heard revelations that words may not utter, and you have returned to terra firma with its duller hues.

I recall reading an article about the T-groups at Esalen, those totally, bluntly honest encounter groups in which you laid it on the line with others and opened yourself up to hear the unvarnished truth from them. Participants testified that their lives had been changed by these weekend encounters, but they soon found themselves dissatisfied, since as soon as they returned to their families and their jobs, they discovered the hard way that others were not prepared to play the game. They found their total honesty unwelcome and unappreciated. How could they translate their new experience into the real world without losing their jobs, alienating their loved ones?

I conclude that these Esalen grads and Oral Roberts made a fundamental error. They should never have tried to take their experiences out the door with them, like a towel lifted from the hotel. It should have told them something when Elijah and Moses vanished from the Mount of Transfiguration and Jesus stopped glowing. Then there was nothing to do but go. They had to leave the zone of spiritual ecstasy where it was.

RICK FELL DOWN AND BROKE HIS CROWN

The worship service is what Berger and Luckmann call a "finite province of meaning,"[3] much like attending a movie or a play. It is precisely a special "eleven o'clock Sunday morning world." It is conjured into being when the organist begins playing the prelude, when the lay reader speaks the call to worship. It ends with the benediction and the postlude. And between that rising and falling of the curtain people do and say things they would never do the rest of the week. When else do you sing out loud with other people, for example? While the curtain is up, while the Bible is read from, the sermon is preached, the bread and the cup are served, we naturally imagine ourselves contemporaries of Jesus Christ, of Moses and Elijah. Once church is over, we return to a world where, like Rhett Butler or Captain Kirk, these great characters return to the fiction page.

Some churches don't sing as much or as loudly and enthusiastically as other churches. Some employ a full orchestra, others a rock band. Why the difference? They are "really getting into it," because some have farther to get into it than others do! They must do a lot of singing to reach escape velocity. They use emotions to fuel the great leap from the world of radios, electricity, and computers, to the first-century world of angels, demons, and miracles. And they expect to be able to take it with them when they leave for home again. Like Oral Roberts, they will go out and attempt to gain divine healing, to speak in tongues of angels and obtain signs and portents from dreams or from some infallible book. But I think they need not bother working themselves up so much. There is no need to try to leap to another world. There is simply no need to try to continue to believe the unbelievable: that Jesus, Moses, and Elijah continue to exist in the outside, mundane world with us.

Literalists like Rick Warren have made faith into a cognitive work, a matter of managing to believe things that you know and can see are not true in the public reality, the reality *out there*. And one cannot do that without cheating, suppressing the truth, denying your better judgment with the excuse of "faith." It is a sacrifice of the intellect, of common sense, or at least of consistency, since, unless you are

David Koresh, Oral Roberts, or one of those guys wearing a sandwich board in the bus terminal, you won't really keep on believing it, living as if it were all literally true, once the eleven o'clock world is over. Many of us are unwilling to make that sacrifice of the intellect, to undertake that intellectual schizophrenia.

SUSPENSION OF DISBELIEF

And yet we, too, even we, have a kind of faith. It is what Samuel Taylor Coleridge called "that willing suspension of disbelief for the moment, which constitutes poetic faith." We have agreed to be strung along for a while, to believe *as if*, to let a part of ourselves believe. We give ourselves over to become characters in the play we are witnessing, the novel we are reading. We must if we are to take the plot as seriously as the characters are taking it. You have consented to be "taken in" by that which you know quite well to be fiction and artifice. You have become clay in the hands of the author, the director, to let them shape you, to manipulate your emotions and thus to galvanize your conscience or open your eyes to some new realization. Aristotle called it catharsis: the cleansing of the soul of pity and terror by means of induced pity and terror. Psychodrama has rediscovered this, and I am saying that religion should rediscover it, too, or, actually, just wake up to what has really been going on all the time. Worship, liturgy, religion, it seems to me, are essentially dramatic and literary in nature. It is no coincidence that all drama began as religious ritual: miracle plays and mystery plays. Religious life is a matter of reading the great fictions and joining in the great dramas of a religious tradition.

Are you an unbeliever? In my book you are not an unbeliever merely because you do not take the script as literal fact. If it engages you and inspires you as you watch it and become caught up in it, then you have the only relevant kind of belief.

Rick Warren does not see it. In his thirteenth chapter, he tells us true worship must be based on correct belief in God as derived from the Bible, as if the Bible were a definitive revelation of God and what he is like. I say no. I say that worship remains aesthetic and dramatic in nature. I think that what one may or may not believe philosophically is simply irrelevant to worship. Where is the only relevant God? In history? In science? In the physical universe? Is he just to the left of the planet Jupiter? Is he like a gremlin, an unseen cause of plane crashes and disasters? No, if we are to seek him where he may be found, we must seek him *in worship.* "Yes, You are holy, O You who are enthroned upon the praises of Israel" (Psalms 22:3, NASB).

THE PLAY'S THE THING

I have already suggested that you are living your life on the model of some story you have heard or read, whether an epic poem or a soap opera. The "meaning" of your life is its conformity, at least its attempt to conform, to a certain literary or biographical prototype. I know a man who modeled himself on Sheridan Whiteside from *The Man Who Came to Dinner.* I know another who modeled himself on Kierkegaard, another on H. P. Lovecraft, another on certain characters from Bergman, another on Eva Perone, believe it or not. Hearing the story of Jesus who served others, not himself, may galvanize you to imitate him, to take up your cross and follow him, as the gospels say, envisioning just this possibility.

You may find in the stories and dramas of the Bible some path to follow through the rest of the week. You cannot take out the door the sacred experience, the moment of inspiration, but the lesson you learned can go with you. You may find a word of rebuke in what you hear in church. Like David with his guilty conscience, you may find yourself skewered by some prophetic parable, as when the prophet Nathan decides, like Hamlet, "The play's the thing wherein I'll catch the conscience of the king."

Suppose all is out of kilter with you because of some offense committed against you. You have a festering wound. You have lost a friend. You bear a burden of bitterness that you can neither carry nor let go. The pattern of your relationships is altered, misaligned, because of your alienation from your ex-friend. Those who side with him or her bear your enmity as well. What a mess! How has your life come to such a pass? And then you hear again the Parable of the Prodigal Son. It is a story much like yours in some ways. Here is a son who bears disgrace and so cannot really count as a son. But which is worse: his entire absence in a far land or his presence as a slave on the farm? Why can't things be the way they were before? Well, maybe they can be. There is one little thing you can do, one magic wand you can wave. It is called forgiveness, and sometimes it is able to turn back time and heal great wounds. Once you see that, you can take it away with you into the mundane world for the rest of the week. Maybe it wouldn't have come alive, wouldn't have come to appear to you as a live option without hearing that parable again. But now that it has, it will not vanish when the weekly Brigadoon of the church hour has vanished.

THE FINE ART OF WORSHIP

So worship, I'm saying, though it has moral dimensions, is essentially aesthetic in nature. The aesthetics are the "special effects" that give power to the moral message. Did you know there is a *spirituality of beauty*? It is what many cultured, secular people cultivate instead of overtly religious worship. It fills the same need. Let me explain why.

First, as you contemplate a poem, or a painting, or a living landscape outspread before you, don't you experience a rising sense of wonder beginning to sweep over you and carry you away? There are certain poems that are a revelatory experience for me. The spine tingles and the soul marvels that words can be so associated. Great music awakens something within and stirs it up. Art causes you to transcend yourself, and that, in religious terms, is a reaching up of the soul to God.

Have you ever felt a certain ache, a certain sense of yearning connected with some vision of great beauty? If you analyze it, I wager you will find that the yearning is a strange feeling of frustration. Frustration at what? That you can't put this great beauty into words? Possibly. But I rather suspect that the ego inside you is reacting, if only for a moment, in the only primitive way it knows how. It desires that beauty, to possess it, to consume it. It sees a great good and wants to own it. It wants to devour it. And in a sense the soul does feast on it by its sheer openness to beauty.

But one immediately realizes that one cannot possess the beauty of a landscape. And one soon forgets the self, lost in wonder. Prevented from possessing, the ego withers away for the moment, and the beauty shines unobstructed. Self no longer stands in its way, blocking the view.

Beauty, then, because it overwhelms the self, decenters the self. Beauty frees you from self-fixation. Self is forced off the stage so the show can begin.

And worship is the same way. Consider Isaiah 6:1–5. The prophet is meditating in the courts of the temple in Jerusalem, trying to gain some perspective on the tumultuous events of the day, when suddenly what is usually invisible to human eyes becomes for a moment visible. He has a vision of God enthroned above the Ark of the Covenant and surrounded by flaming spirits! And they are discussing *him*. What is Isaiah's first reaction? It is *the hasty retirement of the ego from the field*. He exclaims, as his knees give way and he raises a forearm to shield his eyes, "Woe is me! For I am undone!"

Isaiah's words "I am undone" strike me as especially fortunate. What do they mean? "I," that is, the ego, is like a tightly fastened knot that keeps intact the rope net of selfishness, the roped-off zone of defensiveness. It is a noose that hangs, a bond that restricts my movement toward that which is greater than me. But in the moment of wonder, worship, and holy amazement, the clenched knot of the "I" is undone, the fetters slip off, and I stand free before eternity.[4]

ICONOGRAPHY

But not only is worship an exercise in momentary ego forgetfulness; it is also a factor in the process of *individuation*, the goal of which is to transcend the ego and become a mature Self. As Carl Jung explained, the human mind matures by accessing certain powerful images ("archetypes") hardwired into the human brain. They come to the surface in dreams, artwork, myths, and religious symbols. Crosses, mandalas, the holy number three, the questing hero, the wise man or woman, the dragon, and so on, all serve as something like icons on the mind's computer screen, denoting the deep presence of complex programs built into the machine. But we, like novice computer users, have a lot of learning to do if we are to get the most use out of it. And to learn the programs, we must see the icons, then click on them. What religious myths and symbols do is to provide those icons. Religious rituals are opportunities to "click on" those icons and bring ever more complex and deeper "programs" into play. Maturity, individuation, occurs gradually as we bring more and more of the built-in programs on line. Role playing is therapeutic, the entrance to another realm, a world of regeneration and respite, of catharsis and inspiration. The best commentary on the doctrine of the atonement is the Communion service.

This has not a thing to do with belief in the factual character of the powerful symbols. The Buddha and the Christ may never have lived in history for all we can prove, but they are powerful symbols for transforming lives. God may exist nowhere but in worship, but then that is the only relevant place one ought to seek him anyway. It is an aesthetic affair, becoming part, as it were, of a psychodrama, a great and transformative drama in which one plays for a few moments a supermundane role as "a worshiper of God." In following the "script" of liturgy and prayer one becomes momentarily lost in the role. One transcends the ego.

You do as you wish, but I have staked out my position. On the one hand, I do not plan to let the fundamentalists bully me out of a wholesome experience because I don't pay their admission price of literal belief. On the other, I'm not about to allow secularists to deny me the joy of churchgoing because they cringe from it like Dracula from the cross.

Day Thirteen

Point to Ponder: The church service is like Las Vegas: what happens there stays there.

Quote to Remember: "Therefore, if God is to exercise his divine property by his gifts, he may well need my humility; for apart from humility he can give me nothing—without it I am not prepared to receive his gift. That is why it is true that by humility I give divinity to God." (*Meister Eckhart*, Fragment 2)

Question to Consider: You mean, I have the right to enjoy church even without being sure about God?

NOTES

1. Rudolf Bultmann, "New Testament and Mythology," in *New Testament and Mythology and Other Basic Writings*, ed. and trans. Schubert M. Ogden (Philadelphia: Fortress Press, 1989), pp. 3–4.

2. Oral Roberts, *The Call* (New York: Avon, 1971), pp. 37–38, 40.

3. Peter L. Berger and Thomas Luckmann, *The Social Construction of Reality: A Treatise in the Sociology of Knowledge* (Garden City, NY: Doubleday Anchor, 1967), p. 25.

4. They cut the moment's thongs and leave me free
   To stand alone before eternity.
                        —H. P. Lovecraft, *Fungi from Yuggoth*, XXX "Background"

I Can't Get No Sanctification

I am convinced that this anxiety running through my life is the tension between what I "should be" and what I am. My anxiety does not come from thinking about the future but from wanting to control it. It seems to begin whenever I smuggle an "I want to become" into my mind. It is the tension between my desire to control what I will be and the recognition that I can't. "I will be what I will be"—where is the anxiety in that?
—Hugh Prather, *Notes to Myself*

DISAPPOINTMENT WITH GOD

Pastor Warren tells us that we can get as close to God as we want to. But in due time, I suggest, you will find yourself against a blank wall. You will conclude that with your mind you serve the law of God, but with the flesh you obey the commands of sin and death. And then what are you to conclude? You may look back in shame, or perhaps in bitterness, at what now seem the overoptimistic and inflated terms of the promise of sanctification that you once embraced. You may find that the straight and narrow path of sanctification is none other than the boulevard of broken dreams!

There is such a thing as spiritual disillusionment, disappointment with God. You feel far from God, but you know that despite the face-saving slogan, it was not you who moved. Rather, you take as your own the plaintive words of George Harrison's psalm: "I really want to know you, but it takes so long, my Lord." If you have reached this point, I have some things to say to you. Or, even if you aren't there yet, perhaps you can remember them in case that rainy day ever comes.

The first is this: remember that spiritual growth is receptivity, and that receptivity requires emptiness, poverty of spirit, an empty cup.

For spiritual fullness is a plenitude of emptiness. The sense of hunger and longing is itself the satisfaction. Or, at least, that is certainly my experience. I have found a greater spirituality in seeking answers I knew I did not have and was not likely to get than in assuring myself that I did have them. The intellectual quest for answers that will never come is another form of the fullness of emptiness, the blessed poverty of spirit. When Antonius Block (played by Max von Sydow in Bergman's *The Seventh Seal*) asks in his travail, "What will become of those of us who want to believe but are unable?" blessed is he.

It is only those who continue to seek who continue to find. They are like Diogenes of Sinope, holding aloft his lantern as he walked the ways of the world in search of an honest man. He himself was the man he sought, and if he ever realized this and stopped, the world would have forfeited its single honest man.

In all this I am not talking about a mere period of "spiritual dryness" that one might expect to endure for a while, a dark night of the soul one hopes will end but fears will not. I am talking about the result of maturity, a "mid-religious-life crisis," if you will, when you just have to realize that you are not going to become the pious angel you once thought you might be. You realize that it was never a realistic goal. You come to accept that Karl Barth wasn't being pessimistic; he was being realistic, not unbelieving, but free of "childish things," when he said:

> Let us be honest. If we relate to ourselves, to you and me, to this or that Christian (even the best), that which is said about the conversion of man in the New Testament . . . it will have the inevitable smack of hyperbole and even illusion—and the more so the more we try to introduce it . . . [into] the Christian life. What are we with our little conversion, our little repentance and reviving, our little ending and new beginning, our changed lives . . . ? How feeble is the relationship, even in the best of cases between the great categories in which the conversion of man is described in the New Testament, and the corresponding event in our own inner and outer life![1]

Let's turn it the other way around. Let's look at the preface of Monsignor Knox's classic study of religious fanaticism, *Enthusiasm*. Listen to his description of the typical enthusiast:

He expects more from the grace of God than we others. He sees what effect religion can have, does sometimes have, in transforming a man's whole life and outlook; these exceptional cases (so we are content to think them) are for him the average standard of religious achievement. He will have no 'almost-Christians,' no weaker brethren who plod and stumble, . . . whose ambition is to qualify, not to excel. He has before his eyes a picture of the Early Church, visibly penetrated with supernatural influences; and nothing less will serve him as a model . . . Quoting a hundred texts—we also use them, but with more of embarrassment—he insists that the members of his society, saved members of a perishing world, should live a life of angelic purity, of apostolic simplicity.[2]

What immediately occurred to me the first time I read these lines is a possibility that it would also explain the distressing gap measured by Karl Barth: perhaps the New Testament writers were sectarians and enthusiasts (religious fanatics, in short) of the kind Knox describes. Indeed, they must have been. The initial fervor of any new religious movement glows with fever heat in the pages of the New Testament. When enthusiasts read it, they find the page a mirror, and they hear the Spirit say to come join the sect, imbibe the heady wine of its fervor.

But inevitably the fire burns low, and one adjusts to reality even as the early Christian sect itself did, and one (as Knox and Barth say so well) finds oneself quoting those passages with embarrassment. The claims made for "entire sanctification," for Christian perfection, in the pages of the New Testament, become as much a stumbling block as its statements about demons and a flat earth. We have to take them as equally mythical.

There are plenty of people who do a passable job mimicking New Testament Christianity in our day. They are the pietists, the literalists, the adventists, the dogmatists, the exclusivists, the tongue speakers and miracle believers. Anyone else they regard as mere worldlings, half-Christians. They point to their greater numbers and condescendingly tell mainline churches that if they would embrace full-bodied evangelicalism they would be growing. There is a great irony in that claim, for sooner or later, it is they (the evangelicals) who will be jumping ship.

The adolescent grandiosity that colors their religious life now will eventually die down, and they will become contemptible "half-Christians" like those they now pity. But they will be worse hypocrites than those others because, unlike them, they will continue to quote the fanatical texts of the New Testament as if they really believed them.

END OF THE ROPE

Let me draw attention to one pitfall of the spiritual life, indeed perhaps the very one that has led so many to despair of sanctification. It is the dynamic of *striving and resting*. In the literature of religious conversions and "deeper-life" experiences, one finds story after story of frustrated seekers who just could not receive the blessing of spiritual power they sought, no matter how they prayed and fasted. At length they just threw in the towel—and, what do you know, that was precisely what it took to gain the blessing! Pietist literature explains it this way: all one's own efforts at spirituality are the efforts of the flesh, of sinful human nature, which unwittingly exalts itself as it seeks God, foolishly imagining that it might produce him like a product by enough strenuous effort. One must come to the point of exhaustion to see the limits of the flesh and to make room for something better to replace it: the grace of God, which then pours through an unclogged conduit unopposed. Psychologist William James explained it this way:

> A man's conscious wit and will, so far as they strain towards the ideal, are aiming at something only dimly and inaccurately imagined. Yet all the while the forces . . . ripening within him are going on towards their own prefigured result. . . . It may consequently be actually interfered with (jammed, as it were like the lost word when we seek too energetically to recall it), by his voluntary efforts. . . . "Man's extremity is God's opportunity" is the theological way of putting this fact of the need for self-surrender; whilst the physiological way of stating it would be, "Let one do all in one's power, and one's nervous system will do the rest."[3]

James thinks nothing is lost to conversion-religion by admitting this. But even Bultmann's existential gospel could not survive it. Even Bultmann insists that as long as we rely on what we believe are our own human resources, we can never find grace. James is popping the bubble by revealing that what you thought were extrahuman forces of divine grace are themselves, after all, simply reinforcements from the subconscious.

But we did not need to wait for William James to come along to throw a wrench into the mechanism of pietism. If one reads closely enough such handbooks as Andrew Murray's *Abide in Christ*, one will sooner or later become uneasily aware of precisely the same catch-22. Murray tells us that the secret of the victorious Christian life is "simply" to stop trying to live it in one's own strength ("the arm of flesh will fail you; ye dare not trust your own"). Instead one must resign oneself to utter spiritual impotence and let the indwelling grace of Christ emerge to transfigure and sanctify. "Let go and let God." Simply rest in the everlasting arms.

But then one finds oneself unable to make the leap, unable to rest, to be forever mindful of the benefits of Christ, to practice God's presence—whatever devotional idiom you prefer. And then inevitably—one *strives to rest*, and the whole maddening cycle begins again. Before, one strove for victory, gave up striving and surrendered, then received the victory. But now this very act of self-surrender, no longer a wonderful surprise to the despairing soul, is too well known. One is led to expect it as part of the process of sanctification, one of the necessary stages, one of the preliminary things one must do. It becomes a holy charade. It worked once, when it happened spontaneously, unexpectedly. But it's too late for that now. And devotional systems based upon it merely torture their adherents with a will-o'-the-wisp of a victorious Christian life that never comes, and thus they send the seeker into a profounder Slough of Despond.

But, as Gandhi once said to a despairing man, "I know a way out of hell." Surrender the whole endeavor of piety. Face it: it doesn't work. I say unto you: Drop it. Follow the example of Pontius Pilate and wash your hands of the whole stinking matter.

I have always enjoyed C. S. Lewis's advice in *The Screwtape Letters* on how one ought to react to a vicious cycle of spiritual frustration. The veteran tempter Screwtape instructs the novice Wormwood thusly:

> Catch him at the moment when he is really poor in spirit and smuggle into his mind the gratifying reflection, "By jove! I'm being humble," and almost immediately pride—pride at his own humility—will appear. If he awakes to the danger and tries to smother this new form of pride, make him proud of his attempt— and so on, through as many stages as you please. But don't try this too long, for fear you awake his sense of humour and proportion, in which case he will merely laugh at you and go to bed.[4]

What should the earnest pietist do when he realizes the trap he's in, striving to rest from strife? Awake to the absurdity of his predicament! Laugh it off and go on to something else, anything else, in fact, except more pietism.

Do you remember the strange words of the Sermon on the Mount that advocate a secret piety? Matthew tells us to hide any religious devotion we may have from the approving or disapproving eyes of others, and then to hide it even from oneself! "Let not your left hand know what your right hand is doing." The person who is pious in a Sermon-on-the-Mount sort of way might be the one who would be surprised to hear himself or herself described as Christian or righteous or spiritual. Here's how Lewis puts it in another book, *Mere Christianity*:

> Do not imagine that if you meet a really humble man he will be what most people call "humble" nowadays: he will not be a sort of greasy, smarmy person, who is always telling you that, of course, he is nobody. Probably all you will think about him [i.e., the truly humble] is that he seemed a cheerful intelligent chap who took a real interest in what you said to him. If you do dislike him it will be because you feel a little envious of someone who seems to enjoy life so easily. He will not be thinking about humility: he will not be thinking about himself at all.[5]

Or as Bonhoeffer put it in his *Letters and Papers from Prison*:

> To be a Christian does not mean to be religious in a particular way, to cultivate some particular form of asceticism . . . , but to be a [human being]. It is not some religious act which makes a Christian what he is, but participation in the suffering of God in the life of the world.[6]

There is the essence of Bonhoeffer's "religionless Christianity," to do what Christ did and leave the magic circle of heaven where only religion matters, where religion sets the parameters of discussion, and to enter into worldly, profane existence, truly incarnate as a human being, not trying to be something else, an angel walking the earth mindful only of God.

Maybe that is the true sanctification: *no* sanctification.

That's what I say.

Day Fourteen

Point to Ponder: Is the Christian life reducible to a kind of fantasy role-playing game inside my head?

Quote to Remember: "Christ's virtue, the virtue of discipleship, can only be accomplished so long as you are entirely unconscious of what you are doing." (Dietrich Bonhoeffer, *The Cost of Discipleship*)

Question to Consider: If my Christian experience is a constant struggle of dissatisfaction, frustration, and seeking forgiveness for sin, aren't I being a hypocrite when I witness, telling people that Christ gives you inner peace?

NOTES

1. Karl Barth, *Church Dogmatics*, vol. 4, part. 2, pp. 582–83. Quoted in James M. Gustafson, *Christ and the Moral Life* (Chicago: University of Chicago Press, 1968), p. 95.

2. Ronald A. Knox, *Enthusiasm: A Chapter in the History of Religion* (New York: Oxford University Press, 1950), p. 2.

3. William James, *The Varieties of Religious Experience* (New York: New American Library, 1958), p. 171.

4. C. S. Lewis, *The Screwtape Letters and Screwtape Proposes a Toast* (New York: Macmillan, 1970), p. 63.

5. C. S. Lewis, *Mere Christianity* (New York: Macmillan, 1960), p. 114.

6. Dietrich Bonhoeffer, *Letters and Papers from Prison*, trans. Reginald H. Fuller (New York: Macmillan, 1953), pp. 222–23.

Joining the Sect

When der Führer says,
"Ve ist da master race!"
Then we Heil! (Spit!) Heil! (Spit!)
Right in der Führer's face.
—Spike Jones

WATER FELLOWSHIP, WATER JOY DIVINE

Evangelical Christians like Rick Warren have a bit of a problem when it comes to baptism. The impossibility of neatly systematizing all the disparate, almost random, New Testament texts really comes home to roost here. Warren and his compatriots want to put their rational faculties in the faculty parking lot and just take orders from the Bible, but here ambiguity and contradiction force them to choose. You see, their favorite parts of the New Testament (John 3:16; Acts 16:30–31; Romans 5:1, 10:10; Ephesians 2:8–9; etc.) say that faith alone is necessary for an individual's salvation. Having faith in Christ (which they gratuitously translate into "having a personal relationship with Christ") is supposed to cause God to regenerate, to justify, and to supply the Holy Spirit. It is an existential moment of decision that initiates an invisible transaction in the spirit world. But then there are those passages like John 3:3, Acts 2:38, Romans 6:4–5, and 1 Corinthians 12:13 (and if you read the King James Version, Mark 16:16) that speak of water baptism (apparently by immersion) as the means of entry into salvation.

Warren, like traditional Baptists, Pentecostals, Plymouth Brethren, and other adult-baptizers, adopts a surprisingly rationalistic theology at this point, making the water immersion a mere public declaration of the faith one has already accepted and by which one has already been saved. Campbellite evangelicals (Church of Christ and Disciples of Christ), on the other hand, give the second set of passages their due weight and deny that faith by itself is effective. Both no doubt feel uneasy with the apparent magical materialism of sacramentalism and the notion that washing the body could possibly have anything to do with one's spiritual state. You see, that is part of the "disenchantment of the world" unleashed by Protestant Rationalism at the time of the Reformation. It is just a question of how far a particular Protestant sect is willing to take it consistently. Most eventually draw the line somewhere and dare tread no farther.

Evangelicals have largely replaced baptism even as a symbol of conversion with raising one's hand or walking to the front in an evangelistic rally, or with "praying the sinner's prayer." These are now the operative rituals. They are stuck with baptism (and the Lord's Supper) because they cannot dispense with the gospel scenes in which Jesus commands their observance. But if he did not, why, I have no doubt they would dispense with them at once. There can be no sacramental theology for evangelicals who want everything settled in "the hour I first believed." Baptism is redundant, and communion is for them merely one more occasion to do what they are doing all the time anyway: doting on the crucifixion of Jesus on their behalf. But they continue both, and Rick Warren provides a thumbnail sketch of his view of baptism as one of the hoops to jump through in order to join the fellowship of the saved, at least in its visible, organized form.

THE INFANCY OF BAPTISM

Where did the rite of water immersion originate? In a general way, early Christian baptism, like that of John the Baptist, comes from the various purification rites of the Old Testament. At some unknown date, Judaism began requiring baptism by immersion for adult converts from paganism. For John the Baptist, the Essenes, the Mandaeans, the Masbotheans, Hemerobaptists, Sabeans, and other first-century Jewish sects, water baptism, whether once or daily repeated, was an important devotional act, washing away sins and marking one as an inheritor of the soon-coming kingdom of God. Here we are dealing with an intra-Jewish rite, not an initiation of non-Jews into the Jewish community. Mark 1:8 ("I have baptized you with water, but he will baptize you with the Holy Spirit." RSV) must stem from some Christian faction who had renounced John's baptism as a foreshadowing of Christian spirit baptism. Such Christians as these would not have practiced water baptism at all. That would have been consigned to the same theological-ritual museum with animal sacrifices as outmoded theological charades (Colossians 2:16–19). But, of all Christian denominations known to me, only the Society of Friends (Quakers), the Salvation Army, and the Kimbanguist Church of Congo (Kinshasa) have caught on to this and have abolished water baptism. We cannot know which was the first or original Christian posture on water baptism, but the variety of opinions on the question certainly implies Jesus had said nothing about it. Rather, the commandment to baptize (Matthew 28:19) is like the Great Commission in the context of which it appears, certainly a later speech attributed to Jesus fictively precisely in order to settle such disputes by pulling rank. "Oh, Jesus said to do it? I didn't know! Okay, I guess that settles it." "Uh, yeah, that's right. He said so, all right!"

The way Paul speaks of baptism makes it plain that, at least as practiced on Hellenistic soil, Christian baptism had much in common with the initiation rites of other popular religions called the Mystery Cults. In such a context, by the way, "cult" implies no value judgment, but only denotes the recently imported, foreign origin of a religion. These religions included those of Isis and Osiris (from Egypt), Mithras (from Persia), Attis and Cybele (from Phrygia), and Sabazius (from Thrace). "Mystery" is just the Greek work (*musterion*) for "initiation rite." All these religions, in their original homes, had been agricultural religions. Originally their dying-and-rising god myths symbolized the death and return of vegetation, or the shortening and lengthening of the daylight. The same societies had various rites of passage, like all societies do. There are christening or naming rituals for newborn infants, puberty rites in which young men and women leave adolescence and assume adult responsibility, learning the secrets of sex, death, and the sacred, with diverse and symbolically appropriate (and sometimes quite harrowing) actions. Next come marriage rites, retirement rites, and burial rites, sending off the individual to a successful life in the next world.

The Hellenistic world, in the wake of Alexander the Great, saw a great mixing of cultures and communication of ideas, not least religious ones. There was an unprecedented shifting of populations, with individuals traveling as a result of commerce, war, immigration, or evangelism. When a sufficient nucleus of immigrants from the same old homeland found one another in a foreign city, they would get together and start an assembly based on their common, religious identity. Jewish synagogues were exactly such ethnoreligious conclaves. Since the religion, like its adherents, had been uprooted from the old homeland and transplanted in foreign soil, the nature of the rituals changed, especially if the people found themselves in urban areas of the Roman Empire. What once symbolized the *ex*ternal, the death and rebirth of nature, now came to symbolize the *in*ternal, the death and rebirth of the soul. Now the death and resurrection of the deities came to symbolize the spiritual rebirth of the individual who sought initiation into higher secrets of the faith. It was like a second puberty rite, admission into a higher level of maturity, spiritual maturity (the same word as "perfection" in Greek).

The common thread in initiation rituals was the initiate's dramatic reenactment of the saving victory of the god. Hercules initiates would don a lion skin, commemorating their hero's victory over the Nemean Lion. Attis initiates would castrate themselves in the course of an induced frenzy. Then, three days later, they would retrieve a ritually entombed effigy of Attis and rejoice in his resurrection, a token of their own. The Maenads (female devotees) of Dionysus would enter a frenzy in which they would tear live animals limb from limb, imitating the dismemberment of Dionysus Zagreus by the Giants, which led to his rebirth. All such rituals sacramentally united the initiate with the god and his saving deed or passion and exaltation. Communion was the same way. Osiris worshipers consumed bread and beer symbolizing the body and blood of the god of the grain. Mithras's sectarians also had a sacred meal of bread and wine. The New Testament linkage is obvious. While the Last Supper/Lord's Supper consumption of the savior's body and blood cannot have come from any form of Judaism, where such symbolism must be absolutely abhorrent, it fits beautifully into the context of Dionysus worship (long familiar in Palestine). The function of baptism in Romans and 1 Corinthians, the mystical uniting of the initiate with the death and resurrection, then the cosmic body, of the savior, has nothing to do with Judaism either, but it fits quite well into the sacramentalism of the Mystery Cults, whence it must have been borrowed.

The imagined result of the Mystery rites was to impart salvation by inaugurating an inner alchemy whereby the old nature would be gradually transformed and replaced by a new *doxa*, or "glory" nature. The culmination of the process would come after the death of the physical body, coincident with the soul's ascension through the heavenly spheres to the Godhead. Gnosticism promised more or less the same thing. And so does Christianity. Athanasius, champion of Orthodoxy against the Arians in the fourth century, explained how the incarnation of Jesus saves those who appropriate it through faith and the sacraments: "God became man so that man might become God." Later Eastern Orthodox theology modified this broad statement, explaining that mortals would be transformed by being taken, not into the very nature of the Trinity, but rather into the divine "energies," or attributes of God, so as to preserve an eternal distinction between Creator and creatures. Still, the basic understanding of salvation was what theologians called *theosis*, or "divinization," as Eastern theologians still call it today. Western theologians (Roman Catholics and Protestants) tend to use different terminology but agree in substance: salvation culminates in receiving an immortal "spiritual body" at the time of the resurrection.

And Rick Warren is a loyal son of the tradition. In chapter 15 of *The Purpose-Driven Life* he reiterates these promises and more. Great indeed is the destiny of born-again Christians. How different for those who do not enjoy a personal relationship with Jesus Christ: the undying maggots of Gehenna are their portion. The white-hot griddles of hell will be their resting place.

BORN-AGAIN SUPERRACE

Warren, like all evangelical Christians, is clear on the point that it takes more than mere membership in the human race to make one a child of God. No, that elite category is only for born-again Christians, those who will adopt a particular seventeenth-century pietistic idiom and devotional style. No one else is a true Christian. No one else is a child of God, only a creature of God. This means Warren implicitly draws the line not between animals and humans but between praying and singing fundamentalists on the one hand and everybody else, beasts and humans, scoundrels and philanthropists, serial killers and humanitarians, all lumped together, on the other. "World-class Christians are the only *fully alive* people on the planet."[1] The outrageous arrogance of this insane boast never seems to dawn on him. Eric Hoffer has Warren pegged: "The impression somehow prevails that the true believer, particularly the religious individual, is a humble person. The truth is that the surrendering and humbling of the self breed pride and arrogance. The true believer is apt to see himself as one of the chosen, the salt of the earth, the light of the world, a prince disguised in meekness, who is destined to inherit the earth and the kingdom of heaven, too. He who is not of his faith is evil; he who will not listen shall perish."[2]

One sees Reverend Warren placidly and humbly sitting before the cameras, being interviewed by Neil Cavuto, and you just wish Cavuto would ask him, "Uh, Reverend Warren, you sit here smiling like some benign humanitarian, and all the while you plan on soaking up the tanning rays of heavenly glory for all eternity, while the screams of most of the human race are wafting up from hell in the background! Where the hell do you get off with that stuff?" I'd love to hear Larry King suddenly snap out of it and ask Warren, "Rick, tell us, what on earth gives you the right to condemn the human race to eternal torture—all because they don't have the cozy love affair with Jesus that you do?"

Well, you know what he'd say. It's what they all say: "Larry, I can't *help* it! I don't *want* all those folks to fricassee in hell. But it's not my idea. I just have to go by what the Bible says. I can't change the word of God." No, Reverend Warren. No, evangelical Christians, you can't. But can't you see you are evading responsibility for your beliefs? You are like Nazi soldiers who invoked the terrible defense, "I was only following orders!" Like it or not, you are responsible for rejecting any hateful screed that damns billions of people because they don't practice your latecomer version of Protestantism. You are responsible to take a sober look at this detestable doctrine and recognize that no such belief can be the word of God, any more than the Aztecs could have really been obeying God's orders by slicing the hearts out of their sacrificial victims from another tribe. No more than it could have been the voice of God that told Saul to butcher every last Amalekite. No more than it could have been the revealed will of God that sent Mohammed Atta flying an airliner into the World Trade Center. If there is no ethical test for alleged revelations, then it is just dumb luck keeping us out of the arms of Jim Jones and Charlie Manson.

In his parable of the Grand Inquisitor (part of the novel *The Brothers Karamazov*), Dostoyevsky has his character Ivan explain to his brother Alyosha why he wants no more to do with the church. Even though it offers a ticket to salvation, Ivan cannot in good conscience accept it, because it will require his complicity in God's guilt. He will have to stop being indignant over the fact that "God" allows the terrible suffering of innocent children. If he becomes an obedient lackey of God, he will have to become a spin doctor, a yes-man for God. He will have to agree in advance with whatever his heavenly Patron, who gives out the tickets, does. He will have to start mouthing strained apologetics for God's actions and, worse, his *in*action: "Oh, that suffering is not *God's* fault, but *ours*!" "If God did not allow pain and torture, then how would we learn from them?" And so on. Anything to cover God's almighty butt. Well, no thanks, said Ivan. He wasn't going to trade his integrity for a berth in heaven. That would be losing his soul in order to save it. So he said he had to hand back the ticket. It was too expensive. Rick Warren and his millions of coreligionists, on the other hand, are tragically willing to pay it. But it's hard to be mad at them: they are cowed into submission. Poor wretches, they are afraid *they'd* wind up in hell if they questioned it.

Day Fifteen

Point to Ponder: Any God who could torment hapless mortals for failing to believe in a savior of whom there is no proof, for not belonging to a sect of whose superiority there is no evidence, is no better than the devil.

Quote to Remember: "He who begins by loving Christianity better than truth, will proceed by loving his own sect or church better than Christianity, and end in loving himself better than all." (Samuel Taylor Coleridge)

Question to Consider: You wouldn't be a member of a club that banned Jews from membership. Is it any better belonging to a religion that bars nonfundamentalists from eternal life?

NOTES

1. Rick Warren, *The Purpose-Driven Life: What on Earth Am I Here For?* (Grand Rapids, MI: Zondervan, 2002), p. 298.

2. Eric Hoffer, *The True Believer: Thoughts on the Nature of Mass Movements* (New York: Harper & Row, 1951), pp. 97–98.

The Greatest of These

*It is therefore natural that for John the believer has no duties toward
'the world,' but only towards those who like himself are saved from
it. The new commandment (xiii, 34f.) is not that the neighbor is to
be loved . . . , still less the enemy (Matt. V, 44; Luke vi, 27), but
rather the fellow-Christian. . . . Looked at from John's perspective, it
could not be otherwise: his ethics followed straight from his
theological convictions.*
—J. L. Houlden, *Ethics and the New Testament*

THE HEART HAS ITS REASONS, BUT THEY'RE WRONG

Why is it so difficult to get one's fundamentalist friends to listen to
reason? For one thing, they are coached into believing that any questions or criticisms of their faith are either seeds of doubt Satan wants
to plant within them or smokescreen tactics on the part of desperate
sinners who, faced with the gospel, want to evade it. If they are pre-
disposed to dismiss all questions in this way, they have been relieved
of the burden of thinking through their faith.

But we must go back a step. Why would someone want to put in
place fail-safes like these? Since it is the intellectual issues they want
to short-circuit, it must be something other than intellectual factors
that are in control. And of course it is a matter of emotions. On the
one hand, every evangelical Christian is in the game for the certainty
and security the fundamentalist gospel affords. (By saying this I in no
way mean to minimize the genuine moral challenges their faith sets
for them, much less the admirable progress many make in meeting
them. But I suspect that the overriding motive for membership in
such a faith community is the need for certainty.)

On the other hand, born-again Christians have rooted themselves in a new, fictive family. By that I mean simply that it is an intentional, voluntary association that is given familylike allegiance. It becomes a substitute for the blood-relation family and is often even preferred to it. It is the same with so-called cultists. At least if my own long and pleasant experience in church youth groups and campus ministry chapters is representative, such ties are the source of great satisfaction. And there is much to be praised in such associations. But there is a dark side as well. First, the loyalty one properly feels for one's partners in Christian fellowship comes to overrule one's duty to consider intellectual questions with the necessary impartiality. If a person is to be intellectually honest with himself, he needs to set aside his preferences, what he would wish to be true, and consider matters as objectively as possible. But to do this would seem to the average evangelical a betrayal of his commitment. Two things have been fatally confused here. The best example of this confusion is an essay by C. S. Lewis, "On Obstinacy in Belief."[2] In it he reiterates his apparently broad-minded stance from *Mere Christianity* where he said, "I am not asking anyone to accept Christianity if his best reasoning tells him that the weight of the evidence is against it."[3] But then, astonishingly, Lewis says that such open-mindedness holds good only for a trial probation period. Once one commits oneself to Christian faith, one no longer gives any other viewpoint a fair hearing, because conversion is like marriage. Afterward, you're done shopping around. Rethinking your beliefs, considering the possible viability of rival viewpoints would amount to adultery! Lewis has switched metaphors. What began as a matter of rational consideration has become a matter of emotional loyalty to a cherished doctrine. Surely Uncle Screwtape has blinded him.

It is a gross category error to embrace beliefs just because one wants to pay intellectual admission to an emotionally attractive group, say, some group that tells you that you can experience a vigorous sense of purpose, provided you accept Christ as your personal savior. And once you have taken the bait, you will have entered into a bubble-reality whose ground rules redefine everything. Once your purpose is thus defined, you will of course find satisfaction in pursuing it, not least because of the positive reinforcement offered by your fellow members. And since you got into the whole thing because of emotional attraction, mere appeals to reason will likely fall on deaf ears.

Cults are sometimes accused of "love bombing," which amounts to showering attention, approval, and praise on prospective new members, to lure them into the fold. I do not doubt the truth of it. But the same thing happens in evangelical groups. In neither case is there anything particularly insidious about it. We need not question anyone's sincerity. I doubt very seriously if any born-again Christian or Moonie or anyone else consciously approaches some repulsive creep with feigned smiles and lying compliments. Sure, they may be pouring it on a bit thick, but they are sincerely delighted at the prospect of a new person joining. There is no blame to assign. Nonetheless, I believe the love bombers are predisposing the potential convert to "stumble," to start the new life of faith on the wrong foot. If it were simply a matter of membership in a club or a team, emotions would be quite sufficient as a basis for joining. But if one is henceforth to promote and defend a set of cognitive theories and positions to which no thinking, but only emotional loyalty, has led one, then such a disjuncture is dishonest. It is inauthentic. And it promotes a bad conscience, for instance, as one, motivated mainly by love for the group and its deity, offers intellectual apologetics one is in no position to evaluate. Just ammunition for propaganda.

CONDITIONAL CHRISTIAN LOVE

Another shadow of the innocent-seeming wonder of Christian agape, the love of the brethren, is its *artificiality*. It sounds noble to say that Christian love is, like God's ostensible love for us, based not on any inherent worth of the beloved, but rather on the uncritical, self-giving love of the lover. Agape is a love rendered by moral obligation. Of course, such a commitment has moved people to do great things, such as Reverend Warren's excellent work on behalf of AIDS/HIV sufferers. I mean only to suggest that, whatever its fruits, its roots may be unsound.

The fundamentalist welcomed into the fold with ample love bombing will rejoice that his new compatriots are united only by common faith in Christ, not by any natural ties, common interests, or shared opinions. Praise the Lord! What a miracle! Think here of the oft-repeated boast that only Christ could have united a mismatched pair like quisling tax collector Matthew and revolutionist Simon Zelotes. "Charlie here and I would have nothing at all in common if we weren't both Christians, praise the Lord!" Only let that earnest Christian start questioning the party line, and he will find a pink slip enclosed in the next handshake. He is henceforth a leper. That ought to be no surprise, since he has dared unravel the only bond tying him to his ostensible brothers and sisters. Weren't these people his precious siblings in Christ? What happened? They didn't love him or each other. They always admitted that what they loved was "Christ in you." It is the same kind of regard that led them to view you, in your "unsaved" days, primarily as a recruit. They never liked you for yourself, and, when you think about it, they even made a virtue of the fact that they didn't. Remember the slogans like "Jesus in me loves you"? So it ought not surprise you that, minus your faith and conformity, they don't like you now. Such was the quality of that "love" by which, as the chorus says, "they'll *kno*-ow we are *Chris*tians."

GOOD COP, BAD COP

Friedrich Nietzsche, as is well known, condemned Christian ethics as a cowardly slave morality born of *ressentiment*, the kind of impotent bitterness that dares not strike back but sublimates itself into feigned superiority and spurious forgiveness. Turning the other cheek, he said, was a self-deceptive strategy for disguising a cowardly avoidance of deserved conflict. I tend to agree with Protestant philosopher Max Scheler that the Christian stance is not automatically vitiated in this way. I believe, by contrast, that Scheler was right and the Christian ethic is itself a Nietzschean-type Superman ethic that presupposes a true greatness of spirit that cannot lower itself to take offense at the offender but pities him and forgives him, even seeks to win him over.[4] The Superman has no need for protecting his ego, saving face, and so forth.

But this is not to say Nietzsche was mistaken. No, I feel quite sure that much of what passes for Christian love and forgiveness is really cowardly *ressentiment*. This is not a judgment I would presume to level against anyone in particular. It is a suspicion each person must direct toward his or her own motives.

But it is a suspicion I must direct toward the broad outline of fundamentalist belief in divine love and Christian forgiveness insofar as these fine sentiments are held simultaneously with the belief in an eternal hell of torment. As Scheler summarizes: "the *ressentiment*-laden man transfers to God the vengeance he himself cannot wreak. . . . In this way, he can satisfy his revenge at least in imagination with the aid of an otherworldly mechanism of rewards and punishments. The core of the *ressentiment*-Christian's idea of God is still the avenging Jehovah."[5] When one says, on the one hand, "I love the world and God loves the world," then says, "The wicked will be turned into hell, and all the nations that forget God" (Psalms 9:17, KJV), one wonders how to resolve the cognitive dissonance. Old Testament Psalmists were forthright in their disdain for the wicked: "I hate those who are double-minded, but I love your law" (Psalms 119:113, NASB). "How happy shall he be who seizes your infants and dashes their brains out against the rocks!" (Psalms 137:9). That is not a pretty picture. But in some ways it is better than the pious dodges one hears from hell believers. That was Nietzsche's point: if, deep down, like a Wahabi jihadist, you really do despise the "sinners" who commit the sin of not belonging to your sect, then why not have the guts to say so instead of hiding it under the smarmy veneer of feigned love and compassion?

John Beversluis is willing to give C. S. Lewis's remarks on hell the benefit of the doubt: "The humaneness of Lewis's view is clearly preferable to the chop-licking attitude of such religionists as Tertullian and company who bubble with anticipation at the torments awaiting those who do not believe."[6] But I am not so sure. Genuine compassion would be the best, but frank hatred is better than hypocrisy, at least better in terms of one's own integrity.

But someone will say: "God does not *send* anyone to hell! They choose it themselves!" Yeah, right. Like any sinner really decided he wanted to fry in hell, even believed seriously that it was a possible consequence of his actions. As if the sinners would not be taken by nasty surprise when they awoke screaming in the magma pit. C. S. Lewis even stooped to this silliness: hell is God's way of letting the sinner have his way. "I willingly believe that the damned are, in one sense, successful, rebels to the end; that the doors of hell are locked on the *inside*. . . . They enjoy forever the horrible freedom they have demanded, and are therefore self-enslaved: just as the blessed, forever submitting to obedience, become through all eternity more and more free. In the long run the answer to all those who object to the doctrine of hell, is itself a question: 'what are you asking God to do?' To wipe out their past sins and, at all costs, to give them a fresh start, smoothing every difficulty and offering every miraculous help? But He has done so, on Calvary. To forgive them? They will not be forgiven. To leave them alone? Alas, I am afraid that is what He does."[7] He wanted to be away from God, so now here's his opportunity! In the first place, sinners do not want to avoid the reproving company of God. They just do not believe it is a question of that. They don't take seriously the preaching of the pious. In the second place, Lewis and his fans are entering into just the sort of hateful spite Nietzsche claimed underlay the pretension of Christian forgiveness: "You wanted it? You *got* it, bastards! Let's see how you like being away from God *now!*" Hell is a fulfillment of the wish of the sinner in precisely the same fashion as the backfiring wishes in W. W. Jacobs's chiller, "The Monkey's Paw."

Then there is the "I can't help it" defense: "Look, I'm not *happy* people are going to hell! In fact, it's because I don't want you to end up there that I'm witnessing to you!" It's as if the born-again Christian agrees with you that hell is unjust, so don't blame him. But there it is, so what are you going to do about it? This is in effect the old "good cop, bad cop" strategy. One interrogator warns the suspect to come clean now, before he has no choice but to turn him over to his out-of-control partner.

But why is the divine "bad cop" such a hard case? What forces him to send anybody to hell? Is he subject, like the Greek gods, to the dictates of Fate? Hasn't he satisfied his own justice on the cross? What's the matter: didn't it work? Why does he still plan on sending people to hell? Look, if he's going to force them into some post-mortem destiny they never saw coming and, despite the dodge, didn't choose, then why the heck doesn't he subject them to an involuntary, postmortem process of *sanctification*? Suppose Hitler and Stalin (not to mention Gandhi and all the other folks fundamentalists have booked into hell) instead woke up in heaven, surprised to be there, but awakened from the nightmare of wickedness. Who's the loser in this scenario? What's the problem? Is God a forgiving God or not? Are his followers really forgiving either?

One last thing: once you realize that fundamentalism, despite all its talk of love, love, love, enshrines as its ultimate paragon of morality an entity whose "goodness" is compatible with torturing billions of people for eternity, you begin to understand those bigots holding their picket signs that say GOD HATES FAGS. They aren't exactly hypocrites. Their inconsistency, though gross, occurs on a deeper level than that. They are holding together two diametrically opposed convictions about God: he is loving and he is the Lord of Damnation. It is an unstable, schizophrenic mix. No wonder it can tip now to one side, now to the other. Once again we see the fundamentalist God of Reverend Warren and his pals as the prototype of the abusive father, he who professes his love and demonstrates it with his fists.

Day Sixteen

Point to Ponder: If love accommodates even hell, what *can't* it accommodate? And then, what does it even *mean*?

Quote to Remember: JESUS LOVES YOU, BUT EVERYONE ELSE THINKS YOU'RE AN ASSHOLE. (bumper sticker)

Question to Consider: Do I really witness to people because I love them? Or am I afraid of guilt if I don't?

NOTES

1. C. S. Lewis, "On Obstinacy in Belief," in *The World's Last Night* (New York: Harcourt, Brace, Jovanovich, 1990), pp. 13–30.

2. C. S. Lewis, *Mere Christianity* (New York: Macmillan, 1960), p. 123.

3. Max Scheler, *Ressentiment*, Marquette Studies in Philosophy IV, trans. Lewis B. Coser and William W. Holdheim (Milwaukee: Marquette University Press, 1994), pp. 67–73.

4. Ibid., p. 75.

5. John Beversluis, *C. S. Lewis and the Search for Rational Religion* (Grand Rapids, MI: William B. Eerdmans, 1985), p. 24.

6. C. S. Lewis, *The Problem of Pain* (London: Fount, 1940), pp. 101–102. Emphasis in original.

A Place to Conform

Then Amaziah said to Amos, "Go, you seer, flee away to the land of Judah and there eat bread and there do your prophesying! But no longer prophesy at Bethel, for it is a sanctuary of the king and a royal residence." Then Amos replied to Amaziah, "I am not a prophet, nor am I the son of a prophet; for I am a herdsman and a grower of sycamore figs. But the LORD took me from following the flock, and the LORD said to me, 'Go, prophesy to my people Israel.'"
—Amos 7:12–15 (NASB)

Woe to you! For you build the tombs of the prophets, and it was your fathers who killed them. So you are witnesses and approve the deeds of your fathers; because it was they who killed them, and you build their tombs.
—Luke 11:47–48 (NASB)

JOHN Q. PIOUS

It is quite revealing for Pastor Warren to warn his readers that, if they want to maintain spiritual health and keep the flame of their Christian devotion stoked, they need to make sure they do not miss church. The path of Christian Individualism, as Otis Sellers used to call it, is a dead end. I'm not sure Kierkegaard would agree with that assessment. In fact, I think there are pretty strong arguments against this sort of religious collectivism. But first, let me mention another keen critic of organized religion: Bart Simpson. In one episode of *The Simpsons* he and his pal Milhouse have been punished for a church prank. (It's the one called "Bart Sells His Soul," where they tricked the organist into playing "In-A-Gadda-Da-Vida" instead of the morning hymn. Recently, I got the visiting organist at my church to sneak a few bars of the *Star Wars* theme into the prelude with no such repercussions.)

Bart and Milhouse are assigned some menial chore in the back room, and the two lads begin discussing hell. Bart expresses his doubts that any such place exists, whereupon Milhouse asks why on earth anyone would make such a thing up? Immediately the camera switches to Reverend Lovejoy counting the morning plate offering.

I hardly think it's as easy as that, for the simple reason that few pastors get rich off their ministries. It is usually not a very lucrative field. Reverend Warren's books have made him a good deal of money, and I for one wouldn't complain if he kept the fruits of his labor and enjoyed them. In fact, though, he gives away by far the most of it. And, as for the offerings, a church has to pay the light bills the same as everybody else. Nonetheless, there is something about religious institutionalism that is inimical to intellectual honesty.

Why is it better for the health of one's faith to remain within the Camp of the Saints? Because you will be much less inclined to doubt your beliefs while surrounded by others who are constantly affirming them. Like plants in a greenhouse, they are generating an atmosphere of belief. It is what sociologists Berger and Luckmann call a "plausibility structure." The idea is that we naturally tend to accommodate ourselves to the opinions of those around us because basically we are "social animals" and need to fit in with the herd. Many experiments have shown how powerful peer pressure is. A test subject is placed in a group of what he imagines are random volunteers like himself. As they wait for the test to begin (or so he thinks!), someone strikes up a conversation about politics. To his surprise, most present start talking up Communism, a doctrine of which he knows little save that all "good" Americans hate it. Before long such a test subject finds himself warming to the philosophy of Karl Marx, though after the session is over, he will likely wonder what on earth he could have been thinking.

The same dynamic explains the odd phenomenon of which one occasionally reads, of field anthropologists "going native" and embracing the customs and beliefs of the alien culture they are living with. As Berger and Luckmann say, the witch doctor may begin to doubt himself when standing amid a circle of Logical Positivist philosophers, but then again, the Logical Positivist may do the doubting if the positions are reversed, and it is he who is standing in the midst of a circle of witch doctors! It is no mere question of relativism, as if beliefs were nothing more than social reflections. No, the whole point is that *they ought to be more*. Properly one holds a belief for good reasons, appropriate to the sort of belief it is. A belief about allegedly historical events must be settled on the basis of evidence and historiography, not on faith, or we will have no defense against Holocaust deniers and believers in the lost continent of Mu. The thing is, though, that very often we do not embrace beliefs on the basis of evidence. We hold them instead on the basis of peer pressure and the desire to join or remain in a group that holds them. We may have been born into the group or we may have joined it after a period of searching, crisis, or loneliness. But the warm feeling of belonging and affirmation one feels from one's compatriots has nothing to do with the beliefs they espouse. They might be right, but it would be by some stroke of luck.

So a plausibility structure is a social framework in which any notion may seem believable because of the cognitive atmosphere generated by one's fellows. And that is the wrong reason. I myself remain acutely aware of the temptation here. Any time I find myself beginning to think that, of course such and such a belief of mine and my valued colleagues is obviously true, I stand back and ask myself if it is just the result of a mutual admiration society we have going. I try to guard against that. I constantly try to review and reevaluate the reasons and evidence for any theory I hold, so I don't continue to espouse it out of brand loyalty or, worse yet, fear of having to back up and admit I was wrong.

Do you suppose church is an environment where honest scrutiny of beliefs is liable to happen? Is it even possible there? I realize a church congregation is not a debating society, that it exists for other reasons. My point is, however, that churches do promote beliefs that would more appropriately find a place in a context of intellectual debate. They wind up cheerleading for highly dubious opinions on historical, scientific, and metaphysical matters, simply on the bases of emotional preference and the inertia of tradition. They demand conformity to these beliefs, and if you cannot swim with the current, then, well partner, maybe you'd be happier in another pool, another lake in fact, the one ablaze with burning sulfur.

Kierkegaard saw things just the opposite way from Reverend Warren. For Kierkegaard, the shoe was on the other foot: the hardest place to be a Christian, he wrote, was in Christendom. Why should that be? Among other reasons, it is because the church as a nest of comfortable belief, a plausibility structure built to reinforce belief, is hardly conducive to the growth of original thinking. Orthodoxy never welcomes new ideas. Surely there are plenty of evangelical scholars and thinkers. But in my experience, theologians and apologists value logic and scholarship in precisely the same way TV evangelists value one particular aspect of science: broadcast technology—anything to aid in the propaganda effort. Kierkegaard knew that the religious institution inevitably alienates its most creative members. He was one of them. So were the biblical prophets.

PILLARS OF THE CHURCH, TOMBS OF THE PROPHETS

Amos 7:12–15 presents a fascinating scene: a showdown between Amos, a self-appointed prophet, as we might deem him, and Amaziah, an official prophet of the royal court of Israel. He had all the prophetic credentials one might ask, not to mention an official post in the government. The trouble is that Amos, a loud-mouthed upstart and an outsider from Judah, was appearing in public, on a soapbox so to speak, railing against the government, its foreign policy, and its official worship. It is all a sham, he says, and for that reason an abomination in the sight of God. Amaziah tries to shoo his unlettered rival away. What business has Amos, with no prophetic ID card, no official sanction, in declaring the word of God, especially since it made the state and the state church look bad?

How, you might ask, could Amaziah be so sure Amos was wrong? Simply this: he *had* to be wrong. By definition a true prophecy was one that toed the party line. You see, prophecy was an institution. The court prophets were a group of oracles whose job it was, ostensibly, to advise the king in light of God's wisdom. But the Bible itself makes clear that prophethood had degenerated into a group of well-paid yes-men who were supposed to pronounce God's blessing on any plan the king might float (1 Kings 22:1–18). Prophecy was the party line. Amaziah followed that line well. Amos called its bluff. No wonder he didn't have credentials. He wouldn't play the game.

The prophets were simply the embodiment of the divine right of kings, living proof, as it were. In modern terms we would call them spin doctors. You know, the political handlers who talk to the media after every debate and assure them that an obvious defeat for their man was really a victory if you see it their way. Press secretaries who defend the president's policies no matter how bad they look. Reporters ask them for a candid opinion, but it is their job never to give one. It is all PR.

Notice that Amaziah tells Amos he'd better stop bad-mouthing Bethel, because, after all, it's the king's own chapel. Significant choice of words. You know the difference between a chaplain and a prophet? Jim Wallis is good on this in his book *Agenda for Biblical People.*[1] A chaplain is a clergyman retained by an institution to perform religious functions for them. Billy Graham praying at the inauguration, Tom Skinner praying at a football game. That sort of thing. A chaplain is the functionary of the institution that pays him. Just like Amaziah. And there is no problem with this as long as there is no question of speaking the truth. There are plenty of aspects of religion that are ceremonial, ornamental, aesthetic. And a chaplain does these things quite properly. But the trouble comes when the minister is *told* to prophesy, that is, speak the truth as he or she sees it, and yet is *really* expected to speak the comforting affirmations of a chaplain. This is going to mean that sooner or later the preacher is going to say things that make the congregation, or at least the major shareholders in it, mighty nervous, and then it's time for a search committee.

HERDING CATS

And if you gather a group of freethinkers who will allow a preacher to speak his mind—people who want no party line—what's going to happen? You're going to have a loose collection of individualists (which is what you want) who will gradually drift away. They will shun the responsibilities of making an institution and keeping it going. And they will be right! Many of us have seen the institution of a church become an albatross around our necks till the congregation exists simply as the maintenance crew for the institution. We don't want that, so instead we want to travel light. But there will be no future to such a group.

I think there is no irony in a short-lived collection of freethinking religionists who eventually go their own ways enriched by their common experience. This was what I promoted at First Baptist Church in Montclair, New Jersey, and it was no wonder the church never grew. New members would come, but they were pilgrims, searchers. And inevitably they would continue their search—elsewhere! Of course! The whole idea was freedom!

But this simply did not serve the purposes of the institution we had. Various church bureaucrats complained that we had to fill those pews to get new bureaucrats and new funds. And we should spend our efforts getting the sort of members who would settle down in a church and shoulder those responsibilities: young families with children. It all came down to marketing. It always does in an institution. It *has* to.

However understandable, even inevitable it may be, it is nonetheless insidious. It leads to ironies and hypocrisies such as Jesus condemns in Luke 11: 47–48. Religious institutions venerate the prophets of the dead past, the ones who can no longer speak inconvenient and embarrassing things. And the old things they said? Well, they can be defused with the proper exegesis. But let any new prophet say what the old ones said and he will share the same fate as the old ones. "Blessed are you when people hate you, and when they exclude you and revile you, and cast out your name as evil, on account of the Son of Man! . . . [F]or so their fathers did to the prophets" (Luke 6:22–23, RSV).

Again, what would you *expect*? Are you naïve enough to believe that an institution can take seriously what the prophet says and survive as an institution? A group that *does* take it seriously will not long survive as a group. And that's the way it must be. The church of seekers must be ephemeral. If it becomes permanent, it fossilizes.

When it comes to its natural end there is nothing to regret; nothing has gone wrong. As Thomas Jefferson said, each generation must have its own revolution. This is no less true spiritually. Let the truth of the spirit be discovered again and again, whether discovered in an old book or not, it doesn't matter. Each new seeker has to see it for himself; you can't inherit it.

Jesus points out the irony of those undertakers of the prophets who venerate their safely silent corpses. "You who erect the tombs of the prophets! You say you would never have killed them? Then tell me why you're building that new one over there!" Maybe that's the point of the business about Joseph of Arimathea burying Jesus in a brand-new tomb: it was just waiting for him, since it was only a matter of time.

THE PERILS OF PAUL

Which finally brings us to Paul and his encounter with the so-called Pillars—James, John, and Peter—recorded in Galatians 2:1–14. Let me draw a contrast between the great Apostle to the Gentiles and the satraps of Jesus in the Holy City Jerusalem, the home office. Liberal Protestants like to call Paul the second founder of Christianity. They say that he transformed the religion of Jesus, a simple moral piety, into a dogmatic religion about Jesus. But it doesn't mean Paul was a villain. It doesn't mean that, even if we disagree with what he taught. You see, what this means is that Paul was like Jesus: an original thinker, a charismatic religious genius. For him, Jesus was no longer a human being. He had already become a god. And that meant Paul was to his Christ as Jesus of Nazareth had been to his Father. Like Jesus, Paul was a radical, a lone wolf, a loose canon. Not an organization man. He struck out in a new direction, his own direction.

What about James, John, and Peter? These are mere names. What shadowy existence they went on to have in Christian history was simply as—you guessed it—symbolic figureheads for religious institutions, James as the founder of Ebionite Jewish Christianity and Peter as the pedigree of the Roman popes. And John? The big name affixed to the fourth gospel to give it legitimacy when some thought it was a piece of Gnostic blasphemy penned by Cerinthus.

Look at the titles of these three, James, John, and Peter. James and John are called "the Pillars." This is a mythic/cosmic allusion, referring to the great pillars holding up the vault of heaven. The pillars of heaven are frequently mentioned in the Bible. The two pillars in Solomon's temple, Boaz and Jachin, were meant to represent them, just as the Temple itself, like all ancient temples, was supposed to be a microcosm of the universe. In fact, this is most likely what "Boanerges" means, the epithet given to James and John in Mark 3:17—"upholders of the vault of heaven."

Peter is also called Cephas, the Rock. This is supposed to represent the great foundation stone of the cosmos, on which, again, the Jerusalem temple, as a copy of the world, was supposed to rest. And what is the significance of Simon (Peter) being the cosmic Rock? "You are Peter, and upon this Rock I will build my church. . . . I will give you the keys of the kingdom of heaven, and whatever you bind on earth shall be bound in heaven, and whatever you loose on earth shall be loosed in heaven" (Matthew 16:18–19, RSV). This was not lost on the popes. The whole point of James, John, and Peter being the Pillars and the foundation stone was to guarantee their *institutional* authority.

And with this, Paul was destined to *collide*, just as Jesus collided with the authorities of *his* day. In 1 Corinthians Paul is already fending off Peter's claim to be the foundation stone of the church. He says that no one can possibly lay another foundation than that of Christ himself (1 Corinthians 3:11).

But one day Paul finds it advisable to go to the home office and try to gain the recognition of the Pillars (Galatians 2:1–2). It will save him some needless friction if he can get their blessing. If he can get them to accept his credentials. And it works. He is glad to accept the one condition they place on him—to gather a relief fund for the Jerusalem church. He is faithful in carrying out the mission, as you can see in several of his letters.

Then imagine his shock when in Antioch the whole thing blows up in his face. Peter visits and circulates freely among Paul's Gentile converts. They don't keep kosher. What of it? If Paul told them they didn't have to, Peter's not going to undermine him. But then some representatives of James appear, and Peter changes his tune. He seems to realize that the Pillars do not really look at Paul as a legitimate colleague at all, and so he falls in line with James's party line and tells the Gentiles that, on second thought, they'd better adopt Jewish customs, do it the way the Pillars do it—and to hell with Paul. Paul charges him with hypocrisy on the spot (Galatians 2:11–14).

One wonders whether Peter at that moment found himself experiencing a bit of déjà vu. Didn't he used to hear Jesus say such things to the scribes? Back then, in Galilee, Peter cheered him on. And yet now here he is—on the *receiving* end!

And indeed we may ask what on earth could have happened to *bring* Peter to such a point? *I'll* tell you: he had become one of the custodians of an institution, *that's* what. He no longer had the freedom to tell the emperor that he had no clothes on. He no longer had the luxury of speaking his mind. He had become the very sort of nameless functionary whose nervous scrupulosity about the rules Jesus used to lampoon. What is the scripture of the churches today? The Bible? Sorry, not even close! Try *Roberts' Rules of Order*. That's the holy Torah.

Any New Testament scholar will tell you Jesus never meant to found a church, and it was no accident. A church, an institution, could never have kept his insights, his truth, alive. An institution can only become a mausoleum for a suffocated truth. Peter, James, and John were Pillars of the church. But by the same token, in the very same moment, they were also the builders of the tomb of the prophet Jesus.

Nietzsche explained why it happens: the Superman transvaluates the values of his day, but the mass, the herd, cannot live for long on that exalted mount of transfiguration. The atmosphere is just too rare. So the first thought of the disciples, the followers, is to build a tabernacle, a shrine, for the prophet atop the mountain, a tomb for his truth, and then to descend the hillside as quickly as possible. And then it's business as usual. *Roberts' Rules*, full speed ahead.

Abraham Maslow (in *Religions, Values, and Peak Experiences*) sees it in terms of prophets like Isaiah, the Buddha, and Jesus being "peakers," people with peak experiences of revelation or enlightenment, ecstasy in which they are lifted outside the limits of their selfhood. But one cannot pass this experience on to others. They must find it for themselves. And they don't want to. The mass who follow the prophetic peaker will only admire the prophet's experience from afar. Soon they will be saying *they* could *never* experience it. And then they will say that the prophet was a savior, that because *he* had the peak experience we need not try to have it for ourselves. It would be presumptuous to try.

It is what Max Weber called "the routinization of charisma." The original power of the prophet, after he dies, becomes channeled into routine, institutional structures, administered in the form of sacraments by duly appointed, certified representatives. And no one notices that it has long since drained away. We retain the form of religion while denying the power thereof.

And then we get to the jest of Kierkegaard, and the joke is on us: "Imagine a man who preaches that the teacher of truth can have no disciples—and immediately 50 men apply to preach his doctrine in his name!" Isn't that precisely where we got Christianity and all the other religions? Built on the bones of the prophets.

Institutions survive, but what are they surviving *for*? One cannot pass down peak experiences or prophecy. It is useless to expect those trained as ships' captains to rock the boat. They can only be obedient crewmen, maybe galley slaves.

Day Seventeen

Point to Ponder: You have to admire the courage of a radical, not that it makes his opinions correct.

Quote to Remember: "What after all are these churches now if they are not the tombs and sepulchers of God?" (Friedrich Nietzsche, *The Gay Science*, 3:125)

Question to Consider: Is your church or group on the verge of buying a building to meet in? Are you sure you want to do that?

NOTE

1. Jim Wallis, *Agenda for Biblical People* (New York: Harper & Row, 1976), p. 24.

Heretics Anonymous

I've searched for community in many places, Jesus. I was often looking in the wrong places, but I don't think my motive was altogether wrong. I was looking futilely and hopelessly there for fellowship, belonging, and acceptance. Now, in this moment, which many people would label "loneliness," or "nothingness," I want to thank you, Jesus. In this moment—in this place and with these other persons—I have found community where and as it is. It seems to me it is your gift. I am here with these others for only a few hours. I will be gone tomorrow. But I won't be searching so desperately any more. I know I must accept community where you offer it to me. I accept it in this moment. Thank you, Jesus.
—Malcolm Boyd, *Are You Running with Me, Jesus?*

JESUS AT ESALEN

One of the major criticisms aimed at megachurches like Reverend Warren's is that they are so huge, it is inevitable for a lone member to get lost in the shuffle. Well, I think that criticism is unfair. Of course, that's just what many people want, and the sheer size of the congregation makes it easy for them to take the path of anonymity with no strings attached. Such churches always subdivide into small groups that meet for Bible study, prayer, and discussion during the week. In such cell groups real relationships can form and honest discussion can flourish. That is a healthy development.

I can't resist pointing out, however, another humorous instance of Warren's utterly ahistorical way of reading the Bible, as if it had been written for fundamentalists in the 1970s. Why did Jesus have twelve disciples? "Jesus ministered in the context of a small group of disciples. He could have chosen more, but he knew twelve is about the maximum size you can have in a small group if everyone is to participate."[1] Biblical scholars think the number of the disciples/apostles probably had more to do with the number of the tribes of Israel, but Warren knows better: Jesus was the "with-it" master of group dynamics theory, and that despite the fact that the gospels give no hint that Jesus sought the comments or participation of his men at all.

I think small groups are great, and you don't have to be a bunch of evangelical Christians to have a great small-group experience. For many years my wife, Carol, and I have conducted discussion groups called Heretics Anonymous. As you might expect, the name is a joke. There is no attempt, as in twelve-step groups who suffix their monikers with "Anonymous," to free anyone from their addiction to heresy. We are quite committed to heresy, because the word "heresy," the Greek *hairesis*, simply means "choice." It became a theological cuss word when orthodoxy decided with Luciferian hubris that it could prescribe right belief for everyone. That one should choose one's own belief rather than meekly swallow the catechism of the bishops was deemed the greatest effrontery.

PIZZACOSTALS

The name "Heretics Anonymous" originated in the halls of Gordon-Conwell Theological Seminary, a bastion of stale and arrogant orthodoxy, when a few of the guys (including one who used to do a great Billy Graham imitation—I once took a picture of him shaking hands with Dr. Graham)[2] mused with a gleam in their collective eye that there ought to be a retreat for freethinkers, sort of a "Heretics Anonymous"! I became one of that number, and we would meet in the low-lit recess of Capri Pizza in Beverly, Massachussetts. Ah, the good old days! When I graduated and went on to do campus ministry at Montclair State College, I soon discovered a similar need among the ranks of those disaffected from the more straitlaced Christian groups on campus. I worked for the Protestant Foundation, a mainline denominational outreach that had previously had little student constituency. So I scheduled a meeting room for Heretics Anonymous, soon two, because there were too many attending for one weekly meeting to accommodate.

Ah, those were the good old days, too! We would put up posters promoting the meetings, sheets emblazoned with slogans like "Read this quick before some bigot tears it down!" My favorite was the one that depicted four cartoon characters in the familiar postures of "See no evil, hear no evil, speak no evil"—with a fourth praying with closed eyes and folded hands!

These groups continued to meet for no-holds-barred discussion, sometimes with prepared student presentations, regularly for six years until I moved to North Carolina. We tried to establish a new Heretics group there, inviting some of my students at Mount Olive College, as well as other individuals we had met in our small town. Boy, did it fizzle! None of the students ever darkened the door, and the one meeting we had sank like a stone because the local Methodist minister just would not shut up.

I attended a nearby Episcopalian church, and eventually Carol and I started up a similar group, which we dubbed "the Fellowship of the Holy Grail," thinking that had a nice Anglican ambience. The response was overwhelming at first. But soon this effort, too, was derailed by a persistent fundamentalist in the congregation who came only in order to evangelize the rest of us. She, too, would not shut up, and by the fourth meeting, it was pretty much Carol, me, another couple, and this lady.

Not long after that, Carol and I returned to New Jersey where I was to serve as pastor of a very freethinking Baptist congregation (Harry Emerson Fosdick's first parish, as a matter of fact), and we began to feel that reviving Heretics as a church function might not be a bad idea. It would provide a forum for free discussion and feedback that simply would never be possible on Sunday mornings. An impressive number responded, but at length we were disappointed to find that there was seldom much overlap between those who came to Heretics Anonymous on Friday evenings and those who showed up to church on Sunday mornings. They formed two parallel congregations.

HELLO, MY NAME IS . . .

Many of the heretics were people I met through the philosophy department at Montclair State College, where I taught as an adjunct. Others were former students or colleagues, plus folks I met through Adult School classes I taught, or through a film series I hosted. Still others were invited by friends who enjoyed the group.

One man, an advertising writer who has written commercials you've heard, I met when we were both standing with our little daughters in the pony-ride line at the local Teddy Bear Fair. I happened to be holding a copy of Jacques Derrida's *Dissemination*, and he inquired about it. He soon confided that he was "a Jew who prays to Jesus and believes in reincarnation." I knew Heretics was the place for him and invited him.

Another regular was an English major with a minor in philosophy. Like me, he was a devotee of H. P. Lovecraft, and he was a member of a thrash-metal rock group with its own CDs. Another was a family court judge in New York City. Another was a dance instructor, another a singer and actress, another a writer, another a cabbie who has tales to tell of his chats with Derrida and David Lehmann as he drove them to lectures. There were two psychotherapists, one specializing in helping homosexuals accept their orientation. One man recently returned from a semester in Argentina where he was robbed by *terroristas* twice. There was even one of the original Montclair State College Heretics, who went on to become one of the most celebrated kindergarten teachers in the local school system.

There were a couple of writers, and the group provided the opportunity to share contacts and possible markets. There were two or three literary criticism buffs. Politically you could find ultraliberals as well as conservatives of the most politically incorrect opinions. The most politically liberal also happened to be the most theologically conservative, an articulate evangelical—who also shared the Lovecraft addiction (and so did the judge!). What a crew! With a group like this, there is pretty much no way the discussion is not going to be interesting. More than once Carol and I went to bed and left a marine and a pacifist amiably arguing till the wee hours.

In 2001 my family returned to North Carolina, and it was not long before we tried to start up Heretics again. Before too many months had gone by, we began having tentative meetings, often with pretty shallow and mundane conversations, just so people could get to feel comfortable with each other. Again, there were students and faculty, business associates, people daring to question inherited dogmas, learning to stretch the wings of their minds and to think for themselves, as well as fundamentalists who have this or that odd opinion unwelcome in their own circles but that could be expressed here. Even one or two high school students, friends of my daughters.

The meetings have thrived. Everyone, usually about fifteen people, sat around our living room. Wine, soda, munchies, and cheese circulated freely—as did ideas. Usually the melee began with someone reading an essay or a book review from some source or other. Then the discussion might ricochet anywhere.

Gradually we found we had to circulate a list of ground rules facilitating polite interaction (see the next chapter); but no one minded, and it did some good. For instance, we have always thought it best to avoid politics. It is divisive, mundane, and, besides, there are plenty of other opportunities throughout the week to air your opinions on these matters. So why waste rare evenings when more advanced ethical, spiritual, and existential topics can come up for review?

Over the years, I have often been gratified to hear people exclaim how much they enjoy the meetings, and how unique they are. But what we do, surely anyone can do. As long as you have acquaintances whom you think would enjoy it, just make a list of some topics, clip some columns, choose some book excerpts, set out some snacks, and you're on your way!

Reverend Warren suggests that his readers organize discussion groups focusing on *The Purpose-Driven Life*, and I bet you'd profit from a series of discussions based on *The Reason-Driven Life*. You could read a chapter aloud for everyone to discuss (or not), I don't care.

Also, I mentioned that Heretics Anonymous has functioned as a port in the storm for people dissatisfied with dogmatic religion to speak their minds and to share experiences. This book could certainly provide a nucleus for such a group. Another possibility, though, is to check out some of the online discussion forums maintained by ex-evangelicals for the same purpose.

Ex-Christian Stories
  http://www.infidels.org/electronic/email/ex-tian/stories.html
Ex-Christian WebRing
  http://k.webring.com/hub?ring=exchristian
Ex-Tian Homepage
  http://www.infidels.org/electronic/email/ex-tian/index.html
Fundamentalism and Deconversion WebRing
  http://a.webring.com/hub?ring=leavingfundament
Leaving Fundamentalist born-again Christianity WebRing
  http://a.webring.com/hub?ring=lbafc
More Deconversion Stories
  http://www.users.globalnet.co.uk/~slocks/individual_decon_stories.html
Recovering from Religion WebRing
  http://x.webring.com/hub?ring=recoveringfromre
The Secular Web
  http://www.infidels.org/library/modern/testimonials/index.shtml
Walk Away
  http://web.archive.org/web/20020802040806/www.ifas.org/wa/index.html

Day Eighteen

Point to Ponder: The moment you can no longer take your beliefs for granted, you have become a heretic.

Quote to Remember: "For premodern man, heresy is a possibility—usually a rather remote one; for modern man, heresy typically becomes a necessity." (Peter L. Berger, *The Heretical Imperative*)

Question to Consider: Evangelists tell me I have to choose Christ for myself. Why don't they want me to make up my own mind about anything afterward?

NOTES

1. Rick Warren, *The Purpose-Driven Life: What on Earth Am I Here For?* (Grand Rapids, MI: Zondervan, 2002), p. 139.

2. Kevin Bausman was his name. He used to do this hilarious rant in Billy's voice, as if turning down a proposal by Cornelius Van Til to do "cooperative evangelism": "Corny! Ah'm afraid I can't wuhk with ya! Our theol-ah-lugies ah just too diffrunt!"

Price's Ten Commandments

Let two or three prophets speak, and let the others weigh what is said. If a revelation is made to another sitting by, let the first be silent. For you can all prophesy one by one, so that all may learn and all may be encouraged.
—1 Corinthians 14:29–31

When it comes to small discussion groups, I tend toward Taoism: the doctrine that the least direction is the best. I like to allow things to take their natural course. But one does have to establish some few guidelines in order to keep things running smoothly. They are just reminders for individuals who may get so carried away with what they are saying that they become insensitive to how they are coming across and what effect they are having on the group as a whole—namely, ruining it! These ground rules are common sense, but that is just what slips away quickest when we find ourselves in the heat of exciting discussion.

First Commandment: Thou shalt get to thy point as quickly and succinctly as possible. I'm not talking about monosyllables. And I know you have to explain so as to head off misunderstanding right off the bat. But you should aim for brevity for the simple reason that you have a room full of others who want to speak their piece, too. We haven't got all night! And try to make it a single point. Make your other comments later, after people have had a chance to respond to the first one.

Second Commandment: Thou shalt try to stay on topic at least for a while. After all, someone went to some trouble to design the kickoff presentation, and it would be enormously rude to toss it aside in favor of something that pops into your head. Eventually the announced discussion will disintegrate into a general chatfest, but let's see if we can hold that off as long as possible, enough to explore the announced topic.

Third Commandment: Thou shalt avoid politics like the plague! This is a divisive family of topics, likely to alienate people from one another and to generate more heat than light. We can't avoid politics; we hear it and talk about it in every other forum. So let's give it a rest already! Remember, you probably don't get many opportunities to discuss deeper issues of belief and meaning. Don't squander this one.

Fourth Commandment: Thou shalt give heed unto the person talking. Neither shalt thou merely wait till they're done so that thou mayest launch into thine own planned soliloquy. I recall the time, in an InterVarsity Christian Fellowship "action group," that I found myself bemoaning the long-windedness of a pal and suddenly realized I was just waiting impatiently for my own turn to sound off! Why not actually *listen* to the other person? You might learn something. You might find something new to think about.

Fifth Commandment: Thou shalt esteem individual persons above their opinions and beliefs. In this manner thou mayest abstain from personal enmity and avoid waxing wrathful. Remember, theological discussion is great sport! You can get pretty animated about the issues without getting mad and offended. Think of it more like tennis than football: you are batting the *ball* around, not the players on the other team. In retrospect, you might feel you pursued those with an opposing viewpoint pretty hard. You may have hurt their feelings. Why not be big enough to apologize? At least find them afterward and trade some friendly small talk. That way you can remind them and yourself that you are still friends.

Sixth Commandment: Thou shalt not fracture the group discussion into two or more. But thou shalt all have one conversation going on until the informal aftermath of the main event. Granted, this is sort of tough, the more people you have. But we are talking about small groups, not an auditorium. Splitting off into smaller discussions is rude to whomever is ostensibly addressing the whole group, and it creates a noisy chaos no one can ignore, given the close confines. If you find you just cannot contain yourself, why don't you and your buddy quietly drift off into the kitchen and talk briefly as you get more coffee? At least you won't be distracting everybody else that way.

Seventh Commandment: Thou shalt not grandstand. I have had uncomfortable meetings in which someone arrived with a bee in his bonnet and just felt like he had to lecture everybody. This might not be a problem, but the host ought to have the prerogative to make that decision. It might be a topic outside the parameters of the group and its common interests. It might be otherwise inappropriate. The farther outside the parameters it is, the greater the likelihood that the person is going to invite misunderstanding or even abuse. But anyhow, if you already have something scheduled, you have no choice but to ask the person to stop hijacking the discussion. Maybe you can ask him to come back next time prepared to lead a discussion of his own. Everybody gets his or her turn.

Eighth Commandment: Thou shalt not aim to convert the group to thine own faith or opinion. Remember, the point is dialogue. The goal is for representatives of rival viewpoints to understand one another's opinions. At least, that is the case if you are lucky enough not to be ideologically monochrome. Whatever your evangelistic zeal, it makes your cause look mighty bad if you are a boorish, one-track-minded representative of it. Go find someone else to set straight.

Ninth Commandment: Thou shalt make sure all present know that they are not expected to speak, though their participation is most welcome. What the heck, you're not grading them on class participation—or anything else! If they want to soak up what everybody else is saying for a while, let them. Pretty soon, I bet they'll feel bold enough that, like Elihu, hitherto content to listen to the great debate between Job, Eliphaz, Bildad, and Zophar, the quiet one will burst into speech and enrich the conversation with a new voice. But it will happen in its own time. You can lead a horse to water, but you can't make him drink. But if you hang around the watering hole long enough, you can be pretty sure he will. And then, for Pete's sake, let everybody defer to the new voice! Let him or her speak, or the new voice will never try again.

Tenth Commandment: Thou shalt not interrupt thy brother or thy sister! This is trickier than it looks. The greatest temptation to interrupt is presented by someone who makes more than one point in a single turn at speaking. Somebody is going to want to comment on the first point and is afraid he will forget what you said by the time you get to the end of your rant. Or the discussion will have moved on to something else. And the more people have to say, "Uh, I'd like to return to something Eggbert said ten minutes ago . . . ," well, the messier the whole thing gets. On the other hand, if someone seems to want to address something you just said, you might not mind letting him. Perhaps there could be a discrete signal, the would-be interrupter raising his hand or making eye contact, and you answering by a "just a second" index finger, as I do when I'm teaching and want to let a student know I will stop in a moment for his question if he'll just let me finish my point.

How much of a traffic cop do you have to be for the meeting to chug along pleasantly? You don't have to be the heavy if you review the Commandments before each meeting, or e-mail them to everybody in advance. That way, if you do have to point out that somebody's hogging the floor, you can turn it into a bit of fun. "Remember the First Commandment?" "Oh yeah! Sorry!"

The evening you introduce the Commandments, you might make them the topic of discussion. Ask for ideas and criticism. Better yet, why not start with an empty slate and ask those present what *they* think would be good conversational ground rules? If they arise from the group, it will never seem they are being imposed *on* the group. In fact, the whole thing can become a striking illustration of the pragmatic character of moral and civil rules: just enough regulation to facilitate maximum individual self-expression without stepping on the other person's right to do the same. To paraphrase Pink Floyd, "We don't need no revelation."

Day Nineteen

Point to Ponder: Don't hesitate to request clarification; if you're mystified, chances are most others present are, too.

Quote to Remember: "No one is wrong. At most someone is uninformed. If I think a man is wrong, either I am unaware, or he is. So unless I want to play a superiority game I had best find out what he is looking at." (Hugh Prather, *Notes to Myself*)

Question to Consider: So *what* if I make a fool of myself?

Healing Religious Divisions

He drew a circle that shut me out—
Heretic, rebel, a thing to flout.
But Love and I had the wit to win:
We drew a circle that took him in!
—Edwin Markham, "Outwitted"

NO SINNERS NEED APPLY

Have you ever noticed the contradiction between Matthew 9:10–13 and Matthew 18:15–17?

> And as he sat at the table in the house, behold, many tax collectors and sinners came down and sat with Jesus and his disciples. And when the Pharisees saw this, they said to his disciples, "Why does he eat with tax collectors and sinners?" But when he heard it, he said, "Those who are well have no need of a physician, but those who are sick. Go and learn what this means, 'I desire mercy, and not sacrifice.' For I came not to call righteous but sinners." (Matthew 9:10–13, RSV)

> "If your brother sins against you, go and tell him his fault, between you and him alone. If he listens to you, you have gained your brother. But if he does not listen take one or two others along with you, that every word may be confirmed by the evidence of two or three witnesses. If he refuses to listen to them, tell it to the church; and if he refuses to listen even to the church, let him be to you as a Gentile or a tax collector." (Matthew 18:15–17, RSV)

In the first one, Jesus scandalizes the religious authorities by associating with the "wrong people." They were, first, the despised tax collectors (Jewish "scalawags" who worked for the Roman occupation) and, second, the "sinners" (common people indifferent to the piety of the devout Pharisees). Jesus defends his actions by pointing out it is better to befriend these people. It is better to get close enough to influence them for good than to boycott them. Why despise them for the sinfulness you refuse to help them escape? But in the second passage, he is shown taking for granted precisely the policy of the blue-nosed Pharisees! He urges that a coreligionist who will not admit he is in the wrong should be shunned just like the tax collectors and sinners. Huh? Aren't they the ones Jesus made a point of *not* shunning? Talk about "What would Jesus do?"

Well, it's pretty clear what has happened: the first passage describes the freedom Jesus had as a maverick prophet who cared nothing for the biases of an entrenched institution. The second passage ascribes to Jesus (falsely, no doubt) the hard-heartedness of an entrenched institution. Between the two, the Christian church has been founded (Matthew 16:18), and Jesus has been made into the mouthpiece for the very same hard-line policies he once happily flouted. He himself had been pleased to associate with the outsiders. But those who built an institution with his name on it built a new wall to keep a proper distance between the outsiders and the new in-group. Reverend Warren is speaking not for Jesus the outsider, but for Jesus the institutional figurehead when he quotes Matthew 18:15–17 as a guide for congregational discipline.[1] It's not that he doesn't have a point about what to do in extreme cases of discipline, as we'll see in the next chapter. I just want to point out the irony of his "us versus them" posture.

In his twentieth meditation, Reverend Warren devotes space to some tips for keeping relationships healthy within the church, that is, among the believers, isolated from the big bad world of sinners outside. He doesn't want the temple of born-again Christians to become a den of thieves no better than the devil's scorched earth outside. I chafe at this disdainful view of nonfundamentalists, as if you couldn't tell. I remember quite specifically when I stopped seeing things the way he does.

Nearly thirty years ago I was in the last stages of my evangelicalism while attending Gordon-Conwell Theological Seminary. A few of us had taken the train down into Cambridge, Massachussetts, to hear liberal theologian Harvey Cox. We were having supper in some café, filled with students pretty much like ourselves. They were talking animatedly about interesting things, books on the tables, having a good time. I had for years been used to regarding any such public crowd as a population of sinners who needed me to convey the gospel to them. It had been as if a translucent wall had separated us from "them," the worldly crowd. Don't get me wrong: I had viewed them with concern, not hatred, but the effect was still fundamentally divisive. It was almost as if they were a different species: poor mortals with nothing to live for and no hope of heaven.

Well, on this particular autumn night, in the eyes of my imagination that wall suddenly fell down. All of us were all of a sudden just people! People with problems, sure. But also people with potential, all the more lovable for our flaws. People more authentic for not denying our shortcomings for the sake of a party-line claim of redemption and sanctification. I can only tell you that, from that moment on, every subway ride I took, every lunch in a pizza joint or a deli I enjoyed, was a wide-eyed thrill of discovery. I was living in a new world, surrounded by fascinating people, people who were *just people*. They were neither the "unsaved" nor members of some elect superrace such as I had thought for many years that I belonged to.

But here's an irony! From there on in, the temptation was to keep the "us versus them" attitude, but merely switch sides. I found myself resentful for having been taken for a ride by well-meaning zealots. I guess that was inevitable. Still, I tried to guard against seeing my former compatriots as my new opponents. I remembered to be grateful for the many good things my born-again experience (all dozen years of it) had given me. Above all, I sought to engage born-again people as genuine friends, whether they were my old compatriots or new ones I'd met. *I didn't want to build a new wall.* It would have been pathetic to view fundamentalists as the "unsaved" from my new perspective. I felt—and still believe—the goal ought to be to minimize the interpersonal divisions, not just *within* one's narrow sectarian confines (whether those of religion, nonreligion, or antireligion), but *between* those warring camps as well. I want to come to the place where I can agree to disagree with people and not to regard them as the enemy. So in this chapter I want to offer some suggestions as to how you might try the same thing with the zealous believers in your life.

CALLING A CEASE-FIRE

First off, with your fundamentalist relatives, acquaintances, friends, whatever, you need to resign yourself to the fact that their beliefs have become absolutely central to them. You and I may bemoan that centrality. We may think it has, in a sense, lobotomized them, giving them a false sense of direction and assurance, and at much too great a price. But let's keep this opinion to ourselves, shall we? We'll just have to get over it.

Another important fact to keep in mind is that their opinions about God, and the like, are not intellectual *in origin*, though they are intellectual *in character*. The fundamentalist believes what he believes because of a prior decision to join a community that accepts him, not because he has simply changed his mind on some theoretical issues regarding the Bible. But this fact remains strangely hidden from him. As soon as he learns of apologetical rationalizations buttressing faith, he starts to profess these as the reasons for his belief (because he has been implicitly coached to do so). This contradiction accounts for how frustrating it is to argue with our fundamentalist friends intellectually. They are quite intelligent, but they employ that intelligence in *rationalization*, defending at any cost a set of beliefs they hold for emotional reasons. You will never get anywhere with intellectual arguments. But if you understand the emotional origin of their faith, you are granted a wide window into understanding their faith. If you feel you should try to prompt them to rethink their commitment, then the way to do it might be to show them that the (imagined or real) benefits of their faith are readily available elsewhere and without such a price tag.

In saying "*if* you want to prompt a reevaluation," I imply that you might *not* want to disabuse a born-again Christian of his or her faith.

Right, because it might be that it is the only thing keeping the person going. Once an emotionally fragile fundamentalist friend announced that he had decided I was right and he was wrong. What had brought him to this point? He said, "I ran out of bullshit." But I was afraid for him! I didn't know what he might do without the old security blanket. So I said, "Now, let's not be hasty!" and went on to discuss his problems with him. I figured that the day might come for him to reassess his beliefs, but that this probably wasn't it.

TURNING THE TABLES

If you are to get anywhere restoring normal friendly relations between you and a born-again Christian, you are going to have to devise ways of defying his stereotypes, bucking her expectations of you. How? As you know, fundamentalists are given a straw-man picture of unbelievers. We are dupes of Satan. Our objections to their beliefs are merely moral smoke screens to avoid having to admit the truth of their ("the") gospel and repent. We must hate the Bible as much as the born-again Christian loves it. If we are religious, it must be a self-deceived condition of moral complacency. We must be self-satisfied and trusting in our own good works to deserve salvation. They somehow imagine that they need to "tell us about Jesus," as if fundamentalists had something new to say. As if many of us had not choked on that same stale bread years ago. Well, I for one refuse to play the role in which they have cast me in their little play. I am determined not to be their enemy but to become their friend.

I want to knock them off balance by showing them that I know the nature of evangelical faith inside and out and that I have reasons for turning from it. They usually don't know what to do with that. It never occurs to them that such a thing might be! What reasons other than willful backsliding, tiring of the straight and narrow path, could one have for exiting fundamentalism? Tell them. And do so in a sincere tone of concern. Let *them* be the object of therapeutic concern for once.

I try to show (if I am in an academic context) that I, the critical scholar, am the true champion of the Bible, not the fundamentalist with his straitjacketed, gagged Bible that speaks with all the spontaneity of a hostage. Like him, I seek to unravel the puzzles of the Bible, and, unlike the literalist, my methods work. I can explain why it says one thing in one passage and the opposite in another. I can solve the puzzles.

But this approach, though enlightening, also happens to make fundamentalism impossible. The more you understand scripture, the less amenable it is to fundamentalism. And this forces the question: what is it born-again Christians really want? Membership in a familiar sect? Or getting the Bible right? I suspect, as I have said, that it is the former, but they claim it is the latter. They only want to be biblical. In other words, they have convinced themselves their belief is paramountly an intellectual matter. Well, maybe I can help them see for the first time how they have sliced the pie wrong. Do you love the Bible? So do I! Welcome to the Higher Criticism! You won't have to wait till you get to heaven to find all those answers.

I want to make fundamentalists see that they are defaming and blaspheming God by crowning him the Lord of Damnation. I urge them to stop spreading the slander that God is planning to torment most of his hapless creatures in an eternal hell. Don't get holier-than-thou with *me*, if *this* is what you are preaching. It is *you* who need to repent, Hellmonger, not me! It is you who are blaspheming the Spirit by calling all other religions false, not me, buster! born-again Christians need to have the shoe placed on the other foot, where in fact it belongs. I don't believe many of them are used to treatment like this, and it may surprise them into rethinking things.

FRIENDLY PERSUASION

Born-again Christians are often urged to witness to their acquaintances by means of "friendship evangelism." This is a tricky matter. I am not saying one could not engage in such a strategy with sincerity, but I'd be surprised. It seems to me it is essentially a manipulative ploy. I remember some years ago, after I had dropped evangelicalism,

I became friends with a strong creationist. We knew each other's opinions well and even debated them in a friendly way. He was a funny guy, unassuming, fun to be around: in short, a natural friend. But as I began sharing with him my various youthful anxieties, such as dating, careers, and so forth, and asking him of his experiences, I suddenly found he had little to say, as if he weren't really interested in a deepening friendship. I began to suspect that he felt reluctant to open up to a "non-Christian." I dared ask him in a letter once if I were misreading him: was he possibly feigning a greater friendship than he felt, just to get me "saved"? I hoped not, I said, and if he were, it would certainly be disappointing. I heard nothing else from him. Not until a few years later, when he, too, had come to see the errors of fundamentalism and creationism. And then our friendship was back on track. I'm glad to have him back, but I wasn't the one who was playing some game.

MR. FUNDAMENTALIST, TEAR DOWN THIS WALL!

So I'm suggesting my own brand of "friendship evangelism." That is, to win back your friend whose dogmatic stance has alienated you, just determine to approach her in friendship and win her back *as a friend*. Don't let her shut the door in your face just because you don't accept her faith. I'm not prescribing this strategy for someone you don't know. That would be phony. I'm saying it might repair a bridge that used to connect the two of you, but that her faith has demolished. She drew the circle narrow, to exclude you. Now you draw one around the both of you.

It may be that your once-estranged friend or relative may come to the same crossroads I did that night in Cambridge. The wall may fall, once he or she sees how cruel and arbitrary it was. This may lead to your friend's rethinking everything. But then that's not the real goal, is it? We just want to mend the severed ties of friendship, not to deconvert the "heathen" who doesn't share our opinions.

I bet you still have common interests or shared opinions about some matters. Why don't you avoid religion and discuss the other stuff instead? A "saved" relative and I never get too far talking about theology, so I try to avoid it. But we have a great time trading jokes about the political party we both oppose!

Another possibility for easing tensions is to propose a common service project that does not involve faith differences. I have noticed at town clergy association meetings how representatives of the most widely different beliefs will set them aside to roll up their sleeves on a common project for social improvement. The same thing will surely happen if you and your born-again friend can work together on some volunteer project. You will share the innocent joy of helping people, and your friend will see that to do so does not require a specific faith.

Or, if you *can* civilly discuss matters of religion, why don't you open up a dialogue with the other person? Trade books and promise to seriously consider the book the other offers. Then discuss what you can agree with, and what you can't, and why. The other will see that you have taken his beliefs seriously and that you have honest reasons for declining them where you feel you have to. Dialogue is not second best to agreement. No, the only important thing is *getting along* with each other, not sharing particular beliefs and opinions. Because, as we will consider in the next chapter, sharing beliefs is no guarantee at all of being able to get along!

Day Twenty

Point to Ponder: It's more important to have good relations than to have shared beliefs.

Quote to Remember: "Only Nixon could go to China." (Old Vulcan Proverb)

Question to Consider: Do you want to win an argument? Or do you want to win a friend?

NOTE

1. Rick Warren, *The Purpose-Driven Life: What on Earth Am I Here For?* (Grand Rapids, MI: Zondervan, 2002), p. 165.

Damage Control

Faith allows the greatest latitude in philosophic speculation, allowing us without blame to think what we like about anything, and only condemning, as heretics and schismatics, those who teach opinions which tend to produce obstinacy, hatred, strife, and anger; while, on the other hand, only considering as faithful those who persuade us, as far as their reason and faculties will permit, to follow justice and charity.

—Baruch Spinoza, *A Theologico-Political Treatise*

WHAT'S SO GREAT ABOUT UNITY?

I can't remember when it was that stopped thinking what a shame it was for Christianity to have divided up into thousands of different sects and denominations. One still often reads that such a condition is an abomination and a living reproach to the Christian community whose hallmark is supposed to be love.

I don't see that at all. As Ernst Käsemann once argued, the diversity of thought and conviction among the New Testament writers is surely responsible for the analogous diversity among the churches who appeal to the New Testament.[1] If most Protestants explain their indifference to Sabbath observance by appeal to passages like Colossians 12:16 ("No one is to act as your judge in regard to food or drink or in respect to a festival or a new moon or a Sabbath day." NASB), Seventh-Day Adventists can with equal justification cite Matthew 5:18–19 ("Truly I say to you, until heaven and earth pass away, not the smallest letter or stroke shall pass from the Law until all is accomplished. Whoever then annuls one of the least of these commandments, and teaches others to do the same, shall be called least in the kingdom of heaven; but whoever keeps and teaches them, he shall be called great in the kingdom of heaven." NASB). Still other issues involve complexities that the Bible just does not address, so what wonder is it that well-meaning Christians over the centuries have set-tled them in different ways? Such issues include the organization of church government, the manner in which sacraments are to be observed, if at all, and a thousand other things. What is scandalous about different groups of Christians hanging out their separate shin-gles to denote that they behave and believe in their own distinctive ways? It's not as if they'd all fit under the same roof otherwise!

No, surely the scandalous thing is the acrimony and ill will that have accompanied such divisions. That leads one to ask: why were the splits so bitter? I think the answer is the very assumption that there is something wrong with schism, splitting, diversity. There is an implicit totalitarian conformism in the historic Catholic tradition, and when the Protestant movements emerged from it, they carried that DNA with them. The result is the otherwise gratuitous assumption that dif-ference is a bad thing. Thus an impending split seemed ipso facto like a crime or a tragedy.

FROM MACROCOSM TO MICROCOSM

The sort of disunity from which Rick Warren wishes to safeguard the church has less to do with theological or liturgical differences, over which even he, presumably, does not lose much sleep. No, it is a matter of group dynamics, or "life together," to use (as Warren does) Dietrich Bonhoeffer's almost copyrighted phrase. Pastor Warren has much wisdom to share on this topic, applicable whether one is a Christian or not, religious or not. People are people, and in any group, many of the same issues are going to occur, and with the same dangers. Let me illustrate one of these perennial issues with a sur-prising anecdote I heard during my college days.

I was talking to my pal Kevin, then the vice president of the Montclair State College Student Government Association, a great guy, and as Pentecostal as the day is long, even in Daylight Savings Time. I mean, this guy would not go to the doctor, believing that "Doctor Jesus" would cure what ailed him. Pentecostalism to him was very serious business. He attended R. W. Schambach's Miracle

Temple in Newark, New Jersey, a bastion of militant, even slightly weird, Pentecostalism. Now imagine my astonishment when Kevin commented one day that he did not believe in the charismatic gift of prophecy. Huh? How could that be? He spoke in tongues (though not during Student Government meetings) and accepted pretty much the whole party line. Why no prophecy? Well, as he explained it, he had seen lone wolf "prophets" drop in at Miracle Temple once too often, claiming that God had sent them to take control of the church! Thus saith the Lord. The old "prophetic ramrod," as I like to call it. Kevin had faith sufficient to move mountains, but he wasn't born yesterday. And he recognized that a belief in prophetic authority leaves any church open to chicanery and the worst abuses. He had learned a lesson that second-century Christianity had similarly learned the hard way, which is why it retreated from charismatic to institutional authority.

But surely the battle of prophets in Miracle Temple cannot be paradigmatic for conflicts outside such a parochial context? Yes it can. It is merely drawn in more vivid colors. The same issue arises when a new member of your group pops up with some new idea, plan, or project that the group is not too keen on. It may be a good idea, but too much of a stretch for the group as it is currently constituted. It might involve more of a shake-up than people are comfortable with. Essentially the new, enthusiastic person wants to set the agenda for the whole group, and he cannot understand when they do not share his enthusiasm. Well, of course, it's no mystery. He or she is new to the group and shares no past with them, thus cherishes none. The new enthusiast has only the future to consider. It is not a question of identity for him as it is for everyone else. So ill will erupts. The zealot cannot help seeing the group and its leaders as mossbacks afraid to risk anything new. He becomes impatient and disgusted. The group, thrilled to see his enthusiasm, will probably wish he would stay and channel such enthusiasm into already-established programs and such. But he will not. He is off to try another group, or to start his own.

The hothead cannot really be blamed for failing to see what is naturally invisible to him. All he can see is an apparent attempt to co-opt his energy and ability for the maintenance of the precious status quo.

And it's probably going to happen with every group he seeks out to share his vision. So what will eventually happen? He will end up starting his own new group. And that ain't bad! He should have seen from the first that this would be the needful outcome. But it's hard to leap out of the nest to fly by oneself. And it may not work. But if it does, we have a new sect or group, sacred or secular, alongside all the other ones. It will have something new to offer. It will appeal to a new "market niche" of people whose needs hadn't been satisfied by any older option.

This development need not be acrimonious, though it usually is. I guess I am saying that there might be less tension and ill will if both sides saw earlier on what is really going on: the coming to birth of a new thing. I noticed this the very first time I attended the Jesus Seminar. I was sitting at a booth in Santa Rosa's Roundtable Pizza (one of many stops there over the years), and I was reading Earl Morse Wilbur's *History of Unitarianism*, the part about how Miguel Servetus pestered Martin Bucer, Calvin, and other Reformers[2] until it became clear he had no place in their movements and would have to move out on his own, do his own thing. I remember looking up from the page and thinking how, as much as I loved the Jesus Seminar and the wonderful colleagues in it, sooner or later I should have to promote a more radical approach of my own. Soon thereafter I founded the *Journal of Higher Criticism* and the Institute for Higher-Critical Studies. I've taken a different direction. There was no reason for me to insist they derail their operation, based on the founder's own vision, to follow mine. No, then I should have been like Kevin's sheep-stealing prophet at Miracle Temple.

If the leadership of a group could see the implicit potential of an enthusiastic new member proposing new directions they don't want to pursue, I can imagine not only an amicable parting of the ways, but even a positive affirmation of the new zealot. The group might help him see his own mission in a way he had not so far thought of. And then we would not only have headed off a nasty tiff; we would have also midwifed something new and good into the world.

THE PINK SLIP

We have a mirror-opposite situation when some new, talented person enters the group and shows herself able to do a better job at some task than the person who is already doing it. It is bad to stifle the new member's exercise of her talents for the benefit of the group. Your group exists, at least partly, to be a place where individuals can let their potential blossom. And your group might really need superior expertise, let's say in advertising or Web site maintenance. The group might have a more effective outreach if you gave the job to the new member. But, as you know, such a move will mortally alienate the one already doing the job. He will surely quit the group in a huff. You would, too. But suppose the new one volunteers, and you explain you won't accept her help because you don't want to offend the one already doing it. Well, now you're stuck! Which one do you mind offending less? You'll be lucky finding something else for either person to do, something that is not superfluous busywork, which would obviously be just an attempt to smooth ruffled feathers.

Let's just take the Web site example. Suppose you can see that the new person's work would make the site look much more professional. And that would, presumably, increase the attractiveness of your group to outsiders. As a leader of the group, you're now stuck with deciding which way the group should go. Is it an organic family of acquaintances with whose randomly distributed talents you will do the best you can? In that case, the mediocre Web site efforts may send exactly the message you want: we're a mom-and-pop operation, not Mega-lo-Mart. Or do you think there is no excuse for not having the highest degree of professionalism you can get in this day and age, where people expect the slickest productions? I don't know which way to go. I had a humanist group in this situation once, and when one of our founding members began criticizing the Web mistress, another founding member, she got her back up and left. But the site started vastly improving. Was it an even exchange? Maybe so. I don't know.

I think it ultimately comes down to this: what is more important to you? The group as a collection of friends? Or the imagined "mission" of the group? If it is the former, then you may want to just do as well as you can with the resources you have in-house. If the mission is paramount, individuals must be sacrificed to it if someone new seems able to do a job better. I love the TV show *King of the Hill*, and I can't help thinking of the episode ("Peggy's Pageant Fever") in which Peggy Hill, with typical delusions of grandeur, enters the "Mrs. Heimlich County" beauty contest. At first, her beautician is her niece, Luanne. But as she gets closer to the pageant, she realizes she is going to require a transformation far beyond Luanne's amateur abilities, so she fires her in favor of a professional. Peggy tries in vain to reassure Luanne that she will still be "an important part of Team Peggy Hill," but Luanne sees through it. Luanne is pretty stupid, but not quite that stupid. And neither will be a member of your group, when you ask him or her to step aside.

Perhaps there is something to be said for the "half-baked but authentic" option. Last night I saw a TV ad for some local church congregation that they must have paid a bundle for. My first thought was that the real message being conveyed was not "C'mon in! We're the friendly church!" but rather "C'mon in! We're the church with the biggest advertising budget!" Is that the kind you'd feel comfortable in? I mean, pushy evangelism is bad enough, but maybe flat-out marketing is even worse.

In the end, I feel that a freethought group, like a church congregation, is more of a family that exists as a matrix for the common life of its members, and that it needs no further "purpose" to justify its existence. There may be all sorts of reasons to adopt a group mission, but I hope it is not merely a distraction from the vapid state of group-life, like the 1980s Iran-Iraq War, which Iran used to keep its citizens' minds off what a mess the mullahs had made of the country.

EXCOMMUNICATION AS EXORCISM

There are a number of intragroup pitfalls that really boil down to interpersonal situations. If things get weird between two people in the group there will be an element of tension, at least between them, as long as both continue to attend the group. The worst-case scenario might be dating within the group. Once it goes bad, one or the other is likely to leave since they'll feel sheepish or bitter or frustrated seeing the other at meetings. But I don't see how the leadership of the group has anything to say on that score.

Suppose there is someone whose behavior irritates the entire group: such a person is poison to the group. If he or she is really annoying, and nothing is done, you can expect more and more people to stop attending. The meetings will have become more of an unpleasant experience than a pleasant one. I had been asked to speak two Sundays in a row at an Ethical Culture group in a nearby town. Carol and I liked the atmosphere of the group. But both times one particular gent latched on to me and would not stop with the political rant that was near and dear to his heart. I knew right then and there I would never attend the meetings again because there would be no way to avoid this guy and his endless, albeit friendly, harangues. It just wouldn't be worth the trouble. I wonder how many other visitors had been turned away by this self-appointed welcoming committee. Nice guy, but tiring, and after only one visit I was already way too tired of him.

That was a pretty easy decision to make. It was much harder in our own group. Following a local debate between myself and an evangelical writer, I had met a bright fellow who professed himself interested in any other events I might be offering in the area. I mentioned our Sunday morning group, the Grail, and our Friday evening group, Heretics Anonymous. He became one of the most regular attendees. He was very, very intelligent as well as learned. He liked our topics and had many other questions for me. But he was completely oblivious, a social misfit with no sense of decorum. Someone else would be asking me something, and this guy would butt right in with his own question. He would derail conversations and bring up arcane questions of interest to him and to me but hardly appropriate for the whole group. After the meetings, he would make a beeline for me and talk, talk, talk. And then he wouldn't leave! There were one or two others with similar problems, including one who acted even worse, but because he had more than an hour's drive to come to the meeting, he seldom attended, fortunately. Or think back to that charismatic woman who single-handedly destroyed our group in North Carolina.

But I guess it wasn't really single-handed. We helped her by not having the guts to *do* something. We should have taken her aside and leveled with her. "Look, Pat, we know you have our best interests at heart. But you're hijacking the conversation, and people resent it. We have to ask you not to come if you're not going to stick to the topic, okay?" I don't know why we didn't. But it might not have worked, anyway. Later, as a church pastor and as ringleader of our Heretics groups, I had two or three times accepted the role of hatchet-man to go talk with troublesome individuals. It virtually never worked. Personally, I hate and dread confrontation. At length I did issue a rebuke to one fellow. I spoke to him and e-mailed him a couple of times. It seems such admonitions were nothing new to him. He was used to them, but eventually it seemed like he did improve somewhat.

It might be better to have the whole group confront such a person, an "intervention," as some call it. That way, everything's out on the table. Even if one person goes to talk to him, it will be evident that the whole group thinks he's being a jerk. Why not have them all say so—in so many words—to his face? After all, it's everyone's problem, and if the whole group confronts him with concern, telling him that they want to find a way they can all continue together, then what might have been a horrible humiliation may end amazingly well, as an affirmation of loving concern.

But even if your troublesome member does find it terminally humiliating and leaves in a huff, what the hey? Consider it a matter of triage! Ruffling one guy's feathers is better than allowing him to slowly destroy the group. Just find out if he's a loner and a gun enthusiast first!

GIVE ME YOUR TIRED, YOUR POOR, THE WRETCHED REFUSE

Seriously, though: it seems the same problems occur in all small groups. Churches or freethought groups, herpetology clubs or science fiction geeks, we are susceptible to eccentric members, and we have to deal with them. I wonder if sports teams, garden clubs, and bridge players are as worried about "space cadets" as we are. Members of our groups often flatter themselves that they have a hard time acting in concert because "it's like trying to herd cats." Sometimes I think "herding skunks" might be more to the point, to tell you the truth. Why do we get more than our fair share of prima donnas, tin gods, know-it-alls, and geeks? Actually, it's pretty simple in principle. Any way you cut it, all of our groups are made of marginalized people, folks who feel some need beyond those met by television, shopping malls, and football games. Just as born-again Christians speak of the church versus "the world," so do science fiction fans refer to nonfans as "mundanes." It is a syndrome: if you hanker for the transcendent, you may be more "heavenly minded" than earthly good. And the same holds true if your mind is in the Matrix or aboard the Starship Enterprise—or the Kingdom of God. All have the same, analogous place in the imagination. The things of the "real" world pale in interest beside the more colorful worlds in which the imagination dwells. By this I do not mean to reduce all these "nonmundane" realms and concerns to the same level of facticity or importance. It's just that preoccupation with "alternate realities" (is that neutral enough?) can result in the person being ill prepared for and ill at ease with the public world. Such a person is likely to be a nerd, oblivious of social niceties. Scientists are often the same way. I am not criticizing anyone; people just are what they are.

Remember, eccentrics and geeks are sometimes geniuses. Their spiritual and intellectual gifts may be great and their creative talents may be impressive. And though it may be difficult to have them in your group, they will still add value and diversity and thus it will be worthwhile to make extra efforts for them. If they can't fit in with us, where *can* they go? And if they are made to feel unwelcome, I have a hunch it is we who may be the poorer for it. It is, after all, always easier to get along if there are no challenges in one's path.

Day Twenty-one

Point to Ponder: It is easy to disguise cowardice as forbearance.

Quote to Remember: "Drive out the scoffer, and contention will go out." (Proverbs 22:10, NASB)

Question to Consider: How do I know whether I ought to consider a troublesome member more like the demoniac in the Capernaum synagogue (Mark 1:23–26), to be expelled, or more like the Lost Sheep (Matthew 18:12–13), to be pursued and persuaded?

NOTES

1. Ernst Käsemann, "The Canon of the New Testament and the Unity of the Church," in *Essays on New Testament Themes*, Studies in Biblical Theology 41, trans. W. J. Montague (London: SCM Press, 1964), pp. 95–107.

2. Earl Morse Wilbur, *A History of Unitarianism: Socinianism and Its Antecedents* (Cambridge, MA: Harvard University Press, 1947), pp. 63–67, 132–37.

The Character of Christ

Every man partakes of the divine nature in both his spirit and his flesh. That is why the mystery of Christ is not simply a mystery for a particular creed: it is universal.
—Nikos Kazantzakis, *The Last Temptation of Christ*

THE WORD MADE FLESH

Pastor Warren reiterates what classical Christian theology says, that Jesus Christ is the ideal for humanity. This is what is implied in all the talk about him being the heavenly Adam. Not the way humans actually are, but the way they were meant to be. Human character unsullied by the Fall, untainted by sin. But I wonder if it is not the other way around, if "Jesus Christ" does not represent a historical personage so much as an artificial portrait of ideal virtue. I suspect that "Jesus Christ" is largely an abstraction given apparent human warmth and vitality by becoming a literary character. In this sense he was indeed "the Word made flesh." He is the human moral ideal by virtue of the fact that Christians have externalized their best traits, their own moral perfections, so they could gain a better perspective on them. Sure, they could draw up lists of virtues, such as the famous "fruits of the Spirit" list in Galatians 5:22–23. But to create a fictional character who would manifest these traits in action would be much more powerful.

Nor do we need to limit this way of interpreting the "Jesus Christ" character to the vivid stories about him. We can understand the more theoretical, doctrinal statements about him in the same manner. Here, in broad outline, is Immanuel Kant's own reconstruction of Christology and soteriology on a moral basis.[1]

The "Son of God" is the archetypal idea of *righteous humanity*. In fact, humans are radically evil; even when they do the right thing, it is

209

for the wrong reasons. But we *could* be godlike in moral holiness. The fact that this human idea/ideal exists in the conscience of even evil humans is, so to speak, the Son of God descending from heaven into our midst, into the likeness of sinful flesh. Since we know we *ought* to be living up to this moral ideal, it must be possible for us to do so—else why should we feel guilty for not being this way? Salvation will assist in doing so. The historical Jesus would have been an individual who *did* incarnate this "Word" or Son of God, the moral ideal of humanity.

But what about his death for sin, and his resurrection? For Kant it is moral symbolism. It refers to an individual's *repentance*. Paul speaks of repentance as a crucifying of the flesh, a putting to death of the "old man" and a resurrection of the "new man." When we repent, our old self dies, and our new self rises (or is born).

What do we mean when we say "the Son of God bore our sins"? Remember, the "Son of God" is the morally ideal persona, the reformed you. Now, you must really have already become the new you to have been able to repent in the first place. Repentance, paradoxically, is a righteous act. A real sinner wouldn't be sorry. As long as you remain a sinner, you do not repent. You repent only once you have turned about to become righteous. The one who sheds tears of remorse is none other than the Son of God bearing the sins and sorrows of the old man. So you are already the "Son of God" (a person conforming to the moral ideal) when you bear the bitter sorrows of repentance. Both are aspects of the same individual. It is symbolically represented in the gospels as the story of Jesus, the supernatural Son of God, bearing sin as the representative of humanity.

JESUS VERSUS JESUS

Rick Warren summons us to strive after "Christlike character" in all that we do. That sounds good, but let us not jump the gun. Exactly what sort of a character standard should we associate with the name of Jesus Christ? I have already said I think the early Christians molded an image of Christ to embody their highest moral ideals. The model thus created facilitated Christian living. It made it possible to ask one-self, "What would Jesus do?" But who did this? Who composed this Christ? I believe that in many if not most cases the stories and sayings of Jesus in the gospels are really based on the prototypes of wandering Christian apostles and prophets in the early church. Their deeds and words have been attributed to the Lord Jesus in whose name they acted and spoke. And eventually the line between them and the Son of man whom they claimed to represent has become completely blurred.

So as likely as not, a saying attributed to Jesus was originally the utterance of someone else "channeling" the Risen Christ. A prophecy, in other words. When the gospel text says, "Jesus said . . ." I view it as equivalent to when the Old Testament text has Jeremiah or Isaiah begin an oracle, "Thus says the Lord . . ." The prophets did not always agree. If you asked one prophet speaking in Jesus's name what he thought it meant to behave in a "Christlike way," he might give you a very different answer than the last prophet you had asked. I think it will be illuminating to look briefly at two rather different sayings ascribed to Jesus.

The first of the sayings occurs in Mark 9:40, "John said to him, 'Teacher, we saw someone casting out demons in your name, and we tried to prevent him because he was not following us.' But Jesus said, 'Do not hinder him; for there is no one who will perform a miracle in my name, and be able soon after to speak evil of me. For he who is not against us is for us" (Mark 9:38–40, NASB).

But over in Luke 11:23, Jesus is rebutting charges that he casts out demons only as a show, that in fact he is a magician in league with the devil. "He who is not with me is against me, and he who does not gather with me, scatters" (NASB), says Jesus.

Which way is it? Are you counted as being on Jesus's side if you do not actively oppose and reject him? That seems to be the implica-tion of Mark. Or is it as Luke has it? That if you do not "stand up, stand up for Jesus," you are implicitly and unwittingly leaguing your-self against him? What sense can we make of these warring sayings? On one level, the solution is simple: the two sayings stem from two rival Jesus-prophets who differed as much as Jeremiah and his opposite number Hananiah had in the sixth century BCE (see Jeremiah chapter 28). Both posed as spokesmen for Jehovah, but their messages were diametrically opposed. Now we have two opposed Jesus-prophets similarly deadlocked. We have dueling Jesuses, and we must decide which, if either, we will serve.

Once I heard Hans Küng give a lecture in which he effectively proof-texted Jesus as being firmly in his corner, painting him as pretty much a situational ethicist and a humanist. His Jesus was much like Dostoyevsky's Jesus. As he spoke, I thought that, though Küng didn't have to twist any texts to get the result he wanted, he had ignored a very different set of texts where the gospels depict Jesus in a very different light.

Did Jesus tell us that human need takes precedence over the Sabbath rules? Yes, but then there is that text in which he crushes women beneath the mailed fist of the divorce prohibition. Does he welcome despised Samaritans? In Luke and John, yes. But in Matthew he tells his missionaries not to set foot in Samaria. Was he a precursor of feminism? Then why no women among the Twelve? You get the picture. We must decide which Jesus we are going to follow, because they are legion. Hans Küng had decided which Jesus he was going to follow.

Listen to the utterances of the two Jesuses. Each seems to say that there is no neutrality. Only the one Jesus excludes all who are not explicitly committed to him, his name, his cause. "Whoever is not with me is against me." Do you see what has happened here? Why is it not enough simply to agree with the moral agenda or the religious principles of Jesus? Most Pharisees probably did!

Why do the Pharisees come in for such a pasting in the gospels? Because they committed the one unforgivable sin in the eyes of this Jesus and those who created him: they did not believe in Jesus himself as being more important than his principles, his teachings. For Christians it no longer mattered what Jesus said so much as that it was he, the Son of God, the Christ, the Superstar, who had said it. As Judas says in *Jesus Christ Superstar*, "You've begun to matter more than the things you say."

Suppose you heard Jesus denounce hypocrisy and uphold unconditional love, the Fatherhood of God, and the infinite value of the human soul, and this you accepted whole-heartedly. But then someone asked you whether you thought Jesus of Nazareth was the promised Messiah. That's a rather different matter, isn't it? How could you form an opinion? Why should you have to? And if you did, what would it add to what you had learned from Jesus?

What is attributed to Jesus in Luke is a kind of summons to discipleship. Like that earlier Jesus, the Joshua of the Old Testament, this one is throwing down the gauntlet: Choose! Not to decide is to decide! Not to decide for me is to decide against me!

I'm sorry, but I don't buy it. Have you ever heard the joke "I wouldn't want to join any club that would have someone like me as a member"? Well, sorry, Jesus Number One: I wouldn't want to join a group that would only attract me if I were a religious bigot. If the price of joining the club is to condemn all nonmembers to hell, I don't think that's the kind of club I want to join.

CEASE AND DESIST

So, ironically, it is the very summons to join up that repels me from the group! Now what about Jesus Number Two? The Jesus of Mark 9 makes no summons for anyone to join. Instead he asks the shepherd to go retrieve the lone lamb that John had driven forth from the flock. This is interesting to me: John tells Jesus that the unknown exorcist had not been following Jesus and the disciples. So to John he seemed to be poaching, violating the disciples' copyright on the name of Jesus. It is obvious that John considered the man a nonmember. But it is equally apparent that the exorcist did not think himself a member either. He seems to have accepted John's right to forbid him. For him the name Jesus simply seemed a powerful incantation for use in his profession. He was exactly like the exorcists in Acts 19 who have appropriated the divine name of Jesus because Paul seems to get results with it. Like a comedian who steals a good joke from a colleague.

Have you ever wondered why John did not rather invite the exorcist to join the group of followers of Jesus? He doesn't even say he asked the man and that the man refused. We might put this down to the motif of the thick-headedness of the disciples, but that will not do. For Jesus does not suggest that the man should have joined up either! And that is the great point: as far as Jesus is concerned, the man does not *need* to join. Since he is doing the work that Jesus does, he is already a member! As the Epistle of James says, "I will show you my faith by my works" (James 2:18, NASB). Jesus has drawn a circle that counts him in. Here is the liberal Jesus, Küng's Jesus, Karl Rahner's Jesus, in whose eyes one may be as Christian as one needs to be even if one's faith is anonymous or wears another name altogether. If he is not against us, he is for us.

From this Jesus we hear no invitation to join up, no summons to decide. No, what we hear is that such an explicit joining is super-fluous, altogether unnecessary. What an irony! This nonsummons, this noninvitation, is far more attractive, much more winsome than the Olympian ultimatum of Jesus Number One! Though he has not required you to join him, this very openness makes you think that maybe it would not be a bad thing to follow this Jesus.

And there is a third Jesus to be heard from. We hear his voice in the book of Revelation. He says, "I know your works: you are neither cold nor hot. Would that you were cold or hot! So, because you are lukewarm, and neither cold nor hot, I will spew you out of my mouth" (Revelation 3:15–16, RSV). Here is an amazing thing! A Jesus who goes even farther, who rejects only the complacent Christian. It is the lukewarm disciple he cannot stomach.

It is no surprise that he would rather have the lukewarm become hot, fervent in commitment. But how can it be that he prefers the cold? Is it perhaps possible that he yields the rejector of Christianity a certain measure of grudging respect? Could it be that he recognizes in the Christ-rejector a seeker after truth? Don't tell me Jerry Falwell is more acceptable to Jesus than Bertrand Russell! If he is, then I will tell you I prefer Bertrand Russell to Jesus.

Suppose one is, suppose you are, a seeker after truth who point-edly does not follow Jesus and his church. Christians may, like John, forbid you because they think Christians have the exclusive copyright on the name of Truth. But no, even if you do not follow with the church, even if relative to Christianity you are cold, perhaps Jesus prefers you, considers you one of his flock. How? Because you invoke the name of Truth, and he answers to that name as well.

Day Twenty-two

Point to Ponder: Jesus is too important to be left to Christians.

Quote to Remember: "Like beauty, perhaps Jesus is in the eye of the beholder." (Harry Reasoner)

Question to Consider: When I ask myself, "What would Jesus do?" am I perhaps doing just what the gospel writers did?

NOTE

1. Immanuel Kant, *Religion within the Limits of Reason Alone*, trans. Theodore M. Greene and Hoyt H. Hutchinson (New York: Harper & Row, 1960), pp. 54–72.

When Is a Religion
Not a Religion?

The attempt to reduce Judaism to a religion is a betrayal of its true nature.
—Milton Steinberg, *The Making of the Modern Jew*

We must reject the assumption that Judaism is, or can be reduced to, a religion only.
—Mordecai M. Kaplan, *Judaism as a Civilization*

It is hardly possible . . . to say whether [Hinduism] is a religion or not, in the usual sense of the word.
—Jawaharlal Nehru, *The Discovery of India*

Buddhism is not a religion in the sense in which religion is commonly understood.
—U Thittila, "The Fundamental Principles of Theravada Buddhism"

Islam is not merely a "religion" in the sense in which this term is understood in the West.
—Said Ramadan, *Islam, Doctrine and Way of Life*

YEAH, THAT'S THE TICKET

Rick Warren deals with other matters in his twenty-third chapter, but I feel obliged to clear the rest away to zero in on his reiteration of the cliché: "Christianity is not a religion or a philosophy, but a relationship and a lifestyle."[1] There is a sense in which this old saw is quite true, but hardly in the sense Reverend Warren imagines. I will even-

216

tually return to this other possible meaning. But first, let's play target practice with his claim.

Any reader of the present volume, unless he never heard of fundamentalism before picking up *The Purpose-Driven Life*, will be quite familiar with the evangelistic slogan, "It's not a religion; it's a relationship," that is, with Jesus Christ, one's personal savior. You know the drill. What you may be surprised to learn is that born-again Christians are by no means the only ones to say this about their faith. I was stunned some years ago to read a collection of similar statements from representatives of several major world religions, compiled by the great comparative religion scholar Wilfred Cantwell Smith.[2] I have reproduced them at the head of this chapter. Of course, what this means is that no one thinks his religion is merely one more cookie from the same cutter. And they are right. Each faith is unique with many treasures and charms to commend it. None is merely "another one of those."

But just because they aren't all the same, that doesn't mean they don't have a great deal in common. We can still draw up an abstract textbook definition that will outline certain common features of those very different entities we call "religions." Nor will this minimize the differences. Once we do formulate such a yardstick, it will help us to measure each religion's unique traits and differences from the other faiths. The result will be that we will understand each one better. For instance, in general a religion would seem to entail dealings with a God or some other analogous superhuman Reality. Most in fact do. But then we run smack dab into Theravada Buddhism or Jainism, neither of which has any such thing. Why on earth not? We do not conclude that the "ideal type" of "religion" does not apply to Theravada Buddhism; rather, we now know to zero in right here and find out why and at what point this religion came to differ so drastically from the others. (And there are good reasons, too elaborate to pursue here.)

Religions in general would seem to possess a diagnosis of some root problem that plagues the human race, whether it be named sin, desire, ignorance, or what have you. And as far as I know, there are no exceptions to this rule. Again, religions would seem to offer communal rituals as well as some kind of individual spiritual exercises. There are exceptions, but they appear to be temporary, as if a vacuum has been created that begs to be filled. For instance, the eleventh-century Druze religion began by wiping away every symbol and outward ritual, proclaiming that henceforth believers would have a direct, unmediated vision of divine Truth. It did not take long for popular piety to fill the gap by creating new symbols and prayers. Jainists at first regarded their saints (jinas) as great heroes and exemplars now at rest in heaven, paying no attention to human beings, who must see to their own enlightenment. But it didn't take long for the laity to supply each one of the saints with a pair of attendant godlings who did answer prayers. You see, it is as if there is a basic anatomy of religion, so that departures from it are very extraordinary or else temporary until nature reasserts itself. If some system of belief possesses these basic traits, one will not be libeling it, to point to it and say, "There is a religion." And in this sense, it would be insane to deny that Christianity is a religion.

When Warren and company claim they are not members of a religion, they might mean simply that "Christianity is not like the rest of the religions, which are man-made shams, while Christianity alone is revealed truth." Then you wouldn't need to deny that Christianity is a religion, any more than you would deny that a Cadillac is a car even if it is the best one. Why go farther, to the point of the apparently nonsensical denial that Christianity is a religion at all? It sounds as silly as it once did for Transcendental Meditation spokesmen to claim their invocations of Vishnu ought not to be deemed a religion when they were teaching it for credit in New Jersey public schools. It sounds as deceptive as when so-called Scientific Creationists insist their Genesis-based antievolutionism is not religious in character. So why make such an outlandish claim?

I think Paul Tillich provides the clue in his essay "The Conquest of the Concept of Religion in the Philosophy of Religion" when he explains how no religion wants to be categorized as "one of the religions," because that way of understanding any particular faith logically relativizes it. Understanding Christianity (or any other faith) as "a religion, one of the religions," means you are no longer allowing Christianity to set its own ground rules for understanding it. You are understanding Christianity in terms derived from elsewhere, if only from the inductive study of several religions, or perhaps from history or philosophy, sociology, or psychology. And indeed the scientific study of religion does and must place Christianity under all these microscopes. It cannot just take orders from Christian theologians, who would rather ignore the fingerprints of their religion's human origin. Like the Tablets of the Law, Christians want their faith to have come straight down from the sky as the handiwork of the Living God. They don't want Christianity to be understood in terms of *something else*. "Just as the concept of religion dissolves the unconditionality of faith into the relativity of the various spiritual functions, so it also dissolves the unconditionality of revelation into the continuous evolution and alteration within the history of religion and culture. 'Religion' as a general concept is indifferent to the revelatory claims of the particular religions." "This is what is involved in the protest that religion raises against the spirit of the concept of religion."[3]

SOUND FAMILIAR?

Ultimately, it's a question of semantics as to whether you want to call your faith a religion. Mainly it hinges on how you define "religion." Well, let's take a look at one of the most persuasive and useful definitions of religion, the model proposed by anthropologist Clifford Geertz in his famous essay "Religion as a Cultural System." Basically Geertz suggests that a religion is a system of symbols that enables any given culture to deal with three perennial challenges: *ignorance, injustice*, and *adversity*. The symbolic (or mythic or theological) system adopted by the culture will cushion these ever-recurring blows. It does this by positing the existence of a larger, invisible dimension outside of and adjacent to our visible world. The idea is that the crises that challenge our worldview get referred to the larger, adjacent, invisible realm, where one may believe they are resolved, though one knows not how.

To take *ignorance* first, it is obvious that religion helps with this one every time we commiserate with a mourning friend and comfort her with the assurance, "We know God had a reason for it!" We are not actually claiming we know what the reason is. It is just more comforting to believe there *is* some reason; at least it's better, most people seem to believe, than admitting the tragedies of life are random blows, like meteorites falling from space. Or think of nagging theological puzzles that, left unanswered, might seem to threaten faith. Contradictions in the Bible, for example. How many times have you heard someone confess he is stumped over an apparent contradiction, with no stopgap harmonization to offer; and then he says, "I suppose we'll just have to wait till we get to heaven to find that out!" Anyone who says this wishes he had an actual solution, but it's second best to assure oneself that one day there will be an answer. It's better than nothing. You see, in all these cases, the supposed answer, though not available here and now, is assumed to exist in an invisible, adjacent dimension, either in heaven or in the future. And that seems to be enough of a shock absorber for most people.

Injustice presents a similar challenge. If a felon evades justice in the here and now, let's say, O. J. Simpson or Ugandan dictator Idi Amin, we might be tempted to wonder if our much-vaunted sense of justice is all a naïve mistake. But that would be a very dangerous conclusion to reach. We might give up striving for justice if we came to believe there was no justice built into the universe. So we posit that there is an unseen extension of this world and that, in that realm, justice will be done, even if we cannot see it. The doctrine of reincarnation is a prime example of such a face-saving rationalization. I love an old Sikh story in which Guru Nanak recruits a new disciple.

> One day the new disciple's neighbor accompanied him to meet the Guru, but on the way stopped instead at a prostitute's house. Thereafter the two would go out together, one to the Guru, the other to his mistress, until one day they decided to test the merits of the radically different habits they were following. The same day the neighbor discovered a pot filled with coal, but containing also a gold coin, whereas the disciple had the misfortune to pierce his foot with a thorn. Guru Nanak explained to them that the neighbor's gift of a gold coin to a sadhu in his previous existence had earned him a pot of gold coins. The disciple, on the other hand, had performed deeds meriting an impaling stake. The neighbor's subsequent immorality

had, however, converted all but the original gold coin to coal, and the disciple's piety had reduced the impaling stake to a thorn.[4]

That is a pretty neat solution to the problem of apparent injustice. It relieves the anxiety that justice is a figment of wishful thinking. If it appears that the wrong man is getting the gold, don't worry: if you could see what the Guru sees, it would be evident that everything is coming out just right. The solution is to be found in the adjacent, invisible dimension of *past lives*. The solution of the book of Job is no less clever. In that one, the reader knows what Job does not: he is the butt of a kind of *Candid Camera* prank to settle a bet between God and Satan. The negotiation has been made offstage, up in heaven, where Job cannot see or hear it. And so the reader is bidden to believe that, whenever undeserved suffering strikes him, it is likely a similar test of his mettle. Heaven is the invisible realm up above the earth where the answer to our earthly dilemma is parked.

What about the Christian doctrines of postmortem bliss in heaven (or at the resurrection) and punishment of the wicked in hell below us, now or in a hotter hell after Judgment Day, off in the future? Do nice guys finish last here on earth? Well, it would solve the problem if we knew they were getting rewarded up above, in the invisible heaven. Are the bad guys getting away with murder and living it up in our visible world? Don't worry, hell awaits them, invisibly, below. So inequities are equalized in the hidden realms above and below. If you prefer the apocalyptic version, the invisible realm containing the solution is the future.

The problem of *adversity* isn't really much of a third, separate category, I guess, since basically it presents us with an overlap of the other two: ignorance and injustice. Usually what we are talking about with adversity is the puzzle (lack of explanation, thus ignorance) for a case of undeserved suffering, for example, from a tsunami (i.e., injustice). And you know what they always say: the suffering of this world is like the chaotic-seeming reverse side of a tapestry. From heaven's viewpoint, one will be able to view the finished product and see the beauty of the hitherto-hidden design. Again, the problem will be solved in the unseen dimension on top of this one.

It seems to me that perhaps Bonhoeffer anticipated Geertz: "Religious people speak of God when human perception is (often just from laziness) at an end, or human resources fail: it is really the *Deus ex machina* they call to their aid, either for the so-called solving of insoluble problems or as support in human failure—always, that is to say, helping out human weakness or on the borders of human existence."[5]

Considered in general terms this way, especially with reference to the doctrines of non-Christian religions, these beliefs in a hidden realm where faith-shattering difficulties are ironed out certainly sound like face-saving (or faith-saving) rationalizations. It sounds like different thinkers in different cultures have fabricated slightly different versions of the same basic set of dodges. Can you see Tillich's point? As long as you look only at the Christian version, not the Hindu or Sikh or whatever, you may have no trouble taking it seriously as revealed truth. But once you look at the whole category in which these doctrines fall as mere specific examples, it is a lot harder. The apparent absoluteness of revelation drains away from the doctrines. It begins to dawn on you that there's no particular reason to exempt your own inherited doctrines from the suspicions that attach to the others. You might feel tempted to give your favorite version, the Christian version, the benefit of the doubt, but don't you feel guilty? Can't you tell you are being arbitrary?

I'd say that if the other faiths are religions, there is no way to say, at least not with a straight face, that Christianity isn't one, too.

BUT SUPPOSE IT WASN'T A RELIGION?

Rick Warren raises, unwittingly I'm sure, a fascinating possibility. What if you decided you felt the compelling call of Jesus as you read the gospels, but you were one of those poor chaps C. S. Lewis anticipated whose best judgment tells him the evidence is against Christianity as a set of beliefs? Should you just shake your head and walk away? You have to give up Jesus, however reluctantly, because you can't buy the whole package? That would be an honest response. A friend of mine back in college felt he had to make it. Bert had many fundamentalist friends who were constantly witnessing to him. He did not find them particularly obnoxious, but neither did he succumb to their gentle pressure. Among other objections he had was creationism. As a biology student (now a professor), he knew too much about the evidence to be able to take creationist arguments seriously. He told me a dream he had one night. In it, Jesus himself appeared to him—for some reason wearing a business suit! Jesus asked Bert to believe in him, to accept him as his savior. And Bert was quite moved. He felt momentarily that he must yield to Jesus. But then he stopped and asked the savior, "But what about the *truth?*" Jesus had no reply to that—and vanished!

Imagine the dilemma, then, of someone who reads the Sermon on the Mount and likes what he hears, but he just does not find the arguments for God or the Trinity or immortality persuasive. I have warned more than once that it is a fatal misstep to start off the life of faith by letting emotional conviction lead one to swallow a whole bill of goods without sufficient, subject-appropriate reasons. I think you could avoid that cheat, you could be honest with the evidence, and still adopt Jesus as your ideal without any particular metaphysical beliefs at all. At least, you could if it's true that Christianity is a lifestyle, *not a religion* or a philosophical system.

I think that's what Albert Schweitzer did. He did not hold conventional Christian beliefs; in fact, he believed the historical Jesus was something of a deluded zealot. But here is what he said at the conclusion of his famous work, *The Quest of the Historical Jesus*: "He comes to us as One unknown, without a name, as of old, by the lake-side, He came to those men who knew Him not. He speaks to us the same word: 'Follow thou me!' and sets us to the tasks which He has to fulfill for our time. He commands. And to those who obey Him, whether they be wise or simple, He will reveal himself in the toils, the conflicts, the sufferings which they shall pass through in His fellowship, and, as an ineffable mystery, they shall learn in their own experience Who He is."[6] This is what motivated Schweitzer to set aside a cushy life of fame and fortune in Europe and move to French Equatorial Africa, where he founded the first hospital and brought medicine to the suffering. Ironically, the mission board that sent him refused to allow him to teach the Bible because of his heretical views!

Or suppose going to church or engaging in religious practices like prayer and meditation left one cold, despite one's interest in Jesus. If Christianity is indeed *not a religion*, then church shouldn't matter much! Why not accept Christianity as a lifestyle, a moral stance, an existential posture, but *not as a religion, not as a philosophy*? Warren, without wanting to, seems to have opened up the door of what Bonhoeffer called "religionless Christianity." "How do we speak of God without religion, i.e., without the temporally-influenced presuppositions of metaphysics, inwardness, and so on?"[7] This was the sort of radical Christianity advocated in the 1960s by Harvey Cox, Thomas J. J. Altizer, Paul Van Buren, and William Hamilton. Eschewing all claims to know what did or didn't happen historically on Easter morning, dismissing far-fetched doctrines about the incarnation of a divine being, Van Buren says, "The man who says, 'Jesus is Lord,' is saying that the history [i.e., the story] of Jesus and of what happened on Easter has exercised a liberating effect upon him, and that he has been so grasped by it that it has become the historical norm of his perspective upon life. His confession is a notification of this perspective and a recommendation to his listener to see Jesus, the world, and himself in this same way and to act accordingly."[8] R. B. Braithwaite saw things similarly: "A man is not, I think, a professing Christian unless he both proposes to live according to Christian moral principles and associates his intention with thinking of Christian stories; but he need not believe that the empirical propositions presented by the stories correspond to empirical fact."[9] There is someone who truly believes Christianity is not a religion but a lifestyle.

THINK AGAIN

In conclusion, on the other hand, it might not be such a bad idea to rethink the value of Christianity as a religion. I mean, we've already seen what a self-deluded fantasy it is to imagine you are having a "personal relationship" with anybody but yourself. If it isn't a relationship, and it isn't a religion, either, you might have just painted yourself into a corner.

Day Twenty-three

Point to Ponder: If justice is not built into the structure of the universe, then our duty to establish it as best we can here on earth is all the greater.

Quote to Remember: "In this respect fundamentalism has demonic traits. It destroys the humble honesty of the search for truth, it splits the conscience of its thoughtful adherents, and it makes them fanatical because they are forced to suppress elements of truth of which they are dimly aware." (Paul Tillich)

Question to Consider: Why would it be bad to admit that Christianity is a religion after all?

NOTES

1. Rick Warren, *The Purpose-Driven Life: What on Earth Am I Here For?* (Grand Rapids, MI: Zondervan, 2002), p. 183.

2. Wilfred Cantwell Smith, *The Meaning and End of Religion: A New Approach to the Religious Traditions of Mankind* (New York: New American Library, 1964), pp. 115, 307, 308.

3. Paul Tillich, "The Conquest of the Concept of Religion in the Philosophy of Religion," in *What Is Religion?* trans. Kenneth Schedler and Charles W. Fox (New York: Harper & Row, 1973), p. 127.

4. W. H. McLeod, *Guru Nanak and the Sikh Religion* (Delhi: Oxford University Press, 1976), p. 40.

5. Dietrich Bonhoeffer, *Letters and Papers from Prison*, trans. Reginald H. Fuller (New York: Macmillan, 1953), p. 165.

6. Albert Schweitzer, *The Quest of the Historical Jesus: A Critical Study of Its Progress from Reimarus to Wrede*, trans. W. Montgomery (1906; repr., New York: Macmillan, 1968), p. 403.

7. Bonhoeffer, *Letters and Papers from Prison*, p. 164.

8. Paul M. van Buren, *The Secular Meaning of the Gospel, Based on an Analysis of Its Language* (New York: Macmillan, 1966), p. 141.

9. R. B. Braithwaite, *An Empiricist's View of the Nature of Religious Belief* (Cambridge: Cambridge University Press, 1955), p. 27.

This Paper Idol

Too great praise challenges attention, and often brings to light a thousand faults that otherwise the general eye would never see. Were we allowed to read the Bible as we do all other books, we would admire its beauties, treasure its worthy thoughts, and account for all its absurd, grotesque and cruel things, by saying that its authors lived in rude, barbaric times. But we are told that it was written by inspired men; that it contains the will of God; that it is perfect, pure, and true in all its parts; the source and standard of all religious truth; that it is the star and anchor of all human hope; the only guide for man, the only torch in Nature's night. These claims are so at variance with every known recorded fact, so palpably absurd, that every free, unbiased soul is forced to raise the standard of revolt.
—Robert Green Ingersoll, *Some Mistakes of Moses*

I have not the slightest doubt that the reason we have anything at all to do with Christianity today is not that we have swallowed what Christianity has told us to believe and do, but that out of our own sense of how to live we have come to look seriously at Christianity because it seems in part at least to be saying the same thing we know to be right.
—Robin Scroggs, "Traditon, Freedom, and the Abyss"

I love the Bible. I have devoted my life to the study of it. I wrote one PhD dissertation on the various evangelical theories of biblical authority, and a second one focusing on themes in Luke and Acts. None of this means my views must be correct. But it does show I do not approach this sensitive topic as an opponent of the Bible. Just the reverse. I disagree sharply with many Bible devotees, but we both love it and want to know it better. I know it will sound to many readers as if I am attacking the Bible in what follows. I do not mean to. The

226

problem is, as Robert G. Ingersoll remarked, that people have magnified the Bible beyond reason, elevating it to an idol and praising it with extravagant flattery. And then they have wielded their Bible like a club against those they feel are disobedient to it. Given this use of the Bible as a tool of oppression, it becomes necessary to show that the Bible is after all a paper tiger. But, just because there are grotesque abuses of the Bible, that hardly means there are not also valuable and wholesome uses of it. I will return to that point.

But first I must challenge the traditional fundamentalist bibliolatry set forth in Rick Warren's twenty-fourth chapter. In it he claims the Bible is the infallible word of God and that it must rule our lives at every point. By contrast, I want to suggest that, first, the claim that the Bible is divinely inspired is *spurious*; second, that it is *pernicious*; and, third, that it is *moot*. The Bible and our study of it will be better off without that claim.

RECORDED REVELATION OR REVEALED RECORD?

First, the claim is *spurious*, false. Not in the sense that it claims something is true that is not true, but rather that the *claim itself* is bogus, inappropriate, inapplicable. We are only *mistakenly* told that "the Bible claims to be inspired." There is less to this grand pronouncement than meets the eye. Granted, very often the Hebrew prophets are quoted as claiming their spoken oracles are the very word of God, which indeed they may have been. But in context, such claims refer strictly to the spoken words as originally delivered. They in no way contain a guarantee that these oracles may not have been inaccurately copied, altered or corrupted, or mixed with words from later prophets. There is no claim at all that the writing down and editing of their oracles was divinely inspired or supervised. In fact, John, in Revelation 22:18–19, expresses the fear that someone might tamper with his text and threatens such a one with damnation. He knew it was a real danger.

To make the inspiration claim on the basis of the prophets is to confuse spoken delivery with scribal preservation. And, worse yet, it is to beg the whole question, for when we say "'*The*' 'Bible' claims its own inspiration," we smuggle in the assumption that scripture is a single, canonical unit in which any claim made by one writer automatically applies equally to all, as if Jeremiah's "Thus saith the Lord" applied equally to 2 Chronicles or the Song of Solomon. Not so fast, if you please!

Some say the New Testament must be inspired because in John 16:12–14 Jesus predicts the coming of the Paraclete who will inspire the apostles with his teachings, new and remembered. But this promise says nothing of any writings they might commit to paper. And even if it did, Paul, Mark, and Luke were not in the room at the time. And it is hotly debated whether any New Testament document was actually written by any of the Twelve. The authorship of 1 and 2 Peter is very likely pseudonymous. The ascriptions of two gospels to Matthew and John are merely traditional, not even contained in the texts. Like the Epistle to the Hebrews, the gospel texts actually contain no authors' names.

The author of 2 Timothy 3:16 certainly considered the contents of whatever the Jewish scripture canon was at the time to be divinely inspired, but he says nothing about any *New* Testament writings being inspired. That is no real surprise, but it leaves us without the claim to "plenary" biblical inspiration that some pretend to find in this verse. There is no biblical claim that the whole biblical canon as we know it is inspired. And to claim that there is, is circular, making the Bible into a univocal, canonical monolith. It is a spurious claim.

DAMNING WITH EXTRAVAGANT PRAISE

The claim to inspiration is *pernicious*. First, it implicitly insults the very book it seeks to praise, as if one need not take the Bible seriously unless one could be persuaded that a superhuman entity wrote it. Much of the Bible is so profound, so wise, so beautiful, so edifying that any claim of miraculous inspiration adds absolutely nothing to the inherent force of its words. As Father Abraham said to Dives, those who already have Moses and the Prophets and remain deaf to them will not start listening if one rises from the dead (Luke 16:31). And claims to divine inspiration will make no *more* difference. Conversely, some of the Bible, such as its vengeful commands to genocide, its threats of eternal torture, its easy toleration of slavery and the oppression of women, are so defective that no claim to inspiration can make them better and only places a halo over bad texts. Such claims to plenary inspiration corrupt biblical morality itself by teaching us to call the bad good. Such claims debase the Bible by making us pretend that it is all on the same level when in fact any sensitive reader, until bullied by theologians, can see that it is not. If Isaiah's ringing oracles and the wisdom of the Sermon on the Mount do not command your conscience by their own merit, claims of divine inspiration are not going to help. Nor should they make the superstitious scare stories of Leviticus sound any better to us. The good parts of the Bible do not need your help, nor do you have the right to become a disingenuous spin doctor for the bad ones.

Second, the claim for biblical inspiration is pernicious because it straitjackets the open-ended, inductive reading of the Bible. Once one holds normative beliefs about what an inspired book may or may not be found saying, one has abandoned both the Protestant axioms of *Sola Scriptura* and the grammatico-historical method. *Sola Scriptura* ("Scripture alone") means that the text of scripture shall have precedence over any theological claim. The grammatico-historical method means that scripture must be read in a public, secular manner, the same way we interpret any ancient literature. We cannot admit of secret meanings and special rules appropriate to Holy Scripture, just as Martin Luther ruled out Roman Catholics' reading their own doctrines into a text that, plainly read, said nothing of purgatory or popes. So when fundamentalists forbid any reading of the text that would imply biblical error or contradiction because "Scripture cannot err," they themselves are trying to control the reading of the Bible according to prior doctrine. Again, claims to inspiration dishonor the Bible since they prevent us from reading it honestly and without prejudice.

SO WHAT?

Finally, claims about biblical inspiration are *moot*. Even if we had reason to believe the whole canon was equally inspired, this should not make any real difference to our understanding of the text. Would an inspired book necessarily be historically and scientifically inerrant? There is no particular reason to think so. Fundamentalists wouldn't relish the notion, but one cannot be sure that an inspired book doesn't contain "inspired" myths and legends, even fiction. There are other nonfactual genres in the Bible, after all, like the Psalms. Who is the theologian to tell God that he cannot have included certain genres in his book? If we know God's literary tastes in such detail, then I suggest the Bible is altogether superfluous. We already know the very mind of God before we even open the Bible! Aren't we clever?

Similarly, how can we be so sure that, if, as B. B. Warfield said, God chose real human beings, with real biographies, educations, and opinions, to write his book, that he wouldn't have allowed their opinions to conflict, as godly people piously differ today? Just because it would make it less convenient for us?

In fact, as is well known, fundamentalists readily admit that it *appears* that the Bible writers do contradict one another, for instance, James and Paul on the question of whether faith alone or faith plus works justifies. But this, they say, is only an *apparent* contradiction. They then proceed to spin. They say that if we took James's words in some less than obvious way we might be able to make it sound like he is saying the same thing as Paul, only in different words. But wait a second! I thought the Bible was authoritative *as taken literally*. That is, on the *face* of it, the *surface* sense. Not some subtle, less than literal meaning that would be convenient for our theology. Again, if we can do that, we have rejected the grammatico-historical method. We can make the Bible say anything we want.

And why do they always make James agree with Paul? Why not twist Paul to make him sound like James? Because Reformation theology controls their interpretation, and that theology prefers Paul. In any case, in practice, fundamentalists wind up saying implicitly what I am saying explicitly: that the whole Bible cannot be taken as equally authoritative.

Anyone knows that a claim for the inspiration of the Bible does nothing to mitigate the frequent *ambiguity* of the Bible. Can you get a divorce or not? Is warfare allowed or not? Can women be ordained? Do charismatic gifts linger to our own day? Is there predestination or free will? Does John 1:1 mean Jesus is God himself, or *a* god? At Dallas Theological Seminary they debate whether it is sufficient to accept Jesus as savior only, or whether one must accept him as Lord also. None of these debates has ever been resolved, but both sides in all these debates are defended by believers in the inspiration of the Bible. I ask you, *if it leaves even such questions as these uncertain, what is the doctrine worth?* What difference does it actually make? None that I can see.

THE BAD NEWS BIBLE

Why will this conclusion dismay many people? So much so, in fact, that they cannot even bring themselves to consider the possible merits of my argument? Why do they feel at once the urgent need to find some refutation, if not to dismiss it out of hand? I think it is because they are impatient and afraid.

Some wish to use the Bible as a weapon to silence others and their viewpoints. They know that if they ever took seriously even the fact of the Bible's frequent ambiguity, they would never be able to say with Billy Graham's ringing certitude, "The Bible says . . . " Careful study shows that it is not so simple a matter to decide what the Bible says. Sometimes it says more than one thing per topic. People want to be able to teach like Jesus, "with authority, and not as the scribes." But they are not the Son of God. Like me, they are at best scribes, and the better a scribe knows his text, the more hesitant he will be to pontificate from it.

Some are afraid. They are afraid of having to use their own wits to decide what is the right thing to do, or to believe. They would like to think they have a supernatural answer book. Why not admit with the rest of us that we are all in the same boat? We are all stuck using our best wits to decide those tough ethical and theological questions.

Everyone knows we are left to our own resources when it comes to questions not mentioned in the Bible, like abortion, cloning, genetic engineering, the fate of those who never hear the gospel. Why would it be so terrible if we had to approach all the big questions the same way?

Some people seem to imagine, whether consciously or not, that God is a cranky theology professor, and that he has assigned us the task of answering all the questions of existence by a deadline: the day we die. And some are afraid that if they show up at the pearly gates and hand in the exam book, and if there are enough wrong answers, especially on some big-ticket questions (like the deity of Christ and the atonement), they will get a big red "F" and go down the shoot to hell. Where did this crazy idea of God come from? I know: from church. But it is a bad idea. But what on earth does this have to do with grace? It is a form of Gnosticism, salvation by knowledge.

This is the root of the urgency of biblicism. As I have tried to show, there is not much logic to it, just psychologic. The psychology of superstitious fear. The claim to biblical inspiration is a rationalization whereby we allow ourselves not to hear the things we fear to hear from the Bible. But I am not afraid. I love the Bible, and perfect love casts out fear.

BIBLINE BLOOD

There remains much of very great value in the Bible, and I have never for an instant regretted that my teenage period of fundamentalism awakened in me an insatiable thirst for better and better knowledge of the Bible. I have learned not to cower before whatever it may say, but then we are urged in the Bible itself to test the spirits and prophecies we hear. John R. W. Stott once urged Christians to see to it that their very blood become "Bibline,"[1] as saturated with scripture as the seawater is with salt. Not a bad idea. It has always profited me to have biblical texts and insights ready at hand, intruding upon my consciousness as I considered what to do.

And let me recommend as well that you bathe your mind in the

Buddhist Dhammapada and in certain Upanishads. Certainly the Tao Te-Ching and the Bhagavad Gita, Hasidic Jewish tales, and definitely the wonderful Gospel according to Thomas would repay your study. I like to read both New Testament and Koran through in their entirety in different translations every once in a while. I have gotten through the Koran only four times, but I plan to read it more. Yes, I know it's quite the reading list, but come on: you've got the time.

Day Twenty-four

Point to Ponder: If you believe the Bible is an infallible authority because your pastor said so, then *he* is really your infallible authority, isn't he?

Quote to Remember: "That which does not preach Christ is not apostolic, though it be the work of Peter or Paul; and conversely, that which does teach Christ is apostolic even though it be written by Judas, Annas, Pilate, or Herod." (Martin Luther, preface to James)

Question to Consider: Why isn't any true statement just as good as the "Word of God"? What makes any true statement something *other* than the word of God?

NOTE

1. John R.W. Stott, *The Preacher's Portrait* (Grand Rapids, MI: William B. Eerdmans, 1961), p. 31.

Jesus with a Jackhammer

The soul attracts that which it secretly harbors, that which it loves, and also that which it fears; it reaches the height of its cherished aspirations; it falls to the level of its unchastened desires—and circumstances are the means by which the soul receives its own.
—James Allen, *As a Man Thinketh*

As I read Rick Warren's twenty-fifth meditation, I could not help thinking of one of Stephen King's early short stories, "Quitters, Inc.," in which a man is given a business card for a stop-smoking outfit and told that it will without question succeed where all others have failed. It has an astonishing 98 percent success rate. He makes an appointment and signs up. It turns out that the foundation was the brainchild of a mob boss diagnosed with inoperable lung cancer. This death sentence galvanized him to play hardball with other smokers, to save as many as possible from his terrible fate. Why is the program so darn effective? Because they have mob thugs constantly watching you, hiding in your closet, following your car with telescopes, and so on, and if they ever see you lapse and light up, they will grab you and beat the stuffing out of you! Next infraction: they start on your loved ones. No tearful begging deters them. It always works. What a parable for Rick Warren's benevolent tyrant of a God! "We are like jewels, shaped with the hammer and chisel of adversity. If a jeweler's hammer isn't strong enough to chip off our rough edges, God will use a sledgehammer. If we're really stubborn, he uses a jackhammer. He will use whatever it takes."[1]

Now you might be tempted to give Reverend Warren a break and say, "Oh, come on, Price! He's just saying that, if someone insists on being so obtuse that he fails to learn from experience over and over again, it may take some major turbulence to knock some sense through his thick skull!" Uh, no, he's *not* just saying that. There is a crucial element of difference between that and what Warren is saying. That is the factor of a personal being pulling the strings and engineering the events of your life. If there is none, then it is right and proper to tell someone he'd best start learning from life's reproofs (about his drinking, let's say), before it takes some major tragedy to wake him up. That is a lesson anyone should learn. Amen! But Pastor Warren is mucking up the whole thing by bringing heavy-duty superstition into it. The way he tells it, you have an interfering God, almost a plaguing demon on your tail, conditioning you with increasingly potent jolts of a cattle prod.

It is precisely this superstitious primitivism that creates theology's biggest headache: how can a loving God treat his creatures this way? But the problem is purely artificial. It is created by the superimposition of a personal God onto the morally neutral universe. But if you admit that events occur haphazardly, with you inevitably getting in their way, there is nothing to accuse anyone of. There is nothing to chafe at, nothing to resent. Trouble strikes? Too bad; it strikes everybody. Now be a man and see what you can learn from the experience. You don't start whining about life being unfair. Life cannot be either "fair" or "unfair." Only a *person* could be, and once we posit a controlling God, we have created a superfluous and insoluble fairness issue. We have created a Frankenstein monster, a divine bully and an obsessive stalker. Warren assures us, "You know you are maturing when you begin to see the hand of God in the random, baffling, and seemingly pointless circumstances of life."[2] But surely it is just the reverse! Could Warren be more wrong? It is the immature, the superstitious person who starts reading the random events of day-to-day existence as if he were a shaman reading the intestines of a sacrificial animal to tell the will of the gods.

WHO'S IN CHARGE HERE?

Reverend Warren is quick to denounce one of his leading competitors, the optimism-driven life: "Our hope in difficult times is not based on positive thinking, wishful thinking, or natural optimism. It is a certainty based on the truths that God is in complete control of our universe and that he loves us."[3] But I should say that the very notion of God being in control of the universe is itself one of the most blatant examples of "wishful thinking." I will return to Warren's disdain for positive thinking in a moment. But first, what about this wild claim that a loving God is in control of the universe? Exactly what is being claimed here? Let's talk about something called the falsifiability principle. This means that, in order to define any claim, you have to be able to specify some state of affairs whose occurrence would be recognized as debunking the claim. If you can't think of any turn of events that would falsify your claim, you aren't making much of a claim. If we can't think of what the opposite of your claimed reality would be, then we can't tell what it is you have in mind.

For instance, if I claim that my wife is faithful to me, but then you show me photographs of her having sex with you and other men as well, this would be so incompatible with the notion of her fidelity as to debunk it. If she is indeed faithful to me, which is my claim, then no such liaisons or photos will exist. But suppose you can produce the incriminating pictures, and I confront my wife with them, saying, "You said you were being faithful to me! What about *this*?" And suppose she says, "Oh, but I *am* being faithful—in my way!" Yeah, that really helps. She has smuggled in a private definition of "faithfulness" that may make sense to *her*, but not to me. But let's say I am desperate to believe the best of her, and I adopt her version of fidelity, so that I no longer object to her escapades. Then some friend, hearing about her scandalous behavior, confronts me, saying, "Have you no self-respect at all, man? She is grossly unfaithful to you!" But I say, "It's okay, she is faithful—in her way." My friend will shake his head in disgust and walk away, rightly convinced that I am a bigger fool than he thought. What he will have seen that I haven't is that, *by adopting a definition of "fidelity" that is so broad and flexible as to be compatible with any and every state of affairs, I have evacuated my claim of any sense whatever.* If my claim that my wife is being faithful to me is compatible with her sleeping with every man she meets, then my claim does not mean much at all, does it? What is it I am even *asserting* anymore? Nothing much. I *am* communicating *some*thing, though: I am signaling that my loyalty to my wife, however undeserved, is nonetheless unwavering, even to the point of my making a hopeless and pathetic fool of myself.

That, it seems to me, is just the way it is with Warren's shapeless claim that a loving God is in control of this world. Most people, innocent of the twisted shenanigans of Christian apologetics, would admit that claiming a loving God is in control would be incompatible with certain bad things happening. They would say they have faith that God is not going to allow some certain level of damage to them or to the human race. And if such did befall us, we would have been shown we were wrong about the loving, divine control of the world. They don't expect to be proven wrong, though, because they have faith in Divine Providence going their way. It may take only one tragedy to change their mind and make them start down the rationalizing path of apologetics such as Warren's. But, who knows? They might give up the claim altogether, as Jewish theologian Richard L. Rubenstein did in his gutsy book, *After Auschwitz*, in which he said Jews have been flat wrong about the notion of being God's chosen people because, if it meant anything at all, it certainly must be incompatible with the Nazi Holocaust. Rubenstein preferred to drop the cherished claim rather than "defend" it by evacuating it of all meaning.

To their credit, Warren and his cohorts seem to have cast off all childish illusions about God sending the cavalry over the hill at the last minute to rescue us. They know from personal as well as pastoral experience that it just doesn't work that way, so they are trying to substitute an unfalsifiable version of Divine Providence. Anything at all may happen, whether an AIDS pandemic, a nuclear exchange, Hitler, Saddam Hussein, you name it, and it will not prove that no loving deity is in charge of the world.

Finally, they are revealed as making no meaningful claim at all about the way things would be turning out if there were a loving God in charge. No, they admit, the principle of Divine Providence is no guide whatever to expecting that one sort of events will occur and another sort will not. It all boils down to store-brand Stoicism, Stoicism with the Christian label pasted onto it after the fact. But it is Stoicism tainted with superstition, since Warren simply will not give up the oppressive business of God as ready to "love" you with a jackhammer.

Let me provide a bit of historical perspective to what's going on here. About a century ago Sir James Frazer came up with a possible explanation of the decline of magic and the rise of religion.[4] The difference between them is that magic thinks it is dealing with abstract forces, analogous to electricity or water pressure, whereas religion thinks to persuade personal beings, like us, but invisible and more powerful. Why the changeover? It was a matter of falsifiability pure and simple. Witch doctors would do the rain dance or the war dance, expecting in this way to manipulate hidden forces and to effect the desired outcome. It was a mechanical process, so it pretty much *had* to work. On the frequent occasions when it didn't, they would just go "back to the drawing board" and try to eliminate a few more variables. Maybe spin the dead cat around three times, not just two. But eventually the jig was up. Nothing seemed to improve the success rate. So they moved on to a new paradigm, the religious one. They were no longer dealing with things like occult energy, where it should have been as predictable as plugging an appliance into an outlet. Now they figured they were petitioning gods or spirits, who were personal entities and could turn down human requests for reasons of their own, just as our parents always did, unpredictably to us, their kids. Now how is the religious paradigm better than the magical one? Only in that it is *less susceptible to debunking by results*. There is a built-in likelihood that it will not work. There is a variable you can never eliminate: the inscrutable will of the gods. They may know something you don't, that your request, if granted, would backfire on you. So they refuse, and you just have to trust them.

Sound familiar? God is in loving control of the world, but that doesn't mean he will won't prevent your getting tortured to death. In fact, he may cause the deaths of loved ones in order to teach you a lesson. But who are you to second-guess him? So you are really left in the dark. Whatever he does must be the best thing, no matter how it hurts. Whatever he does must deserve the adjective "loving" simply because he is the one doing it. "Loving," then, is no longer defined by ordinary use of the word and need not even bear any resemblance to what the dictionary says. It seems to me a worthless mess of glossolalia, but you're welcome to it if you really want it.

Here's another Warrenesque "claim": you can pray for something to happen or not to happen, and you can be sure he will hear you, his beloved child. But of course you can only be sure he'll grant your request if it coincides with his will, that is, if it is something he had already decided to do anyway. The belief that God will answer prayer is so flexible as to allow God to do anything, so flexible as to be meaningless. Whatever meaning it may have is hidden in that walled-off invisible zone adjacent to our world, just like Clifford Geertz said. Basically, it's still just superstition, superstition with better spin.

ALWAYS LOOK ON THE BRIGHT SIDE OF LIFE

Rick Warren reassures the poor Christian reader, who is now nervously looking to the sky to see what divine love bomb may descend upon him next, that he need not worry: everything that befalls him is screened by God's permissive will. It is "Father filtered." Here is another one of those nauseating trivializations of doctrine that invite such scorn. Fundamentalism seems to treat its own beliefs with all the seriousness of an advertising slogan. It seems sometimes that its enemies have more regard for its traditions. Anyway, I think Warren has once again gotten things exactly backward. There is a "Father filter" all right, but it is not out there in the world, between God in heaven and you here on earth. No, the Father filter is *inside your head*. It is the mythic picture of the world you use to interpret the otherwise random raining down of events.

Why does one person say "Life is good!" while another says "This world is hell!"? Partly because their experiences are different, but also partly, if not mainly, because their mental filters, the grids by which they interpret events, are very different. If you are defensive, you will take everything you hear as a slight or an insult. If you are generous of spirit, you will have patience with people's shortcomings and just hope they mature. There are many possible filters through which to make sense of your experiences. It does not have to be the jackhammering demiurge of Rick Warren and his fundamentalist colleagues. It could be (gasp) . . . *positive thinking*!

New Age gurus have popularized the notion that we create our own reality. Unfortunately, the fact that it is *they* who endorse it automatically tends to scare some of us off. But you remember the stopped watch—even it is right twice a day. And this time they are right, at least partly. I have long noticed how different friends and colleagues, faced with the same circumstances, have totally different experiences.

What accounted for the differences? I began to suspect it was a question of the mind-set they brought to the situation. They *expected* people would give them trouble, and by gosh, they *did!* They feared they would fail, or that people would reject their ideas, and what do you know, they did! On the other hand, some people took setbacks in stride, viewed unexpected events as challenges rather than obstacles, and they won out. Let's face it, your attitudes about yourself and others, your expectations about how your plans will turn out, they all come back to you. Circumstances form a mirror reflecting you. Is it any wonder that people can pick up even on the most subtle signals you send out, even subconsciously? Can't they pick up and reflect what you send out about your winsomeness or repulsiveness, your interest in them or impatience with them? Should it surprise you that an innate pessimism will tend to make you dismiss or ignore possibilities lying in your path? There is absolutely nothing spooky or metaphysical about this. It is just like all wisdom, based on long-term, inductive observation.

Once you realize that, to a significant degree, you can and do create your own reality by reading events in a certain way or sending out certain signals, you can change things. You can begin to examine yourself. You can seek feedback from others. Study others who have accomplished great things and ask how they did it. There are patterns and attitudes of success, and you can learn them. For one thing, you can stop whining and complaining. Even if you have reason to complain: you were really wronged or ripped off. But remember our discussion of forgiveness. It's the same issue: bitterness will preoccupy you to no purpose. It is a simple "business decision" to concentrate your attention on the positive: positive things that happen, positive lessons from unpleasant happenings, positive plans for the future. It has nothing to do with being a giddy Pollyanna.

You can gradually, through positive self-reminders ("affirmations," though I hate to use that word after seeing Stuart Smalley skits on *Saturday Night Live*), begin to change your mind-set from one that expects failure and rejection, to one that expects success and plans on it. There will be setbacks, but then who needs to look at them that way? Setbacks are challenges, enabling you to assess and increase your strengths, to reassess your outlook. It is all a matter of the direction you choose. You determine to look forward, onward, and upward, and to make everything grist for your mill. There is no question of self-delusion here, nothing of forcing yourself to believe arbitrary and insupportable "promises." It is simply a matter of creating your agenda and determining to pursue it, come hell or high water.

And it reinforces itself as things go better and better, as you *make* them go better and better. I am not talking about gaining greater influence over your life. No, you already *have* that influence. Your attitudes and expectations are *already* making a huge difference, though it may not be a good one. As with so many areas of life, you need to stop and reassess what you are doing. Only then can you take things in hand and do with purposeful skill what you were making a mess of by doing it haphazardly.

You are the attentive "deity" who filters input from the outside world. *You* are the one who causes all things to work together for your good. Take responsibility for your world, for you are busily engaged, whether you know it or not, in creating it.

Day Twenty-five

Point to Ponder: What happens to me is "good" if I decide it is.

Quote to Remember: "A theory is a theory, not a reality. All a theory can do is remind me of certain thoughts that were a part of my reality *then*. A statement or a 'fact' is an emphasis—one way of looking at something. At worst it is a kind of myopia. A name is also just one way of seeing something. I can't make a statement about reality without omitting many other things which are also true about it. Even if it were possible to say everything that is true about a reality, I still would not have the reality; I would only have the words. In fact, the reality changes even as I talk about it. When I outgrow my names and facts and theories, or when reality leaves them behind, I become dead if I don't go on to new ways of seeing things." (Hugh Prather, *Notes to Myself*)

Question to Consider: Is Warren saying that things will actually turn out "good" for me in some way, or that I will have to redefine "good" as meaning "whatever happens to me"?

NOTES

1. Rick Warren, *The Purpose-Driven Life: What on Earth Am I Here For?* (Grand Rapids, MI: Zondervan, 2002), p. 196.

2. Ibid., p. 199.

3. Ibid., p. 195.

4. James G. Frazer, *The Golden Bough: A Study in Comparative Religion* (London: Macmillan, 1890), pp. 30–32.

Satan's Sunday School

But your daughter doesn't say she's a demon; she insists she's the devil himself, and that's the same thing as saying you're Napoleon Bonaparte! You see?
—William Peter Blatty, *The Exorcist*

Rick Warren's first chapter on temptation is preoccupied with Satan. It is almost more of a chapter on Satan than on temptation. So I begin with Satan. I want to argue that Rick Warren, representing his fundamentalist tradition, believes way too much about Satan, more than the Bible itself justifies and even more than classical Christian theism would naturally allow for. Then, in the next chapter, I will propose a couple of alternate ways of looking at the challenge of temptation.

DEVILUTION

In outline, the story of Lucifer's Fall and transformation into Satan is as follows. God created Adam and bade all the angels bow down to him, as he represented the living image of God. Lucifer ("Light Bearer") was God's chief lieutenant, the most glorious of the archangels. But he refused to obey God, despising the creature Adam. He took God's demand to denote that the Almighty had lost all judgment. Thus Lucifer staged a palace revolution, recruiting as his allies one-third of the angels. Naturally the action failed, resulting in the expulsion of Lucifer, now become Satan ("the Adversary"), and his confederates, who then became the demons and busied themselves with possessing unfortunate wretches, inflicting illnesses, seizures, or bizarre behaviors. To vindicate his opinion that Adam was unworthy of God's honor, Satan took the form of a serpent, infiltrating the paradise of Eden, and lured Adam and Eve into disobeying God's command not to eat of the Tree of the Knowledge of Good and Evil. This

243

plan succeeded, initiating the whole epic of salvation and the restoration of humankind to the good graces of God. At the end of the age, Satan will lead one last battle against God and will be defeated, incarcerated in the bottomless pit, and finally consigned to the fiery lake of eternal torment.

How much of this story is spelled out in the Bible? I should say very little of it. Rather, various bits and pieces of scripture were eventually lifted out of context and cobbled together by imaginative scribes to create the Satan story. The whole story appears only in later writings, such as the Secrets of Enoch (2 Enoch) 18:3, the Life of Adam and Eve 12–17, the Apocalypse of Moses 16–17, which appear to be a bit later than the New Testament, and the Koran 7:11–27 (seventh century). We cannot be sure just how much of the whole tale had been pieced together by New Testament times. Though we do find occasional New Testament references to the scriptural building blocks of the story, we never find mentions of the midrashic mortar holding them together in the full-blown structure. For instance, 2 Corinthians 11:3 ("But I am afraid that as the serpent deceived Eve by his cunning, your thoughts will be led astray from a sincere and pure devotion to Christ." RSV) does have Eve tempted, presumably in the Garden of Eden, but there is no identification of the serpent as Satan. Satan is mentioned in 2 Corinthians 11:14b ("even Satan disguises himself as an angel of light," RSV), but with no connection to the serpent or Eden. Besides, that verse seems to deny Satan's previous role as an angel of light. He does not disguise himself as a snake, but as an angel, implying that, whoever he was, he hadn't been a glorious angel. We will see more of the same in the ensuing survey: the building blocks are there in the New Testament all right, but they are being put together in different ways. The final form has not yet been finished, not within the New Testament canon. But let's take a look at the rest of the pieces, shall we?

ON THE CASE

First, it is important to note that *ha Satan* is not a proper Hebrew name, but a title, "the Adversary." But whose adversary? Not the enemy of *God*. That connection, as far as we can show, was first made in 2 Enoch 18:3, where his name became "Satanil," or "enemy of God." No, his original Old Testament role is to act as God's special agent for testing (tempting) God's favorites, to see if they are really worthy of the faith he has placed in them. The "devil" (Greek, *ho diabalos*) means the same thing: "the [mud] slinger," "the caster [of aspersions]." But in all this there is no suggestion of Satan being evil. For instance, in Job 1:6–12 and 2:1–8, Satan is included among the Sons of God, each of whom rules one of the seventy nations (as the ancient Jews reckoned the number) as God's deputies. Satan is constantly making his rounds, scrutinizing the human race. He wonders if the apparently pious Job is sincere or rather perhaps making a fool of the Almighty, rendering him lip service for the sake of the fringe benefits. God agrees to test Job's true intentions, and Job passes. Similarly, in Zechariah 3:1–5, we see a courtroom scene, with God as judge, his angel as defense attorney (foreshadowing the Holy Spirit's role as "Paraclete," i.e., advocate or defense attorney), and Satan as prosecutor (which is what "the Adversary" really denotes). Satan is not so sure the high priest–elect Joshua really deserves the honor God plans to bestow upon him. Joshua's stained robe symbolically implies the criticism is justified, but God's decision is to purify his chosen instrument instead of disqualifying him. Likewise, 1 Chronicles 21:1ff has Satan tempt David with the idea of inventorying his military resources, a lack of faith in God to protect Israel. If you compare this passage with 2 Samuel 24:1, which the 1 Chronicles version rewrites, you find that it is God who has tempted David. But this is no contradiction. The Chronicler naturally assumed that God must have used the agency of his servant, Satan, for the job. Neither God nor Satan is trying to *get* David to sin. Their purpose is to see *if* he will sin, given the opportunity. It is like FBI sting operations, setting up congressmen, mayors, and the like, about whom some suspicion gathers. Will they fall for the sting? You hope they don't, but it's better to know.

Actually, though other aspects have been added to the Satan character in New Testament times, he maintains his primary role as God's investigator and evaluator. This is what he is doing when he tests (or "tempts"—same word in Greek) Jesus in the wilderness after his baptism (Mark 1:12–13, Matthew 4:1–11, and Luke 4:1–13). Will he pass the test and comport himself as God's Son? Of course, he does, with flying colors. Again, in Mark 8:31–33, when Jesus announces his coming crucifixion, and Peter discourages the idea, Jesus calls him "Satan," because he is unwittingly playing the role of testing Jesus's resolve. Luke 22:31–32 depicts Jesus as privy to what is going on in heaven: just as in the beginning of Job, Satan has claimed his prerogative of testing the professed loyalty of the disciples. They will fail. Note that Satan has "demanded" to test them, denoting his proper duty and prerogative as God's servant. In Revelation 12:10, Christ warns the Smyrnaean believers that "the devil is about to throw some of you into prison, that you may be tested" (RSV). He is not said to be their enemy, only their examiner. Revelation 12:10 has the saints rejoicing at the downfall of "the Accuser of our brethren, . . . who accuses them night and day before our God." He has, as he did with Job, Joshua, and David, been urging the case for their lukewarm faith, but they prevailed, disproving these allegations by the sheer fact of their martyrdom: "they loved not their lives even unto death" (verse 11, RSV).

THE HYDE SIDE

In all this, Satan is not evil, not God's arch-foe, but rather his servant. Where do these other notions first enter the biblical stream? We can pinpoint it very accurately. Toward the end of the Babylonian Exile (fifth century BCE), Cyrus the Persian took over the throne from the Babylonians. He was a Zoroastrian, and this faith posited two, almost equally matched, deities: *Ahura Mazda*, the Lord of Light, the Wise Lord, and *Ahriman*, the Lord of Darkness. This theology was a way of dealing with the problem of evil: why does God allow suffering? The Zoroastrian answer was the theory that God wants only good and would never tolerate evil, but he is not all-powerful. He must reckon with an evil counterpart who is constantly thwarting his will. Ahura Mazda and Ahriman are pitted against each other in a cosmic struggle stretching throughout history. Every mortal man and woman is also engaged in this struggle whether they know it or not. Every good deed is a blow struck on behalf of Ahura Mazda, while every evil deed is a point scored for Ahriman. Well, the Exile was a crucial period in the history of Jewish thought. The monotheistic preaching of Jeremiah and the Second Isaiah was taking root among the exiles, with the result that it seemed one would have to ascribe evil as well as good to Jehovah. His "holiness" had previously denoted only his fearsome, unapproachable majesty (which is why even priests had had to undertake elaborate rituals before they could appear before him at the altar). About this time, though, "holiness" began to take on the moral meaning it has for us now, as when we say someone is a very holy Christian. For the One God to be holy, then, he could not be in charge of evil. Jewish theologians could see how useful the Zoroastrian idea of Ahriman was in this respect: it removed the onus for evil from God. Yet the exiles were now firmly committed to monotheism. They couldn't very well add a second, an evil, god to their system. But then maybe they didn't have to. The Zoroastrian idea of Ahura Mazda having legions of angels to serve him came in very handy, too. Jews decided the Old Testament's "Sons of God" must be angels, and that Satan was one of them, hence an angel. And an angel, though created good, could certainly go bad. So Satan became assimilated to Ahriman, but made into an angel. God's counterpart, but not his equal. He might be on a long leash, but he was not God's equal in power. Satan as the owner and implicitly the creator of snakes and scorpions in Luke 10:18 is a telltale vestige of the Zoroastrian influence on the Satan concept. Ahriman, they believed, had created the vermin, what the Bible calls "creeping things," including snakes and scorpions.

But when *in the story* did Satan go bad? When did he fall from God's graces, and how? You know the traditional version, which I summarized above. At this point, let's just note that the New Testament never mentions the circumstances of Satan's fall. And its only two hints do not fit the familiar version very well at all, implying the familiar (to us) version wasn't around yet. First, Luke 10:18 again depicts Jesus with second sight, able to witness heavenly goings-on. The seventy-two disciples are reporting on their evangelistic journeys, including their miracles, and Jesus says that he saw Satan going down in defeat as they drove him from the field: "I saw Satan fall like lightning!" There is absolutely nothing in the passage to suggest he is telling them that "before Abraham was, I am, and I witnessed the primordial fall of Lucifer thousands of years ago." No, in context, he seems to mean he had seen the fall of Satan occurring during their mission, as the result of their Spirit-inspired ministry. Revelation 12:7–12 explicitly places the heavenly skirmish between Michael and Satan, each with his loyalists, at the *end* of world history ("the devil has come down to you in great wrath, because he knows that *his time is short,*" RSV), not the beginning.

But would the New Testament writers not have known of Satan's fall from reading the Old Testament? The key question there is whether Jewish scribes had already reinterpreted a few passages as referring to Satan. The first of these is Genesis chapters 2–3, the Garden of Eden story. The snake is nowhere identified with Satan. Nor does 2 Corinthians 11:3 so identify him. Romans 5:12–19 speaks of "one man" (Adam) committing some "trespass" and so ushering sin into the world, and this must be the disobedience in Eden, but nothing is said of who or what might have instigated this disobedience. Revelation 12:10 calls Satan "the old serpent," but the reference seems to be to Leviathan "the fleeing serpent" (Isaiah 27:1) rather than to the serpent of Eden, though the latter identification is made in the Apocalypse of Moses.

Isaiah 14, our second major text, is a mock funeral dirge making sport of the fate of the overthrown king of Babylon. The prophet compares the pride and fall of the late king with the well-known astrological myth of Helal, son of Shahar (i.e., Venus, son of the dawn goddess). "Lucifer" (Light Bearer, Morning Star) is no title of Satan, but of the planetary god Venus (Helal). The Helal myth was based on the daily ascent of Venus as the brightest object in the sky—but not for long. It reigned in glory only until the Sun arose, obliterating any sight of it. The sun and Venus were personified in allegorical form. It is as if Venus were a cocky upstart, too big for his britches, and his descent turns out to be fully as meteoric as his short-lived rise. The winged dawn goddess Shahar (also Istahar, Ishtar) is mentioned in

Psalms 110:3 and 139:9). Worshiped in Jerusalem, she was said to be Helal's mother because Venus rises coincident with the first light, the wings of Shahar, just like the Greek goddess Eos, the Roman Aurora, or the Vedic Ushas. The "mountain of the north," Mount Zaphon, (verse 13) was the traditional Olympus of Canaanite myth, and the Most High, as in Israel, was the name of the king of gods, El Elyon ("God Most High"). So Helal, a petty godling, dared to dream of usurping God's throne, at the zenith of heaven, only to be ignominiously cast down at sunrise. This story was an excellent metaphor for the overweening pride of the fallen Babylonian king, who is explicitly said to be the object of the satire in Isaiah 14:4. Satan doesn't come into it at all.

Ezekiel 28 is a similar denunciation of the doomed king of Tyre, who is said to have been the object of God's special favor in the past but is now to be flung away because of his pride. He is compared both to Adam in Eden and to the signet ring of God. The "anointed guardian cherub" mentioned here was Adam's protector until Adam became ruined with pride and was cast out of Eden, whereupon the cherub was set to guard the Tree of Life from Adam himself (Genesis 3:24). The fall depicted in Ezekiel 28 is that of Adam, not Satan, who is nowhere mentioned in the passage. It is to proud and apostate Adam that the king of Tyre is compared. But later scribal interpreters, for whom the long-ago defeats of the kings of Babylon and Tyre were irrelevant old news, gave these passages a new lease on life as part of the growing story of the fall of Satan.

SEXUAL HARASSMENT

But perhaps the most important reused scripture passage for this purpose was Genesis 6:1–4. There the mighty Sons of God mate with mortal women and beget the Nephilim, mythical ancestors of the Anakim, a Canaanite people of great stature. They are mentioned in Numbers 13:28, 32–33; Deuteronomy 3:11; and 2 Samuel 21:15–22. Originally the story of the intermarriage of gods and mortals was an attempt to explain the great height (six feet—pretty tall back then!) of these Canaanites and Philistines. There was nothing untoward about the mating, any more than there was about the cohabitation of Zeus with various mortal women, producing the "mighty men," the heroic demigods of Greek mythology. The point was exactly the same. But once Jews during the Exile had accepted the monotheism of Jeremiah and the Second Isaiah, they began to find polytheistic passages like Genesis 6:1–4 theologically troublesome. They decided the Sons of God must be angels, and that their sexual adventuring must have been a vile sin. It is at this stage of reinterpretation that the Genesis editor decided to use the story to introduce the Flood of Noah, as an explanation of the corruption of the race that led God to unleash the waters of destruction. Even at this stage, however, there was as yet no connection with Satan. That comes later.

In 1 Enoch chapters 6, 7, and 8 we are explicitly told that the Sons of God, or Watchers, seduced women, then taught them cosmetics and arts of seduction in order to induce mortal men, poor creatures, to sin. Their leader is named Semjaza. That might be intended as an alternate name for Satan. Or someone may have later decided to combine the two characters, or to replace Semjaza with the more familiar Satan. (The Testament of Reuben 5:5–7 turns it around. Now the women seduce the Sons of God!)

The Book of Jubilees 10:11 mentions an evil entity called Mastema as one of the demons, sons of the Watchers who fell. Most of the Watchers are then consigned to imprisonment in subterranean caverns, but Mastema successfully petitions God to allow him 10 percent of them to help him plague and punish the human race. Mastema may be Satan, or Satan may be a later replacement for Mastema. At any rate, 1 Enoch and Jubilees at least give us our first stories of a leader of fallen angels spearheading a fall of some kind, but it is not identified as a war in heaven against God (naturally, since Genesis 6:1–4, the source of these later texts, does not contain the war element either). Satan finally enters the picture by name in 1 Enoch 54, where we read that the Watchers sinned by making themselves servants of Satan, not one of themselves, but already a distinct evil being. Nothing is said of how he became an evil being. Finally, Apocalypse of Moses 16–17 merges the Genesis 6 story of the Sons of God with the Genesis 3 story of the Garden of Eden, retaining the element of sexual seduction. Now for the first time the serpent is made the innocent dupe, as it were, the demon-possessed mouthpiece of Satan to tempt Eve. In fact, it is sexual seduction. And she goes on to seduce Adam into sin.

HORNED HEAD HONCHO

Is Satan the ruler of the demons? Mark 3:22–27 seems to make Satan tantamount to Beelzebul, prince of demons, but take a second look: the initial subject is Beelzebul. The scribes allege that Jesus is invoking his power to drive out his subordinate demons. The scribes say nothing about Satan. Satan appears only in Jesus's answer, which does not exactly seem to fit. The connection between the two looks artificial, as if Mark had two bits of tradition, one charging Jesus with sorcery, the other having him talk about Satan. One reason for thinking so is that Beelzebul was originally a god quite distinct from Satan. Beelzebul ("Lord of the House," i.e., of the inhabited world) was himself the combination of two earlier beings. One was Bel-Ea, once the chief Mesopotamian god. One might call upon him to free one from demons. The other was Baal-mul-lil, the Lord of the Ghost World, a king of demons. Somehow they were mixed together as the improbable composite deity Beelzebul, a prince of demons whom one might bind in order to cast out demons.[1] What I am suggesting is that it looks like someone, perhaps Mark, has effected a similar conflation of Satan with Beelzebul. And he did it by patching two fragments of Jesus-tradition together. Note that Mark 2:23's rhetorical question ("How can Satan cast out Satan?") does not appear in the parallel passages Matthew 12:24–29 and Luke 11:14–22. And Mark adds the sentence, "If Satan has risen up against himself and is divided, he cannot stand but is coming to an end" (Mark 2:26). This seems to imagine Satan "rising up against" himself in court, that is, as his own accuser. (Compare Matthew 12:41, 42, where the men of Nineveh and the Queen of Sheba are imagined as "rising against the men of this generation" to testify against them.) Matthew, who is rewriting Mark's earlier gospel, has tried to reinforce the artificial link between the originally independent Satan saying and the Beelzebul context by rewriting the sentence: "But if Satan should *cast out* Satan" instead of rising up against him, as in Mark. This just makes all the clearer the arbitrariness of Mark's implied identification of Satan with Beelzebul. And thus there is no early evidence that Satan was understood to be the prince of demons. Even in the third-century Gospel of Nicodemus, Satan and Beelzebul are different characters. So, while we can be sure Beelzebul was supposed to be the chief of demons, Satan takes this role only once he is confused with Beelzebul.

Were the demons supposed to be the fallen angels, as modern readers make them? Not necessarily. One can make a better case that the principalities and powers mentioned in the Pauline Epistles are supposed to be the fallen angels. They were understood to rule the Gentile nations, even subsequent to their fall. And it may be they who are in view as the hosts of Mastema in Jubilees or of Satan in 1 Enoch 54, especially since Jubilees assigns them the function of punishing the human race, as if they were authorities of some kind. But they are understood quite differently in Jude 6 (later rewritten as 2 Peter 2:4), which says that the fallen angels (derived from the Sons of God in Genesis 6:1–2,4) have been condemned to Tartarus awaiting trial (just as in the Enoch literature, based in turn on Hesiod's *Theogony* 717–731, in which Zeus binds the Titans in subterranean Tartarus). These do not seem to be the same as the infesting demons and unclean spirits of the gospels. These pitiful spooks, ever seeking a warm, fleshly body to hide in, appear to be more like the desert *jinn* of Arabic folklore, as in the Koran. Josephus regards such demons as the ghosts of the wicked dead. Elsewhere in Jewish literature of the time of Jesus, some do make the demons the ghosts of the mighty Nephilim, those offspring of the fallen angels and mortal women. Others see them as disembodied spirits created as such. On the other hand, Jews in New Testament times explained away the pagan gods as mere demons in disguise (as in 1 Corinthians 10:20), and, given the earlier Jewish belief that the nations were ruled by the fallen Sons of God, it might be implied that they did equate demons with the fallen angels. It is hard to say. As often in trying to put together the hints and scraps of the Bible, it is not easy to be sure of one's results, though you would never know that if you only listened to fundamentalist preachers like Rick Warren, who just take all these things for granted.

The burden of my discussion here is to show you how the Satan figure evolved. We can trace the gradual, folkloric accumulation of originally distinct elements and motifs, just like tracing, for instance, the growth of Santa Claus. That kind of tells you that the end result, whatever it is, cannot be historical fact.

Oh, I know what you might want to say at this point: "Okay, maybe the facts about Satan came together only gradually and piecemeal, but that doesn't mean it's false. It's just progressive revelation." Come on; you'd never think that kind of reasoning looked good if you weren't trying to get out of a tight spot. Besides, it won't really work, since you wind up with an inconsistent picture of Satan, with him being presented, even within the New Testament, as God's servant sometimes, God's archenemy other times. And if the evil characterization of Satan is borrowed from Zoroastrianism, what are you going to say: that the rest of that religion is false, but the idea of an evil anti-God was true, and that God caused Jewish thinkers to detect that one truth amid the trash, to pick it out and adopt it as their own? Why would he take such elaborate measures? Why not just reveal the truth about Satan right from the start? Why not just say in Genesis that it was Satan tempting Adam and Eve? No, this sort of jury-rigged, Scotch-taped theology betrays itself as a piece of after-the-fact rationalization.

I know the predictable reaction at this point, if you've followed me this far, is to just shake your head and dismiss the whole thing, just resolve to think no more about it and go back to believing what your Sunday School teacher told you. But it's really too late for that. You know too much now to just flush it away, at least not with a clean conscience.

SUPER SATAN

Rick Warren's discussion of temptation betrays an implicit belief that Satan is virtually God's equal when it comes to omniscience and omnipresence. Warren, like most fundamentalists, does not think twice about saying again and again that whenever you or anyone else is tempted, it is Satan doing the tempting. Do you see my point? Not Screwtape. Not Pazuzu. Not Etrigan or Mephistopheles. But Satan himself. This is dangerous stuff, both theologically and psychologically. Theologically, to posit such attendance of Satan upon every detail of every Christian life in the world today is to make Satan into an evil God with an all-embracing negative providence. It is to say, virtually, that not a hair of your head will perish without his consent. In short, fundamentalism has, apparently without realizing it, gone the whole way with Zoroastrianism, making Satan into the opposite-but-equal God. Do you really mean to ascribe such all-embracing knowledge and activity to Satan?

One often hears that one ought to "rebuke" Satan. Rick Warren warns, "Don't ever try to argue with the Devil. He's better at arguing than you are, having had thousands of years to practice. You can't bluff Satan with logic."[2] I don't think he is using Satan as a metaphor here. The reference to Satan's superior debating skills and his millennia of practice implies Warren is referring to the real Satan. And he deems it possible, merely unwise, for you to speak to Satan. Get this: one may have a personal relationship, not only with Jesus, but with Satan, too! It's just that Warren wouldn't recommend it. Let's not underestimate this grotesque oddity. Roman Catholics believe one can speak to the departed saints in heaven, but Protestants reject this vehemently. Aren't the Roman Catholics praying to the saints when they do this? And that amounts to polytheism. But doesn't the same logic hold true here? Isn't Warren taking for granted the possibility of *praying to Satan*? Again, he thinks it a futile effort, but it is possible. My point: once again, fundamentalism makes Satan into a god.

HOW CAN SATAN PSYCHE OUT SATAN?

Psychologically, we are talking about paranoia. Look at the symptoms. On the one hand, you believe you are being stalked each moment of each day, Satan's glowing eyes following you from the shadows. Not only that, but, again, remember: you are saying it is the very Prince of Darkness—the Lord of Evil and cosmic chaos—who is trying to induce you, poor slob, into eating that extra slice of chocolate cake. Who is trying his best to get you not to go to church this week. Isn't this a case of what they call "delusions of grandeur"? Are you that important? It's Hitler himself shooting at you, not just some Nazi grunt?

But I don't think fundamentalists are actually paranoid. I think their language about Satan being under every bush, around every corner, ready to tempt, strongly implies the metaphorical nature of the whole enterprise. They use Satan language as a metaphor for the lust of human nature. It is like the cartoon depictions of a little angel on one shoulder, a little devil on the other. One is urging the righteous course of action, while the other is urging you to ignore him and do what you really want. We know these little cartoon creatures are merely metaphorical, denoting conscience and temptation, the wavering of our resolve. Now, if you ask a fundamentalist point-blank, "Do you believe you are being tempted by Satan himself?" I have no doubt that he will say, "Yes." But I suspect it is only that he fears he dare not reject any portion of the doctrinal party line. If it weren't for this, he would at once recognize what he has done. He uses Satan as a metaphor, but when challenged, he will tell himself it is a literal description.

If you want to be convinced that Satan is nothing more than "the Imp of the Perverse," that part of our character that trips us up, just read C. S. Lewis's masterpiece *The Screwtape Letters*. I gather, from reading other material by Lewis, that he did in fact believe in Satan as a literal being. But in the introduction to *Screwtape* he is cagey, and for good reason. He seems to realize that even if there is a Satan, it is impossible to draw a line between his work and that of our own self-destructive foolishness. And that in turn means the Satan business doesn't have any explanatory utility. You don't need Jupiter Pluvius when you know about the water cycle, and you don't need Satan when you know about human venality and cruelty.

Day Twenty-six

Point to Ponder: Believers in Satan are actually pretty optimistic about the world: if only we could get rid of this cosmic troublemaker, everything would be okay.

Quote to Remember: "I cannot omit calling attention to the interesting fact that whereas the central Christian symbolism is a Trinity, the formula of the unconscious mind is a quaternity. As a matter of fact even the orthodox Christian formula is not quite complete, because the dogmatic aspect of the evil principle is absent from the Trinity, the former leading a more or less awkward existence as [the] devil." (Carl Jung, "Dogma and Natural Symbols")

Question to Consider: Doesn't a literal belief in Satan implicitly mitigate the severity of human sinfulness?

NOTES

1. William Menzies Alexander, "The Beelzebul Controversy," in *Demonic Possession in the New Testament: Its Historical, Medical, and Theological Aspects* (1902; repr., Grand Rapids, MI: Baker Book House, 1980), pp. 174–93.

2. Rick Warren, *The Purpose-Driven Life: What on Earth Am I Here For?* (Grand Rapids, MI: Zondervan, 2002), p. 215.

Temp Job

The fool is his own enemy.
The mischief he does is his undoing.
How bitterly he suffers!

Why do what you will regret?
Why bring tears upon yourself?

Do only what you do not regret,
And fill yourself with joy.

For a while the fool's mischief
Tastes sweet, sweet as honey.
But in the end it turns bitter.
And how bitterly he suffers!
—Dhammapada 5, "The Fool"

THE DEVIL DIDN'T MAKE ME DO IT

Rick Warren blames the old devil for tempting us. We saw in the last chapter the great difficulties surmounting this view. Now I want to ask if all the mind games necessary to believe in Satan are worth it, given the fact that he is utterly unnecessary to account for temptation, or even to explain what it is. Reverend Warren quotes a significant passage in the Epistle of James that maps out the psychological process of temptation very well: "Each person is tempted when he is lured and enticed by his own desire. Then desire when it has conceived gives birth to sin; and sin when it is full-grown brings forth death" (James 1:14–15, RSV). Satan is conspicuously absent here. And what role is left for him? I say he is a fifth wheel. Worse yet, when you add him to the mix, aren't you implicitly minimizing human responsibility? If not, then I ask again, what possible role can he have in temptation? Therefore, in the present chapter I would like to show that one may have a mature and even a secular understanding of temptation that is serious, workable, and has nothing to do with Old Scratch. Nor with God, for that matter. In fact, it is all a question of enlightened self-interest. It boils down to considering whether any given act is likely to benefit you in the long run.

Mark 8:36–37 suggests a calculus that will serve us well. "What does it profit a man to gain the whole world and to forfeit his soul?" It's a rhetorical question, one that requires and expects the answer, "nothing." There would be no profit. The proverb doesn't tell us one important thing about the one who has gained the whole earth at the cost of his soul: has he made an even trade, or has he made the same sort of deal the unsuspecting Indians made when they sold Manhattan Island for a few dollars' worth of beads? I think the latter is what's intended. You've come out on the short end of the deal. You're left holding the bag, just like Burgess Meredith in *The Twilight Zone*: there's a devastating war, and the only one to survive is a henpecked bookworm. He had always wanted nothing so much as to be allowed to read in peace. And this small luxury no one would allow him. But now here he is alone with whole libraries full of volumes and no one to interrupt him! And wouldn't you know it? He drops his glasses and picks them up shattered! And no opticians are left! He's got the whole world—but to no purpose.

Interestingly, the same deal is offered to Jesus himself in the Temptation narratives of Matthew and Luke. Satan appears to Jesus and boasts that the whole world is at his personal disposal. Like a newly elected president, he can fill all the posts with his loyal cronies. And if Jesus will swear fealty to him, he can have anything he wants. But there will be one little string attached: he will have mortgaged his soul. No, Jesus decides, it's not worth it. A bad investment.

Mark has appended another saying in a similar vein: "For what can a man give in exchange for his life?" Another rhetorical question. The idea is the same in one of the Psalms that says that all the riches of the wicked cannot buy another day of life for them once the Grim Reaper comes to call (Psalms 49:7–9). You can't bribe him. At most you can play a game of chess with him, and even then you're doomed. He cheats.

Your life is so precious that it cannot be gotten back out of hock. When you try, you realize what a beating you took on the deal. You got only a few measly bucks when you pawned it. But the pawnshop owner recognized the value of this pearl of great price. And he won't part with it no matter how much you offer. It's out of the question for you to redeem it, to buy it back, once it's gone.

IF I ONLY HAD A SOUL

In these Markan sayings the same word, *psuche*, is translated "soul" in the first one, "life" in the second. It could mean either one in either verse. I have just given you the meanings that make most sense to me as I read the text. But it's not absolutely clear. And that lack of clarity is a good reflection of the lack of clarity on a related issue. Namely, what *is* the soul, anyway? And do you have one? Does anybody? Of course, that depends on what it is supposed to be in the first place.

Theravada Buddhism teaches the *anatta* doctrine, the doctrine of no soul. I will let the cat out of the bag and admit right up front that I agree with this. There is none, so we don't have one. But the question remains: what is this soul that we don't have?

The Buddhists aren't denying that you have what it is you are referring to when you call it a soul. They just mean that you're taking a metaphor too literally. Just as Augustine said about evil. There is no such thing as evil. Evil isn't a thing, and we shouldn't think so even though we should go right on resisting evil, fighting evil, hating evil. Because "evil" is a name for a condition, not some kind of an essence or substance. Insofar as anything has become evil it has lost something—namely, the goodness it had by simply existing. Evil is good gone bad. A lack of, a draining away of, good. Just as there is no such thing as silence. Rather, silence is the *absence* of a thing, namely, sound. There is no such thing as cold. It is just a shorthand way of referring to the absence of heat, which *is* something.

In the Theravada text, *The Questions of King Menander*, a Buddhist monk explains to a Hellenistic king that there is no soul as such. To do this, he inspects the king's chariot. He points first to the axle, then to the cab, then to the horses, the wheels, and so on, asking at each point whether this is the chariot. Of course, none of them is. It is the combination of these varied components. And the whole is not really greater than the sum of its parts. It is just a name for the sum of the parts. To make an abstraction like "the chariot" into a substantial thing would be mystification.

What he has done is to deconstruct the concept of the soul or self. He has taken it apart so as better to understand how it functions. And when we do that we discover that we know it better, and yet that we do not know it at all, as there is nothing real to know. There is no Santa; there are generous parents. You get the presents, but it doesn't work the way you thought it did. The rain falls because of the water cycle, not because Zeus pulls a lever. But fall it does.

Buddhists lay bare the composite character of what had seemed whole, simple, single, and perfect, the seamless garment of the soul. It is not transcendental, not presuppositional. It is already *derived*, already a function of something else. It is just a name for the collection of mental phenomena called thoughts, instincts, feelings, and perceptions. These exist, sure they do. But there is nothing holding them together or making them a soul, if by this we imagine some sort of immortal spark that abides unchanging the death of the body.

But direct reference, literal description, as Ludwig Wittgenstein showed, is not the only language game in town. I would like to approach the idea of the soul first from the standpoint of language philosophy, linguistic analysis. The meaning of a term lies in the way we usually use it. What do we seem to be talking about when we use this elusive word, "soul"? And I know no better example of soul-talk than the pair of sayings from Mark's gospel. What is it that is more valuable than the whole world, which to possess is far better than to possess the kingdoms of the world? What is it that can never be bought back once it has been foolishly squandered away?

What profit has been made when one gains the whole world but has to pay for it with his soul? None. No profit, because what you paid *with* is infinitely more precious than what you paid *for*. And the metaphor seems to imply that you are still there, still alive, to feel the chagrin at your stupidity. So I don't think it implies that your soul is simply your life force, your breath, as it does seem to mean in Luke's parable of the Rich Fool. "This night your soul is required of you" (Luke 12:20, RSV). Tonight you have to return that borrowed life you lived. You checked the book out, and now it's due, and the librarian has come for it. Hand it over. The irony is that the Rich Fool spent all his time preparing for a future that would never come. He should have slowed down and enjoyed it while he still had some of it left!

No, I think that Mark's warning about the trade of one's soul for the riches of the world implies something else. What is this soul? It makes most sense to me to suggest that it refers to your *integrity*. It is what Heidegger calls the *authenticity* of your existence. As Tillich puts it, it is the living of your days in obedience to *the law of your own being*. You can disobey yourself, you know. You do, every time you cast aside your better judgment. Every time you decide to stifle your conscience. And when you do, you whittle away at yourself, much as the drug addict wears away his health.

And you experience this as a loss of self-respect. An increase of self-hatred. In the moment of temptation you were divided. You could have gone the way of the law of your being, the real you. But instead you went astray, off the track, as when we say a person who has gone mad is "off his rocker." You became the slacker; you became the black sheep. You turned into Hyde as Jekyll stood by helplessly and watched. But now, now that the deed is done, you despise yourself. You have reverted to Dr. Jekyll. You hate what you did. Even though it was as if someone else had done it, someone named Mr. Hyde, you know it was you, and you hate the you that did it. You hate yourself. You are less than you were.

And the more you give in, the less you become. You have descended a moral stair step. To ease the pain of conscience, to be able to stand living with yourself, you have rationalized: "I guess it wasn't so bad after all." That is a fatal move. From your new position, lower on the scale, things that once seemed really bad start looking better to you, more nearly acceptable. Doing them becomes thinkable. They wouldn't have tempted you before, seeming just too reprehensible.

But now your standards are lower, because you yourself lowered them. So new temptations face you as live options. And every time you give in, the lower you sink and the lower your moral standards become. When you have lost yourself, you have come to the point where you can no longer bear the accusing voice of conscience, so you silence it for good, like Poe's antiheroes in "The Black Cat" and "The Tell-Tale Heart." As the Epistle to Titus says, you have seared your conscience; all the nerve endings are dead. You feel nothing anymore. Like frostbite.

And then you have lost the last precious shred of you. These moral compromises may have been the steps up the ladder to power, to wealth. By them you may have attained the world. The world is your oyster. The world is at your feet. But what is left of your soul? Of yourself? Nothing. You have lost your soul. Satan doesn't have it trapped in a bag or a bottle somewhere, like in "The Devil and Daniel Webster." No, it's not a thing.

It's not ectoplasm, a peculiar notion that refutes itself as soon as you say it. A gas? A mist? That's what Jesus is telling you not to lose? Like the air in a tire? I don't think so. You don't have a soul, because you don't really *have* integrity, authenticity. No, you *live* integrity. You *do* integrity. As John's gospel says, you *do the truth*. So you don't have a soul. But that doesn't mean you shouldn't take care not to lose it.

One of my favorite theological texts is *The Wizard of Oz*, an inexhaustible fund of wisdom. Remember when Dorothy and her friends arrive in the Emerald City, like Jesus and the Twelve arriving in Jerusalem for the Passion? The companions are in need, they think, of three rare substances. The Lion needs courage. The Scarecrow needs a brain; the Tin Man a heart. When informed that no one can grant them these boons because there are no such boons to grant, they are downcast, despairing. Have they really journeyed so far in vain? Not at all.

The journey turns out to be the goal, though they did not know it at the time. Because in the process of overcoming all the obstacles that blocked their way to Oz, they brought forth from within themselves just the things they thought they lacked. The Lion defied danger to rescue his friends. The Scarecrow was the master strategist in outwitting the Wicked Witch. The Tin Man acted out of the very compassion he thought could never exist in his hollow shell. Why should the wizard give them things they already had? They just needed someone to point out the obvious. It wasn't what they *had*, because there was nothing to have. It was what they *did*, what they *were*. And that's just the way it is with your soul.

VENEREAL SINS?

Once, back in a Sunday school class, the teacher asked us Baptists if anyone knew the two categories into which Roman Catholics divide sins. My buddy Dean lost no time chiming in: "Uh, mortal and *venereal!*" Well, come to think of it, I guess there might be some truth to that! But technically, what he was referring to is "venial" sin, lesser sin, something short of be mortal sin, which would land you in hell should you die without having received absolution. Unconfessed venial sin would only send you to purgatory. I have just been discussing what I believe to be mortal sin, that which destroys the soul, one's integrity. Now for venial sins, which do not have quite so terrible a price tag. Here, too, we need bring in neither Satan nor even the notion of offending God.

It is absolutely crucial to a reason-driven life that one shall regard nothing as morally wrong that seems to have no destructive effects on self or others. Otherwise we would be talking about arbitrary cultic taboos dictated by the inscrutable fiat of God. There is a famous story of Rabbi Johanan ben Zakkai, who was approached one day by a sarcastic Gentile. The man asked him about the atonement ritual of burning a red heifer to ashes, then mixing them with water and washing the sinner with them. How could the rabbi defend this practice as anything but the same sort of superstitious magic Jews condemn pagans for practicing? To the astonishment of the Gentile as well as the rabbi's disciple, Johanan freely admitted that he was right: the ashes of a cow have nothing to do with purifying people from sin. Once the skeptic left, the disciple asked his master how he could say such a thing. Johanan replied that such a ritual does not make any moral difference, that "the corpse does not have the power by itself to defile, nor does the mixture of ash and water have the power by itself to cleanse. The truth is that the purifying power of the red cow is a decree of the Holy One, who said, 'I have set it as a statute, I have issued it as a decree. You are not permitted to transgress My decree." (Midrash on Numbers 19:2). So why do it? The answer: "Because it is a commandment of God!" That is a good statement of the piety that does not question God or tradition. For such a mind-set, it makes no difference *why* a thing has been commanded or forbidden. It is simply a question of what Paul calls "the obedience of faith" (Romans 1:5).

This is just the point where the reason-driven life takes the other path at the fork. We are responsible for our decisions and for our advice to others. If we suffer from our adherence to some arbitrary ancient taboo, or others do at our advice, then we are to blame. We prize moral autonomy, which means that our moral duty is not simply to obey the stipulations of a rule book (admittedly a challenge in its own right), but to decide for ourselves what stipulations belong in our book. I like what Kant had to say on the subject. I fear I must quote him at some length.

> Enlightenment is man's release from his self-imposed tutelage. Tutelage is man's inability to make use of his understanding without direction from another. . . . Laziness and cowardice are the reason why so great a portion of mankind, after nature has long since discharged them from external direction, nevertheless remains under lifelong tutelage, and why it is so easy for others to set themselves up as their guardians. It is so easy not to be of age. If I have a book which understands for me, a pastor who has a conscience for me . . . , and so forth, I need not trouble myself. I need not think, if I can only pay— others will readily undertake the irksome work for me.
>
> After the guardians have first made their domestic cattle dumb and have made sure that these placid creatures will not dare take a single step without the harness of the cart to which they are confined, the guardians then show them the danger which threatens if they try to go alone. Actually, however, this danger is not so great, for by falling a few times they would finally learn to walk alone. But an example of this failure makes them timid and ordinarily frightens them away from all further trials.

For any single individual to work himself out of the life under tutelage which has become almost his nature is very difficult. He has come to be fond of this state, and he is for the present really incapable of making use of his reason, for no one has ever let him try it out. Statutes and formulas, those mechanical tools of the rational employment or rather misemployment of his natural gifts, are the fetters of an everlasting tutelage. Whoever throws them off makes only an uncertain leap over the narrowest ditch because he is not accustomed to that kind of free motion. Therefore, there are only few who have succeeded by their own exercise of mind both in freeing themselves from incompetence and in achieving a steady pace.[1]

A model of an independent thinker such as Kant eulogizes is the founder of Epicureanism, the third-century BCE philosopher Epicurus, who founded an ethic based unabashedly upon enlightened self-interest. It is an ethic that proceeds inductively from felt human need and requires no revelation. It posits simply that society needs laws to maximize freedom and to minimize fear, anxiety, and danger. Thus all societies have laws against theft, murder, rape, kidnapping, and so on. These things are conducive to the kind of world everyone wants to live in. You hardly need any metaphysical standards of right and wrong. In such a world there will be friendships in which we truly care for one another, for that is pleasing to do. It is much more pleasing in the long run, and even in the short run, than exploiting other people (though it may take certain confused individuals longer to see it). I should look after my own best interests without trying to trick you into looking out for my interests. It will be better for me if you look to your own interests. This way, society will function like an orchestra in which each one plays his own portion of the common musical score, leaving it to all others to pay attention to theirs.

Epicurus advised that one ought to prefer pleasures that are long-lasting and with the least possible entailed suffering, as when we resist the temptation to overeat for fear of suffering all night from heartburn. Obviously, any rational person would by this token eschew all drug use. Nor would one get drunk, wanting to avoid a hangover. None of this would be prudery; only prudence. Eating a lot of food is not sinful. It is just ill advised if it is going to make you fat, assuming it would be more pleasant for you not to be fat. What is it you want? Ethics is a matter of acting wisely to pursue that end, not working against yourself. It sounds easy in principle but may be hard to practice. That is the usual way with any ethic.[2]

So the reason-driven life is one in which moral actions are defined by inductive reasoning. Rational individuals will not always agree on the right thing to do. But no ethical system, not even one based on alleged revelation, can avoid that, as all the intra-Christian, even intra-evangelical ethical debates attest. And that is no shame. Things are not always so clear, and it is no use pretending otherwise. Everyone is left with gray areas, and then the best thing to do is to follow Luther's advice and "sin boldly." Take the risk. Take your best shot. Who can ask more than that of you? The reason-driven life differs from the religion-driven life primarily in its inductive approach. It rejects any attempt to derive what you ought to do from dogmatic pronouncements based on faith. These are arbitrary and dangerous, as the deeds of religious terrorists make all too clear.

THE IMP OF THE PERVERSE

Ever since Socrates taught that "knowledge is virtue," the rational approach to ethics has invited one major criticism. That is the accurate observation that human nature is not entirely rational! As in Romans 7, even the best of us sometimes finds herself doing what, with her better judgment, she hates. You don't think the alcoholic knows good and well he is doing something unwise? He just can't seem to control himself. You think the neurotic doesn't know he is making himself pointlessly miserable? You think the clinically depressed wretch doesn't know there is no factual reason for feeling so bad? What gives?

Here is where we have to switch our categories from *morality and immorality* to *health and sickness*. You may not be able to isolate a physical basis for the affliction, but the perceived involuntary nature of it, the powerlessness, is no longer something you can blame on the sufferer. You have to adopt the "illness" model, even if it is a metaphor.

It is an apt one, and it means that you have to try some new measures, no longer simple moral exhortation. Psychiatric counseling may be necessary, or antidepressant drugs. Or, as Reverend Warren wisely suggests, membership in a peer support group like Alcoholics Anonymous, Secular Sobriety, or Rational Recovery may be the reinforcement one needs. Good luck in any case!

But when it does come to true ethical choices, I do not see what is lacking in Epicureanism, for example, as a wise system of ethics. It gives us a good compass for detecting moral dilemmas and for navigating our way through them. There need be no devil, no revelation, no supervision from a watching God, no fear of hell, no obedience to antique commands for which one possesses no rationale. One can see what makes for individual and social happiness (and a good society makes for individual happiness!), and the decision on what to do is a calculus for attaining the result we love best. Sounds good to me!

Day Twenty-seven

Point to Ponder: When I "sin," I am sinning against myself.

Quote to Remember: "Jesus says, 'Do not lie, and do not do what you hate, for everything is observed from heaven.'" (Gospel of Thomas, saying 6)

Question to Consider: If we are really supposed to let the Bible be our only moral guide, what are we supposed to do when the Bible doesn't address some moral issue?

NOTES

1. Immanuel Kant, "What Is Enlightenment?" in *The Portable Age of Reason Reader*, ed. Crane Brinton, trans. Lewis White Beck (New York: Viking Press, 1956), pp. 299–300.

2. Kant, by the way, did not accept Epicurean ethics and did not even consider it an ethic. He believed all morality proceeds from a sense of duty to obey absolute rules, with which human nature is congenitally, intuitively acquainted. Morality for Kant was a matter of heeding the categorical imperative regardless of the consequences, whereas Epicureanism is completely a

game of hypothetical imperative: provided you want A, you "should" choose B, though this "should" does not denote moral obligation. I don't mean to misrepresent Epicurus and Kant by associating them. I only mean that both showed one can build a workable, even a noble, ethic upon reason alone, without the aid of revelation. And besides, most ethical systems disagree not on specific provisions of right and wrong action but rather over how one accounts for the fact that an act appears to most people as right or wrong.

Jerusalem Wasn't Built in a Day

There can be no depth without the way to the depth.
Truth without the way to truth is dead.
—Paul Tillich, "The Depth of Existence"

MOVING TARGET

In his twenty-eighth meditation, Pastor Warren counsels the would-be Christian seeker not to grow impatient, because that would lead to despair. Spiritual maturity, character growth, he wisely says, must come slowly if it is to be genuine, solid growth and not some spiritual steroid nightmare. He addresses our fear of change and the growing pains that inevitably accompany it. What I regret, though, is his persistence in using the awful metaphor of God aiming one thunderbolt after another at you in order to shape you up. I cannot help regarding this view of life as grossly superstitious. It promotes a view of God as B. F. Skinner putting his lab rats through the paces of operant conditioning: "Behave, damn you!" Any parent who treated his or her children in this way would be brought to court for child abuse. The metaphor applies only to animal training.

This paranoid fantasy masquerading as piety is made necessary only by the prior personification of life, with its random vicissitudes, as God, who must be aiming events at you, one after another. If you eliminate this superstition, I have already said, you eliminate the problem. You can face the challenges life poses quite adequately (even better, I think) if you just resign yourself to their inevitable occurrence. Just resolve with a grin that you will try to learn from your experiences. This way, the real truth of Reverend Warren's advice survives, but transposed into a rational, adult perspective. It is still proper to view your maturing process as growth, facilitated by change, into a new self, a new you. There are even nonparanoid scripture models to which we may appeal. I find one of them in Luke 21:19: "By your endurance you will gain your lives" (RSV).

In the context I suppose this means that you will save your skin if you hang on long enough in the time of religious persecution. If you give in, if you knuckle under, if you finally renounce your faith, you will be damned. I guess that's the point. But the relevance of that is pretty limited. You can leave it in the mothballs till some unlikely persecution erupts. Is anything implied here that would be more applicable to daily life? Can it be that the passage implies something about personal growth through adversity? Could the point be that you will not finally become your real self unless you are willing to endure some unpleasant things?

What unpleasant things? Anything will qualify as long as it is something that is likely to spell change for you. Ask yourself which phrase feels more natural to you. Do you find yourself thinking that current developments *promise* change or *threaten* change? Much is implied in your attitude toward change.

If you perceive change as a promise, chances are that you see in it a prospect for growth. Perhaps you are dissatisfied with the self you currently are, and you look forward to becoming a better self. Think about that for a moment. Suppose you could be rid of a certain problem, a particular idiosyncrasy, that troubles you or your loved ones. Imagine what your life would be like without that crippling thing. That annoying thing. That besetting sin, whatever. I don't know what conditioned you to have it, but it may be that the next hand of cards dealt you by circumstances will not include that one. After the next shake-up of things, you may be different. You will finally learn that lesson that could never sink in before. Things change, and you will change with them. Why not for the better?

It may be suffering that will cause this change that will wipe the lens clean, that will untie the repeating, neurotic loop. It may be someone else's suffering that will shadow forth your own future. Like Scrooge, you may be moved to say at long last, "I see: that unfortunate man's fate might be my own."

But if change seems like a threat to you, I wonder if it is because you think you will not survive the changes with the self you have been so far intact. You fear that you will have to bid your present self adieu if you move on into the future. If you open up your sails to the future. Well, that is the only way to stop fighting change and instead let change propel you into the future.

Luke has another, similar persecution and martyrdom saying: "Whoever seeks to gain his life will lose it, but whoever loses his life will preserve it" (17:33, RSV). Does this one contradict the one we are considering in 21:19? One says to act in such a way as to gain your life, while the other warns you not to try it. But then it says the only way to preserve it in the long run is to be willing to sacrifice it in the short run. The point, then, is really the same after all. But the saying in chapter 17 provides an important key to understanding the one in chapter 21.

What is it you are afraid of losing if you are afraid of change? It is a self, but it is not your real self. It is not a lasting self, because you will lose it precisely by trying to hold on to it. It is like yesterday's newspaper. If you want to be well informed, you have to toss yesterday's paper aside when today comes with a fresh edition. Maybe you preferred yesterday's news. But it is not news anymore when yesterday is past. Pretending it is still yesterday isn't going to do you any good.

The only way to keep your self, to gain your emerging self, is to let the process of change do its work. You must simply trust that the new self that emerges will be the real one. And it will be replaced in due time by an even more real, a more true you.

Whatever can be threatened, whatever can be shaken, whatever you fear cannot stand, is destined to crash. Do not go down with the ship. Let that which is destined to become the past slip away. Believe that the real you is that which beckons from the future. If it is a sadder you, it will be a wiser one. And dawn will follow the darkness sooner or later. Rebirth can never come without death.

Tillich said that it is not really a question of whether someone believes in God. That is putting the matter all wrong. Everyone has a god, an ultimate concern. The real question is whether what you are living for is adequate to nourish and sustain you. Can it provide for you the courage to be? In the present case, likewise, believing in God is beside the point. What matters is whether you trust the future to bring you to your true selfhood. Will you trust the future? Something new will begin. That is clear. But let it be equally clear to you that you, too, you as an individual, will be born again from the womb of the future. There may be birth pangs, but let it happen. Let it come. Welcome yourself. Your future self knocks even now upon the door; do not turn it away, thinking there is no room left. Unless you open the door, the room you are in will soon be empty.

INTELLECTUAL MATURITY

It happens that some beliefs, no matter how cherished, like a loved one, eventually become outworn and die. And just as you may repress your grief and go into denial at the death of a loved one, so you may go into denial about an outgrown belief. You may hang onto biblical literalism long after you should have graduated to something else. If you do, you are retarding your own religious growth. You are fearing to face the new, more mature self that is waiting to be formed in you.

The great, glaring irony in chapter 28 of *The Purpose-Driven Life* is the utter obliviousness of the need to grow intellectually, in one's beliefs and opinions, rather than accepting a creed full of unverifiable beliefs overnight. This is a fatal course of action. You may feel a great sense of relief that you no longer have to trouble your head deciding among the vast smorgasbord of philosophies and worldviews, now that you have "accepted Christ." But you are kidding yourself to think it can be as easy as that. There are at least two major insidious results of emotional conversion to opinions properly held on intellectual grounds. The first is a fundamental dishonesty. You committed your loyalty to a party line of beliefs because you felt you could find rest for your conscience and purpose for your life in the community that believes these things. But eventually, if you are like most evangelical apologists, whether informal or paid professionals, you will start handing out intellectual and evidential arguments that you supposedly find convincing. And this makes you a hypocrite, because, in fact, you were not convinced this way at all. How could you escape hypocrisy? You could try suspending your faith, putting it on the shelf for the moment, to take the unbeliever's position and see if you *would* find the arguments convincing. I challenge you to do that. Be honest with yourself. Do you dare?

Second, you are taking a terrible risk of character if you just decide to swallow in one big gulp a whole theology and worldview. You won't have earned your convictions. You will be cocky and arrogant. Don't tell me you have not detected such a spirit among your fellow born-again Christians when you speak piteously and disdainfully of all those poor intellectuals out there who don't have the absolute Truth you think you have! Don't you see that *absolute truth corrupts absolutely*? Gotthold Lessing once said that "if God held all truth in his right hand and in his left the everlasting striving after truth, so that I should always and everlastingly be mistaken, and said to me, 'Choose,' with humility I would pick on the left hand and say, 'Father, grant me that. Absolute truth is for thee alone.'"[1] He was right! Just look at the people who glibly claim to know the ultimate and certain truth about the universe. Eric Hoffer adds, "The fanatic is also mentally cocky. . . . At the root of his cockiness is the conviction that life and the universe conform to a simple formula—his formula."[2]

Do you think anyone would hold up a sign saying GOD SAYS KILL FAGS if he didn't believe he had the infallible truth of God in his hip pocket? Do you think that thoughtful individuals who carefully reason out evidence and come to provisional, tentative conclusions, the only kind science allows, would ever be found howling for the blood of homosexuals? You begin to see that the very belief of mortals that they have God's certain truth is a corrupting hubris. And it short-circuits the process of intellectual growth. Even character growth.

Tillich says, "The decisive step to maturity is risking the break away from spiritual infancy with its protective traditions and guiding authorities. Without a 'no' to authority, there is no maturity." He adds, "And, certainly, the way to maturity in thinking is a difficult path. Much must be left behind: early dreams, poetic imaginations,

cherished legends, favored doctrines, accustomed laws and ritual traditions. Some of them must be restored on a deeper level, some must
be given up."[3]

EMOTIONAL MATURITY

Again, fundamentalism, alive and well in *The Purpose-Driven Life*, is a
retarding factor when it comes to emotional growth. It is no use reas-
suring the faithful that they need time to grow when your own
teaching is hindering that growth. Note how Reverend Warren and
his colleagues uphold "spiritual maturity" as the goal of development.
The ideal to be pursued is being "Christlike," a good Christian. There
is less emphasis, if any, on becoming a mature *person*. Nor is that an
accident. The one who grows up in a born-again Christian
family/church environment is being told, explicitly or implicitly, to
concentrate on religiosity at the expense of everything else. Moral
codes, life priorities, value judgments, and so forth are all presented as
a fait accompli, prescribed, prefabricated, predigested. If this were not
so we would not hear all the boasting about the clear Christian sense
of purpose and direction that ostensibly safeguards evangelical youth
from the worldly climate surrounding them. Similarly, evangelical
Christians are always told not even to attempt to deal with their problems, major or minor, from their own imagined wisdom, derogated as
"the strength of the flesh." Rather, she must "lay them on the altar"
and let God take care of them while the Christian busies herself with
more important tasks, like Bible study, prayer, and personal evangelism. But this is a costly trade-off in the long run.

There is just something about the maturation process: you have to
frame your own questions from your own fresh observations about
life. You have to find your own answers, or you will be sitting out the
most important learning experiences of life. As Jung said, one's ultimate goal is to approximate the compassionate Self who lives to serve
others. But on the way to that goal one must first consolidate one's
own ego from whence to go the rest of the way. But this is just not
going to happen if you obediently accept the programming fed to

Christian youth. They will be ill equipped to deal with life's real difficulties when, inevitably, they face them. Personal anxieties that were repressed in the name of "giving them to God" are going to explode sooner or later for not having been dealt with when they arose. One will be able to defer only so long one's personal growth for the sake of maturing as a Christian. And then the rest of the psyche will demand attention. Psychiatrist Eli S. Chesen says it well:

> Throughout a person's life one very real source of frustration can be the great number of unanswered philosophical questions about the meaning of life. I prefer to think of these questions as man's ultimate inquiries or frustrations. They are ultimate not only in a religious-philosophical sense, but in a psychiatric sense also; for if one has no reasonable answers to these questions, one may indeed be depressed or suicidal. The questions I refer to are: Who am I? How did I get here? How should I live? Where am I going? Why am I going there? Where am I going after I have been there? If a person can independently find satisfactory answers, he will possess the essential ingredients to promote stability in his life. If, however, he seeks out preset arbitrary answers from the church, there will be two effects: [First,] his frustration and anxiety will have been reduced or extinguished. [But, second,] he will not have found it necessary to think through these questions to his own satisfaction and therefore shall have learned nothing about himself. As religion is so often preoccupied with rigid arbitrary answers to these ponderings, the religious person need not figure these things out for himself.[4]

MORAL MATURITY

I have already argued that fundamentalism is just making it impossible to get anywhere near moral maturity as long as it holds the threat of an unending furnace of torment over the heads of its cowed adherents. I mean, the legalism of "biblical authority" is bad enough. If righteousness is simply a matter of obeying the dictates of your heavenly daddy, rather than inductively compiling and evolving your own moral posture, you are stuck at a retrograde, childish stage of moral development. But with the hell nonsense thrown in, it is immeasurably worse. Now it would be positively foolish to dare to think for oneself, whether morally, theologically, or any other way, lest one rue it for uncounted billions of years of screaming madness. Why on earth take the risk? Who would be so foolish? But, alas, moral growth is impossible without risk and raising one's own questions, and tentatively framing one's answers.

And so it is that Reverend Warren praises maturity while his theology at every point requires regression into manipulable infantilism. When Jesus advised his disciples to become as little children, I sure hope he didn't have this stuff in mind.

Day Twenty-eight

Point to Ponder: You will never mature morally or intellectually as long as you just take orders from some authority.

Quote to Remember: "When I was a child, I used to speak like a child, think like a child, reason like a child; when I became a man, I did away with childish things." (1 Corinthians 13:11, NASB)

Question to Consider: You wouldn't want your child to make mistakes, but would it be better to tell him to just obey your orders to make sure he doesn't err?

NOTES

1. Gotthold Lessing, *Lessing's Theological Writings*, ed. Henry Chadwick (Stanford, CA: Stanford University Press, 1972), p. 43.

2. Eric Hoffer, *The True Believer: Thoughts on the Nature of Mass Movements* (New York: Harper & Row, 1951), p. 154.

3. Paul Tillich, "In Thinking Be Mature," in *The Eternal Now* (New York: Scribners, 1956), p. 158.

4. Eli S. Chesen, *Religion May Be Hazardous to Your Health: A Psychiatric Guide to the Uses and Abuses of God, Prayer, and the Church or Synagogue* (New York: Collier Macmillan, 1973), pp. 27–28.

Service Industry

As we all know, priests are the most evil enemies to have—why should this be so? Because they are the most impotent. It is their impotence that makes their hate so violent and sinister, so cerebral and poisonous.
—Friedrich Nietzsche, *The Genealogy of Morals*

SLAVE RACE

I am a devout fan of science fiction. Mainly because it is fun and expands the horizon of my imagination, but there is much to be learned there, too. For instance, one finds frequent treatments of the ethical puzzles that might one day accompany the creation of self-aware robots, like Commander Data, the android crewman in *Star Trek: The Next Generation*. The moral dilemma is: do we have the right to create what would in effect be a slave race? Intended as mere functionaries, if they had the capability for independent thought and initiative, wouldn't we be slave drivers if we used them to perform our will? It is a good question to ponder before it one day faces us in the (synthetic) flesh. At any rate, certain creation myths tell us that this is precisely what God did. In creating the human race all he had in mind was a servitor race to make his own maintenance tasks easier. In the Babylonian creation epic, *Enuma Elish*, the god Marduk created the human race and spoke thus: "Blood to blood I join, blood to blood I form an original thing; its name is Man; aboriginal man is mine in making. All his occupations are faithful service." It is pretty much the same in the later Yahwist account in Genesis chapters 2–3. "Then the LORD God took the man and put him into the garden of Eden to cultivate it and keep it" (Genesis 2:15, NASB).

Thus it is no surprise that Rick Warren thinks our primary purpose as human beings is to *serve*. To serve God, and to serve one another. In fact, to serve God *is* to serve one another, since God, of course, has no needs we might satisfy, but he has made us our brother's keeper, and to serve God is to perform the task he has assigned us. I believe it is a high privilege to serve others. But this business of defining ourselves as slaves to God is quite another matter. It is a holdover from the ancient societies that gave birth to our religions. In them, the mass of people were slaves and serfs, and power lay in the hands of tyrants and monarchs whom one hoped might be feeling benevolent on any particular day. God's grace was not much different from Nero's—sometimes he gave the "thumbs up" sign, and you praised him for his gratuitous magnanimity.

One also detects, however, an occasional opposition note in the Bible, a sense of humanity chafing at its slave role and striving to realize its own inherent greatness. The prime example is Genesis 3, the episode of the Prometheus-like Serpent bringing knowledge to Adam and Eve, against God's wishes, defeating his precautions, and kindling his peevish fury. The other is in Genesis 11:1–9, in which a jealous Jehovah notices the technological progress of the humans, whom he had not imagined capable of such things, and conspires with his fellow deities to put a stop to it. They hobble human progress by a "divide and conquer" strategy, making communication impossible. Who would have written such stories, making God look insecure, panicking at human potential and trying to snuff it out? Well, obviously, the stories reflect the struggle in all eras of independent thinkers against the "priestcraft" of religious-royal elites who want to keep the masses pliant, docile, and ignorant. Most people, as Dostoyevsky showed so well in his parable of the Grand Inquisitor, are only too happy to be relieved of the burden of free thought, free decision, and moral responsibility. That is why fundamentalists like Warren are so enamored of the myth of an infallible word of God. They fear it would be too dangerous to think for themselves, given a vengeful God grading their finals. But some have always been willing to call the bluff. Korah, Dathan, and Abiram (Numbers 16) are mythic vestiges of dissenters in ancient Israel, those who dared question the unique prerogatives of the religious power-elite. All these upstarts against "God" (i.e., his representatives, the men behind the curtain) now star in superstitious cautionary tales. In them the reader is warned never to get too uppity lest he, too, slide down the shoot to Sheol. But don't worry: Rick Warren and the churches he represents are firmly on the side of the biblical status quo!

IT'S A BIRD! IT'S A PLANE! IT'S . . .

Friedrich Nietzsche wrote about the two kinds of morality that stem from either side of this great divide. He extolled the morality of the "aristocrat," the independent thinker, the daring product of his own creation. The "superman" is the one who dares to create his own values. The aristocrat is the one who takes responsibility for his own standards of right and wrong. They are values reflecting freethinking, artistic inspiration, and the ascending spirit unafraid of climbing too high. On the other hand, there is Rick Warren's type of Christian morality: the morality of the slaves, of the huddling herd. This is the code of the cringing, the cowardly, those who herd together for mutual sympathy and comfort, who dare not rise above the common level of mediocrity lest they be struck down. They want to play it safe. They worship the tyrant that enslaves them, being infected with what we now call the Stockholm syndrome, the pathetic transfer of affection to one's captors and tormentors. The slave professes himself, and truly believes himself, happy to suffer punishment from his masters, since he must have deserved it, and it must be for his own good. He does not presume to think any thought not preapproved by the guardians of orthodoxy, and he whispers warnings to questioning souls not to heed the seductions of Satan. He exalts humility as it is usually defined, a self-abnegating dismissal of one's own value, for this is a way of internalizing the contempt of one's master and thus avoiding the risk of being struck down by him.

The slave morality includes sympathy and fellow feeling of a particular kind, the kind that amounts to misery loving company. Moral slaves praise the so-called virtue of forgiveness, because it guarantees them tolerance for the mediocrity of their virtue and obliges them in turn to turn a blind eye to the failings of their fellows, a mutual non-admiration society. The slave's vaunted compassion bleeds even for the murderer and the molester, because they, too, are "only human." This decadence erases the line between innocent and guilty so as to clear the way for the slaves' own retreat into the moral fog thus invoked. If not even the evil are to be treated as evil, then what have the mediocre and the cowardly to fear? Most of all, the slave morality universalizes its code of mediocrity so as to exclude and, if possible, destroy, lobotomize, and clip the wings of the true aristocrat, the superman who has perforce broken with their sickroom worldview.

The superman must guard against the attempts of the freedom-fearing herd to take him down. Apart from this, though, he need not despise them and will in fact view them with compassion. This is the role and the fate of Jesus Christ himself, whom Nietzsche by no means blamed for Christianity. Dostoyevsky depicts Jesus as such a compassionate superman, seeking to raise the level of the herd, though you see where it got him. The superman, the moral aristocrat, is like the Buddhist bodhisattva, one seeking and gaining Buddha-hood, a high perch from which to exercise impartial compassion for those below him. The aristocrat is Plato's escapee from the allegorical cave, who eventually returns to the shadows to try to lead more of the troglodytes to freedom, though inevitably few heed him, having grown accustomed to the dark. As James Fowler shows, the superman has ascended to Jung's pinnacle of maturity where the center and the circumference of his world have coincided, and he no longer champions private concerns but makes the needs of all his own.

The ancient Gnostics understood all this. They repudiated the peevish deity of priestcraft and pious ignorance. They sought to regain a forgotten unity of essence with the High God above and beyond the god of religious conventionalism, whether Jewish or Christian. The Sethians called themselves "the kingless race," because they sought to realize their own inner divinity (what we should call human potential) and bowed to no god outside themselves.

FILLING UP THE COMMITTEES

Part of Reverend Warren's passion for servitude is readily understandable in terms of his long experience as a church pastor with many positions in the congregational bureaucracy to fill. Your best members eventually get burned out, and their retreat leaves some gaping holes to fill. This is true of any organization. I know atheist leaders in precisely the same bind. As a leader, you ask yourself, "Don't these dear people realize it takes more than the captain to keep the ship going?" Yet they seem to expect just that. And so it comes in handy, as Durkheim said it would, to produce a divine mandate to reinforce the sense of social obligation people ought to feel to hold up their end of the thing. Thus Reverend Warren and his colleagues wave that Bible and use terms like "your ministry," "your spiritual gift," "a member of the Body of Christ," and so on, to motivate the pew potatoes to get off their duffs and get involved. It shouldn't take such implicit scare tactics, but one can sympathize with the poor clergy. These terms all tend to "mystify" what is a simple matter of fairness, but sometimes kids won't be good unless they think Santa is really coming to town.

But what if we dropped this distasteful metaphor of slavery altogether? Would we have lost the sense of obligation to one another that Rick Warren urges upon us? No, not at all. Martin Luther, though he would not have rejected Warrenism as I do, did have something a bit more subtle to say on this subject. Luther taught the doctrine of "vocation," or divine calling. Like Warren, Luther stressed that God calls the bricklayer as surely as he does the missionary, the street sweeper as surely as he does the pastor. Why? Simply because the society he created has need for all these jobs. The missionary has the job with more immediately obvious spiritual relevance, trying to convert souls. But if his shoes do not possess soles, his efforts will not be worth much. Thus the missionary needs the shoemaker. "How lovely on the mountains are the feet of him who brings good news" (Isaiah 52:7, NASB). They're not going to stay that way for long, though, unless "All God's chilluns got shoes."

In this way, Luther was harking back to an earlier, more naturalistic version of the same insight. Aristotle had pointed out the obvious long centuries before: any society must divide up the labor for everyone's needs to be met. We will not have scribes and priests with time enough to teach if they have to hunt their own food and sew their own clothes. Nor is the shoemaker liable to ply his trade very well unless somebody else is securing and supplying leather, and so on. You don't especially need to inject God into the formula to see how all of us must serve one another for our society to get along. You don't need an infallible and inerrant revelation to tell you that, either. Common sense ought to do just fine.

Day Twenty-nine

Point to Ponder: Slavery, even slavery to God, is degrading to human dignity.

Quote to Remember: "All truly noble morality grows out of triumphant self-affirmation." (Friedrich Nietzsche, *The Genealogy of Morals*)

Question to Consider: If I feel disdain toward someone who needs my help, what is it I am afraid of?

Cut Out the Holy Ghost Noise!

*We counteract a deep feeling of insecurity by making of our existence
a fixed routine. We hereby acquire the illusion that we have tamed
the unpredictable.*
—Eric Hoffer, *The True Believer*

RESSENTIMENT IN CORINTH

In the 1970s anyone in evangelical circles was used to hearing discussions of "spiritual gifts" and how to determine which, if any, one possessed. It was the dawn of the charismatic movement, and everybody had something to say about it. Most discussions sooner or later got around to 1 Corinthians chapters 12 through 14. In these chapters I think we have in effect a self-contained essay with a kind of subtitle, "Concerning Pneumatics." As is well known, the word *pneumatikon* (if intended as a neuter) could denote "spiritual gifts/manifestations," but I think it is more likely intended as a masculine and thus means "spiritual persons" like those in view already in 1 Corinthians 3:1. I hope to demonstrate that the goal of these chapters is to level the field, to extinguish the privileges of the Gnostic pneumatics, the spiritual adepts in the congregation, and to exalt the ungifted by redefining mundane duties (unconvincingly) as equally "spiritual." Thus all become "pneumatics." There can be no stronger brethren once weakness has been exalted as strength, strength redefined as weakness according to the manipulative euphemisms of Orwellian piety. We will see a prime case of the conflict Nietzsche described between the aristocratic stance of the virtuosi, the supermen (in this case, Corinthian charismatics and Gnostics), on the one hand, and the slave herd, the pew potatoes who envy and stigmatize those who dare to prophesy and speak in angelic tongues. Our author himself is one of the latter, though he claims disingenuously to be one of the former.

Like Rick Warren himself, he is utterly clueless as to the real nature of charismatic, spiritual gifts, and seeks to suppress them in favor of bureaucratic authority.

THAT DARN JESUS

1 Corinthians 12:3 just may take the cake as the single strangest-sounding verse of the New Testament: "I want you to understand that no one speaking by the Spirit of God ever says, 'Jesus be cursed!' and no one can say 'Jesus is Lord' except by the Holy Spirit" (RSV). Walter Schmithals[1] is certainly correct in understanding the verse as a disapproving reference to the practice of "separationist" Gnostics who exalted the Christ-Spirit over against the human Jesus (whom they regarded as merely his channeler). To stress their point, they would ritually curse the fleshly Jesus. Origen already understood that such a practice, still familiar in his own day from the Ophite Gnostics, underlay the passage: "they do not admit anyone into their meeting unless he has first pronounced curses against Jesus."[2] "There is a certain sect that does not admit a convert unless he pronounces anathemas on Jesus; and that sect is worthy of the name which it has chosen; for it is the sect of the so-called Ophites, who utter blasphemous words in praise of the serpent."[3]

1 Corinthians 12:3 thus cites the most extreme example of unpredictable, heretical prophecy in order, ultimately, to discredit all early Christian prophecy. What is gaining steam here is an attempt, which finally prevailed in the early church, to squelch prophecy that threatened to upset the consensus of emerging orthodox beliefs. That is what happens in all sectarian movements founded on new prophecies, like the Latter-day Saints, the Assemblies of God, and so on. New prophecy inspires doctrinal innovations, which then harden as a new orthodoxy. Still newer prophets arise within the sect, only to be silenced since the elders don't want to have to go back to the drawing board and start over every time some loose cannon claims to be speaking a word of knowledge from God.

THE EARS HAVE IT

The burden of the chapter is a co-opting polemic against pneumatics ("spiritual ones") and their elitism. Thus it proceeds from the direction of the mundane, the so-called natural men (1 Corinthians 2:14), not from that of the pneumatics, who are here perceived *from outside* as troublemakers, boat rockers. We are hearing from the custodians of the institution, the Catholic *psuchikoi* ("natural ones") and their leaders.

We see the group dynamics of the situation drawn acutely first in 12:15–16. The dejected pew potatoes, the *psuchikoi*, keenly aware of their lack of rare spiritual powers, wallow in self-reproach: "Because I am not a hand, I am not of the body. . . . Because I am not an eye, I am not of the body." By contrast, we hear the imagined self-satisfaction of the pneumatic elite in verse 21, "I have no need of you." But it may be doubted whether the Gnostic spiritual ones thus disdained their ungifted brethren.

For one thing, everything we know about Gnostics from their own writings (the Nag Hammadi texts) suggests they viewed themselves on analogy with the Buddhist bodhisattvas, obliged by their degree of illumination to seek to raise the *psuchikoi* up to their own level. The great Gnostic theologian Valentinus (who claimed to be the direct disciple of one Theodas, a disciple of Paul) did not curse Jesus, and it was precisely because he allowed that the crucifixion of Jesus provided a "Plan B" salvation for the *psuchikoi*. The Corinthian levelers of the anathema upon Jesus need not have held Valentinus's particular tourist-class soteriology, but they may well have held out their own brand of hope toward their unenlightened brethren.

For another, it is difficult to see the point of these pneumatics lingering among the ranks of the *psuchikoi* in the same congregation (as Gnostics still did in Irenaeus's time, to his consternation), unless it was to win others to their cause. That means they cannot have simply disdained them. One observes the same dynamic among charismatics and fundamentalists who remain members of staid denominational churches today, where by their own account they cannot possibly derive spiritual nourishment: they remain behind only to use the congregation as a mission field. Thus the pneumatics cannot have regarded their unenlightened coreligionists as beyond redemption. Again, if we look at the instincts of modern glossolalists, it is to shepherd their ungifted brethren into the experience they themselves so cherish. There is no obvious reason to suppose ancient tongues speakers would have had a different attitude.

Things haven't changed much. More mundane Christians still aim the "elitism" slander against those who think themselves charismatically endowed. Again, it is the representatives of staid denominations like the Baptists, Presbyterians, and Lutherans who seek to vilify the charismatic revivalists in their own ranks as conceited elitists. It is a case of extrapolating the worst possible inferences from a doctrine one does not oneself hold. In the same way, the ancient Gnostics were characteristically derided as sexual libertines, though the Nag Hammadi Gnostic texts provide absolutely no evidence of such practices. If anything, Gnostics drew from their flesh-negation the opposite inference of asceticism. Protestants assume Catholics must abuse the sacrament of penance by sinning heedlessly on Saturday night, all the while planning on cynically confessing it all the next morning. Believers in hell professed not to be able to fathom how Universalists, discounting hell, would not yield to every temptation. But Gnostics, Catholics, and Universalists themselves drew no such inferences. The Corinthian pneumatics probably did not either. No, what we are reading in these charges of elitism is the projection of the ungifted herd who covet the superior abilities of the virtuosi and turn that resentment back against those whom they envy.

Note the structure of the argument in 1 Corinthians 12. We have an initial list of charismatic gifts: the utterance of wisdom (*sophia*), the utterance of knowledge (*gnosis*), faith (if that is how *pistis*, a key term in Gnostic philosophy, ought to be translated here), gifts of healing, workings of miracles, prophecy, distinguishing spirits, varieties of tongues, interpretation of tongues (12:8–10). This list represents the Gnostic repertoire. Then follows the simile of the body and how feet are as important as hands, ears as eyes, naturals as much as spirituals. And then comes a second list that includes the endowments of both categories of church members: *apostles*, prophets, *teachers*, miracles, gifts of healings, *helps*, *administrations*, varieties of tongues (12:28). The four italicized terms are distinctly noncharismatic. *Apostles* are accredited leaders, as witness the battle over credentials already in Acts 1:21–22 and 1 Corinthians 9:1. *Teachers* have command of the faith once and for all delivered unto the saints, the rule of faith that prophecy threatens to undermine. *Helps* and *administrations*—the church treasurer and the organizer of potluck suppers are every bit as important as the bearer of living revelation. But it seems so only from the standpoint of the one who really esteems the potluck supper above prophecy, the one who does not want to see the boat rocked. It is the voice of the herd, not that of the prophetic superman. The same thinking leads today's educators to tell children that all participants in the game are winners, oblivious that no one can excel when the playing field is leveled.

I once heard a great example of the same pseudo-egalitarianism from a politically correct campus minister, who insisted that every staff member of a college was on the same level, the custodian as much as the president. Admittedly, you need both. But you can't tell me the search committee to fill each position has the same challenge. No wonder one is paid more highly, given the broader range of skills required. And what really underlined the phoniness of the whole thing was that the campus minister kept referring to the janitor as "the gardener," as if he himself felt he had to whitewash some low-class taint from the janitor's supposedly important and virtuous job!

And this is the approach to "spiritual gifts" we read in *The Purpose-Driven Life*: "Since your natural abilities are from God, they are just as important and as 'spiritual' as your spiritual gifts. The only difference is that you were given them at birth."[4] The only difference, huh? These words denote that Warren sees no difference in kind between natural and spiritual abilities, and he has chosen which of the two categories under which he will subsume the other. Notice that he places "spiritual" in quotation marks, not "natural." So-called spiritual gifts, then, are for him no different from the kind of talents one is born with. That pretty well rules out prophecy, speaking in tongues, gifts of healing, mountain-moving acts of faith, words of gnosis, oracles of wisdom, discerning false spirits, interpreting glossolalia. This should not surprise us too much, I guess, since Rick Warren is a Southern Baptist, to whom such spiritual "excesses" are fully as anathema as they are to Boston Unitarians. In fact, this chapter of *The Purpose-Driven Life* must be the one and only published discussion of "spiritual gifts" that does not deal with charismatic gifts like tongues.

WORD VERSUS SPIRIT

I have said that the author of 1 Corinthians 12–14 utterly fails to grasp the nature and intent of charismatic worship. He has misunderstood the function of glossolalia and reinterpreted prophecy in a tendentious, "Protestantizing" way. For our author, as for institutional churchmen from the second century up to Rick Warren, inspired speech is that which "is profitable for teaching, for reproof, for correction, for instruction in righteousness" (2 Timothy 3:16). It must therefore, he thinks, be intelligible "propositional revelation." Prophecy he imagines as rational discourse, tongues as worthless pyrotechnics unless it be converted into intelligible speech. Modern Protestant exegetes who interpret Corinthian prophecy as exposition of salvation history, of the gospel, and so on are viewing the passage just as our author did, but they are alike mistaking the nature of prophecy as the original prophets and ecstatics experienced it. I believe that, in the eyes of those whom the writer of our text sought to regulate, prophecy was, along with glossolalia, a subset of ecstatic speech, as in 1 Samuel 10:9–12, not the other way around (tongues plus interpretation equals prophecy). It was not some imagined *content*, but the *mode* of oracular delivery that marked it as the word of God. The reason an interloper in the house of the prophets might fall to his knees, cut to his heart with the penetrating presence of God (1 Corinthians 14:24–25), was the same as caused Saul to succumb to the prophetic afflatus. And what is that?

In Peter L. Berger and Thomas Luckmann's terms, the ecstatics will have created a "finite province of meaning,"[5] a small bubble-reality of the Kingdom of God on earth, by means of their ecstatic behaviors, especially glossolalia, prophecy, and accusations of demonic possession (implied in the distinguishing of spirits and explicit in Pentecostal churches the world over). The gifted will have entered upon a trance state, collectively shared, which creates the effect for them (as for the bystanders) of an alternative world, a zone of sacred space come to earth. The outsider stumbling onto the spectacle might indeed imagine himself to have wandered into the local insane asylum (1 Corinthians 14:23), but he might just as well find himself staggered with the presence of God (14:25–26). It wouldn't matter whether all within were speaking in tongues or prophesying, and it is very doubtful one could tell the difference. Luke knew that it was the spiritual predisposition of the observer that made him think he heard either prophets or raving drunks (Acts 2:11–13; cf., 2 Corinthians 2:15–16).

When the writer of 1 Corinthians 12–14 imagines that tongues utterances are merely half-prophecies, when he thinks glossolalia cannot edify until it be made intelligible, when he thinks one can and should stifle the impulse to speak in tongues or to prophesy (three at most, one by one, etc.), he shows he has not the faintest acquaintance with the genuine life of a charismatic community. The actual life setting of charismatic utterance has been revealingly mapped by anthropologist Felicitas D. Goodman (though members of countless Pentecostal and charismatic storefront churches already knew it well). Her participant-observer research lays bare the logic of charismatic worship: all or most must speak in tongues in order to conjure the alternate reality in which the angels attend one's worship and one may sing in their heavenly dialects (1 Corinthians 13:1; *Testament of Job* 48:3, 49:2, 50:1). In such a hothouse atmosphere the content of the prophecy matters as little as the gist of the Latin Mass did in the numinous pre–Vatican II Catholic Church.

Thus it mattered not if a number of prophets spoke forth their revelations all at once. To imagine that they should stand in line so that everyone can consider each one's sermonette in turn is preposterous, as is the notion that one must needs await the interpretation of glossolalia before it could be considered edifying. What we have in 1 Corinthians 12–14 is a Presbyterian trying to regulate Pentecostals. By contrast, 1 Corinthians 2:12–14 supplies the exact logic of glossolalic prophecy: "Now we have received not the spirit of the world, but the Spirit which is from God, that we might understand the gifts [i.e., the secrets—cf., verse 9] bestowed on us by God. And we impart this in words not taught by human wisdom but taught by the Spirit, interpreting spiritual truths to those who possess the Spirit. The natural man does not receive the gifts of the Spirit of God, for they are folly to him, and he is not able to understand them, because they are spiritually discerned" (RSV). Thus genuine charismatics would not have troubled themselves to await some interpreter to perform the impossible task of making the secrets of God available to the *psuchikoi.* They would know that the deep things of God were made known precisely in words suited to angels, not in human speech. These things will be foolishness to the natural man. Were he to stumble into the midst of glossolalic oracles, he might indeed think them mad because only fellow pneumatics could appraise their revelations correctly. But these things become dangerous when one is trying to construct a church like a well-oiled machine turning out orthodox dogma.

COMFORTABLY NUMB

A friend of mine once told me how he happened to catch the tail end of a broadcast church service on the weird end of the radio dial late one Sunday evening.[6] He had tuned in to the weekly taped service of one of those churches with long names filled with theological adjectives. You know, something like "The Holy Ghost Fire-Baptized John 3:16 Tabernacle of Deliverance, Pillar and Ground of the Truth, Inc." Well, it's plain at once that the preacher has completely lost control of the tongue-speaking congregation. His voice is almost lost amid the echoes of prophesying, tongues utterances, Hallelujahs, and general shouting. But he is manfully trying to restore order so he can get to his sermon: "Cut out the Holy Ghost *noise!* Cut out the Holy Ghost *noise*, I say!" So they finally start to simmer down, and just as the preacher announces his text, you hear a big thump, as one of the saints comes along, dancing in the Spirit, and knocks the lectern over! Then comes the voiceover: "Thank you for being with us at the Holy

Ghost Fire-Baptized John 3:16 Tabernacle of Deliverance. Join us again next week!" They had just sent in the tape as it was!

Well, that, it seems to me, is exactly what is going on in 1 Corinthians 12–14. It is an attempt to get the unruly charismatics of the early church to "cut out the Holy Ghost noise" and to acquiesce to the self-appointed authority of the emerging institution. Don't get me wrong. Personally, I prefer the dignified pageantry of the Episcopal liturgy. But I do not dismiss Pentecostals as a bunch of weirdos. I understand what they are doing, as I would try to do with the behavior of any group alien to me. And I must give them credit for actually doing what most evangelicals merely *say* they are doing: trying to recreate New Testament supernaturalism in the here and now. Most evangelicals, especially the Southern Baptists, are as skeptical of modern supernaturalism as Rudolf Bultmann and D. F. Strauss were. I only wish they'd be consistent and admit that, if these phenomena do not happen now, then there is no historical reason to say they ever did. But if one is not prepared to do that, then you have to admire the Pentecostals for at least putting their money where their mouth is, being consistent supernaturalists.

I'm just trying to make it clear that I am no advocate of charismatic bedlam, but that I can still recognize that the Corinthian Gnostics and charismatics were the genuine spiritual aristocrats, and that 1 Corinthians 12–14 is trying either to cut them off as heretics or to drag them back down to the mediocrity of the herd in the name of a spurious spiritual democracy. Historically, institutionalism won out, and the Gnostics were forced out of the churches, then persecuted to death. Today, Rick Warren is a spokesperson for the kind of homogenized, mundane, "safe" religion that triumphed. He is "the organization man." So it is just what you'd expect when he defines "spiritual gifts" as abilities you can use to build up the church, period. Can you imagine the scene if someone were to write a "book of acts" detailing the spiritual triumphs of Warren's Saddleback Church? Pastor Warren hears that the sinners of some local suburb have repented and received the gospel. So the Apostle Rick journeys there to place the seal of the Spirit upon them. He prays over them and lays hands on them, whereupon they are filled with the Spirit and speak boldly,

"Why, now I have the gift of *administration*! I can run a *committee*, praise God!"

Day Thirty

Point to Ponder: For Rick Warren, "spiritual" gifts are simply talents your church wants to exploit.

Quote to Remember: "Men of thought seldom work well together, whereas between men of action there is usually an easy sense of cama-raderie. Teamwork is rare in intellectual and artistic undertakings, but common and almost indispensable among men of action." (Eric Hoffer, *The True Believer*)

Question to Consider: Is the Pentecostal belief in spiritual gifts essentially any less strange than belief in parapsychology or pyramid power?

NOTES

1. Walter Schmithals, *Gnosticism in Corinth*, trans. John E. Steely (New York: Abingdon Press, 1971), pp. 126–28, 297.

2. Origen *Against Celsus* VI: 28.

3. Origen *Catena fragm.* 47 in I Corinthians xii.3. *Ophos* is Greek for "serpent."

4. Rick Warren, *The Purpose-Driven Life: What on Earth Am I Here For?* (Grand Rapids, MI: Zondervan, 2002), p. 242.

5. Peter L. Berger and Thomas Luckmann, *The Social Construction of Reality: A Treatise in the Sociology of Knowledge* (Garden City, NY: Doubleday Anchor, 1967), p. 25.

6. Kenneth C. Blank, who is the only one who could really do justice to this story!

Cogs for Christ

We are the all-singing, all-dancing crap of the universe.
You are not a beautiful and unique snowflake.
We are all a part of the same compost heap.
—Tyler Durden

[The fervor of a mass movement] subordinates creative work to the
advancement of the movement. Literature, art and science must be
propagandistic and they must be "practical." The true-believing
writer, artist or scientist does not create to express himself . . . or to
discover the true and the beautiful. His task, as he sees it, is to warn,
to advise, to urge, to glorify and to denounce.
—Eric Hoffer, *The True Believer*

THE INBORN DRIVE

C. S. Lewis was right in advising us not to neglect the old books in favor of the new.[1] All you need to know about your individuality and its treasures, Aristotle said long before Rick Warren turned his hand to the task. Aristotle was amazingly prescient. St. Thomas Aquinas found him so persuasive that he based his whole Christian ethics upon Aristotle's "pagan" ethics. He figured God hadn't parceled out smarts to ancient Israel alone, and that insofar as the Bible had anything to add to Aristotle's reasoning, it was only on subjects that were never amenable to human reason anyway, things like the Trinity or the plan of salvation. Not being either inducible from evidence or deducible from logical premises, such doctrines could never be discovered by unaided reason. Modern science, too, has to stand in awe of Aristotle's gray matter. How much he was able to surmise that modern science has only recently verified or accounted for! For instance, Aristotle didn't and couldn't have known a thing about DNA, but he did under-

293

stand the result of it. He taught that every entity has a particular innate property or trajectory inherent in its form, the way its matter is organized. The inner drive of the bird is to fly. That of the rock is merely to fall toward the center of the earth. That of human beings is to do whatever they do rationally.

Furthermore, if properly nourished (if you're talking about living things), each creature will inevitably pursue its natural trajectory, becoming better and better at it as it matures. And it cannot change course. The acorn cannot grow into a spruce or a pine; it can only become an oak, a mighty one if it is sufficiently nourished. Its *entelechy*, or inner goal, is set, as we now know, by its DNA. No one designed it. The particular mix of gifts, talents, weaknesses, defects, assets, and liabilities that make up the individual appearing on your driver's license and in your mirror is no one's invention; nonetheless, your uniqueness is precious.

What does any of this have to do with God? The mechanics of genetic inheritance and mutation are quite enough to explain the whole thing. It is sheerest superstition, raw mythical thinking, to drag God into the equation. It is no more necessary than to believe Apollo is driving the sun across the sky. No more reasonable than to believe elves are painting the grass green. We know what happens, and God is conspicuous by his absence. I possess various talents my parents did not have. I also have Milroy's disease, no thanks to them. It's a mutation. I don't thank or blame anybody for either the blessing of the one or the nuisance of the other. There is nobody to blame or to thank, least of all, me. So I agree with 1 Corinthians 4:7, "What have you that you did not receive? If then you received it, why do you boast as if it were not a gift?" (RSV). Exactly right. As C. S. Lewis adds, it would be as stupid as patting yourself on the back for your hair color.[2] But no one picked out that gift for you. It's the luck of the draw.

Aristotle had a very abstract concept roughly corresponding to a creator God. He spoke of the Prime Mover, a beacon of self-contained, static perfection that, by the simple fact of its existence, draws all material things to move through their paces to attain their own greatest degree of perfection, to come as close as they can to perfection, each in its own way. That, however, as August Comte said, sounds no less mythical than the Creator God version—just less colorful! There is no reason to believe in the need for an outside magnet drawing things toward perfection. It works better as a figure of speech. Genetics explains it well enough, and the key thing to remember out of all this is that while there is randomness, there is not chaos. There is no purpose, no design, but there is a rational structure to the way things work.

Thus, dear reader, you do not have a purpose assigned to you by some Geppetto who constructed you. But you do have a raison d'être. There is a law of your being, and the way to joy and fulfillment is to obey it. The way of unfolding one's potential is the way of satisfaction. If we may speak of a God even in a metaphorical sense, surely it would make the most sense to speak of "serving" one's creator simply by doing a good job of being what you are. Jesus speaks of God's provision for the birds and the flowers, lazy louts that they are. They do not toil or spin, but they are nonetheless doing their jobs by simply doing what a sparrow does, being what a lily is. I should say that is the way of things for human beings, too. Your "assignment," assigned only by your DNA, is to grow into your mature self, and along the way to discover and develop your innate talents.

UNCLE RICK SAYS, "I WANT YOU!"

The notion that this is not enough is another manifestation of Rick Warren's "interim ethic." He admits that there would be no other reason at all for us to continue upon this earth, after receiving Jesus Christ as our imaginary friend, if not for this: "Have you ever wondered why God doesn't just immediately take us to heaven the moment we accept his grace? Why does he leave us in a fallen world? He leaves us here to fulfill his purposes. Once you are saved, God intends to use you for his goals. [Or at least, Pastor Warren does; see below.] God has a *ministry* for you in his church and a *mission* for you in the world."[3] Yup, your reason for taking up space on planet earth is to do religious work. You are a Christian cog. "Whatever you're good at, you should be doing for your church!"[4]

Here is Rick Warren, Grand Inquisitor, a man who can see the human race only as a vast Amway sales force for fundamentalism. Life as a theater for artistic greatness, for simple human feeling, for stimulating the imagination, simply does not exist for him. He is very much like Albert Schweitzer's reconstruction of the historical Jesus, a preacher of extreme piety, allowing time for nothing but repentance and the preaching of repentance, for the end was at hand. Only Warren's gospel is implicitly even more fanatical, since his call to one-track-mindedness is not even predicated upon a belief that the world must soon end. His nothing-but-religion lifestyle can last as long as it has to, leaving one with a generous life expectancy full of one-dimensional religiosity. But get your nose out of your copy of *The Purpose-Driven Life* and take in the bigger picture for a moment. Do you think it is an accident that a book that tells you your chief reason for *existing* is to do volunteer church work is authored by the pastor of a seven-thousand-member congregation? I tell you, it's priestcraft.

Pastor Warren wants us to know how much he prizes the great diversity of personalities and gifts that occurs in the human race and, more important for him, among the born-again master race, the church. What an irony! All it turns out meaning for him is that he has plenty of round pegs for the round holes of church work and square pegs for the square holes. All differences amount to the spices that get homogenized into a great conformist sausage. Who can look at the white-bread, machine-generated character of evangelical "art" or "music," generic, orthodox drivel that has managed to make it through the strainers of pious prudery and hypersensitivities, and think otherwise? If you're saved and you know it, wear a tie.

PITY PARTY

We cannot help thinking of Nietzsche when we get to the part about our ministries being largely a matter of finding the similarly afflicted and probing our bleeding wounds with them. "If you really desire to be used by God, you *must* understand a powerful truth: The very experiences that you have resented or regretted most—the ones you've wanted to hide and forget—are the experiences God wants to use to help others. They *are* your ministry."[5] Here we breathe the fetid atmosphere of the Christian sickroom Nietzsche condemned. Here the slaves find fellowship in wallowing in one another's competing yarns of spectacular preconversion sins and postconversion failures. Bonhoeffer, precisely as he languished in a Nazi prison, waiting for the noose, expressed his disgust with such Christianity: "Are we to fall upon one or two unhappy people in their weakest moment and force upon them a sort of religious coercion?"[6] He says a few pages later, "I should like to speak of God not on the borders of life but at its centre, not in weakness but in strength, not therefore, in man's suffering and death but in his life and prosperity."[7]

Day Thirty-one

Point to Ponder: I am not a robot programmed by God.

Quote to Remember: "Flee, my friend, into your solitude: I see you stung all over by poisonous flies. Flee where the air is raw and strong. Flee into your solitude! You have lived too close to the small and the miserable. Flee their invisible revenge! . . . They hum around you with their praise, too: obtrusiveness is their praise. They want the proximity of your skin and your blood. . . . Often they affect charm. But that has always been the cleverness of cowards. Indeed, cowards are clever! . . . They punish you for all your virtues. They forgive you entirely—your mistakes." (Friedrich Nietzsche, *Thus Spoke Zarathustra*)

Question to Consider: Why is some abstraction called "the meaning of life" better than just *life*?

NOTES

1. C. S. Lewis, "On the Reading of Old Books," in *God in the Dock: Essays on Theology and Ethics* (Grand Rapids, MI: William B. Eerdmans, 1970), p. 201.

2. C. S. Lewis, *The Screwtape Letters and Screwtape Proposes a Toast* (New York: Macmillan, 1970), p. 65.

3. Rick Warren, *The Purpose-Driven Life: What on Earth Am I Here For?* (Grand Rapids, MI: Zondervan, 2002), p. 229.

4. Ibid., p. 244.

5. Ibid., p. 247.

6. Dietrich Bonhoeffer, *Letters and Papers from Prison*, trans. Reginald H. Fuller (New York: Macmillan, 1953), p. 163.

7. Ibid., p. 166.

Being Who You Are

Yes, you're a good boy, Oscar, and I grieved terribly when you died.
That was a strange part to play. My feelings came from my body and
although I could control them they shattered reality, if you know
what I mean. Reality has been broken ever since, and oddly enough it
feels better that way. So I don't bother to mend it.
I just don't care if nothing makes sense.
—Ingmar Bergman, Fanny and Alexander

WHICH ONE'S THE MASK, AND WHICH THE FACE?

I have already signaled my divergence from the Warren Way in that I believe you ought to be more concerned with who you are being in this world than with where to plug yourself into the Borg Collective. And yet I find a few of Rick Warren's questions for self-reflection useful, even for my alternate agenda. Reverend Warren wants you to discover your best avenue of church usefulness (which is what "serving Christ" means to him), and to that end he suggests that you "Ask yourself questions: What do I really enjoy doing most? When do I feel the most fully alive?"[1] Well, at least it's not as bad as an earlier model of fundamentalist introspection, when they used to tell you to imagine the kind of Christian service you'd hate most, and then figure that's God's will for you. Rick Warren's fundamentalism has been more influenced by seventies pop psychology and serendipity theology than by the older Watchman Nee style of spiritual masochism where anything you liked had to be abandoned as an idol, any natural inclination as the worthless "strength of the flesh." For that, at least, we can be grateful.

But I would still modify these self-diagnostics. I suggest you expand the question a bit. Ask yourself when it is that you feel most truly *yourself,* less like you are trying to fit into someone else's clothes. Do you feel most authentically yourself when you are a religious pietist, or when you are just *you*, not especially religious, not particularly trying to govern every thought and impulse, free to speculate on the meaning of things, not fixated on church work, and so on.

I am automatically excluding the possibility of someone deciding they feel most truly themselves when they are getting drunk or smoking crack. No, it ought to be pretty apparent that degenerate pursuits like these, with which I certainly have not the slightest patience, only serve to deface and destroy one's native personality, to degrade one's character, to put you out of kilter. But I wonder if religious devotion is another kind of drug. I'm not saying it is for you. I'm no mind reader. I only wonder if your experience might be like mine. For years I was a born-again Christian, leading others to Christ, seeking sanctification, trying to conform myself to what I was told was a standard of Christlikeness. I struggled to have daily devotions and a meaningful prayer life. I read the Bible and then some! In fact, the deeper I got into the Bible, the less sense all the evangelical beliefs about it made to me. So I finally decided to continue my love affair with the Bible and to kiss evangelicalism good-bye.

But that wasn't the only thing that made me drop born-again Christianity. Another was the realization that I just didn't feel like *me* when I was trying my best to be a good evangelical, born-again pietist. I realized I was delaying personal maturity by fixing my attention solely on religious pursuits. I realized I was suppressing aspects of my personality that I missed. I missed *me*! I felt I had not seen me in a long time. There was, among other things, a great joy in simply being who I am. I never felt able to enjoy that when I had to be on paranoid watch lest the bugaboo "pride" raise its horned head. My constant refrain of the self-abnegating mantra "He must increase and I must decrease" robbed me of the sense of adventurous self-confidence I had once felt. My concern to conform every thought to Christian orthodoxy made me afraid to read the fantasy fiction I had once so enjoyed (Robert E. Howard, H. P. Lovecraft, Lin Carter, and others). If I thought someone was a jerk, I couldn't admit it, lest I commit the sin of "judging." I had to curb and clip my natural sarcasm and self-censor jokes (not even dirty ones) in a pathetically prudish way (nor was I alone in that; have you ever read through one of those terrible Christian joke collections?). And sex? What was *that*? I was getting closer and closer to plaster sainthood, but I was alienating myself from myself.

My utter disillusionment with bogus Christian apologetics meant I had to renounce them to remain intellectually honest (something InterVarsity had always told me I ought to be, God bless them). In the same way, I now found I had to put away the born-again Christian who had taken over my identity like one of the pod aliens from *Invasion of the Body Snatchers*. On the margins of a notebook page from seminary, I wrote one day, "I feel less like a Christian named Bob Price than Bob Price who is a Christian." And from there it was inevitable. I was soon just Bob Price again, not so sure whether to call myself a Christian or not, and thinking maybe ambiguity was a better place to be. And in the meantime, as I said in an earlier chapter, the world assumed brighter colors. People, whether my born-again buddies (the ones who would still speak to me, that is) or anybody else, were just *people* fascinating in their own right, no longer targets for evangelism, prospects for recruitment.

Let me hasten to add that, a few years later, I began to realize I had lost something by rejecting the evangelicalism I had embraced for some dozen years. And so I began to accept that as part of myself, too, as a set of experiences that had helped make me what I am. I became associated with secularists and atheists, very delightful people in the main, but there, too, I found I just could not be hostile to religion as many of them were. That wasn't me, either. So I started attending church again. I love the myths and symbols, none of which I take literally, some of which I cannot even take seriously, but I find it edifying. I am long past the idea that religion entails belief in impossible things (see chapter 13). I don't have everything figured out, and I think that any attempt to organize things and make them completely consistent would be premature closure. The universe is way too big for me to think I've got it figured out. Even the microcosm of myself is too much to think I've got settled. But one thing I'm sure of is that for me fundamentalism, Warrenism, is a straitjacket. Whatever my authentic self is, I can tell it's not going to fit into that constrictive harness. How about you?

IS IT REAL, OR IS IT MEMOREX?

Here is another bit of Warren's advice that I fear I must twist against his intent: "Instead of trying to reshape yourself to be like someone else, you should celebrate the shape God has given only to you."[2] ("Shape" is Warren jargon, an acronym for spiritual gifts, heart, abilities, personality, experiences.) So one must not allow oneself to be intimidated into copying someone else, since that would be a betrayal of one's own unique identity. Yes! By golly, I like the sound of that! Hmmm . . . do you suppose Reverend Warren is including *Jesus* in the deal? Or isn't he a major exception? Elsewhere in the book he tirelessly reiterates that our whole purpose is to "be conformed to the image of Christ." But, once again, to strive to approximate a strictly religious ego ideal is to neglect and suppress all the many areas of life that find no echo in the gospel portraits of Jesus. It is fine to say that he was tempted in all points as we are, like us in every respect save sin (Hebrews 4:15), but the fact remains that we have no precedent to follow when we ask what Jesus might do, faced with many situations we face today. Jesus is not much use in questions of sexual ethics or marriage problems, much less politics. Ron Sider, founder of evangelicals for Social Action, may feel sure Jesus would not be caught resurrected driving a gas-guzzling SUV, but he has no way of knowing. He's just using Jesus as a ventriloquist dummy.

And it would be a waste of time anyway. If Jesus was anything, he was an independent thinker with daring and courage to defy the status quo. We simply cannot imagine him as the first evangelical Christian, taking orders from God as he studied his *Pocket Torah Promise Book*. So how dare we think we are being Christlike when we strive to be obedient sheep? If we are to emulate Jesus, we must go our own way, not his way, because that's what he did! I ask you again: have you accepted yourself as your personal savior?

LET'S PLAY RISK

Rick Warren closes with one of my favorite parables, the Parable of the Talents (Matthew 25:14–30). Let me share with you my own translation for a change.

> For it is just like a man going away from home. He summoned his own slaves and entrusted his goods to them. And to one he gave five talents, to another two, to another one, each according to his ability, and he left home. At once the one receiving the five talents, going off, traded with them and made another five. Similarly, the one receiving two made another two. But the one receiving one went away and dug a hole in the ground and buried his master's silver. Then, after a long time, the lord of those slaves comes and settles accounts with them. And the one receiving five talents approached and presented the five additional talents, saying, "Lord, you entrusted five talents to me; look, I made five more!" His lord said to him, "Well done, good and faithful slave! You have proven yourself responsible with a few things; I will place you in charge of many! Enter into your lord's favor!" The one with two talents also approached, saying, "Lord, you entrusted me with two talents; look, I made another two!" His lord said to him, "Well done, good and faithful slave! You proved yourself responsible with a few things; I will place you in charge of many! Enter into your lord's favor!" And the one having received one talent also approached and said, "Lord, I knew you, that you are a ruthless man, reaping crops that others sowed, harvesting fields that others planted. And fearing to risk it, I went away and hid your talent in the ground. Look, here it is, safe and sound!" But answering, his lord said to him, "Wicked slave! Lazy lout! You say you knew that I reap fields that others sowed? That I harvest crops that others planted? Then surely you must have known at least to leave my silver with the exchange tables, and when I returned I should have recovered my money with interest! So, you there! Take the talent from him and give it to the one with the ten talents. The know-how that brought the wealthy his success will get him even more abundance. But the one not knowing what to do with it will lose even the pittance he has. And the useless slave? Throw him outside into the dark night. Let him lament his error and grind his teeth in chagrin!"

When your life is done, what will you be remembered for? What will be the judgment of history on you? People will judge you by what you did with what you had. They will shake their heads at your failure to live up to your potential, as sports fans do today with Mickey Mantle. He was so great, but he never lived up to his potential, and given how great his potential was, that measures up as quite a lapse. Or they may wonder at what you accomplished with apparently so little to work with. On that score, consider Helen Keller, lost in solipsistic shadow until someone, like Orpheus rescuing Eurydice from the pit of darkness, taught her to communicate by touch. And then there was no stopping her. Or consider Albert Schweitzer, a man with the potential of ten men, who used every ounce of it.

That is what I take from the story. But there is one more thing. I see how the common thread in the story is the element of *risk*. What the first two slaves did was not simply to hand in more money than they started with. No, what they did was *risk* what they had been given, and it paid off. By contrast, I do not get the impression that if, say, the first slave had told his lord, "Master, look! I have doubled the money by stealing from innocent passersby!" he would still have received the accolade "good and faithful slave." Or if the second had said, "Master, look! I have doubled what you gave me by selling your children into slavery while you were gone!" I don't think he would have been invited to share the joy of his lord. Simple increase by itself was not the sufficient condition of blessing. They had to invest wisely, and these two did.

But neither does it seem that increase was even a *necessary* condition for their master's favor. The third slave is condemned for his laziness and cowardice. He should have taken the risk the others took. Now suppose he *had* taken it, and that his financial sense was just as bad as he feared. Picture him approaching his lord empty-handed and confessing, "Lord, I tried to multiply what you entrusted to me. I invested the money in a farmer's crop of figs, but the harvest was bad, and I lost the investment!" Don't you think the master would have blessed him, too? Because he *tried*. He *ventured*. That's why they call it "venture capital."

That's what you are responsible to do with your life. If you play it safe and try to stay within the narrow lines of orthodox belief, valuing the positive peer pressure of your church, afraid to think for yourself, you may think you are going to get a pat on the head for your faithfulness, but I say you have only buried the money in the ground and waited. You took no risk, and you will be the poorer for it.

If you take the risk and fail, what of it? Clarence Darrow, the notorious agnostic lawyer who squared off against his old friend William Jennings Bryan in the famous 1925 Scopes trial, was once asked how he would feel if, after death, he were to find himself surrounded by a jury of biblical prophets and apostles, demanding of him, "Well, Mr. Darrow, what have you got to say for yourself *now?*" He said he would reply, "Gentlemen, I was mistaken." He had done his best. He had called them as he saw them. I say he had nothing to be ashamed of, but if you think he would have been promptly shown the door to hell, then you do.

Day Thirty-two

Point to Ponder: Who am I when I feel most authentically myself?

Quote to Remember: "Idolatrous faith has a definite dynamic: it can be extremely passionate and exercise a preliminary healing power. . . . But the basis of the integration is too narrow. Idolatrous faith breaks down sooner or later and the disease is worse than before. The one limited element which has been elevated to ultimacy is attacked by other limited elements. . . . The fulfillment of the unconscious drives does not last; they are repressed or explode chaotically." (Paul Tillich, *Dynamics of Faith*)

Question to Consider: Reverend Warren warns: "You will find that people who do not understand your shape for ministry will criticize you and try to get you to conform to what *they* think you should be doing. Ignore them" (p. 254). Should that include Reverend Warren himself?

NOTES

1. Rick Warren, *The Purpose-Driven Life: What on Earth Am I Here For?* (Grand Rapids, MI: Zondervan, 2002), p. 251.
    2. Ibid., p. 252.

How Twisted Texts Scream

Things that you're liable to read in the [Living] Bible ain't necessarily so.
—Porgy and Bess

YOUR HIGH HORSE

I am inclined to go easier on Pastor Warren in his thirty-third chapter. I applaud his disdain for the pathetic spectacle of people jockeying for greatness, posturing for recognition. How right he is to lampoon the insecure windbags who insist on being addressed by their titles as "*Doctor* Frankenstein" or "*Reverend* Hargis." A colleague of mine at Bergen Community College once told me how he had sat through a wearying discussion among the faculty about who should be addressed by what title.[1] He quipped that you can be pretty sure they don't have such discussions at Harvard. Indeed they don't. I took a course at Harvard Divinity School once and was astonished to hear students commonly call scholarly titans like Helmut Koester and Harvey Cox by their (*gasp*) first names!

And Pastor Warren is certainly right when he urges that you are too high and mighty if you regard yourself as exempt from any menial task that requires doing. If there is someone who needs help, no matter how distastefully stinky that person might be, you don't have the right to say "Yecch!" and leave it to somebody else. (Actually, you kind of learn this fast once you have to change your baby's diapers!) Think of the pious villains who carefully stepped over the beaten man before the Good Samaritan got there.

It's never beneath your dignity to help someone or to do your share of the common task. Mahatma Gandhi organized a racially integrated commune in South Africa, and one day the chore of raking out the latrine (pretty much a human litter box) fell to his wife. Yikes! They were Brahmins by caste, the highest, priestly tier of Hindus. She exploded, "It is the work of Untouchables!" Not Elliot Ness's Untouchables, you understand, but the folks at the opposite end of the Hindu caste system. Gandhi didn't let her get away with it. She hadn't gotten the point of the whole endeavor. But Rick Warren has.

I always got a chuckle out of an anecdote I read about Chairman Mao Zedong in his early years, long before the Communist revolution in China. As a young soldier in the field, Mao would pay other soldiers to go to the river and draw his water for him, because he felt it was beneath the dignity of a scholar to do menial work—even on his own behalf! I used to invoke the example of the Great Helmsman when my folks suggested I mow the lawn. But that's about as close as I ever got to being a Commie.

And I really resonate with what Rick Warren says about the greatness of those who have not a thought about being great, who know it would be absolutely comical to think of themselves in that way. My father, Noel B. Price, was like that. He spent his adult life working for gainful employment opportunities for the blind. He was a great dad with a great sense of humor. He whiled away his retirement flyfishing. I had the high privilege of giving the eulogy when he died. My text for the occasion was taken from the Chinese scripture the *Tao Te-Ching* (The Book of the Way and Its Power):

> The sage keeps to the deed that consists in taking no action and practices the teaching that uses no words.

> > The myriad creatures arise from it yet it claims no authority;
> > It gives them life yet claims no possession;
> > It benefits them yet exacts no gratitude;
> > It accomplishes its task yet lays claim to no merit.
> > It is because it lays claim to no merit
> > That its merit never deserts it. (II:6–7)

> Therefore it is because the sage never attempts to be great that he succeeds in becoming great. (LXIII:150)

PSYCHING OUT SCRIPTURE

But I must admit I am mighty irritated at the glib way in which Pastor Warren cites the biblical text. Those who psychologize the text play a dubious game with it. They start with some psychological point of which the text is oblivious. Then they find a passage that might be taken as illustrating that psychological point simply because some relevant behavior is depicted in it. Finally, they imply that their cosmetic citation of the Bible somehow proves the larger point they are making. They have some point to make about anger, so they cite a verse showing someone getting angry, and that is supposed to lend biblical support to their theory. But the text only mentions anger, not their theory about it, so it is a sleight-of-hand trick. The abuse is especially egregious when the interpreter ignores the ancient context or the likely point the biblical author was trying to make. It's uncomfortably close to Immanuel Velikovsky citing Bible stories to prove his quack astronomy. Let me review a few cases of what I regard as Warren's frivolous appeals to the Bible. "Jesus specialized in menial tasks that everyone else tried to avoid: washing feet, helping children, fixing breakfast, and serving lepers. Nothing was *beneath* him, because he came to serve."[2] Warren is suggesting that these are typical behaviors for Jesus. But is that the impression one would gain from a contextual reading of any of the relevant texts? Let's see.

First, was Jesus in the habit of washing the feet of his disciples each day when they retired from the dusty road? No, of course not. In John 13:1–17 it is plain Jesus is doing something he has not done before, and obviously he is not going to have much of a chance to do it again, given that the Passion narrative is about to start. Peter is horrified at Jesus's seeming violation of master-disciple protocol. He has certainly never seen Jesus do such a thing before. It is a unique demonstration, an object lesson. Obviously, mutual humility is the point. But the act hardly counts as evidence of the sort of thing Jesus usually did.

Second, did Jesus "help children"? I don't know what Warren may have in mind here. Perhaps he has seen one too many Vacation Bible School posters depicting Jesus helping some kid perfect his baseball swing. If, however, he is thinking of Mark 10:13–16, the passage shows Jesus laying holy hands upon the infants. Their parents had brought them to him for a blessing none but a holy man could give. There is nothing about him offering to change their diapers.

Third, was Jesus in the habit of "fixing breakfast"? Of course, Warren has in mind John 21:9, where the Risen Jesus eerily manifests himself on the shore as his dumbfounded disciples are returning from a fishing outing. It is a powerful scene in which we are to recognize the presence of the numinous barely veiled in a mundane circumstance. But there is no hint at all that Jesus regularly manned the chuck wagon.

Fourth, did Jesus "serve lepers"? This recalls the sort of selfless work we associate with those compassionate souls who take frail AIDS patients to the bathroom, who change the bandages of decaying scarecrows. Such people are nobly Christlike in a genuine way I can never imagine being. But in fact Jesus is not shown doing such things. "Leprosy" in the Bible refers to skin conditions like psoriasis and exema, not Hansen's disease such as one sees depicted in *Ben-Hur*. Not that disgusting. Besides, all Jesus does is touch the poor wretches or even just speak to them.

"Your servant's heart is revealed in little acts that others don't think of doing, as when Paul gathered brushwood for a fire to warm everyone after a shipwreck. He was just as exhausted as everyone else, but he did what everyone needed. No task is beneath you when you have a servant's heart."[3] I don't know about you, but this "servant's heart" stuff is beginning to creep me out. I mean, I don't plan to make it a hobby to seek out the most disgusting jobs I can find. And I'd be even more creeped out at anyone who did. But what about Paul on the island of Malta? The story is a piece of fiction, cut from the same cloth as Hellenistic travel novels of the period. It plays Paul's near-divinity off against the gullible "the gods must be crazy" savages. The wood gathering Paul does is simply a narrative prop, setting up the scene for his snakebite and the subsequent gawking of the yokels. It tells us nothing about the historical Paul or his habits.

Did Paul have "bouts of depression"?[4] The passages in 2 Corinthians 1:8–10 certainly do not suggest it. Paul there refers simply to some unnamed danger that had made him think the jig was up and he was about to meet his maker. "Despaired of life" doesn't mean Paul was clinically depressed; in context it just means he could see his whole life flash before him, before God delivered him in the nick of time. "If Paul had kept his experiences of doubt and depression a secret, millions of people would never have benefited from it."[5] Warren is rewriting the text so it will seem to give his touchy-feely encounter group spirituality some biblical legitimation—as if it needed it. Why not just present your favorite psychological theory as is, without the out-of-context Bible verses to close the deal? The quoted verses have about as much to do with it as half-naked women do with the products they sell on TV.

But the worst ventriloquism Warren perpetrates in *The Purpose-Driven Life* must be his constant quotation of loose paraphrases of the Bible. These are essentially commentaries from a born-again viewpoint, sneaking the interpretations into the text. They erase the line between text and interpretation. I find I am constantly stopping at Warren's declarations that "the Bible says this" or "Paul said that" and scratching my head, thinking: "I don't ever remember reading *that*! Sounds more like something out of a fundamentalist devotional manual to me!" So I look it up in the endnotes, only to find some Bible chapter and verse numbers with initials standing for something like "Today's Slang Version" or "Contemporary Dumbed-Down Version." These people are rewriting the Bible to make it more "useful," and any sense of its historical integrity is out the window. The tighter and tighter they close the gap between the Bible text and the evangelical platitudes their paraphrases make it sound like, the more overtly they are admitting, "By 'the word of God,' all we mean is 'evangelical doctrine.'"

Maybe the most outrageous example is a "quote" from Matthew 20:28, or at least it would be if the text actually read the way Warren has it, from the Living Bible: "Your attitude must be like my own, for I, the Messiah, did not come to be served, but to serve and to give my life."[6] What Matthew 20:28 actually says is "even as the son of man came not to be served but to serve, and to give his life as a ransom for many" (RSV). Once in class I remarked that, whatever you want to make of it, the fact is that Jesus never, in any canonical gospel, says flat-out, "I am the Messiah." A student raised his hand and said, "What about Matthew 20:28?" I asked him, "Uh, what version of the Bible are you reading?"

He answered, "The Living Bible." I replied, "I thought so. In the *real* Bible it doesn't say that." Anyone familiar with New Testament scholarship knows that the "son of man" sayings are open to many interpretations. Is the phrase supposed to be a Christological title? Does it refer to the speaker as a typical human being, as when we say, "You really know how to hurt *a guy*"? Does it refer to the human race in general, as in Psalms 8:4, "What is man that you take thought of him, and the son of man that you care for him?" (NASB). Actually, one could read Matthew 20:28 in any of these ways without too much trouble. It is far from clear that Jesus is claiming to be the Messiah, or that "son of man" denotes that here. But Reverend Warren, it is safe to say, is impatient of all such questions. If you are committed, as I am, to the careful study of the Bible, it is highly annoying to find that the most vocal Bible quoters like Warren neither know nor care about important issues of interpretation. As long as some book has "Bible" on the cover, no matter how far it wanders from the Hebrew or Greek text, Warren and his colleagues are happy to quote it in the pragmatic interests of fundamentalism.

Day Thirty-three

Point to Ponder: Whenever you are tempted to think how great you are, just think of Peggy Hill on *King of the Hill*.

Quote to Remember: "I'm humble—and proud *of* it!" (Wheaton College lapel button)

Question to Consider: Does *The Living Bible* even count as a Bible?

NOTES

1. The wise and witty George Cronk. You may remember him from playing bass and singing backup on *Peppermint Twist*.

2. Rick Warren, *The Purpose-Driven Life: What on Earth Am I Here For?* (Grand Rapids, MI: Zondervan, 2002), p. 260.

3. Ibid., p. 261.

4. Ibid., p. 247.

5. Ibid., p. 248.

6. Ibid., p. 230.

Meetings with
Unremarkable Men

*But when Jesus heard this He turned upon Judas, and His face was
filled with wrath. And he spoke in a voice terrible as the thunder of
the sky and He said, "Get you behind me Satan. Think you that I
came down the years to rule an ant-hill for a day?*

*"My throne is a throne beyond your vision. Shall he whose wings
circle the earth seek shelter in a nest abandoned and forgotten?*

"Shall the living be honored and exalted by the wearer of shrouds? . . .

*"Dare you tempt me with a crown of dross, when my forehead seeks
the Pleiades, or else your thorns?"*
—Kahlil Gibran, *Jesus the Son of Man*

AT THE SERVICE DESK

Once, for about nine months, I worked at the Montclair Public
Library. I learned some interesting things there. But I guess the best
thing I learned there, or had reinforced there, was the joy of serving
others. As a rule in life, my goal is to get along as smoothly as I can
with everyone I meet. I like a well-oiled progression through the
course of every day. I don't want to irritate anybody. I live by the
maxim "A soft answer turneth away wrath" (Proverbs 15:1, KJV). I
find it refreshing to be shown kindness and courtesy by others, and I
enjoy showing others the same consideration. It is a mutual language,
a game where everyone wins. And so at the library I enjoyed dealing
with patrons, making them feel at ease, assuring them that their ques-

tions were not stupid, lighting a way for them through a seeming labyrinth of what I knew to be simple steps, helping them use technology they would never come to see as user-friendly. None of it was menial work, all of it meaningful, since all of it gave me the opportunity to serve. But most of those I served in the library were, as far as I am concerned, unremarkable. I say this not to their discredit; indeed it was their mundaneness that made it a privilege to serve them.

During those months, I found myself compelled to attend a Memorial Day cookout hosted by my beloved brother-in-law Scott and his wonderful wife Laura. I always enjoy seeing them. But I resist events like this, mainly since I didn't really know anybody in Laura's huge Staten Island family. They are pleasant people, but I find myself feeling like a sideshow freak. I can't stand the small talk. As I knew it would, the interminable chat turned ineluctably to golf, the heliotropism of the mundane, of beer drinkers. I brought a book. And, thank God, the day was a boiling hell, which meant I could retreat into the air-conditioning and nap. My wife, Carol, whom I envy, is a chameleon. She can speak the language of linoleum if she has to. But I cannot. Why do I not try to turn the conversation to matters that interest me? "How can we sing the Lord's song in a foreign land?"

Actually, Carol had goaded me to scandalize the assembled mundanes by spouting my opinions on religion. Give 'em a shock; at least it would relieve the boredom. Well, maybe it was just too hot. Maybe it was just that, as I say, I like to avoid needless strife. So in the end, I didn't do it. Sure, to get a couple of hot dogs I eventually moseyed out onto the deck and sat down. Between munches I fired off a couple of smart-ass remarks (which is *my* version of small talk). Then I went back in, complaining about that blessed heat and humidity.

This, too, was a meeting with unremarkable men. From this one, I fear I learned nothing. Some might say I ought to learn to "play well with others." But I have no intention of doing so. I don't mean to make a big deal out of conscripted social gatherings. The larger question is that of whether one owes it to the mundane crowd of unremarkable men to seek to subsume oneself in their mass, to feel guilty for *not* fitting in, as if one's transcendence of the norm were clinically, and not merely statistically, abnormal.

Let me tell you the day I knew that I was not a theologian but rather a philosopher of religion. I was presenting a paper on postmodern theology in Unitarianism. A respondent pointed out that my paper presupposed a certain independent individualism of thinking. It did not speak for the collective community of faith, for even Unitarianism is a community of faith. Theology is the discipline of explicating the faith one shares with one's flock, even though the theologian may act as a kind of vanguard of the proletariat. This is what gives liberal theology its stench in my nostrils. It is patronizing, manipulative, asking what the pew potatoes ought to be fed as the latest politically correct party line.

The philosopher of religion, on the other hand, is like Nietzsche's prophet Zarathustra. He resides in his cave alone and apart. There may be those who wish to consider his words for themselves, but he is not beholden to them. If he does become concerned with them and what they will think, he is, as Nietzsche said, in danger of being sucked dry by them. The crowd wants one of themselves elevated like a scarecrow crucifix, a Clintonian messiah whose flaws are held up like the enormities on *The Jerry Springer Show*, so they can see themselves both magnified and minimized. In a funhouse magnification their flaws assume gigantic proportions like Bill Clinton's, and the fools comfort themselves with the relief that their own sins are smaller and more modest than his. But it is only a trick of the light. At any rate, as Zarathustra said, this is why the mob is happy to forgive the sins of the great, but never their virtues.

I knew, when I heard the respondent's words, that he was right: I was not pursuing religious thought in the interest of the mass, even that mass that falsely imagines itself to be a mass of individuals as they march lockstep. I was the more horrified to hear him say that Unitarians had thought it best to leave individualism behind in favor of interdependence. Sorry to say, Ayn Rand was right on this one: collectivity equals mediocrity and slave morality.

THERE AND BACK AGAIN

There is a two-way path, I think, along which one meets unremarkable men. In his spiritual autobiography, *Meetings with Remarkable*

Men, George Gurdjieff symbolized the various stages of illumination in the guise of gurus and dervishes he had encountered here and there along a spiritual quest. He made it all up. *Meetings with Remarkable Men* is his version of *Pilgrim's Progress* and almost as fictitious. But the point is that in his spiritual search he had to break with the mass of the unremarkable and attach himself to the occasional remarkable individual he met along the way. The time comes when one must play the role of James and John, Peter and Andrew, and leave a mystified Zebedee holding the bag.

But then one reaches Pentecost or the Sarmung Brotherhood, or Shamballah or Zarathustra's cave, or whatever symbol you prefer for spiritual enlightenment. What do you do then? You may start picking your way back along the same path. This is what the Buddha did when he attained enlightenment. He had left his home and family to seek the truth. He chanced to meet one guru and studied with him. Becoming dissatisfied, he attached himself to another remarkable man, but in time he left him, too. Joining a group of ascetics, he added their technique to his growing repertoire. But he abandoned them, too. Finally, seeking the shade of the Bodhi Tree, he sought and found Satori. Then he arose and went back to the deer park in Sarnath where he knew the ascetics still dwelled. Seeing him approach, they cursed his name as an apostate. But it was they who proved to be unremarkable men that day. The Buddha had in the meantime become a remarkable man himself.

So he first had to set out on a journey beyond the crowd, disengaging himself with difficulty, meeting remarkable men on the way. But gaining his goal, he reversed course, now in the role of the remarkable men such as he himself first met. He hoped in this manner to play for others the role his gurus had played for him. He might have different degrees of success with different people. Some simply joined him. Others, like Hermann Hesse's character Siddhartha, finally decided to follow his example more than his teaching, and struck out on their own paths.

But was it obvious that the Buddha, once enlightened, should have returned to the world along the path of the unremarkable? Why not rather shake the dust from his feet and make straight for Nirvana?

Briefly he considered this. Mara the Tempter, his own dark side, whispered into the Buddha's long-lobed ear, "Why bother? None of these worldlings will want to hear what you have to say! Who wants a cure for a disease they love? Your medicine will be to them a poison!" Momentarily the Buddha considered this, for he knew Mara was right. The mass of unremarkable men would view him merely as a curiosity. The great crowds attracted by the Buddha and Jesus were merely crowds of gawkers, like a rubbernecking delay on the highway. But he concluded, "Some will listen." The monks gathered in the deer park did. There was no guarantee anyone would ever do anything more than listen. The Buddha might for all he knew find himself in Nirvana alone. Equally, you may find yourself alone in the silent circle of your own truth.

I AM YOUR DENSITY[1]

Are you one of the remarkable men, or of the unremarkable? José Ortega y Gasset taught that only a precious few have a destiny at all. Let's call it the difference between destiny and dharma. They aren't the same thing. In the Bhagavad Gita, Krishna tells Arjuna it is his dharma to lead the troops into battle. He must put aside his scruples and second thoughts, his humanitarian instincts, and take up the sword boldly!

How are we to interpret Arjuna? In the manner of Kierkegaard's Abraham (in his *Fear and Trembling*), is Arjuna a knight of faith whose special destiny elevates him as an individual above the absolute obligation, "Thou shalt not kill," which applies to everyone else? In that case he would have had a destiny. But I think that is not, after all, the point. Just the opposite, in fact. Arjuna is first thinking precisely of transcending the general duty of his caste. The absolute commandment for him as for the whole warrior caste was "Thou shalt kill!" He had begun to question that duty. He perhaps thought he was rising higher, but his God shot him down. Arjuna had no destiny after all, but only a common dharma. And Krishna insisted that he carry it out.

The unremarkable men have only a dharma. The remarkable have a destiny. Which do you have? That is up to you! Nothing is keeping you chained to the ranks of the unremarkable if you are ill at ease there. Maybe you don't belong there. Maybe, like Heidegger's inner call, it is your destiny whispering to you. If so, there are two temptations facing you.

First, you may resist the call of destiny. You may not like the idea that you owe anything to the future, to the world. You may want to shirk the burden of greatness and prefer to live life passively as a couch potato. Sometimes I think I would. That would be pleasant. At least until, like Jeremiah, who felt himself heartily sick of prophesying, you feel again the urgency smoldering in your very marrow.

Second, you may fall prey to Mara's temptation and refuse to go back among the unremarkable. But if you have escaped Plato's cave, it may be that other troglodytes could escape, too, if they had you to lead them. So why not go back down? But keep an eye on the exit! As Aristotle said, there is no reason that Athens should sin twice against philosophy. No reason, as Jesus said, you should throw your pearls before swine only to have them trample you.

Why should you go among the unremarkable? The Gnostics had a wonderful myth for that. They spoke, and sang, of the Redeemed Redeemer, the savior who entered the dark world of unredeemed mankind like Diogenes with his lantern, looking for those few he knew would listen. He knew that they would be but few. They would be himself, sparks, as the myth puts it, of his own scattered essence. He sought his own face in the faces of those to whom he preached. Occasionally a look of dawning recognition would register, and in that moment the Redeemer would recognize that face as a reflection of his own. For the redeemed and the redeemer were one. And as you meet a receptive ear here and there among the mass of unremarkable men and women, you will have found yourself. This is how I feel when I speak my heresies and am not dismissed as "strange old uncle Bob" by the mundane, the conventional. When I see the bud begin to open, when I see the light dawn, as I occasionally do in class or at a lecture, I have glimpsed *myself* at a different point in time.

The unremarkable will remain unremarkable. But you do not have to remain or, worse yet, become one of them. Turn away from the propaganda lie that it would be better, that you have a duty, to fit in with the mass. Remember the story of the Greek tyrant who used to kill any outstanding person who distinguished himself from the mob in any way. He struck the head off any stalk that dared grow above the level of the field. But we live, as my affectionate Uncle Screwtape said, in a worse trap than that, a reign of the mediocre in which the low stalks themselves decapitate any that rise higher. Do not yield to the reprimand of the collectivity. It may be your destiny as a superior being to serve the unremarkable, as I said at the outset, and that way lies great joy. But do not yield up the knowledge of your superiority at their say-so, for then you will not even be able to serve them.

Day Thirty-four

Point to Ponder: Sometimes you also have to condescend to *be* served.

Quote to Remember: "I do not wish to be mixed up and confused with these preachers of equality. For, to *me* justice speaks thus: 'Men are not equal.' Nor shall they become equal!" (Friedrich Nietzsche, *Thus Spoke Zarathustra*)

Question to Consider: In the Sheep and the Goats Judgment story (Matthew chapter 25), who is the most like Christ: the least of the brethren, or the ones who help them? Or the man on the throne?

NOTE

1. Not a typo for "destiny." I am, of course, quoting George McFly in *Back to the Future*.

War Is Peace
Freedom Is Slavery
Weakness Is Strength

"Churches" they call their sweet-smelling caves. Oh, that falsified
light! That musty air! Here the soul is not allowed to soar to its
height. For thus their faith commands: "Crawl up the stairs on your
knees, ye sinners!"
—Friedrich Nietzsche, *Thus Spoke Zarathustra*

ORWELLIAN GOSPEL

Much of the Bible teaches that victory comes not from the mighty
arm of man but from the considerably mightier arm of God. The
Deuteronomic theology of Joshua, Judges, Samuel, and Kings reflects
the notion over and over again. David, a callow youth with neither
sword nor armor (which would only encumber him), defeats the tow-
ering titan Goliath. He does it by stealth and skill, but in the larger
picture one is to understand that his faith in the living God has won
the victory. Gideon approaches his major battle with a respectable
legion of troops, only God then tells him to dismiss more and more
of them in a brilliantly hilarious scene that compares with the
"marching up and down the square" skit from *Monty Python's The
Meaning of Life*. He does this in order to demonstrate that it is God's
power, not human resources, that wins the day. Of course, here, too,
it is Gideon's strategy that wins the battle, so the message is a trifle
ambiguous. More like a case of brain beating brawn. In the New Testament we find Paul rejoicing in his ailments, vicissitudes, and perils,
because they force the recognition that his apostolic doggedness must
have more than a human source: the all-sufficient grace of Jesus
Christ. In all these cases and more the point would seem to be that
human resources only get in the way. They are a false reed of support,

doomed to give way in the end. Better to begin with a healthy distrust of human strength, to admit, even cultivate, one's weakness. In that way, one may clear the deck for the appearance of God's spiritual power. It seems quite profound in its dialectical sweep.

And yet others have thought differently. What if such a humble embrace of one's utter impotence is not sober and pious realism but rather the most deeply concealed cowardice? What if, deep within, we know that we are fully capable of Sermon on the Mount living (after all, Jesus appeared to expect his hearers to obey him!), and yet we are reluctant to meet the challenge? Could it be that our pious self-abnegation is really a case of what Paul derided as "doing evil that good may abound"? By toadying before God, professing our own weakness to make him look all the stronger, are we renouncing virtue instead of embracing it? After all, the praise thus rendered to God does, as Alfred North Whitehead saw, rather smack of the flattery rendered as lip service to a petty tyrant.

PHLEGETHON

Ludwig Feuerbach was a nineteenth-century philosopher and a religious humanist who aimed a theological argument against belief in God. He began from the fact that theologians always say God in himself is unknown and unknowable to us, that instead we can know only his attributes, his qualities (goodness, power, love, truthfulness, etc.). But then, asked Feuerbach, why should we suppose there is any divine Being at the center of it all? Why believe in some by-definition unknowable being in which all the attributes are supposedly stuck like needles in a pincushion? He proposed that the only real divinity was that of the divine attributes themselves, and that these exist nowhere else but in the human breast, not out there somewhere.

Belief in God, Feuerbach thought, resulted from the moral cowardice and self-hatred of the human race. We refuse to believe in our own potential for goodness, creativity, love, and the like, and so we project all these qualities onto the heavens and make them the exclusive property of an imaginary God. And as a result we see ourselves as miserable, doomed sinners. We must denigrate ourselves in order to make the imaginary God look all the better. But then we project our own evils onto an imaginary devil who we say tempted us to sin. At the same time, we try to make it easy for ourselves. We make God gracious, willing to save us not by our own good merits but by his free love toward us. Having abstracted the longevity of the human species and made it into a single unending life (for God), we selfishly imagine that God will grant it to us as individuals, too.

As for God being merely an imaginary projection, Feuerbach pointed to the history of the God-concept, which seems to change with every generation. God did not create man in his own image, Feuerbach held; rather, we created God in our own image because we found our own potential too great a burden to bear.

He said that *he* was the real believer in the divine, for though he rejected belief in God, he did believe in the *true* divine reality: human nature. To deny the divinity of humanity, the only genuine divinity there is, is to be a real atheist, and that includes traditionally "religious" people.

Jeremiah told us that "the heart is deceitful above all things, and desperately wicked: who can know it?" (Jeremiah 17:9, KJV) Suppose the seeming humility of the bankrupt soul who seeks the grace of God is actually the worst of the wicked heart's cheats?

ADDING A MILLION ZEROES

Remember how Dostoyevsky claimed that the fearful flock of Christians turned aside from the freedom-challenge of Jesus, retreating into the smothering arms of Mother Church, who was only too eager to relieve them (us) of the burden of freedom and autonomy? Eric Hoffer says, "Freedom of choice places the whole blame of failure on the shoulders of the individual. . . . Unless a man has the talents to make something of himself, freedom is an irksome burden. Of what avail is freedom to choose if the self be ineffectual? We join a mass movement to escape individual responsibility, or, in the words of the ardent young Nazi [I. A. R. Wylie], 'to be free from freedom.'"[1]

If there is validity to that picture, as I for one am sure there is, we should not be surprised that such a church and its clergy would catechize us to believe in Original Sin and moral impotence, to ascribe all worthiness to the idol totem they have erected, and to wallow in pious obsequiousness. Nietzsche admired Jesus but christened himself the Antichrist, the implacable foe of debilitating Christian priestcraft. And one may easily see the cowardice Feuerbach described as part and parcel of the slave morality that Nietzsche denounced. It was left for Eric Hoffer to explain how such cherished weakness can nevertheless become the motive power for a mass movement, which is just what Rick Warren wants it to be. Keep in mind that in what follows, Hoffer is outlining the dynamics of mass movements of any and all types, not just religious ones, for he finds that a single psychology underlies them all, Christian, Nazi, Communist, whatever, with no reflection on the positive or negative values each group pursues.

> A mass movement, particularly in its active, revivalist phase, appeals not to those intent on bolstering and advancing a cherished self, but to those who crave to be rid of an unwanted self. A mass movement attracts and holds a following not because it can satisfy the desire for self-advancement, but because it can satisfy the passion for self-renunciation. . . . They look on self-interest as on something tainted and evil; something unclean and unlucky. Anything undertaken under the auspices of the self seems to them foredoomed. Nothing that has its roots and reasons in the self can be good and noble. Their innermost craving is for a new life—a rebirth—or, failing this, a chance to acquire new elements of pride, confidence, hope, a sense of purpose and worth by an identification with a holy cause. An active mass movement offers them opportunities for both. If they join the movement as full converts they are reborn to a new life in its closely-knit collective body.[2]
>   A rising mass movement attracts and holds a following not by its doctrine and promises but by the refuge it offers from the anxieties, barrenness and meaninglessness of an individual existence.[3]

I'd say that searchlight pretty well delineates fundamentalism in general, Rick Warren's Saddleback Church (as he describes it) in particular, and, even more specifically, *The Purpose-Driven Life*, in which

Warren cultivates just these attitudes of self-mistrust and nullification. It is this yielding up of individual thinking, confidence, and initiative, this abandonment of one's own power, that gives strength to the mass movement of Christian fundamentalism. Indeed, weakness is strength. The converted individual yields his strength to the movement that saps it from him. In return he draws from the collective a power he could never have had on his own. The trouble, from my perspective, is that this strength does not fortify the individual again but remains, even in his embrace of it, a sharing of the group mind and collective existence. He has assimilated himself to the group and exists and functions only as an avatar of it.

While Reverend Warren sees close integration into a church group as essential to discipleship, I should conclude just the opposite: one must clear one's head and venture forth alone if there is to be any chance at all of authentic commitment to the truth.

Day Thirty-five

Point to Ponder: Belief in my own weakness is a self-fulfilling promise, and it only allows others to manipulate me.

Quote to Remember: "Except we turn back and become as cows, we shall not enter the kingdom of heaven. For we ought to learn one thing from them: chewing the cud. And verily, what would it profit a man if he gained the whole world and did not learn this one thing: chewing the cud!" (Friedrich Nietzsche, *Thus Spoke Zarathustra*)

Question to Consider: Why should I play into the hands of those who want to keep me weak and dependent?

NOTES

1. Eric Hoffer, *The True Believer: Thoughts on the Nature of Mass Movements* (New York: Harper & Row, 1951), p. 30.

2. Ibid., pp. 12–13.

3. Ibid., p. 39.

Made into Missionaries

They believe that the world is about to come to an end, and that if you don't hear their message you may be lost forever. They freely admit that they will go to practically any lengths to bring that message to your attention. They often shock people, and they mean to. The hour is too late, they say, to stand on false dignity.
—Dan Cohen, *The New Believers*

AD NAUSEAM

Righteousness is one thing, taste is another. I'm an Episcopalian, and we seem to regard the two as equal in importance. Not that I'm complaining. One reason the Episcopal Church has problems growing is that Episcopalians are not particularly big on evangelism. It seems gauche to us to pester people about their religious convictions and how they ought to be more like ours. We want to live and let live. We don't have evangelistic crusades. Charity work is more our kind of thing.

But I wasn't always an Episcopalian. I grew up a Baptist and a fundamentalist. I have witnessed for the faith on street corners, in Boston Commons and Penn Station, in parks, on buses, in rescue missions, to classmates, in shopping malls, and door to door. I learned to have no shame if I thought what I was doing was right. I'm glad for that, though in retrospect I sometimes feel like a jerk. I would never do any of that stuff now. I remember how there was no trick, no gimmick, we wouldn't try if there was a chance it might catch someone's attention "for the gospel." One of the worst gimmicks was phony religious opinion surveys that were merely excuses to trick strangers into talking about religion and give us an excuse to set them straight with the gospel.

326 THE REASON-DRIVEN LIFE

But there were also the terrible tacky slogans. There were posters and stickers that copied the Coca-Cola design and said "Things Go Better with Christ." Surveys (real ones, that is) showed that the average person thought these things were a joke, mockery of Christianity, not a promotion of it. We should have learned a lesson from that: we were unwittingly making our cherished faith into a joke by resorting to tasteless marketing gimmicks. We were not so much casting our pearls before swine as we were trampling them into the mud ourselves.

I thought I had seen everything, but I had seen nothing yet—until recently when in the local paper I beheld an ad for a congregation with the slogan "Nobody does me like Jesus!" I could not believe what I was seeing. I still can't. Can the people responsible for this ad possibly be oblivious to the unspeakably loathsome implications of it? I think of Paul's words in 1 Corinthians 14:23, "Will they not say that you are mad?"

This problem, the greatest fans of the Christian message becoming the worst enemies of it by their inane attempts at spreading it, is a symptom of a much bigger problem.

ALWAYS HOPED THAT I'D BE AN APOSTLE, KNEW THAT I WOULD MAKE IT IF I TRIED.

For a long time my study of the New Testament has led me to believe that there simply is no mandate for the average Christian to take upon himself or herself the specialized task of evangelism. Ephesians 4:11 says that only "some" were appointed to the evangelistic task, just as only "some" were set aside for the pastorate. Matthew 28:18–20, Mark 16:15–18, Luke 24:47, John 20:21–23, and Acts 1:8, the various versions of the Great Commission to evangelize the world, are all pointedly aimed at the apostles and their successors, leaders of the church, not at the rank and file. It is only the Protestant, democratizing way of reading the Bible, as if everything it says, it says to *you*, that makes anyone think otherwise. Essentially, thinking the Great Commission is addressed to any casual reader, even any casual Christian reader, is tantamount to the old joke where the guy opens the Bible at random to find God's will for him and chances upon Matthew 27:5, "He went and hanged himself." Hastily flipping the pages, hoping for something better, he stumbles upon Luke 10:37, "Go and do likewise." Spooked, he now rustles some more pages and comes to John 13:27: "What you are going to do, do quickly." Yikes!

But remember, the gospels were written in an era when, unlike Rick Warren's *The Purpose-Driven Life*, no books could boast on their dust jacket, TWENTY MILLION SOLD! like McDonald's hamburgers. Given the cost of scribal copying, few even wrote books intended for mass audiences, even assuming most people could read. So who constituted the intended audience for the gospels? Let's take Matthew as the clearest example. This gospel seems to have been composed (on the basis of Mark's earlier book) as a kind of handbook and catechism for the missionary preachers of the church at Antioch, a major hub of early Christian missions (Acts 13:1–3). This is why it is arranged in five major sections of teaching, organized by topic. One of them (chapter 18) is a church manual, stipulating measures to mediate disputes, mechanisms for congregational discipline, and so on. As Matthew 10:23–24 shows, the disciples/apostles in the book really stand for their successors, the Antiochene missionaries. It is obviously they, not the original Twelve including Peter, Matthew, Simon, and Thomas, who are being told that their missionary journeys will be cut short by the second coming of Jesus. And it is they who are being sent off with final words of instruction in 28:18–20. It is they who are being sent to convert and baptize Gentiles, and so on. Not you. What, do you think Jesus was handing the keys of the kingdom to you, too?

YOU ARE THE SALT OF THE EARTH

To the laity, the average Christians, what does the New Testament say? 1 Peter is clear on the point. One ought to live an exemplary life and be ready to account for it if someone asks what it is that makes you tick (1 Peter 3:15). Matthew 5:16 says the same: let your life be a beacon so folks will say, "Thank God for people like that!" And yet just down the page Jesus warns, "Take care not to practice your right-eousness before others, to be seen by them" (Matthew 6:1). The difference is between someone who shows kindness to a stranger and someone who buttonholes a stranger to "witness" to him, like it or not. I'd love to know how anybody can read Matthew 6:1 and then go attach to his bumper a sticker that reads, HONK IF YOU LOVE JESUS. What would Jesus do? If Matthew 6:1 is any guide, he would not drive around with bumper stickers about the Rapture and how tailgaters will be abandoned to the wrath of the Antichrist.

For years, at Wednesday night prayer meetings, I would hear devout women telling the congregation how their husbands remained aloof to the gospel despite the women witnessing to them. What? Could they not see that their pious badgering was only making the gospel seem repulsive? Indeed, all such obnoxious evangelism sends one clear message, and it's not what the witness thinks it is. As soon as you knock on that door, pass out that tract, turn a casual conversation to matters of private faith, what you are really saying is, "Why don't you become a vexing fanatic like me?" This is certainly one case where, as Marshall McLuhan said, "The medium is the message." I don't care what you say about the virtues of the gospel, the glories of the redeemed life; the very fact that you are pitching this message that no one asked to hear is communicating something else: "I'm a nut, and you can be one, too!" Most people have a hard time mustering the courage to witness to someone precisely because they fear they will come across as a nut. And they are right! That's exactly how they come across!

I know many readers will want to reply, "But look at the results! Person-to-person evangelism has made evangelical Christianity into a global juggernaut! That must prove it's the right strategy!" Yes, but don't you see the nature of the result? You have recruited legions more of the obnoxious and the narrow-minded, the proselytizers and the pushy. Besides, it has ever been the way of mass movements to thrive on a steady diet of self-condemned "sinners" and self-haters. It is unhealthy growth, like that of a cancer. I've got news for you: it's not hostility toward the gospel that makes outsiders wish born-again Christians *would* suddenly vanish in the Rapture!

LAY THAT BURDEN DOWN!

Leave it to those who feel the call to specialize in evangelism in the proper forum. Otherwise, you may be doing your gospel more harm than good. Far better, I say, to heed the advice of 1 Peter 3:1, to win over others "without a word by [one's] behavior." Or the counsel of James: "I will show you my faith by my works" (James 2:18, NASB). For Pete's sake, and for James's sake, give it a rest!

Day Thirty-six

Point to Ponder: Born-again Christians are basically Jehovah's Witnesses who believe in the Trinity.

Quote to Remember: "God, save me from your followers!" (Lapel button slogan)

Question to Consider: Have you ever wondered why the New Testament does not offer guidance on "personal evangelism"? Is it maybe because the writers never thought of such a thing?

Fabricating
Your Life Message

Search your feelings! You know it to be true![1]
—Darth Vader

SELLING YOUR STORY

In the previous chapter, I argued that the New Testament does not assign the evangelistic task to the rank-and-file Christian. Already in the earliest Christian texts, there is a distinction drawn between average Christians who are simply responsible to live an exemplary life (and to account for if outsiders are impressed and ask about it) and specialists including "evangelists," "apostles," "brethren," and so on. No one can deny there is a great gap between characters like Peter, Paul, Barnabas, Apollos, Priscilla, and Aquila on the one hand and average believers on the other. Modern evangelicalism ignores the distinction, seeking instead to "democratize" evangelism. Why? Rick Warren makes a crucial admission. It is all a marketing ploy. "Actually, your personal testimony is more effective than a sermon, because unbelievers see pastors as professional salesmen, but see you as a 'satisfied customer,' so they give you more credibility."[1] But they shouldn't. They will just be getting taken in by a sneakier sales pitch. Warren is really trying to train something like an Amway sales force. Evangelicals subjecting you to "personal evangelism" are exactly like Ned Ryerson in *Groundhog Day*, exploiting their acquaintance with you to sell you some eternal life insurance. How can these people not see how absolutely odious to outsiders they appear? And, again, the medium is the message. It appears as if they are spontaneously sharing with you what means so much to them, like a pair of housewives in a Clorox commercial. But it is fake. Warren tells you how to formulate and rehearse your testimony. How bogus!

Here is what you do, composing your own gospel, the gospel according to you according to Rick Warren: "The best way to 'be ready' is to write out your testimony and then memorize the main points. Divide it into four parts:

1. What my life was like before I met Jesus
2. How I realized I needed Jesus
3. How I committed my life to Jesus
4. The difference Jesus has made in my life"[2]

Do you see what's going on here? If your experience with Christ did not already conform to an assembly-line pattern, it will now. Whatever happened to bring you to Christ is now to be rewritten according to a formula. And this means your actual experience is being forced into the formula, sacrificed to it, fabricated in its image, reduced in the last analysis to a canned formula with your name penciled into the blank. And you will go forth and parrot this canned spiel with all the spontaneity of a Jehovah's Witness.

In one sense, I suspect, the stereotype testimony-formula does not significantly depart from the actual conversion experience it purports to describe, but that is because a huge amount of so-called Christian experience is hardly experience at all, but really rather a set of ritualized group behaviors (church services, singing hymns, small group Bible studies, daily devotional routines) and, just as crucial, a set of repeated slogans and shibboleths. You soon realize that you are to call your religious life "having a personal relationship with Christ," but I have never seen much reason to believe it is more than a piece of jargon. This was the original meaning of the nickname "Methodist." The Church of England pietist movement prescribed a series of devotional exercises that was considered tantamount to a "personal relationship with Christ"—and still is. There is less to it than meets the eye. It is analogous to speaking in tongues in Pentecostal denominations like the Assemblies of God. Go to their prayer meetings, and I suspect you will seldom behold anything like the book of Acts portrays. It is learned, repeated behavior. The same individuals will say the same nonsense syllables at the same point in the service every week. It is like the Latin Mass in the Catholic Church. Same with the standard evangelical church, where members comfort and condition one another with a constant exchange of shibboleths and clichés. Shibboleths, because if you don't use the right clichés and formulas, you will not be considered "saved." I suspect the "born-again experience" is mere formula all the way down.

IF YOU'RE SAVED NOW, YOU MUST HAVE BEEN LOST BEFORE

Berger and Luckmann explain why and how members of conversionist movements, whether religious or political or anything else, rewrite their preconversion biography to make sense in light of their new beliefs. If the new is good and salvific, the old, simply by virtue of having been different, must have been bad and damning. If you interviewed the person before conversion to Sect A, you might have heard a positive estimate of how things were going. But once she has converted, she must justify such a dramatic change of identity, and so her past must have been sinful and ignorant. It was "sinful" only in the sense of "unclean" or "profane," that is, not yet within the charmed circle of sacred space. Berger and Luckmann call this ideological reevaluation a "nihilation" strategy.

> This reinterpretation brings about a rupture in the subjective biography of the individual in terms of "B.C." and "A.D.," "pre-Damascus" and "post-Damascus." Everything preceding the alternation [=conversion] is now apprehended as leading toward it . . . , everything following it as flowing from its new reality. This involves a reinterpretation of past biography *in toto*, following the formula "Then I *thought* . . . now I *know*." . . . Prealternation biography is typically nihilated *in toto* by subsuming it under a negative category occupying a strategic position in the new legitimating apparatus: "When I was still living a life of sin," "When I was still caught in bourgeois consciousness." . . . Since it is relatively easier to invent things that never happened than to forget those that actually did, the individual may fabricate and insert events wherever they are needed

to harmonize the remembered with the reinterpreted past. Since it is the new reality rather than the old that now appears dominatingly plausible to him, he may be perfectly "sincere" in such a procedure—subjectively he is not telling lies about the past but bringing it in line with *the* truth that, necessarily, embraces both present and past. This point, incidentally, is very important if one wishes to understand adequately the motives behind the historically recurrent falsifications and forgeries of religious documents.[3]

Thus, as soon as you become a Christian, your past also undergoes a conversion and becomes "non-Christian" or "unsaved," though you would never have thought of it that way at the time. There's nothing esoteric about it, nothing to be surprised at. After all, the past always changes its meaning for us as our present perspective changes.

This is why, for instance, when people leave conversionist sects like the Unification Church or Krishna Consciousness and return to mundane society, they often claim they were brainwashed into joining in the first place. There appears to be no evidence that these groups practice anything remotely resembling brainwashing, coercion, hypnotizing, and so forth. But the new de-converts have a lot of explaining to do. Having rejected a once-intense faith allegiance, they now cannot understand how it used to make sense to them. So, just as in the new days of their cult conversion they spoke of their old unenlightened life, now they speak of a pre-deconversion life as the product of brainwashing. They are not lying; they just cannot figure out how else they could once have believed in such outlandish doctrines, as they now seem. Similarly, when porn star Linda Lovelace repudiated making skin flicks, she claimed that her boyfriend had imprisoned her and coerced her into porn. I suppose it might have been true, but I suspected she had just come to think better of what she had done and now tried to exorcise it, along with the responsibility for it, by claiming to have been coerced.

THE MIRROR OF MAN'S DAMNATION

But testimonies cut both ways. Let me challenge you, if you are an evangelical Christian, to read the testimonies of people who have grown disillusioned with born-again Christianity. Ed Babinski, himself an ex-evangelical and ex-creationist, has compiled a collection of these called *Leaving the Fold* from Prometheus Books. It features the stories of many individuals from various backgrounds and various historical eras, many of them biblical scholars.

Naturally, you ought to be on your guard, as you evaluate these testimonies, as to any signs of the authors "nihilating" their religious pasts in order to justify their subsequent rejection of it. Ex-believers are fully as capable of rewriting their "prealternation" autobiographies as ex-unbelievers are. One gauge, as with ex-fundamentalist or ex-cultist autobiographies, is whether the abandoned life is portrayed unremittingly as negative. That just has to be one-sided.

But I think there is nothing quite so revealing and thought-provoking about one's own opinions as reading an account by someone who once held them but has dropped them. What have they seen that you have not? Are they right? Did they jump the gun? Leave for inadequate reasons? What a unique opportunity to see yourself as others see you! I hope you will avail yourself of the opportunity.

C. S. Lewis once remarked: "If you examined a hundred people who had lost their faith in Christianity, I wonder how many of them would turn out to have been reasoned out of it by honest argument? Do not most people simply drift away?"[4] Good question. It would be interesting to know. But let me mention one more thing about "nihilation" just at this point. I know how strong the temptation is among born-again Christians to accuse people of having dropped Christian faith for ulterior motives that they will not admit. It's not necessarily that the ex-believers give some signal, maybe body language or something, to that effect. Nor is the Christian claiming to be a mind reader. They just assume there *cannot* have been a cogent reason for leaving, and so what's left? But that is another "nihilation" strategy. You are once again trying to explain away threatening information by accounting for it in terms of your own belief system. I have the impression that evangelical Christians imagine that, since born-againism was a new experience for them (having perhaps been brought up in some other religion), then it must be equally an unknown quantity to all non-evangelicals, and that these, too, would likely embrace it once they heard the "news." When and if born-again Christians discover someone who has actually been where they are and left, it is *a terrible threat to their faith*, for obvious reasons. It casts doubt like nothing else can that this, too, might turn out to be merely one more in a series of fads or trips or phases. The easiest thing to do, then, is to nihilate the dangerous testimony of an "unsatisfied customer" by attributing base motives. But that is intellectually dishonest, to say the least. You have no right to go that easy on yourself. I hope you will resist that temptation.

Day Thirty-seven

Point to Ponder: Whatever you converted to evangelical Christianity *from*, you can probably find someone who has converted to it from evangelical Christianity.

Quote to Remember: "Do I really think there is anything more profoundly true about my interpretation of the situation, now that I'm in bed, than there was when I was in the middle of it this afternoon?" (Hugh Prather, *Notes to Myself*)

Question to Consider: Chances are you once belonged to some other group, and you felt you had found the final truth. How do you know you will not one day think better of the faith you hold now?

NOTES

1. Rick Warren, *The Purpose-Driven Life: What on Earth Am I Here For?* (Grand Rapids, MI: Zondervan, 2002), p. 290.

2. Ibid., p. 291.

3. Peter L. Berger and Thomas Luckmann, *The Social Construction of Reality: A Treatise in the Sociology of Knowledge* (Garden City, NY: Doubleday Anchor, 1967), pp. 159–60.

4. C. S. Lewis, *Mere Christianity* (New York: Macmillan, 1960), p. 124.

The Hidden Agenda
of Witnessing

*One repays a teacher badly if one always remains nothing but a
pupil. . . . You revere me; but what if your reverence tumbles one
day? Beware lest a statue slay you. You say you believe in
Zarathustra? But what matters Zarathustra? You are my
believers—but what matters all believers? You had not yet sought
yourselves: and you found me. Thus do all believers; therefore all
faith amounts to so little. Now I bid you lose me and find yourselves;
and only when you have all denied me will I return to you.*
—Friedrich Nietzsche, *Thus Spoke Zarathustra*

The Great Committee

Rick Warren is much interested in evangelism, so much so, as we have
seen, that he tries to recruit all born-again Christians as the sales
force. He wags his finger at naughty Christians who would go to a
self-development seminar (even a Christian one) instead of a missionary conference. Some larger local churches that are mission-
minded have long hosted missionary conferences of their own, fea-
turing some of the missionaries their congregation supports while
they are home "on furlough" beating the bushes in church after
church to raise their own support. I always found it pathetic and
unfair that these dedicated individuals who had sacrificed the com-
forts of home had to spend their time singing for their supper, trying
to make enough of a swell pitch to earn a few bucks from the audience, like a flute player on the subway platform.

The climax of missionary conferences is the appeal to the congregation's young people to commit themselves to missionary work.
There is always a strange atmosphere of déjà vu on these occasions,
for it is like an evangelistic rally, only aimed at those who are already

born-again Christians. Now they are being summoned to commit themselves, not to Christ, but to "full-time Christian service." Parents wait anxiously with an eye on the pews where their teenagers are sitting with their friends. Tears come to their eyes when one or another will get up and go forward to the altar, like sinners at a Billy Graham rally. It has long seemed to me that this is a ritual of child sacrifice. Just as Zipporah slices off baby Gershom's foreskin and throws it down before an angry Jehovah as an offering on daddy Moses's behalf (Exodus 4:24–26), so do Baptist parents tearfully offer up their offspring to atone for their own career compromises with the world. (I hope I have made it clear I do not mean in any way to minimize the heroic dedication of the missionaries themselves in anything I have said. My hat's off to them!)

Warren knows he can't send every church member packing to witness to the penguins in Antarctica. But he doesn't need you to make a career of it anymore. He suggests you plan a business trip or a vacation to a foreign land and use it as a missionary expedition. One hopes the heathens thus bagged on safari do not lose their heads to a plaque on the wall of the Saddleback Church fellowship hall!

Warren's schemes and plans for lay world evangelism go further than this, however. He points out that the Internet makes it possible for the born-again Christian who is online to spread the gospel by e-mail. "E-vangelism!" Get a load of this: *Gospel spamming!* Is there no limit to the obnoxiousness of these people? Can they be oblivious of how all this comes across? Christianity already claims roughly a third of the world's population. That isn't enough of the market share?

Some years ago, when the evangelistic juggernaut Key '73, and, then later, the Southern Baptist Convention, announced they were picking Jews as a special target for evangelism, Jews were outraged, and the fundamentalists were taken equally by surprise! Why should Jews mind? After all, the fundies weren't discriminating—they think *every*body but them is going to hell! And in the same way, you don't have to be Jewish to chafe at Reverend Warren's drum-beating for religious imperialism. We are all inclined to reach for our scalp to see if it's still there. I don't think Warren and his legions have any idea how they come across with their designs on us. I am a wiseacre, I admit, but I'm not kidding when I draw a comparison with the science fiction film classic *Invasion of the Body Snatchers*. I can't help thinking of the scene where actor Kevin McCarthy and his girlfriend are trapped in his office by fellow citizens of Santa Mira who have been supplanted by pod-people. They appear normal in every way, aside from a kind of low-key emotionless cool. The aliens are telling the two still-humans not to make such a big deal about the change they're about to undergo. It's nothing to be afraid of! It's even better than before: you don't have silly emotions to make you act foolish. Who needs 'em? Come on and join us. Why hold out? For what? But the man and the woman just don't want to surrender that indefinable something that makes them who they are. That is exactly how we non-evangelicals feel. We know Warren and his legions mean well in their benevolent aggression, but we don't want to buy it. "Ah, but if only you *understood* . . . !" they say. Hey, we *do* understand, especially the many of us who used to be there. The only difference is: we don't think it's good or true. Leave us alone.

KEEPING BUSY

But the biggest irony has to be this: if everybody became born-again Christians, the air would go out of the tire. Their movement would lose all its muscle tone. What would there be left to do? Keep in mind, for Rick Warren, your whole life is intended for one purpose: making more converts. After that, what? Harp playing? That was the self-contradiction of his interim ethic: once the project is complete, what purpose for living is left? Chairman Mao understood the problem. He knew the Chinese masses, to maintain revolutionary zeal, had to be goaded to a constant state of revolution. Once they had driven out their rivals, the corrupt Kuomintang Party, Mao initiated the Cultural Revolution, to keep everybody busy.

What this means for Warrenism is that the much-vaunted excitement of "the Christian life" is the excitement of the soldier on campaign, the party worker during election season. The thrill of Jesus and the Spirit is basically a constant state of excitement generated by evangelistic activities, and if these were to outgrow their usefulness, Christianity would have run out of excitement. E. J. Carnell, one of the greatest of the Neo-evangelicals of the 1950s, saw what was at stake here. Carnell was sick of the excesses of popular fundamentalism and, though still ardently evangelical himself, viewed fundamentalism as "Orthodoxy gone cultic." He wrote: "The fundamentalist's quest for souls is subtly interlarded with a quest for status in the cult, for the soul-winner belongs to a new high-priestly caste. He can rise in prayer meeting and discourse on his accomplishments in the Kingdom. Ordinary human kindness does not have this cash value."[1] Admittedly, that is a bit rough on the poor fundies, but I think Carnell had a point. If born-again Christians simply believed it was their task to live exemplary lives, would they see themselves as engaged in an exciting crusade? I doubt it. If a congregation is calmer and better adjusted to the world, we call them mainline Protestants. Rick Warren calls them "worldly Christians." Is that the bad thing Pastor Warren says it is? I think it is the more mature way. Think back to those missionary conferences for a moment. Those events uniquely reveal and typify the essentially adolescent character of fundamentalist religion. It has a starry-eyed dream of changing the world and solving all the problems bequeathed by the past, as if a simple formula could do the trick. The New Left of the sixties was much the same way. Adults, who have perforce calmed down and accommodated themselves to the workaday world, subtly graduate from this childlike enthusiasm. But they still hear it from the pulpit and so exist in a state of perpetual guilt, like a low-grade fever. This is why they are so delighted when their own children walk up front, committing themselves to missionary service: their own flesh, although not in their persons, have paid the debt they felt they owed ever since they (inwardly) abandoned the toy land of fundamentalist rhetoric years before.

THE INNER LIMITS

Pastor Warren draws an invidious distinction between his good and faithful servants, the "World Class Christians," and the also-rans who will no doubt wind up in heaven wearing dingy sheets and wire halos, the "Worldly Christians." While the latter are supposedly inner-directed and self-preoccupied, the former are always seeking opportunities to take the gospel to those yet undisturbed by it. Well, of course the whole thing is utter hypocrisy; and the Christian who takes the fundamentalism-driven life seriously is constantly hag-ridden (not least by Warren!) toward morbid introspection and iron governance of every stray thought and impulse. No, Warren really has you, poor soul, trying to go both ways at once.

And with the Evangelistic enterprise it is particularly hard to tell inner from outer focus. If you take a close look at evangelism, you begin to see that it has at least as much to do with fortifying the inner conviction of the born-again Christian as it has with saving the "unsaved." Once again, ladies and gentlemen, Eric Hoffer:

> The missionary zeal seems rather an expression of some deep misgiving, some pressing feeling of insufficiency at the center. Proselytizing is more a passionate search for something not yet found than a desire to bestow upon the world something we already have. It is a search for a final and irrefutable demonstration that our absolute truth is indeed the one and only truth. The proselytizing fanatic strengthens his own faith by converting others.[2]

Remember the "plausibility structure"? It is a social peer-support group within which we find a shared belief compelling despite the skeptical jeering of those outside, whose criticisms are put on the shelf while we breathe the heady atmosphere of mutual affirmation. Well, evangelism is an attempt to increase the plausibility structure attendant to our belief so that we may never have any more occasion to doubt it. If I can get everybody to agree with me, then I must be right! They all agree! More votes! A million Mustang owners can't be wrong, can they? So let's sell some Mustangs!

Leon Festinger, Henry W. Riecken, and Stanley Schachter, in *When Prophecy Fails*, a study of a flying-saucer cult that set a date for a space invasion that ignominiously failed to materialize, saw the same dynamic at play. What are you going to do when you've been preaching that people ought to repent or face destruction when

Klaatu gets back with his deadly robot Gort—and he stands you up? They started reinterpreting fast! Just like Jehovah's Witnesses and others whose deadlines for the end of the world fell through in 2000. But this is not enough. One still suffers from a migraine of doubt. The alarms of "cognitive dissonance" keep going off in one's head. Which would be less painful: to give up in shame and embarrassment and admit you were wrong, or to stonewall and hope the facts (and more important, the ridicule) will just go away? Many sects in such a situation (and it happens frequently) choose the latter. And then it is time to redouble one's evangelistic efforts. Even though the product is now much harder to sell, thanks to the public debunking, the believers turn up the juice. Why bother?

> *If more and more people can be persuaded that the system of belief is correct, then clearly it must, after all, be correct.* Consider the extreme case: if everyone in the whole world believed something, there would be no question at all to the validity of this belief. It is for this reason that we observe the increase in proselyte[iz]ing following disconfirmation. If the proselyte[iz]ing proves successful, then by gathering more adherents and effectively surrounding himself with supporters, the believer reduces dissonance to the point where he can live with it.[3]

Naturally, the doubt in question need not arise from this particular source. Evangelicals generally do seem to believe in Chicken Little apocalypticism, but they know better than to saddle themselves with a definite date. So even Hal Lindsay retreats a few steps into vagueness to leave himself some strategic room to wiggle. But there is plenty of room for doubt, and on many grounds; just look at the spate of apologetics books. There must be plenty of intellectual demons for William Lane Craig and Josh McDowell to spend so much ink trying to exorcise them from troubled Christian minds. (Isn't it interesting that, while evangelism and apologetics are both ostensibly aimed at outsiders, trying to bring them into the faith, their real targets seem to be insiders, trying to keep them safely in the fold?)

Nor is this the only way in which evangelism functions to reinforce the walls of the born-again ghetto. As I mentioned briefly in an earlier chapter, we must recognize that evangelism is a distinctive role-playing game that keeps Christians feeling like Christians by manipulating outsiders into the corresponding role of "sinners" and foes of the gospel. If not confronted in this way, outsiders might never seem to fit the stereotype fed to the born-again Christian. Outsiders would be happy to live and let live. One often hears them congratulate fundamentalist friends on the good their faith has done for them: "I'm glad it works for you." That is not exactly hostility to the gospel! But then the fundamentalist springs the trap by insisting that, no, it has to work for everybody, including you, or you're going to hell. Well, then, the outsider is taken aback. He is goaded into replying, "Well, if that's your religion, you can keep it!" And then the fundamentalist can walk away, fatuously congratulating himself for taking such abuse for the sake of the gospel, like the apostles in Acts 5:41. Of course it would be even better if the outsider accepted the gospel and received Jesus Christ as his imaginary playmate, but the rejection was valuable enough in its own right. It reinforced the fundamentalist's self-image as a Christian. It cemented his beliefs more firmly than ever, just as a hazing secures a pledge's loyalty to the frat, since we never want to admit we took such abuse for nothing. And it serves to alienate the fundamentalist from an acquaintance who, if allowed to come closer as a friend, might have influenced him away from fundamentalism.

John Lofland, in *Doomsday Cult*, his famous study of the Unification Church in the San Francisco Bay area, noticed the same thing: "Satan worked hardest against [them] when they were really striking a blow for God. Therefore if it appeared that Satan was really attacking them, e.g., if few prospects were appearing—that must mean that in some way they were really getting close to a victory for God. . . . In general, [they] could not lose. If prospects came along, God was most active. If they did not, Satan was most active. It seemed, however, that Satan was most active most of the time. This meant that God's agents had to work that much harder."[4]

So the goal of evangelism is in the end self-serving; it is to be able, once and for all, to breathe easier believing highly dubious beliefs, since they will no longer *be* dubious once the born-again plausibility structure covers the earth as the waters cover the sea.

Day Thirty-eight

Point to Ponder: Maybe Christians who proclaim their faith most vociferously are "protesting too much."

Quote to Remember: "Woe to you, scribes and Pharisees, hypocrites! For you traverse sea and land to make a single proselyte, and when he becomes a proselyte, you make him twice as much a child of hell as yourselves." (Matthew 23:15, RSV)

Question to Consider: Would I even think twice about missionary evangelism if I weren't afraid of the guilt for letting the heathen fry in hell?

NOTES

1. Edward John Carnell, *The Case for Orthodox Theology* (Philadelphia: Westminster Press, 1959), p. 122.

2. Eric Hoffer, *The True Believer: Thoughts on the Nature of Mass Movements* (New York: Harper & Row, 1951), p. 108.

3. Leon Festinger, Henry W. Riecken, and Stanley Schacter, *When Prophecy Fails: A Social and Psychological Study of a Modern Group That Predicted the Destruction of the World* (New York: Harper & Row, 1964), p. 28.

4. John Lofland, *Doomsday Cult: A Study of Conversion, Proselytization, and Maintenance of Faith* (Englewood Cliffs, NJ: Prentice-Hall, 1966), pp. 208, 209.

Juggling Your Life

They see a Samaritan carrying a lamb on his way to Jerusalem. He says to his disciples, "Why does this man carry the lamb with him?" They say to him, "So he may kill it and eat it." He says to them, "As long as it is alive, he will not eat it, but only if he has killed it and it has become a corpse?" They say, "Otherwise he will not be able to do it." He says to them, "As for yourselves, seek a place of repose for yourselves, so you do not become a corpse and get eaten."
—Gospel according to Thomas, saying 60

THE TIGHTROPE

Rick Warren tells us, "Your life is a pentathlon of five purposes [worship, ministry, evangelism, fellowship, discipleship], which you must keep in balance."[1] Balance? *Balance?* He must be joking!

Remember in high school, you'd always have at least one teacher who seemed to have no idea that she wasn't the only one assigning you homework? She'd give you enough to keep you up late, and you wouldn't even have gotten to your Math or Social Studies. Well, that's Brother Rick! He seems to have forgotten you have only so many hours in a day, so many days in a week. He seems to think all laity have the same leisure he does for a schedule full of religious activities. I've got news for you, Rick—everyone else has a day job! Warren is in charge of a megachurch that is a sect in itself. He keeps it booming by preaching that everyone should, in effect, function as unpaid staff, at least if chapter 39 of *The Purpose-Driven Life* is any indication. A church like this is an all-devouring beast, and I suggest you might want to think twice before offering yourself to its hungry maw.

What are the five preoccupations that should use up all your time? They are the pentad of pious practices that forms the "methodism" that evangelicals call "the born-again Experience." Evangelicals in the nineteenth century used to debate Charles Finney's "New Measure Revivalism." An Arminian believing in free will, Finney unashamedly pitched the gospel in an emotional way, frankly trying to manipulate the crowds, which he did with great results. The more staid, cerebral Calvinists thought he was just whipping up hysteria and that he should instead patiently wait upon God in prayer to spark a revival in his own time. Finney carried the day, as numerical success always does. But the Calvinist objection was more than intransigence, more than being sanctified sticks in the mud. They thought Finney was just cobbling together a so-called Christian experience through a combination of pulpit rhetoric, organ music, long sermons, and so on. Such an "experience," they feared, would be counterfeit, trumped up. People would undergo a superficial conversion and then drift away soon after the revival was over, as Mark Twain depicts in *Tom Sawyer* with the ephemerally repentant Huck. In the same way, it seems to me there is no core to the "born-again Experience." It is simply a combination of several activities geared to keep one safely within the zone of orthodox reinforcement, where certain slogans are repeated with the regularity of a cheerleading rally. Being an evangelical Christian is simply believing the basic theology and *doing these religious things*.

THE FIVE COMMANDMENTS

First is *worship*, the flattering of the invisible Creator, the abasing of oneself, the denial of one's merit so that it may be ascribed to God instead. That's putting it pretty negatively, I know. But I think I have zeroed in on a fundamental and insidious dimension of worship as usually practiced. Tell me it doesn't involve groveling. Not that it absolutely *has* to. As I argued in chapter 13, there is a way to enter into the mythological drama of the thing by means of the temporary, willing suspension of disbelief. In that mode, there is a sublime reverence for the numinous holiness of the occasion. Is it an illusory mood invoked by special effects? That's what they criticized Finney for, isn't it? But there is a major difference. If you approach worship in the mind-set I am suggesting, you *know* it is a drama, and that you are playing a role in it. You are moved and improved (I hope) as you would be by attending the symphony or the art museum. Once I toured the Museum of Modern Art, gazing quietly at Jackson Pollock's mighty canvas *One* with a growing sense of ecstatic joy. Eventually I found myself viewing Vincent van Gogh's original *The Starry Night* and whispering to a friend, "This is a holy place." And so it was, though it is but the spark ignited by the creative hand of man. That's what I look for in church. That's why I sing in the choir.

Second is *ministry*, which, in *The Purpose-Driven Life*, seems to denote some niche in the gigantic structure of Mega-lo-Church. It is good to donate one's time, but I advise anyone to take a frank look to see whether your good nature is being taken advantage of. This is a great danger in growing, militant organizations. The love bombing may stop once you're hooked. From there on in, you're curtly expected to pull your weight, while the love of Jesus PR is transferred to the unsuspecting. If you don't know what I'm talking about, good! I hope you never learn firsthand.

Third, there is *evangelism*, about which I've said way too much already. But this is the one where you are really putting it on the line. Your reputation for witnessing is going to make everyone else think you are a bit off. Long ago, I decided it was worth that to do my duty to fulfill the Great Commission in my corner of the vineyard. But of course now I think I had been misinformed. The fact that I was taking upon my shoulders essentially a clergyman's role, the task of acknowledged, recognized specialists, when I was just some kid, is precisely what made me look like a nut! And you will, too. But Carnell was right: you won't mind it much as long as you are cultivating an alternate peer group of fellow fundamentalists who will appreciate your zeal.

I can only say, for what it may be worth, I have always had the greatest respect for evangelical Christians who did *not* seem to be one-track-minded fanatics, who could talk of other things with sincerity and interest. Anyone could tell their faith was the root of them, but they had a life just as big as the world around them. I think this way of C. S. Lewis, and I feel sure that this is also one of the big reasons Lewis's fundamentalist fans like him so much. They seem to recognize in him something they cannot bring themselves to emulate: an urbanity born of feeling at home in the world and its wonderful culture. I believe even born-again Christians deep down suspect they have things out of kilter and wish they did not have to be so fanatical. I think they are secretly embarrassed by their public displays of piety, into which they have been bullied by pulpit preaching. Lewis, by contrast, though he shared similar views with fundamentalists on many issues, was not impatient with the world, was in less of a rush to leave it for heaven. He did not view it as a barrel full of fish he had to shoot with gospel bullets. The late Richard Quebedeaux, author of the influential manifesto *The Young Evangelicals*, saw the need for such "worldly Christianity" to rescue evangelicalism from its Jehovah's Witness mode.[2]

The *fourth* element in the mix is *fellowship*, distinct from worship in that the former occurs in the context of small group meetings, not in huge church sanctuaries. Who could doubt the value of such intimate gatherings of friends? The only question is whether these groups are to function as incubators, reinforcing the common beliefs of all present, or as centers of stimulation for new thoughts and dialogue between people with different convictions. I believe there is a greater spirituality, a greater stretching of the soul, in questions than in answers. Ready-made answers fed to you by your like-minded group, I regard as sleeping pills. I think you need the No-Doz of fresh ideas. Are you going to get them in the group you attend?

Fifth is *discipleship*, which includes Bible study, the mantra of evangelicalism. I delight in the study of the Bible, and that is how I eventually came to the critical study of it, using all the techniques lambasted as heretical and unbelieving in fundamentalist circles. Born-again pastors and Bible college instructors hate the Higher Criticism of scripture because the new realism makes it impossible ever again to regard the Bible as an infallible answer book. I remember the icy look I got in Sunday school once when I objected that we have no business rejecting some theory just because it would make a lot of trouble for us if it were true. I do not regard a wholesale reevaluation of the Bible too high a price to pay if in return I may understand this ancient text without straitjacketing it in theology and feeding it through the shredder of cherished beliefs. I hope you, too, may come to recognize that eating from the forbidden tree of critical knowledge of the Bible is itself an act of discipleship.

There is only so far one can go plumbing the depths of the Bible when one reads it in the completely ahistorical, out-of-context manner Reverend Warren does in *The Purpose-Driven Life*. It is apparent he is utterly innocent of even the most basic facts of criticism. He routinely attributes all the Psalms to David, all the Proverbs to Solomon, the Pentateuch to Moses, all traditional rabbinical guesswork with no foundation in the text. What an irony that the fundamentalist champions of the Bible seem to care nothing for the text, but only for those doctrines and devotional "promises" they pry out of it. And when the Bible does not actually yield the requisite slogans and the desired devotional idiom, they will rewrite the text so that it does. Clark H. Pinnock, an evangelical theologian who, however, knows things are by no means simple, once quipped, "The fundamentalists don't like the Bible they've got." So now they're rewriting it into a more likable, albeit fake, Bible.

WORLDLY CHRISTIANS AGAIN

Did you ever see the 1976 horror flick *The Omen*? It is lots of fun for Bible fans, as well as horror fans. One of the many memorable scenes in it is one in which actor Gregory Peck, unwitting foster father of Damian, the Antichrist, is searching a shack in which the late Father Brennan had stayed before getting skewered lengthwise with a flagpole during a lightning storm. Every inch of the walls and ceiling was plastered with ripped-out Bible pages! Loads of crosses and crucifixes, too. He had once been in league with Satan and had now turned back to God. He was trying to derail the plans for the rise of Antichrist. And he knew he didn't have long before Satan got back at him. But he was trying to fend off the devil's revenge as long as possible by holing up in this Bible bunker, which he figured Satan's power could not penetrate. He was right, by the way, since it was only while venturing outside one night that he became a Satanic shish kebab.

Anyhow, I sometimes think that is a good symbol for what born-again Christians are doing when they try to live every hour of the day in a born-again world. The irony is that it happens to look just like the big, bad secular world, only with a Christian label pasted on it. Christian teens listen to derivative born-again rock and rap. Born-again housewives read born-again romance novels. Megachurches contain their own born-again bowling alleys so you don't have to pollute yourself through exposure to sinners. And once you convert your friends, there will be minimal readjustment, no different really from switching to a Ford from a Chevrolet.

To me, it would seem the needful "balance" Reverend Warren commands would be, not a juggling of time-consuming religious demands, but a balance of one's faith with genuine engagement with the world and its people, for their own sake. That would make Christianity a lot more attractive to the rest of us. We could almost consider becoming that kind of Christian.

Day Thirty-nine

Point to Ponder: You can become purpose-driven to distraction.

Quote to Remember: "The fanatical state of mind by itself can stifle all forms of creative work. The fanatic's disdain for the present blinds him to the complexity and uniqueness of life. . . . The blindness of the fanatic is a source of strength (he sees no obstacles), but it is the cause of intellectual sterility and emotional monotony." (Eric Hoffer, *The True Believer*)

Question to Consider: Freud characterized religion as "the universal obsessive neurosis of humanity." Would he take you as evidence confirming his theory, or as evidence casting doubt on it?

NOTES

1. Rick Warren, *The Purpose-Driven Life: What on Earth Am I Here For?* (Grand Rapids, MI: Zondervan, 2002), p. 305.

2. Richard Quebedeaux, *The Young Evangelicals: Revolution in Orthodoxy* (New York: Harper & Row, 1974), pp. 62, 64.

Not without Reason

A new pride my ego taught me, and this I teach men: no longer to
bury one's head in the sand of heavenly things, but to bear it freely,
an earthly head, which creates a meaning for the earth.
A new will I teach men: to will this way which man has walked
blindly, and to affirm it, and no longer to sneak away from it like
the sick and decaying.
—Friedrich Nietzsche, *Thus Spoke Zarathustra*

On the Move

The Authentic New Testament by Hugh J. Schonfield is a most
intriguing translation indeed, and as far as I know, the only published
version of the New Testament by a Jew, not a Christian. In Schonfield's version Matthew 8:19–22 reads: "The foxes have lairs, Jesus
replied, the birds of the air have nests, but the Son of Man has not a
floor where he may lay his head." His version is based on the reading
in a medieval Hebrew copy of Matthew, where the idea is that trav-
elers were sometimes assigned the most meager shelter of a raised
wooden platform in the stable, surrounded by animals. The Son of
Man cannot even attain such modest accommodations. Why not?
What does the saying mean?

There have been various guesses. Suppose "the Son of Man"
refers to Jesus. Helmut Koester suggested that the saying means to
portray Jesus in terms of the figure of wisdom in Jewish philosophy:
Wisdom personified has come down from heaven to instruct foolish
mortals who could certainly use her advice. But humans were so
impenetrably wicked and stupid, loving darkness better than light,
that they drove wisdom forth. Finding no welcome extended anywhere, she folded her tent and returned in disgust to heaven, where,
we may imagine, she was welcomed back as the returned prodigal.

Jesus, too, said Koester, had "come unto his own and his own received him not." He was despised and rejected of men, subjected to the only fate Plato said a righteous man could look forward to: crucifixion. So on Koester's reading, Jesus sought an open door and did not find one. But others have seen the saying as paralleling Jesus with the Cynic itinerant Diogenes of Sinope, the strange man who wandered the land holding aloft a lit lantern in the daytime, looking for, and never finding, an honest man. Only Jesus the Son of Man is wandering the land in search of faith. "When the Son of Man comes, will he find faith on earth?" (Luke 18:8, RSV). "Truly, I say to you, not even in Israel have I found such faith" (Matthew 8:10, RSV). But he continues to look.

An interesting and powerful interpretation. I especially like the connection with the Cynics. They were a group of philosophers who had decided to use reason to live in accordance with nature, shunning all of what they deemed as artificial conventions. What are artificial social conventions? All the things that vary with different cultures. If different societies define and practice marriage differently, for example, there must not be anything natural or inevitable about it. It must be a human invention.

Or human shelter: why are dwellings so different? Why are some people nomads? The Cynics thought, as did Jesus, that you ought not to waste your valuable time worrying over "What shall we eat? What shall we drink? What shall we wear?" Let these things take care of themselves, while you seek God's kingdom, that is, his natural plan for human life. The Cynics' view was that human beings do not need any stable address. They do not have an inborn nesting instinct like animals do, and when they nevertheless build a permanent home for themselves, they are losing the freedom nature intended them to have.

Does the gospel passage mean this? I suspect it does. Note the contrast with other species, birds and foxes, who do have a nesting instinct, and the sons of men who do not. When they become homeowners, they have become like Kierkegaard's well-fed geese who can look admiringly at wild geese on the wing but can no longer hoist themselves aloft to join them.

THE WORD ON THE STREET

The wayfaring apostles of the early church must have understood the saying this way, and it governed their practice. But what can it mean to you and me? To me the saying speaks of the inevitability of spiritual existence being in nature a pilgrimage. And that is the note on which I would like to end this book.

The very metaphor of "following Jesus" must entail something of an itinerant style, wouldn't you think? You are not to stay firmly ensconced, parked, with Jesus. You cannot be associated with him, the text says, unless you are willing to move, for Jesus himself is to be found in no one place. He has no one permanent address. So you can never quite be sure where to find him.

Can you be sure of finding him in the halls of the orthodox Protestant denominations? I am not sure. Maybe so, but I wouldn't take it for granted. Can you be sure of finding him in a seminary classroom? Last time I took attendance in one I did not find his name on the list. But he may have been there anyway.

Is there any place you think you can take for granted that he would *not* be? Think again! Perhaps, to stretch another saying, the Son of Man cometh where ye expect not.

Revivalist preachers scare their audiences with the threat, would you want Jesus, at his return, to find you here or there? I think the danger is just the reverse: to find Jesus today, you might very well have to look in places you would be embarrassed to find him! That was the experience of people in the first century who were chagrinned to find Jesus feasting with tax collectors and sinners.

Malcolm Boyd, in *Are You Running with Me, Jesus?* prays,

> This is a homosexual bar, Jesus. It looks like any other bar on the outside, only it isn't. Men stand three and four deep at this bar—some just feeling a sense of belonging here, others making contacts for new sexual partners. This isn't very much like a church, Lord, but many members of the church are also here in this bar. Quite a few of the men here belong to the church as well as to this bar. If they knew how, a number of them would ask you to be with them in both places. Some of them wouldn't, but won't you be with them, too, Jesus?[1]

Jeremiah 2:2–3a speaks of Israel's wanderings in the Sinai desert in a very different way than the Pentateuch does, or Amos. They depict the generation of desert wandering as a dreary period of testing and ignominious failure. By contrast, Jeremiah views it as a honeymoon period when all was right between God and his people. "I remember concerning you the devotion of your youth, the love of your betrothals, your following after me in the wilderness, through a land not sown. Israel was holy to the LORD, the first of his harvest" (NASB). And do you know why? Because they were *on the move*. The nomad existence was particularly favorable to spirituality.

Nomads move from one site to another because the food resources for themselves and their flock sooner or later become exhausted. They have to move on to the next oasis. It is the same way with the individual spiritual pilgrimage, in my judgment. It may be you need to move to a new theology, a new devotional practice—or to the lack of one—in order to gain the new nourishment you need. Even spirituality, when familiar, can grow stale. If you stay where you are, you will starve.

NO PERMANENT CITY

The vagabond apostles of Jesus were sent out with marching orders that they not encumber themselves with superfluous possessions. They were not to be like the shopping-bag-laden street people whom one sees, shuffling along and dreaming of the house they wished they lived in but do not. They are content to move slowly like snails: mobile, but limited by the home they carry with them on their backs. The Christian and Cynic apostles knew that if they wanted to cover much ground they had to travel light. If we want to follow in their wandering footsteps, we must not insist on carrying with us every old belief we believed since we were children. We have to let some of them go, or they will impede our progress. They become biases, prejudices, blinders that prohibit us from seeing the path ahead. They stop us from even seeing that there *is* a path ahead of us, more ground to cover.

For example, I believe that biblical literalism is a belief best left behind since sooner or later it is going to limit how much you can see. Many people reject on principle anything not commanded in scripture, as if a finite book, even the Bible, could cover the Infinite.

If, for example, you let a literalistic adherence to the Bible make you deny the valuable truths to be found in other religions, you are ossifying spiritually, just like the legalists who opposed Jesus because he broke the molds, because he wanted to pour new wine into new wineskins.

One thing I have noticed on my pilgrimage is that you wince looking back on the earlier stages when you were so sure of things you have since seen through and set aside. You didn't hesitate to broadcast your opinions: you must have a personal relationship with Christ to be saved! You must be a political leftist to be a faithful Christian! Another thing I learned, though probably not very well, is to try not to make such a jackass of myself. After a certain point you learn Socratic humility. That, having been wrong so many times, you can't be totally sure you're not wrong now. So what do you do?

A mature spiritual journey is a series of experiments. You come to look at various possible doctrines or disciplines much as a scientist views theories: as working models, as tentative paradigms. The question is not "Is it true?" but rather "Will it produce results?" The results, in this case, are a broader spirit, a higher horizon, moral and spiritual growth. That is the only truth of a doctrine that we may ever test.

Zen Buddhists have learned this lesson well. Hence the striking picture one often sees of the Zen monk tearing up the scroll of scripture. The point is to show that even the holy scripture is not an end in itself (in which case it would be an idol), but simply a means to an end. Once it has produced enlightenment, holiness, it has served its purpose. That is its only purpose.

The strange fact is that many doctrines that logically contradict each other can each be productive of great spiritual growth. This means you have to be tentative, provisional, in your belief in your own beliefs, adopting a different role at different stages, playing a spirituality as a kind of game.

And you can be tolerant of someone else who has assumed a different role than yours, engaged in a different experiment than yours. I have always remembered something from Thomas à Kempis's *The Imitation of Christ.*

> Many things you . . . must pass by with a deaf ear, and think rather of those things which belong to your peace. It is more profitable to turn your eyes from such things as displease you, and to leave to everyone his own way of thinking, than to contend in disputes and arguments. (3:44)

Or, as Jesus says to Peter when Peter asks him about the path and the fate of another disciple, "What is that to you? Follow me" (John 21:22, RSV).

Someone else may be treading a path that you have turned aside from years ago. You think you know the pitfalls that await him. You feel it is your duty to set him straight. All right, but be careful! Is the person at the level of spiritual maturity where they can hear what you are saying? Can they do otherwise than see you as a spiritual threat, like cultists who regard the voice of reason as the seduction of Satan? They are the weaker brethren Paul talks about. Let them be. They may have to learn hard lessons for themselves. I have written this book with a certain audience in mind. I know quite well that if the book should make it into the hands of your typical fundamentalist, coached to dismiss out of hand any challenge to his church's party line, he will laugh it off and pray for me. I would like it if something I say in these pages might serve to dislodge them a bit from their fortress mentality, but I don't expect much. No, I write mainly for those who, reading Rick Warren's *The Purpose-Driven Life*, sense something amiss. I write for those who will not allow Warren to program them as he seeks to in the name of Christ and the Bible. Where such a one may end up is his or her business, not mine. But I would like to help such a seeker on his or her way.

Berger and Luckmann remark that, unlike other animals who have only a physical environment, human beings, with their larger brains, require a larger environment, an environment inside our heads. It is the fountainhead of culture, symbolism, spiritual existence, all of which transcend the purely animal state. We must assume responsibility for creating this nonphysical environment, and different people in different countries do it very differently.[2] It is all another way of saying that "the sons of men have no place to rest their heads," no given belief or worldview they are born with or can take for granted. This means it is only a control freak's fantasy that he can tell everyone else, or anyone else, what their purpose in life must be. You just have to discover it yourself, along your journey, don't you? That is the reason-driven life.

Day Forty

Point to Ponder: What are the chances that Kant, the Buddha, Aristotle, and Nietzsche are wrong, but Rick Warren is right?

Quote to Remember: "It is the true believer's ability to 'shut his eyes and stop his ears' to facts that do not deserve to be either seen or heard that is the source of his unequaled fortitude and constancy." (Eric Hoffer, *The True Believer*)

Question to Consider: Am I really going to dismiss this book as Satan's tool, or some sort of smear job? Deep down, don't I know better than that?

NOTES

1. Malcolm Boyd, *Are You Running with Me, Jesus?* (New York: Avon, 1967), p. 106.

2. Peter L. Berger and Thomas Luckmann, *The Social Construction of Reality: A Treatise in the Sociology of Knowledge* (Garden City, NY: Doubleday Anchor, 1967), pp. 47–52.

Bibliography

à Kempis, Thomas. *The Imitation of Christ*. Translated by Albert J. Nevins. Huntington, IN: Our Sunday Visitor, 1973.

Alexander, William Menzies. *Demonic Possession in the New Testament: Its Historical, Medical, and Theological Aspects*. T & T Clark, 1902. Reprint, Grand Rapids, MI: Baker Book House, 1980. Chapter 6, "The Beelzebul Controversy," pp. 174–93.

Allen, James. *As a Man Thinketh*. Philadelphia: Running Press, 1989.

Altizer, Thomas J. J. *The Descent into Hell: A Study of the Radical Reversal of the Christian Consciousness*. New York: J. B. Lippincott, 1970.

———. *The Gospel of Christian Atheism*. Philadelphia: Westminster Press, 1966.

Altizer, Thomas J. J., and William Hamilton. *Radical Theology and the Death of God*. Indianapolis: Bobbs-Merrill, 1966.

Armstrong, Herbert W. "Is There a Hell?" *Plain Truth* (August 1982): 9–11, 38.

Aurelius, Marcus. *Meditations*. Translated by Maxwell Staniforth. Baltimore: Penguin Books, 1964.

Babinski, Edward T., ed. *Leaving the Fold: Testimonies of Former Fundamentalists*. Amherst, NY: Prometheus Books, 1995.

Ballou, Hosea. *Treatise on Atonement*. Hallowell: C. Spaulding, 1828.

Berger, Peter L. *The Heretical Imperative: Contemporary Possibilities of Religious Affirmation*. Garden City, NY: Doubleday Anchor, 1980.

Berger, Peter L., and Thomas Luckmann. *The Social Construction of Reality: A Treatise in the Sociology of Knowledge*. Garden City, NY: Doubleday Anchor, 1967.

Bergman, Ingmar. *Fanny and Alexander*. Translated by Alan Blair. New York: Pantheon, 1982.

———. *Four Screenplays of Ingmar Bergman: Smiles of a Summer Night. The Seventh Seal. Wild Strawberries. The Magician*. Translated by Lars Malmstrom and David Kushner. New York: Simon & Schuster, 1960.

Bettelheim, Bruno. *The Uses of Enchantment: The Meaning and Importance of*

Fairy Tales. New York: Vintage, 1977. "Tales of Two Brothers," pp. 90–96.

Beversluis, John. *C. S. Lewis and the Search for Rational Religion.* Grand Rapids, MI: William B. Eerdmans, 1985.

Blatty, William Peter. *The Exorcist.* New York: Harper & Row, 1971.

Bonhoeffer, Dietrich. *The Cost of Discipleship.* Translated by R. H. Fuller, revised by Irmgard Booth. 2nd ed. London: SCM Press, 1959. Reprint, New York: Macmillan, 1973.

———. *Letters and Papers from Prison.* Translated by Reginald H. Fuller. New York: Macmillan, 1953.

Boyd, Malcolm. *Are You Running with Me, Jesus?* New York: Avon, 1967.

Braithwaite, R. B. *An Empiricist's View of the Nature of Religious Belief.* Cambridge: Cambridge University Press, 1955.

Bultmann, Rudolf. "New Testament and Mythology." In *New Testament and Mythology and other Basic Writings,* edited and translated by Schubert M. Ogden. Philadelphia: Fortress, 1989, pp. 1–43.

Byrom, Thomas, trans. *Dhammapada: Sayings of the Buddha.* Boston: Shambhala, 1993.

Campbell, Joseph. *The Hero with a Thousand Faces.* London: Sphere Books, 1975.

Carnell, Edward John. *The Case for Orthodox Theology.* Philadelphia: Westminster Press, 1959.

Chesen, Eli S. *Religion May Be Hazardous to Your Health: A Psychiatric Guide to the Uses and Abuses of God, Prayer, and the Church or Synagogue.* New York: Collier Macmillan, 1973.

Cohen, Daniel. *The New Believers: Young Religion in America.* New York: Ballantine, 1975.

Cox, Harvey. *On Not Leaving It to the Snake.* New York: Macmillan, 1969.

———. *The Secular City: Secularization and Urbanization in Theological Perspective.* New York: Macmillan, 1965.

Davis, Winston. *Dojo: Magic and Exorcism in Modern Japan.* Stanford, CA: Stanford University Press, 1982.

Downing, F. Gerald. *Cynics and Christian Origins.* Edinburgh: T & T Clark, 1992.

Durkheim, Emil. *The Elementary Forms of the Religious Life.* Translated by Joseph War Swain. New York: Macmillan, 1915. Reprint, New York: Free Press, 1965.

Eckhart, Meister. *Meister Eckhart.* Translated by Raymond B. Blakney. New York: Harper & Row, 1961.

Evans-Wentz, W. Y., ed. *The Tibetan Book of the Dead, or the After-Death Experiences on the Bardo Plane, According to Lama Kazi Dawa-Samdup's English Rendering.* 1927. Reprint, New York: Oxford University Press, 1960.

Festinger, Leon, Henry W. Riecken, and Stanley Schacter. *When Prophecy Fails: A Social and Psychological Study of a Modern Group That Predicted the Destruction of the World.* New York: Harper & Row, 1964.

Feuerbach, Ludwig. *The Essence of Christianity.* Translated by George Eliot. 1853. Reprint, New York: Harper & Row, 1957.

Fosdick, Harry Emerson. *A Guide to Understanding the Bible: The Development of Ideas within the Old and New Testaments.* New York: Harper & Brothers, 1956.

Fowler, James W. *Stages of Faith: The Psychology of Human Development and the Quest for Meaning.* San Francisco: Harper & Row, 1981.

Frazer, James G. *The Golden Bough: A Study in Comparative Religion.* London: Macmillan, 1890.

French, Reginald Michael, trans. *The Way of a Pilgrim, and The Pilgrim Continues His Way.* New York: Ballantine, 1974.

Freud, Sigmund. *The Future of an Illusion.* Translated by W. D. Robson-Scott, revised edition by James Strachey. Garden City, NY: Doubleday Anchor, 1964.

———. *A General Introduction to Psychoanalysis.* Translated by Joan Riviere. New York: Pocket Books, 1953.

Geertz, Clifford. "Religion as a Cultural System." In *The Interpretation of Cultures.* New York: Basic Books, 1973, pp. 87–125.

Gibran, Kahlil. *Jesus, the Son of Man: His Words and Deeds as Told and Recorded by Those Who Knew Him.* 1928. Reprint, New York: Knopf, 1976.

Gladden, Washington. *How Much Is Left of the Old Doctrines?* Boston: Houghton Mifflin, 1899.

———. *Present-Day Theology.* Columbus, OH: McClelland, 1918.

Goodman, Felicitas D. *Speaking in Tongues: A Cross-Cultural Study of Glossolalia.* Chicago: University of Chicago Press, 1972.

Gurdjieff, G. I. *Meetings with Remarkable Men.* New York: E. P. Dutton, 1963.

Gustafson, James M. *Christ and the Moral Life.* Chicago: University of Chicago Press, 1968.

Hamilton, William. *The New Essence of Christianity.* New York: Association Press, 1966.

Herrmann, Wilhelm. *The Communion of the Christian with God, Described on the Basis of Luther's Statements.* New York: Putnam, 1906.

Hoffer, Eric. *The True Believer: Thoughts on the Nature of Mass Movements*. New York: Harper & Row, 1951.

Houlden, J. L. *Ethics and the New Testament*. New York: Oxford University Press, 1977.

Ingersoll, Robert Green. *Some Mistakes of Moses*. Amherst, NY: Prometheus Books, 1986.

James, William. *The Varieties of Religious Experience*. New York: New American Library, 1958.

Jung, Carl. *The Archetypes and the Collective Unconscious*. Bollingen Series XX, *Collected Works of Jung*, vol. 9, part 1, translated by R. F. C. Hull. Princeton, NJ: Princeton University Press, 1968.

———."Dogma and Natural Symbols." In *Psychology and Religion*. New Haven, CT: Yale University Press, 1938, pp. 40–77.

———. *Symbols of Transformation*. Bollingen Series XX, *Collected Works of Jung*, vol. 5, translated by R. F. C. Hull. Princeton, NJ: Princeton University Press, 1967.

Kant, Immanuel. *Religion within the Limits of Reason Alone*. Translated by Theodore M. Greene and Hoyt H. Hutchinson. New York: Harper & Row, 1960.

———. "What Is Enlightenment?" In *The Portable Age of Reason Reader*, edited by Crane Brinton and translated by Lewis White Beck. New York: Viking Press, 1956, pp. 298–307.

Käsemann, Ernst. "The Canon of the New Testament and the Unity of the Church." In *Essays on New Testament Themes*, translated by W. J. Montague. Studies in Biblical Theology 41. London: SCM Press, 1964, pp. 95–107.

Kaufmann, Walter. *Critique of Religion and Philosophy*. Garden City, NY: Doubleday, 1961.

———. *The Faith of a Heretic*. Garden City, NY: Doubleday Anchor, 1963.

Kazantzakis, Nikos. *The Last Temptation of Christ*. Translated by P. A. Bien. New York: Bantam Books, 1961.

Kierkegaard, Søren. *Fear and Trembling and The Sickness unto Death*. Translated by Walter Lowrie. Garden City, NY: Doubleday Anchor, 1954.

King, Stephen. "Quitters, Inc." In *Night Shift: Excursions into Horror*. New York: New American Library, 1978, pp. 208–27.

Knox, Ronald A. *Enthusiasm: A Chapter in the History of Religion*. New York: Oxford University Press, 1950.

Lau, D. C., trans. *Tao Te Ching*. Baltimore: Penguin Books, 1963.

Leiber, Fritz. "Lean Times in Lankhmar." In *Swords in the Mist*. New York: Ace, 1968, pp. 24–65.

Lessing, Gotthold. *Lessing's Theological Writings*. Selected and edited by Henry Chadwick. A Library of Modern Religious Thought. Stanford, CA: Stanford University Press, 1972.

Lewis, C. S. *Mere Christianity*. New York: Macmillan, 1960.

———. "On Obstinacy in Belief." In *The World's Last Night*. New York: Harcourt, Brace, Jovanovich, 1990, pp. 13–30.

———. "On the Reading of Old Books." In *God in the Dock: Essays on Theology and Ethics*. Grand Rapids, MI: William B. Eerdmans, 1970, pp. 200–207.

———. *The Problem of Pain*. San Francisco: HarperSanFrancisco, 2001.

———. *The Screwtape Letters and Screwtape Proposes a Toast*. New York: Macmillan, 1970.

Lofland, John. *Doomsday Cult: A Study of Conversion, Proselytization, and Maintenance of Faith*. Englewood Cliffs, NJ: Prentice-Hall, 1966.

Malherbe, Abraham J. *Paul and the Popular Philosophers*. Minneapolis: Fortress Press, 1989.

Maslow, Abraham H. *Religions, Values and Peak-Experiences*. New York: Viking, 1970.

McLeod, W. H. *Guru Nanak and the Sikh Religion*. Delhi: Oxford University Press, 1976.

Meredith, Roderick C. "Hell: Man's Idea vs. The Bible." *Plain Truth* (September/October 1982): 15–18, 21.

Moore, Robert A. "The Impossible Voyage of Noah's Ark." *Creation/Evolution* 11(Winter 1983).

Munger, Robert Boyd. *My Heart, Christ's Home*. Downers Grove, IL: InterVarsity Press, 1954.

Murray, Andrew. *Abide in Christ*. Old Tappan, NJ: Fleming H. Revell, 1970.

Nee, Watchman. *The Normal Christian Life*. Wheaton, IL: Tyndale House, 1977.

Nietzsche, Friedrich. *The Birth of Tragedy and The Genealogy of Morals*. Translated by Francis Golffing. Garden City, NY: Doubleday Anchor, 1956.

———. *The Gay Science, With a Prelude in Rhymes and an Appendix of Songs*. Translated by Walter Kauffman. New York: Vintage Books, 1974.

——— *Thus Spoke Zarathustra*. Translated by Walter Kaufmann. Baltimore: Penguin Books, 1978.

Palahniuk, Chuck. *Fight Club*. New York: Henry Holt, 1997.

Prather, Hugh. *Notes to Myself: My Struggle to Become a Person*. New York: Bantam, 1976.

Price, Lucien. *Dialogues of Alfred North Whitehead*. Boston: Little, Brown, 1954.

Quebedeaux, Richard. *The Young Evangelicals: Revolution in Orthodoxy.* New York: Harper & Row, 1974.

Roberts, Oral. *The Call.* New York: Avon, 1971.

Rubenstein, Richard L. *After Auschwitz: Radical Theology and Contemporary Judaism.* Indianapolis: Bobbs-Merrill, 1966.

Russell, Bertrand. "A Free Man's Worship." In *Mysticism and Logic.* Garden City, NY: Doubleday Anchor, nd.

Salinger, J. D. *Franny and Zooey.* New York: Bantam Books, 1964.

Sandars, N. K., trans. *Poems of Heaven and Hell from Ancient Mesopotamia.* Baltimore: Penguin Books, 1971.

Scheler, Max. *Ressentiment.* Marquette Studies in Philosophy IV. Translated by Lewis B. Coser and William W. Holdheim. Milwaukee: Marquette University Press, 1994.

Schmithals, Walter. *Gnosticism in Corinth.* Translated by John E. Steely. New York: Abingdon Press, 1971.

Schweitzer, Albert. *The Mystery of the Kingdom of God: The Secret of Jesus' Messiahship and Passion.* Translated by Walter Lowrie. New York: Macmillan Company, 1914. Reprint, New York: Schocken Books, 1964.

———. *The Quest of the Historical Jesus: A Critical Study of Its Progress from Reimarus to Wrede.* Translated by W. Montgomery. London: Adam and Charles Black, 1910. Reprint, New York: Macmillan, 1968.

Scroggs, Robin. "Tradition, Freedom, and the Abyss." In *New Theology No. 8,* edited by Martin E. Marty and Dean G. Peerman. New York: Macmillan, 1971, pp. 84–101.

Sellers, Otis Q. *Christian Individualism: A Way of Life for the Active Believer in Jesus Christ.* Los Angeles: Word of Truth Ministries, 1961.

Shklovsky, Victor. "Art as Technique." In *Russian Formalist Criticism: Four Essays,* edited and translated by Lee T. Lemon and Marion J. Reis. Lincoln: University of Nebraska Press, 1965, pp. 3–24.

Smith, Wilfred Cantwell. *The Meaning and End of Religion: A New Approach to the Religious Traditions of Mankind.* New York: New American Library, 1964.

Spinoza, Benedict de. *A Theologico-Political Treatise and A Political Treatise.* Translated by R. H. M. Elwes. New York: Dover, 1951.

Stott, John R. W. *The Preacher's Portrait.* Grand Rapids, MI: William B. Eerdmans, 1961.

Tillich, Paul. "'By What Authority?'" In *The New Being.* New York: Scribners, 1955, pp. 79–91.

———. "The Conquest of the Concept of Religion in the Philosophy of

Religion." In *What Is Religion?* translated by Kenneth Schedler and Charles W. Fox. New York: Harper & Row, 1973, pp. 122–54.

———. *The Courage to Be.* New Haven, CT: Yale University Press, 1952.

———. "The Depth of Existence." In *The Shaking of the Foundations.* New York: Scribners, 1948, pp. 52–63.

———. *Dynamics of Faith.* New York: Harper & Row, 1958.

———. "In Thinking Be Mature." In *The Eternal Now.* New York: Scribners, 1956, pp. 155–62.

Van Buren, Paul M. *The Secular Meaning of the Gospel, Based on an Analysis of Its Language.* New York: Macmillan, 1966.

Wallis, Jim. *Agenda for Biblical People.* New York: Harper & Row, 1976.

Warren, Rick. *The Purpose-Driven Life: What on Earth Am I Here For?* Grand Rapids, MI: Zondervan, 2002.

Watzlawick, Paul. *How Real Is Real? Confusion, Disinformation, Communication: An Anecdotal Introduction to Communications Theory.* New York: Vintage Books, 1976.

Weber, Max. *The Sociology of Religion.* Translated by Ephraim Fischoff. Boston: Beacon Press, 1964.

———. *The Theory of Social and Economic Organization.* Translated by A. M. Henderson and Talcott Parsons. New York: Free Press, 1947.

Wilbur, Earl Morse. *A History of Unitarianism: Socinianism and Its Antecedents.* Cambridge, MA: Harvard University Press, 1947.